I0094818

Lord Thomas Mackenzie

Studies in Roman Law

With Comparative Views of the Laws of France, England, and Scotland. Third

Edition

Lord Thomas Mackenzie

Studies in Roman Law
With Comparative Views of the Laws of France, England, and Scotland. Third Edition

ISBN/EAN: 9783744773300

Printed in Europe, USA, Canada, Australia, Japan

Cover: Foto ©Suzi / pixelio.de

More available books at **www.hansebooks.com**

ROMAN LAW

STUDIES IN ROMAN LAW

WITH

COMPARATIVE VIEWS

OF THE

LAWS OF FRANCE, ENGLAND, AND SCOTLAND

BY

LORD MACKENZIE

ONE OF THE JUDGES OF THE COURT OF SESSION IN SCOTLAND

THIRD EDITION

WILLIAM BLACKWOOD AND SONS
EDINBURGH AND LONDON
MDCCCLXX

PRINTED BY WILLIAM BLACKWOOD AND SONS, EDINBURGH.

PREFACE.

DURING the last fifty years the study of Roman law has made great progress on the Continent of Europe, and especially in Germany and France. The discovery of ancient works long buried in oblivion, and the researches of some eminent historians and civilians, have thrown new light on this department of jurisprudence, and materially modified its general aspect. In this country we have certainly not kept pace with our Continental neighbours; but it is gratifying to observe that a strong desire has been recently manifested in professional circles to raise the standard of legal education by devoting more attention to Roman law and general jurisprudence. This has led to the establishment of new chairs in some of our Universities, and of readerships by the Inns of Court in London; while it has called forth from English writers a considerable number of works on Roman law of various degrees of merit, but calculated on the whole to enrich our legal literature.

Without trenching on the ground already occupied by these authors, a good elementary book in English is still much wanted, giving a clear, simple, and accurate view of the general principles of the Roman law, with so much of its history as is necessary for a correct knowledge of the system.

In the present work I have endeavoured to give a concise exposition of the leading doctrines of the Roman law as it existed when it reached its highest development in the age of Justinian ; and great pains have been taken to simplify the subject as much as possible, by a systematic arrangement, by avoiding all abstruse inquiries of an antiquarian character, and by confining myself to such matters as appeared to be useful and instructive.

At the outset I have introduced an historical sketch of the sources of the Roman law and the political changes in the government, from the foundation of Rome to the accession of Justinian,—of the legislative works of that emperor in the middle of the sixth century, when all the existing laws and imperial constitutions were revised and consolidated,— of the fate of Justinian's legislation in the East and West, —and, lastly, of the revival of the study of the Roman law in Europe in the twelfth century, and the progress of this department of knowledge from that epoch down to the present time. Then, after a preliminary chapter devoted to a cursory glance at jurisprudence and the principal divisions of law, I have given a general exposition of the Roman law, divided into Six Parts, and based principally on Justinian's Institutes, but leaving out some titles which appear to be obsolete or useless, and adding supplementary chapters on various important matters drawn from the Pandects, the Code, and the Novels, as well as from the writings of Gaius and other sources. These chapters will be found throughout the book, but chiefly under the Fifth and Sixth Parts.

To this exposition, which is my chief design, I have added a subordinate one, by drawing some comparisons more or less important between the Roman system and the laws of France, England, and Scotland ; and although these illustrations are imperfect, and compressed within narrow limits, it is hoped they will prove more interesting to the general reader, than if I had followed the example of many previous writers on Roman law, by entering into minute technical details regarding ancient institutions and usages which have little or no bearing on modern jurisprudence.

As to the arrangement of the subjects, a short explanation will suffice. Under Part First, which treats of the Law of Persons, are considered political rights so far as they bear on private law, the legal capacity of individuals for acquiring and disposing of property, the rights which concern status and the relations of family, and artificial persons called corporations.

Patrimonial Rights, sometimes called the Law of Things, are naturally divided into three classes—1st, What are called by modern jurists Real Rights; 2d, Rights arising from Obligations; and, 3d, Rights arising from Succession. These three classes of Rights are successively treated under the Second, Third, and Fourth Parts.

Actions and Civil Procedure, being the means which the law affords to enforce our rights, are treated under the Fifth Part; while Criminal Law and Procedure are treated under the Sixth Part; the concluding chapter being devoted to a short account of the Roman Bar.

Of the best works on Roman law within my reach I have freely availed myself. In Dr Smith's 'Dictionary of Greek and Roman Antiquities' there is a useful series of articles on Roman law, contributed by that accomplished scholar, Mr George Long, to which I am indebted for valuable hints. Among modern foreign jurists, my special acknowledgments are due to Marezoll, Mackeldey, Warnkoenig, Ortolan, De Fresquet, and Charles Maynz—all writers who have earned a high reputation on the Continent, though some of them are less known in this country than they deserve to be.

On French law, my information has been derived chiefly from the admirable works of Pothier, the modern French Codes, and the Commentaries published thereon, including Pailliet's celebrated 'Manuel du Droit Français.'

As to English and Scottish law, I have been guided by those writers who are generally regarded by the legal profession as standard authorities. One book, Mr Paterson's 'Compendium of English and Scotch Law,' I found extremely useful in suggesting interesting comparisons between the juridical systems of England and Scotland.

Notwithstanding the extent and variety of the subjects discussed, I have condensed my materials, so as not to exceed the limits of a moderate octavo volume. This plan, no doubt, has its drawbacks, and precludes the possibility of entering into a multitude of details which will be found in works of higher pretensions; but the summary I have attempted will probably be better relished by those for whose use it is intended than a bulkier book. For the errors and imperfections which, notwithstanding every anxiety to prevent them, must inevitably occur in a work of this description, I must throw myself on the indulgence of the reader; while I venture to express a hope that, with all its defects, the present volume may be found to combine a comprehensive general view of Roman law, with some interesting contributions to the difficult science of comparative jurisprudence.

NOTE TO THE SECOND EDITION.

A Second Edition of this work having been called for, the Author has taken the opportunity of making some corrections, and of introducing some additional matter, chiefly in the Historical Sketch and Preliminary Chapter. He has at the same time to acknowledge his obligations to his friend George Monro, Esquire, Advocate, for his kindness in superintending the revisal of this Edition, and seeing it through the press.

NOTE TO THE THIRD EDITION.

When the preparation of this Edition was commenced, the learned Author was still in life, but in a state of health which precluded him from taking any share in that labour.   In these circumstances, the task of superintending this Edition was committed to me, I having had charge of the previous Edition.   In the discharge of that duty I have received, in the department of French law, the assistance of Mr Patrick Fraser, Sheriff of Renfrewshire, author of several learned works on Scottish law. In English law, the notes added in the present Edition have been revised by the Author's brother-in-law, Mr J. O. Jones, Solicitor, Liverpool, who gave valuable aid in the former Editions.

The Second Edition, although it did not receive Lord Mackenzie's superintendence while passing through the press, was entirely printed, both text and notes, from his own carefully - completed manuscript.   In the present Edition the whole text and notes of the Second Edition have been exactly reproduced, and the new matter has been introduced in the form of additional notes, distinguished by asterisks, while Lord Mackenzie's own notes are marked by numerals.   By those notes the statements as to the laws of France, England, and Scotland have been brought down to the present time.   Care has been taken to preserve the paging of this Edition almost exactly the same with that of the Second Edition.

The First Edition of this work was published in 1862, and the Second in 1865.   The Author died in September 1869.

GEORGE MONRO, ADVOCATE,
Sheriff of Linlithgow, Clackmannan, and Kinross.

EDINBURGH, *February* 1870.

CONTENTS.

HISTORICAL SKETCH OF THE ROMAN LAW.

CHAPTER I.

HISTORY OF THE ROMAN LAW DOWN TO JUSTINIAN.

INTRODUCTION.

FIRST PERIOD.

FROM THE FOUNDATION OF ROME TO THE TWELVE TABLES.

SECOND PERIOD.

FROM THE TWELVE TABLES TO AUGUSTUS.

CHAPTER II.

CONSOLIDATION OF THE ROMAN LAW UNDER JUSTINIAN.

CHAPTER III.

FATE OF THE ROMAN LAW AFTER JUSTINIAN, AND REVIVAL OF THE STUDY IN EUROPE.

PRELIMINARY CHAPTER.

ON JURISPRUDENCE AND THE PRINCIPAL DIVISIONS OF LAW.

EXPOSITION OF THE ROMAN LAW;

WITH

COMPARATIVE VIEWS OF THE LAWS OF FRANCE, ENGLAND, AND SCOTLAND.

PART I.

OF THE LAW OF PERSONS.

CHAPTER I.

OF PERSONS IN GENERAL.

CHAPTER II.

OF THE CIVIL CAPACITY OF PERSONS.

CHAPTER III.

OF CITIZENS AND FOREIGNERS.

I.—ROMAN LAW.

II.—FRENCH LAW OF CIVIL RIGHTS.

III.—BRITISH LAW ON SUBJECTS AND ALIENS.

CHAPTER IV.

OF SLAVERY.

CHAPTER V.

OF MARRIAGE.

I.—ROMAN LAW.

II.—FRENCH LAW OF MARRIAGE.

III.—ENGLISH LAW OF MARRIAGE.

IV.—SCOTTISH LAW OF MARRIAGE.

CHAPTER VI.

OF DIVORCE.

I.—ROMAN LAW.

II.—FRENCH LAW.

III.—ENGLISH LAW.

IV.—SCOTTISH LAW.

CHAPTER VII.

OF THE LEGITIMATION OF NATURAL CHILDREN.

CHAPTER VIII.

OF ADOPTION.

CHAPTER IX.

OF PATERNAL POWER.

CHAPTER X.

OF TUTORS AND CURATORS.

CHAPTER XI.

OF CORPORATIONS.

I.—ROMAN LAW.

II.—ENGLISH AND SCOTTISH LAW.

PART II.

OF THE LAW RELATING TO REAL RIGHTS.

CHAPTER I.

OF THE DIVISION OF THINGS.

CHAPTER II.

OF PROPERTY IN GENERAL.

CHAPTER III.

OF THE DIFFERENT MODES OF ACQUIRING PROPERTY.

PART III.

OF THE LAW OF OBLIGATIONS.

CHAPTER I.

OF OBLIGATIONS IN GENERAL.

CHAPTER II.

OF REAL CONTRACTS.

CHAPTER V.

OF DONATIONS.

I.—ROMAN LAW.

II.—FRENCH LAW.

CHAPTER VI.

OF OBLIGATIONS ARISING FROM QUASI CONTRACTS.

CHAPTER VII.

OF OBLIGATIONS EX DELICTO AND QUASI EX DELICTO.

CHAPTER V.

HOW TESTAMENTS ARE REVOKED OR ANNULLED.

I.—ROMAN LAW.

CHAPTER VI.

OF LEGACIES.

I.—ROMAN LAW.

CHAPTER VII.

OF ROMAN INTESTATE SUCCESSION.

PART V.

OF ACTIONS AND PROCEDURE.

CHAPTER I.

OF MAGISTRATES AND JUDGES IN CIVIL SUITS.

CHAPTER II.

MODE OF PROCEDURE IN CIVIL ACTIONS.

CHAPTER III.

DIFFERENT KINDS OF ACTIONS.

CHAPTER IV.

OF INTERDICTS.

PART VI.

OF CRIMINAL LAW AND PROCEDURE.

CHAPTER I.

OF CRIMINAL COURTS.

CHAPTER II.

PROCEDURE IN CRIMINAL TRIALS.

CHAPTER III.

OF CRIMES.

I.—OFFENCES AGAINST THE STATE.

II.—OFFENCES AGAINST INDIVIDUALS.

CHAPTER IV.

PUNISHMENTS IN THE ROMAN LAW.

CHAPTER V.

OF THE CRIMINAL LAW OF FRANCE AND BRITAIN.

I.—FRENCH CRIMINAL LAW.

II.—BRITISH CRIMINAL LAW.

CHAPTER VI.

OF THE ROMAN BAR.

AUTHORS CITED OR CONSULTED.

Addison (C. G., Barrister-at-Law), Treatise on the Law of Contracts, 8vo, 5th edit., London, 1862.

Arnot (Hugo), Criminal Trials in Scotland, 4to, Edinburgh, 1785.

Aulus Gellius, Noctes Atticæ, 8vo.

Austin (John, Barrister-at-Law), The Province of Jurisprudence Determined, 8vo, 2d edit., London, 1860.
—— Outline of Lectures on General Jurisprudence, 1832.
—— Lectures on Jurisprudence, 3 vols., 1863.

Bankton (Lord), Institute of the Laws of Scotland in Civil Rights, 3 vols. folio, 1751.

Beaufort (Louis de), Histoire de la République Romaine, ou Plan Général de l'Ancien Gouvernement de Rome, 2 vols. 4to, Hague, 1766.

Becker (W. A.), Gallus, or Roman Scenes of the Time of Augustus, with Notes illustrative of the Manners and Customs of the Romans, translated from the German by Metcalfe, 8vo, London, 1849.

Bell (Professor George Joseph), Commentaries on the Laws of Scotland, 5th edit., 2 vols. 4to, Edinburgh, 1826. New edit. by Shaw, 1858.
—— Principles of the Law of Scotland, 5th edit. by Shaw, 8vo, 1860.

Bernardi (M.), De l'Origine et des Progrès de la Législation Française, 8vo, Paris, 1816.

Blackstone (Sir William), Commentaries on the Laws of England, 4 vols. 8vo, Dr Kerr's edition, London, 1862.

Böcking (E.), Notitia Dignitatum et Administrationum tam Civilium quàm Militarium in Partibus Orientis et Occidentis (illustrated edition), 2 vols. 8vo, Bonn, 1839-1853.

Bonjean (M.), Traité des Actions, ou Exposition Historique de l'Organisation Judiciaire et de la Procedure Civile chez les Romains, 3d edit., 1846.

Bouillet (M. N.), Dictionnaire Universel des Sciences, des Lettres, et des Arts, 4th edit., 8vo, Paris, 1859.

Bowyer (Sir George), Commentaries on the Modern Civil Law, royal 8vo, London, 1848.

Broom (Herbert), Commentaries on the Common Law, 8vo, London, 1856.
Brougham (Lord), British Constitution, 8vo, London, 1861.
Browne (Dr), Compendious View of the Civil Law, 1 vol. 8vo, 1802.
Burge (W.), Commentaries on Colonial and Foreign Laws, 4 vols. 8vo, London, 1838.

Camus, Lettres sur la Profession d'Avocat, Paris, 1772. 4th edit. in 8vo, par Dupin, Paris, 1818.
Colquhoun (Dr Patrick), Summary of the Roman Civil Law, illustrated by Commentaries on, and Parallels from, the Mosaic, Canon, Mohammedan, English, and Foreign Law, 4 vols. 8vo, London, 1849-1860.
Cujacius (Jac.), Opera Omnia, 2 vols. folio, Venet. 1758-1783.

De Fresquet (R., Professor of Roman Law at Aix), Traité Elémentaire de Droit Romain, 2 vols. 8vo, Paris, 1855.
Dickson (W. G.), Treatise on the Law of Evidence in Scotland, 2 vols. 8vo, Edinburgh, 1855.
Dirksen (Henry Ed., Professor of Law at Koenigsberg), Sketch of the Efforts made to restore the Text of the Twelve Tables, Leipzig, 1824.
Domat (J.), Les Lois Civiles dans leur Ordre Naturel, 2 vols. folio, Paris, 1689-1777. Translated into English by Dr Strahan, 2 vols. folio, London, 1722.
Ducange (Charles Dufresne), Glossarium Mediæ et Infimæ Latinitatis, 3 vols. in folio, 1678. Supplement to the above, by L. Diefenbach, Frankfort, 1857.
Ducaurroy (A. M., Professor of Roman Law at Paris), Les Institutes de Justinien nouvellement expliquées, 3 vols. 8vo, Paris, 1822-1827. 8th edit., 1851.

Encyclopédie Methodique de Jurisprudence, 10 vols. 4to, Paris, 1782-1791.
Erskine (John, Professor of Law at Edinburgh), Institute of the Law of Scotland, 2 vols. folio 1773. New edit., with Notes by Ivory, 1828.
—— Principles of the Law of Scotland, 8vo, 1754. New edit., by J. G. Smith, 8vo, 1860.

Falck, Cours d'Introduction Générale à l'Etude du Droit, ou Encyclopédie Juridique, traduite de l'Allemand par C. A. Pellat, 8vo, Paris, 1841.
Fœlix (M.), Traité du Droit International Privé, ou des Conflits de Lois de Différentes Nations en matière de Droit Privé, 3d edit., revue par Charles Demangeat, 2 vols. 8vo, Paris, 1856.
Fraser (Patrick), Treatise on the Law of Scotland, as applicable to the Personal and Domestic Relations, 2 vols. 8vo, Edinburgh, 1846.

Gaius, Institutionum Commentarii Quatuor, emendavit Eduardus Böcking, 4th edit., 8vo, Lipsiæ, 1855.

Gibbon (Ed.), History of the Decline and Fall of the Roman Empire, ch. 44.

Giraud (Ch.), Dissertation sur la Gentilité Romaine.

Gneist (Dr Rud.), Institutionum et Regularum Juris Romani Syntagma ; exhibens Gaii et Justiniani Institutionum Synopsin, Ulpiani Librum Singularem Regularum, Pauli Sententiarum Delectum, 8vo, Lipsiæ, 1858.

Godefroy (James), Manuale Juris seu Parva Juris Mysteria, 9th edit., Genevæ, 1677.

——— Quatuor Fontes Juris Civilis, Genevæ, 1653.

Grant on Corporations, 8vo, London, 1850.

Greaves (Charles S., Q.C.), The Criminal Law Consolidation and Amendment Acts, 24 & 25 Vict., with Notes, 2d edit., 8vo, London, 1862.

Grellet-Dumazeau (M. Th.), Le Barreau Romain depuis son Origine jusqu'à Justinien, 8vo, Paris, 1851.

Grotius (Hugo), De Jure Belli ac Pacis, 4to, Paris, 1625, translated into French by Barbeyrac.

Hallifax (Dr Samuel), Analysis of the Roman Civil Law, 4th edit., 8vo. Cambridge, 1795. New edit., by Geldart, 1836.

Harris (Dr George), Justinian's Institutions, translated into English, with Notes, 3d edit., 4to, Oxford, 1811.

Haubold (Ch. Got.), Institutiones Juris Romani Literariæ, 8vo, Lips. 1808.

——— Manuale Basilicorum, Lips. 1819.

Hautefeuille (L. B.), Des Droits et des Devoirs des Nations Neutres en temps de Guerre Maritime, 4 vols. 8vo, 1848-1850.

Heineccius (Jo. Gott.), Elementa Juris Civilis secundum ordinem Institutionum, 8vo, Halle, 1785.

——— Elementa Juris Civilis secundum ordinem Pandectarum, 2 vols. 8vo, Rotterodami, 1778.

——— Antiquitatum Romanarum Jurisprudentiam Illustrantium Syntagma, editio nova, 2 vols. 8vo, Argentorati, 1755.

Homberg (And.), De Multitudine Nimia Commentatorum in Institutiones Juris, 4to, Helmstadt, 1701.

Hume's Political Discourses.

Hume (Baron), Commentaries on the Law of Scotland respecting Crimes, 2 vols. 4to, Edinburgh, 1844.

Huschke (Ph. Eduardus), Jurisprudentiæ Antejustinianeæ quæ supersunt, 8vo, Lipsiæ, 1861.

Irving (Dr David), Introduction to the Study of the Civil Law, 4th edit., 8vo, London, 1837.

Jones (Sir William), Essay on Law of Bailments, 4th edit., London, 1833.

Kent (James), Commentaries on American Law, 4 vols. 8vo, 10th edit., Boston, 1860.

Laboulaye (Edouard), Essai sur les Lois Criminelles des Romains, concernant la Responsibilité des Magistrats, 8vo, Paris, 1845.
Leapingwell (Dr George), Manual of the Roman Law, arranged after the Analysis of Dr Hallifax, 8vo, Cambridge, 1859.
Lee (Principal), Lectures on the History of the Church of Scotland, 2 vols. 8vo, Edinburgh, 1860.
Lerminier (E.), Introduction Générale à l'Histoire du Droit, 2d edit., 8vo, Paris, 1835.
Lindley (Nathaniel), Barrister-at-law, Introduction to the Study of Juris-prudence, being a Translation of the general part of Thibaut's System des Pandekten Rechts, with Notes, 8vo, London, 1855.
——— Treatise on the Law of Partnership, 2 vols. 8vo, London, 1860.
Long (Professor George), Articles on Roman Law, in Dr Smith's Dictionary of Greek and Roman Antiquities, 2d edit., 8vo, London, 1856.

Mackeldey (Dr F., Professor of Law at Bonn), Lehrbuch des heutigen Rö-mischen Rechts, Giessen, 1842; or,
——— Manuel de Droit Romain, contenant la Theorie des Institutes, traduit de l'Allemand par Beving, 8vo, Bruxelles, 1846.
Maine (Henry Sumner), Ancient Law, its connection with the Early History of Society, and its relation to Modern Ideas, 8vo, London, 1861.
Mai (Angelo), Vaticana Juris Romani Fragmenta, Paris, 1823.
Marezoll (Theodore, Professor at the University of Leipsic), Lehrbuch der Institutionen des Römischen Rechts, Leipzig, 1850; or,
——— Précis d'un Cours sur l'Ensemble du Droit Privé des Romains, traduit de l'Allemand par C. A. Pellat, 2d edit., 8vo, Paris, 1852.
Martens (George Frederick, Professor at Goetingen), Précis du Droit des Gens Moderne de l'Europe, nouvelle edition, par M. Ch. Vergé, 2 vols. 8vo, Paris, 1858.
Maynz (Charles, Professor of Roman Law at Brussels), Elements du Droit Romain, 2d edit., 2 vols. 8vo, Paris, 1856. A third volume is promised to complete this much-esteemed work.
Meerman (Gerard), Novus Thesaurus Juris Civilis et Canonici, ex Collec-tione et Museo Gerardi Meermanni, 7 vols. folio, Hagæ, 1751-1753.
Supplementary volume published by Meerman's son in 1780.
Montesquieu (Ch. de Secondat, Baron de), Considerations sur les Causes de la Grandeur des Romains et de leur Decadences, 8vo, Paris, 1755.
——— Œuvres de Montesquieu, avec les Notes de tous les Commentateurs. Edition publié par L. Parrelle, 8 vols. 8vo, Paris, 1826.
Montreuil, Histoire du Droit Byzantin, ou du Droit Romain dans l'Empire d'Orient, depuis la mort de Justinien jusqu'à la prise de Constantinople en 1453, 3 vols. 8vo, Paris, 1847.
Mühlenbruch (Chr. Fred.), Doctrina Pandectarum, 3 vols., editio quarta, Halæ, 1834.

Ortolan (M., Professor of Law at Paris), Explication Historique des Institutes de l'Empereur Justinien ; précedée de l'Histoire de la Legislation Romaine, et d'une Généralisation du Droit Romain, 6th edit., 3 vols. 8vo, Paris, 1857.

Ortolan (M.), Eléments du Droit Penal, 8vo, Paris, 1855.

Otto (Ed. Ev., Professor of Law at Utrecht), Thesaurus Juris Romani, continens rariora meliorum interpretum opuscula, in quibus jus Romanorum emendatur, explicatur, illustratur, 5 vols. folio, Basil, 1744.

Pailliet (Jean-Baptiste-Joseph, Judge of the Court of Appeal), Manuel du Droit Français, 8th edit., 4to, Paris, 1838.
    Besides much useful information on other subjects, this work contains—
    1. The History of National Institutions ; 2. The Constitutional Charter of 1830, with the Laws which complete it ; 3. The Seven Codes, with Notes thereon, and numerous decisions by the Court of Cassation and the Royal Courts ; and, 4. The Laws and Ordinances published from the Revolution till the month of December 1837.

Paley (William, D.D.), Principles of Moral and Political Philosophy, 8vo.

Paterson (James, Barrister-at-Law), Compendium of English and Scotch Law, stating their differences, with a Dictionary of parallel terms and phrases, 8vo, Edinburgh, 1860.

Paul (Father), History of the Council of Trent, translated from the Italian into English by Nathaniel Brent, folio, London, 1620.

Perezius (Ant., Professor of Law at Louvaine), Prælectiones in Duodecim Libros Codicis editio nova in 4to, Amst., 1671.

Phillimore (John George), Introduction to the Study and History of the Roman Law, 8vo, London, 1848.

Polson (A.), Principles of the Law of Nations, 8vo, London, 1848.

Pothier (Robert Joseph), Pandectæ Justinianæ in novum ordinem digestæ, cum Legibus Codicis, et Novellis, quæ jus Pandectarum confirmant, explicant, aut abrogant, 3 vols. in folio, Paris, 1748-1752 ; nova editio, 5 vols. 4to, Paris, 1818.

―――― Œuvres Complètes de Pothier, précedées d'une Dissertation sur sa Vie et ses Ecrits, par MM. Rogron et Firbach, Avocats à la Cour de Cassation, 2 vols. 8vo, Paris, 1835.

Rogron, Code Civil Expliqué, Bruxelles, 1838.

Roscoe (Henry, Barrister-at-Law), Digest of the Law of Evidence, 8vo, 10th edit., London, 1861.

Rutherforth (T., D.D.), Institutes of Natural Law, being the substance of a Course of Lectures on Grotius de Jure Belli et Pacis, 2 vols. 8vo, Cambridge, 1756.

Sandars, Translation of Justinian's Institutes, with Notes, 8vo, 2d edit., London, 1859.

Savigny (Frederick Charles), Geschichte des Röm. Rechts im Mittelalter, 6 vols., Heidelberg, 1815-1831 ; or,

―――― Histoire du Droit Romain au Moyen Age, traduit de l'Allemand par M. Charles Guenoux, 8 vols. 8vo, Paris, 1840-1851.

Savigny (Frederick Charles), System des heutigen Römischen Rechts, 9 vols., Berlin, 1840-1850 ; Traité de Droit Romain, traduit par Guenoux, 8 vols., 1840-1851.
——— Treatise on Private International Law, translated by Guthrie, Edinburgh, 1869.
Schultingius (Ant.), Jurisprudentia Vetus ante-Justinianea, ex recensione et cum Notis Schultingii, Lugd. 1717.
Serrigny, Traité du Droit Public des Français, 2 vols. 8vo, 1846.
Sigonius, De Judiciis Romanorum libri tres, in 4to, 1574.
Smith (John William, Barrister-at-Law), Compendium of Mercantile Law, 6th edit., by G. M. Dowdeswell, 8vo, London, 1859.
Stair (Lord, President of the Court of Session), Institutions of the Law of Scotland, 1661. New edition, with Notes and Illustrations, by John S. More, Professor of Law, 2 vols. 4to, Edinburgh, 1832.
Stephen (Henry John, Sergeant-at-Law), New Commentaries on the Laws of England, 4th edit., 4 vols. 8vo, London, 1858.
St Leonards (Lord), Practical Treatise on New Statutes relating to Property, 2d edit., 8vo, London, 1862.
Story (Dr Joseph), Commentaries on the Conflict of Laws, Foreign and Domestic, in regard to Contracts, Rights, and Remedies, 5th edit., 8vo, Boston, 1857.
——— Commentaries on the Law of Bailments, 8vo, Boston, 1846.

Taylor (John, LL.D.), Elements of the Civil Law, 2d edit., 4to, London, 1755.
Troplong (R. Theodore, First President of the Court of Cassation), De l'Influence de Christianisme sur le Droit Civil des Romains, 2d edit., 8vo, Paris, 1855.

Vangerow (Ch. Adolphus, Professor of Law at Heidelberg), Lehrbuch der Pandecten (Treatise on the Pandects), 6th edit., 3 vols., Marbourg, 1855.
Vattel, Le Droit des Gens, ou Principes de la Loi Naturelle appliqués à la Conduite et aux Affaires des Nations et des Souverains, 2 vols. in 4to, 1758 ; English Translation, 2 vols. 4to, London, 1759 ; another Translation, by Chitty, London, 1834.
Vinnius (Arnold, Professor of Law at Leyden), Commentarius in Quatuor Libros Institutionem, editio secunda, 4to, Amstel., Elzevir, 1655.
Voet (John, Professor of Law at Leyden), Commentarius ad Pandectas, 2 vols. in folio, Coloniæ Allobrogum, 1757.

Walter (Ferdinand, Professor at Bonn), Histoire de la Procédure Civile chez les Romains, traduit de l'Allemand par Edouard Laboulaye, 8vo, Paris, 1841.
Warnkoenig (Leopold Augustus, Professor of Law at Tübingen), Institutiones Juris Privati Romani, editio quarta, 8vo, Bonnæ, 1860.
——— Commentarii Juris Romani Privati, 3 vols. 8vo, Leodi, 1825.

Westlake (John, Barrister-at-Law), Private International Law, or the Conflict of Laws, with Principal reference to English Practice, 8vo, London, 1858.

Wheaton (Henry), Elements of International Law, 2 vols. 8vo, London, 1836 ; 3d edit., 8vo, Philadelphia, 1846.

Williams (Edward Vaughan, Judge in the Court of Common Pleas), Treatise on the Law of Executors and Administrators, 5th edit., 2 vols. 8vo, London, 1856.

Zimmern, Traité des Actions, ou Théorie de la Procédure Civile Privée chez les Romains, traduit de l'Allemand par M. Etienne, 1843.

Zouch (Dr Richard, Regius Professor of Civil Law at Oxford), Elementa Jurisprudentiæ, Definitionibus, Regulis, et Sententiis Selectioribus Juris Civilis illustrata, 8vo, Oxford, 1629. Reprinted by the Elzevirs at Leyden, 24mo, 1652.

EXPLANATION OF REFERENCES.

I. 2. 3. 4.	Justinian's Institutes, book 2, title 3, paragraph 4.
D. 1. 4. 15. 2.	Digest or Pandects, book 1, title 4, fragment 15, paragraph 2.
C. 2. 6. 7.	Justinian's Code, book 2, title 6, constitution 7.
N. 118, ch. 1.	Novellæ Constitutiones, number 118, chapter 1.
Cod. Theod.	Theodosian Code.
Gai. 1. 200.	Institutes of Gaius, book 1, paragraph 200.
Ulp. 3. 3.	Fragments of Ulpian, title 3, paragraph 3.
Paul. 5. 6. 3.	Receptæ Sententiæ of Paulus, book 5, title 6, paragraph 3.
Marezoll, § 30.	Marezoll, Institutes, paragraph 30.
Mackeldey, § 64.	Mackeldey, Institutes, paragraph 64.
Warn. Inst. § 85.	Warnkoenig, Institutes, paragraph 85.
Maynz, § 87.	Maynz, Elements of Roman Law, paragraph 87.
De Fresquet.	De Fresquet, Elementary Treatise on Roman Law.
Ortolan.	Ortolan, Institutes.

STUDIES IN ROMAN LAW.

HISTORICAL SKETCH OF THE ROMAN LAW.

CHAPTER I.

HISTORY OF THE ROMAN LAW DOWN TO JUSTINIAN.

INTRODUCTION.

IN various departments of intellectual exertion—in philo- Superiority
sophy, poetry, oratory, and the fine arts—the Greeks have of Romans in law.
never been surpassed. But they contributed almost nothing
to the science of jurisprudence. In speculative philosophy
they greatly excelled the Romans; but in the cultivation of
law, the Romans carried off the palm not only from the
Greeks, but from all the other nations of antiquity. The laws
of Lycurgus were never reduced to writing; and although
the Athenians possessed a considerable body of written laws,
some of which appear to have been incorporated into the
Decemviral Code, they have been of very little use to posterity; and Cicero can hardly be said to exaggerate when,
with pardonable pride, he characterises the Greek laws as
rude, insignificant, and almost ridiculous, when compared
with the enlightened system of jurisprudence which the
Romans of his day inherited from the wisdom of their
ancestors.

A

Mere speculation found little favour among the Romans, who were eminently a practical people. No new system of philosophy sprang up among them; but we are indebted to them for the first successful cultivation of law as a science. Apart from their general ability in the business of legislation, their judicial system was far more favourable than that of the Greeks to the improvement of jurisprudence and to the gradual formation of a body of mild, wise, and equitable laws. For several centuries, under the free republic and the empire, the magistrates who exercised the chief civil jurisdiction at Rome were the prætors, who were changed annually; and it became the practice for every new prætor, on his accession to office, to publish, in the form of edicts, the rules which he intended to observe in administering justice. These rules were handed down by the prætors to their successors, and were modified and improved in the course of time to suit the exigencies of the community. It was chiefly by these edicts, by the decisions of the judges, and by the scientific works of eminent lawyers, aided from time to time by the direct action of the legislature, that the ancient institutions were softened and refined, and the general body of the Roman law was gradually, after long experience, moulded into a system, and brought to that state of perfection which it ultimately attained.

Legal history before Justinian.

Without detracting from the merits of the classical jurists, it may safely be affirmed that the Roman law did not attain its full development till it was consolidated by Justinian near the middle of the sixth century. For us the collections of that emperor have the most immediate interest, not only from their intrinsic value, but from the great influence they have exercised on the jurisprudence of modern Europe. But, before giving an account of Justinian's legislation and the fate which attended it, we think it necessary to take a rapid survey of the history of the Roman law previous to his reign. This may be conveniently considered under three periods, all distinguished by important changes in the political constitution of Rome. 1st, From the foundation of the city to the promulgation of the Twelve Tables,

Division into three periods.

extending over a period of about 300 years; 2d, From the
Twelve Tables to the establishment of the empire under Augustus in the year 722 after the foundation of Rome; 3d, From
the time of Augustus to the accession of Justinian, A.D. 527.

FIRST PERIOD.

FROM THE FOUNDATION OF ROME TO THE TWELVE TABLES.

During the government of the kings the history of Rome
is obscured by doubtful traditions and improbable fictions.
Modern criticism has attacked all the commonly received
opinions as to the primitive state of Rome; and this has
been carried so far, that some ingenious writers, such as Vico
at the commencement of the last century, and Niebuhr in
our own day, have endeavoured to construct an entirely new
theory of Roman history, which, as Ortolan aptly remarks,
has the singular merit of having been wholly unknown to
the Romans themselves.

At first the Romans enjoyed a constitution very liberal in
appearance, though it contained within it the most fruitful
seeds of despotism. The government consisted of an elective
king, a senate composed originally of 100, and afterwards of
300 members, and a general assembly of the people. To the
king belonged the command of the army, the administration
of justice, and the general superintendence of religion. The
senate was an administrative and deliberative council of
nobles or persons distinguished by their rank, their wealth,
and their talents. In the general assembly the chief magistrates were elected, and the measures prepared by the senate
were laid before the people, who might either accept or reject them. Political power was at first entirely confined to
the patricians. Under the constitution of Servius Tullius,
who divided the Roman people into six classes, according to
a valuation of their fortune, all the citizens, whether patricians or plebeians, enjoyed the right of voting by centuries in
the Comitia Centuriata; but, from the mode of collecting the
suffrages, the wealthy classes had an overwhelming ascend-

Political constitution of Rome.

ency in that assembly. On the other hand, the taxes were
chiefly borne by the rich, and a very light share of the
burdens of the state was laid upon the lower orders, so as to
compensate them for the want of political influence.

In the infancy of the Roman state, Pomponius says the
people were governed without any regular system of positive
laws by the absolute authority of their kings.   Customs
founded on general consent are the first rudiments of jurisprudence, and when legislation is resorted to, it is generally
to confirm, add to, or modify, rather than to supersede, these
primitive usages.   During the regal government at Rome,
the laws were prepared by the king with the approbation
of the senate, and confirmed by the people, at first in the
Comitia Curiata, and, after the reforms of Servius Tullius, in
the Comitia Centuriata.   These laws were collected into a
body by Papirius, a Roman lawyer, and called, after his
name, the Jus Civile Papirianum.   Granius Flaccus wrote
a commentary on the royal laws in the time of Julius
Cæsar ; but although some attempts have been made to
collect a few fragments of this ancient legislation, no trustworthy remains of it now exist.[1]

Some historians ascribe particular laws to Romulus, Numa,
Servius Tullius, and other kings ; but they relate chiefly to
changes in the political constitution, and little reliance can
be placed on such vague traditions.[2]   According to the
popular account (which, however, is open to much criticism), the Roman state subsisted under seven successive
kings, during a period of 244 years, when a revolution took
place by the expulsion of Tarquin the Proud, and the royal
authority was abolished.

To supply the place of the king, two consuls were chosen
by the people from the order of patricians : these magistrates
were to remain in office for a year, and exercise most of the
powers previously intrusted to royalty.   Each of them had
equal authority, so as to act as a check upon the other, and
they were changed annually to prevent them from abusing
their powers.

[1] D. 1. 2. 2. Pomponius.   [2] Tac. Ann., iii. c. 26.

The two consuls held the highest place in the republic. All other magistrates and officers, except the tribunes, were subordinate to them. They presided in the senate and executed its decrees; they levied the troops and enforced military discipline; and it was their duty to assemble the senate and the comitia, and command the armies in time of war.

As Rome was constantly engaged in war, and the consuls who commanded the armies were frequently absent from the city, some important duties of administration formerly intrusted to them were distributed among other magistrates. Thus the prætors were appointed to exercise jurisdiction in civil causes; the censors to take the census every five years, and superintend the manners and morals of the people: the ediles took care of the national buildings, public games, and matters of police; and the questors acted under the directions of the senate, as collectors of the revenue.

In the early period of the republic, the Roman constitution, which bore the external appearance of a democracy, was in reality an aristocratical government; for although the plebeians were permitted ostensibly to take a part in the deliberations of the assembly of the centuries, the patricians could always command an overwhelming majority in that assembly as well as in the senate, and, with the exception of the tribunate, they engrossed all the important offices of the state. All political power was thus placed substantially in the hands of the aristocracy, who frequently abused it by oppressing the poorer classes.

The earliest legislation deserving of notice during the Republic was the celebrated code of laws called the Twelve Tables. According to historical tradition, three commissioners were sent from Rome to Athens and other Greek states, for the purpose of inquiring into and collecting what was most useful in their legal systems; and we are told that Hermodorus, a learned Ephesian, then an exile at Rome, contributed valuable aid to the work. On the return of the commissioners, B.C. 452, ten magistrates, called decemvirs, were invested for a year with absolute power to carry on the government, and

The law of the Twelve Tables, A.R. 303.

frame a body of laws for the republic. At first ten tables were completed and made public by the decemvirs, and two other tables were added the following year. These laws, after being approved of by the senate and solemnly confirmed in the Comitia Centuriata, were engraved on twelve tables, and fixed on the most conspicuous part of the forum.

This ancient code, which is highly praised by the Roman writers,[1] and was long considered as the foundation of all law, has not come down to us. Our knowledge of it rests on a few isolated fragments and some historical relations of what has been lost. The best attempt to restore the text is that by James Godefroy;[2] and some additional light has been thrown on this subject in our days by the criticism and research of Haubold and Dirksen.[3]

Only a few provisions of the decemviral code need be noticed here.

(1.) Insolvent debtors were treated with great severity. They were liable to be seized and imprisoned by their creditors, and, after being kept loaded in chains for sixty days, might be sold into foreign slavery.

(2.) The old law or custom which prohibited all marriages between patricians and plebeians was confirmed.

(3.) In bodily injuries the barbarous principle of retaliation was sanctioned—an eye for an eye, a limb for a limb—unless the injured party chose to accept of any other satisfaction.

(4.) Any one who wrote lampoons or libels on his neighbours was liable to be deprived of civil rights.

(5.) An appeal might be made to the people from the sentence of every magistrate; and no citizen was to be tried for his life except before the Comitia of the Centuries.

---

[1] Cicero de Orator., i. 34. Titus Livius, iii. 34. "Fons omnis publici privatique juris."—Tac. Ann., iii. 27.

[2] See Quatuor Fontes Juris Civilis, Geneva, 1653. Otto's Thesaurus, t. iii. p. 1.

[3] Haubold, Institutiones Juris Romani Literariæ, t. i. p. 300 - 306. Dirksen, Sketch of the Efforts made for restoring the Text of the Twelve Tables. See also Ortolan's Institutes, t. i. p. 98.

SECOND PERIOD.

FROM THE TWELVE TABLES TO AUGUSTUS.

By the decemviral code the plebeians gained a consider- Progress of the plebeians. able step towards the adjustment of their differences with the patricians ; but it was nearly eighty years before these differences were settled by the admission of the plebeians to the supreme offices of the state. After a long series of angry contests, the popular party gradually gained ground till they achieved complete political independence. The consuls and higher magistrates, in place of being selected exclusively from the patrician order, were thenceforward chosen from the whole body of the citizens, leaving the field open for men of merit wherever they were to be found.

The reconciliation of the two orders, by an equal distri- Fusion of the two orders. bution of political rights, was followed by two centuries of national prosperity and victory. Rome was long an insignificant state, engaged in waging petty wars with her neighbours. Southern Italy had been peopled with colonies from Greece ; the northern division, which now contains Lombardy and the territories of Venice and Genoa, reaching to the Alps, had been occupied by a colony of Gauls, and on that account was known to the Romans as Cisalpine Gaul. About the close of the fifth century from the foundation of the city, and 250 years after the establishment of the republic, Rome had conquered the whole of Italy from the Alps to its southern extremity ; and, having become a powerful state, began to lay the foundations of that universal dominion which at a later period rendered her the mistress of the civilised world.

At the period when the constitution of the Roman republic Sources of law. had attained its full development, legislation emanated from three different authorities—the Comitia Centuriata, the Comitia Tributa, and the Senate ; so that laws might be promulgated in the three forms of *leges populi*, *plebiscita*, and *senatus-consulta*.

The *leges*, or laws properly so called, were proposed by the Laws of the people— consuls or other senatorial magistrates, and passed by the Leges.

whole body of Roman citizens, patricians and plebeians, in the assembly of the centuries.

Plebiscita.

The *plebiscita* were laws proposed by the tribunes and passed by the assembly of the tribes, which was originally composed of plebeians only. At first these acts were only binding on the plebeians; but after the Lex Hortensia, in the year of Rome 465, both orders recognised the authority of each assembly to pass general laws binding on the whole state. Both the *leges* and the *plebiscita* were usually distinguished by the name of the magistrates who prepared them—as Lex Aquilia, Lex Cincia, and the like.

After the Hortensian law the Roman constitution presented the singular anomaly of having two distinct legislative assemblies, each of which exercised full and absolute authority within itself to make laws for the republic. In the assembly of the centuries the people voted according to their fortunes, as ascertained by the census; so that when the first class was unanimous, as generally happened in all party divisions, though it contained only a small portion of the citizens, it determined everything, and established laws with the sanction of the senate. In the assembly of the tribes every vote was alike; and the democracy, led by the tribunes, had unlimited power to pass acts binding on the whole community, without any negative being allowed either to the consuls or to the senate. This political anomaly of two distinct legislative bodies in the Roman republic, however objectionable in theory, did not practically produce that discord and confusion which might reasonably have been expected from it, mainly in consequence of the prudent conduct of the senate and the aristocracy, who carefully avoided any struggle with the popular assembly after it had acquired authority to give laws to the whole state.[1]

Decrees of the senate.

Modern historians are not quite agreed as to the obligatory force of the ordinances of the senate during the republic. The power of the senate seems to have been different at different times. At first its legislative action was limited to the right, asserted from the most remote times, to grant or

[1] Hume's Political Discourses, Essay 9—Of some Remarkable Customs.

refuse its approbation to laws voted by the people. During the republic the supreme power belonged to the people; but they seldom passed acts without the authority of the senate. In weighty affairs it was common for the senate to deliberate and decree, and for the people to interpose their sanction. But there were many things which the senate determined by its own authority, even during the free republic, if not by express law, at least by the custom of their ancestors. When the popular cause gained ground, the tribunes assumed the right of putting a negative on the decrees of the senate, which rendered them of no effect; and, on the other hand, acts were passed by the people in the assembly of the tribes, which did not require the concurrence or approbation of the senate. Under the empire, when the comitia had disappeared, the senate had, for a time, undoubted authority to make decrees, which had the force of law, but subject to the veto of the emperor under his tribunitian power.

Upon the edicts of the magistrates, at Rome and in the provinces, was built up a system of equity which supplied the deficiencies of the common law, and exercised the most beneficial influence on the development of Roman jurisprudence. This branch of law was called the *jus honorarium*, in opposition to the *jus civile*. When the prætor entered on his office,[1] he published, as already explained, an edict establishing certain rules, according to which he professed to administer justice for the year; and a similar course was followed by the curule ediles at Rome, and the proconsuls and proprætors in the provinces. Each prætor might frame a new edict if he chose; but it was not uncommon for him to adopt the edict of his predecessor, in whole or in part, and to make such additions and changes as circumstances required. The principal object of the edict was to promulgate the changes which custom and the practice of the courts had introduced; and, where no remedy could be obtained by the strict civil law, the prætor explained the manner in which

Edicts of the magistrates.

---

[1] The *prætor urbanus* was first appointed in the year of Rome 387, and the *prætor peregrinus* in the year of Rome 508. The number of prætors was afterwards increased.

rights might be enforced, and what actions would be allowed in given cases. Strictly speaking, the prætor was not entitled to exercise legislative power; he could not abrogate or alter the laws; but in certain instances he was permitted to temper them with equity, to supply what was wanting to give them full effect, and, in matters falling within his jurisdiction, to apply them according to his own ideas of justice.[1] Though the *jus prætorium* is supposed to bear some resemblance to equity in English practice as distinguished from common law, " the equity of Rome, it should be understood, even when most distinct from the civil law, was always administered by the same tribunals. The prætor was the chief equity judge, as well as the great common-law magistrate." [2]

As regards the laws which were established by public authority after the era of the Twelve Tables, in the various forms of leges, plebiscita, senatus-consulta, and edicts of magistrates, our knowledge of them is derived chiefly from the writings of the civilians preserved in the Digest; but some special laws have been collected, by the patient industry of scholars and antiquaries, from inscriptions on marbles and tables found in various parts of Italy.[3]

Customary law.

A great part of the Roman law was founded, not on direct legislation, but on the *mores majorum*—that is, customs long observed and sanctioned by the consent of the people.

Responses of jurisconsults.

The old Roman jurists gave advice to private persons; they were consulted by the judges in cases of difficulty; and they acted as assessors to the magistrates to guide them in their judicial determinations. In their origin the Responsa Prudentum were nothing more than the private opinions of particular lawyers; but after they had been generally adopted by the legal profession, and recognised by the judicial tribunals, they were called *sententiæ receptæ*, and acquired the authority of law.

---

[1] "Jus prætorium est quod prætores introduxerunt adjuvandi vel supplendi, vel corrigendi juris civilis gratia propter utilitatem publicam."—Papinian, D. 1. 1. 7.

[2] Maine's Ancient Law, p. 67.

[3] De Fresquet, Droit Romain, t. i. p. 22. Spangenberg, Antiquitatis Romanæ Monumenta Legalia extra libros juris sparsa; Berlin, 1830.

Two works, apparently collections of forms, the 'Jus Flavi- Writings of jurisconsults. anum,' and the 'Jus Ælianum,' appeared, one in the middle of the fifth century from the foundation of Rome, and the other in the century following.[1] But, properly speaking, the scientific elaboration of law did not commence till about the age of Cicero. Q. Mucius Scævola, Consul, A.R. 657, was the first who published a complete system of civil law.[2] Servius Sulpicius, Consul in 703, who is said to have been equally eminent as an orator and a jurisconsult, wrote a commentary on the edicts of the prætors. His pupil, Ofilius, published a work on the same subject. Alfenus Varus, another of his pupils, acquired celebrity by a book written upon a more extensive plan, called 'Digesta.'[3]

The free republic which succeeded the kings, endured, ac- Fall of the republic. cording to common reckoning, 478 years, during which the political constitution underwent frequent changes. Montesquieu has pointed out with much discrimination the causes which led to the overthrow of the republic. When the Roman legions crossed the Alps, or passed to distant countries beyond seas, and remained absent for years in the conquered states, the troops lost by degrees the spirit of citizens, and the generals, who disposed of armies and kingdoms, became so powerful that they yielded a very reluctant . obedience to the central authority at Rome. The fall of Carthage, and the brilliant conquests of Greece, Egypt, and the Asiatic kingdoms, brought about a revolution in the manners and government of the Romans. The arts and customs, and the enormous riches of the conquered nations, familiarised the Romans with luxury, which opened the way to many vices. As the love of country and the zeal for freedom declined, corruption obtained more pernicious in-

---

[1] D. 1. 2. 2. § 7 and 38.
[2] Cicero studied the civil law under Mucius. He is the most ancient lawyer from whose works extracts have been taken by Justinian in the Digest. There are four fragments from Mucius. From the works of Alfenus Varus and Ælius Gallus, who were both contemporaries of Cicero, some extracts likewise appear in the Digest. Maynz, Droit Romain. t. i. p. 103, notes.
[3] D. 1. 2. 41 et seq.

fluence; powerful and ambitious men fomented internal troubles, and popular tumults were followed by an exhausting series of civil wars, which terminated in the ruin of public liberty.[1]

THIRD PERIOD.

FROM AUGUSTUS TO THE ACCESSION OF JUSTINIAN, A.D. 527.

Transition to absolute monarchy. In the year 722 from the foundation of Rome, Octavius, the grand-nephew of Julius Cæsar, established the Empire. All the powers of the state were concentrated in his person. He was consul, tribune, prætor, censor, pontifex, imperator; and, with the title of Augustus, his commands were obeyed throughout the wide extent of the Roman dominions, which then comprehended the most beautiful countries of Europe and Asia, with Egypt and all the northern parts of Africa.

Augustus gathered round his court the wits, and poets, and learned men who have made his reign illustrious. He used his powers with great moderation, and preferred to govern the Roman state according to the ancient forms of the republic.

But legislation by the popular assemblies, though not wholly discontinued, fell gradually into disuse; and the ordinances of the senate were the usual form in which laws were promulgated. After the experience of two centuries under the empire, Ulpian was justified in declaring that the decrees of the senate had the force of law,[2] though under Tiberius and his successors they had virtually degenerated into imperial ordinances clothed in a more popular form. The power of electing magistrates was transferred by Tiberius from the comitia to the senate. Under Septimus Severus and Caracalla the legislative action of the senate entirely disappeared. By gradual usurpations the power of the emperor became absolute, and the forms of ancient liberty disappeared. Under Hadrian the organisation of the empire was openly despotic; and about the beginning of the third

---

[1] See Montesquieu, Grandeur et Decadence des Romains, ch. 9.

[2] D. 1. 3. 9. "Non ambigitur senatum jus facere posse."—Ulpian.

century his successors frequently issued rescripts in which they asserted they were not subject to the laws.[1]

During the republic the opinions of the great lawyers carried with them no higher authority than what they derived from their own intrinsic merit and good sense. Under Augustus some of the most distinguished jurists were authorised to give legal opinions upon cases submitted to them, so as to become the public expounders of the law. In the time of Gaius the Responsa Prudentum were a recognised source of law, peculiar to the Romans; but it is evident from his account that the functions of these privileged civilians were limited to a declaration of their opinion of what was law in a given case, and did not extend to making new rules of law, which is the proper province of the supreme authority in the state. To this branch of law some encouragement was given by the Emperor Hadrian, who ordained that if the jurists were all agreed upon any question, their opinion should be considered as law by the judge; if they disagreed, the judge was at liberty to follow what opinion he pleased.[2] *New character of Responsa Prudentum.*

Two rival sects or schools of law appeared in the time of Augustus, the one founded by Antistius Labeo and the other by Ateius Capito. Labeo, a scholar of Trebatius, and an ardent republican, was the chief of the Proculians or Pegasians, who were so called after two of his followers. Capito, the pupil of Ofilius and an adherent of the court party, was the chief of the rival sect, called after two of his followers Sabinians or Cassians. Upon various questions of law these two sects differed in opinion; but little is known regarding the character of their differences, beyond what we learn from Pomponius, who says Capito firmly adhered to ancient precedents, while Labeo, with more learning and ingenuity, was disposed to introduce innovations. After the Antonines this division among the jurisconsults disappeared, though we occasionally find partisans of the ancient schools. *Schools of law after Augustus.*

---

[1] I. 2. 17. 8.

[2] "Responsa Prudentum sunt sententiæ et opiniones eorum, quibus permissum est jura condere, quorum omnium si in unum sententiæ concurrant, id quod ita sentiunt, legis vicem obtinet; si vero dissentiunt, judici licet quam velit sententiam sequi; idque rescripto divi Hadriani significatur."—Gai. lib. 1. 7.

Perpetual
Edict, A.D.
131.

Under the empire the edicts of the magistrates, and particularly of the prætors, continued for some time to exercise
the most important influence on the development of the law.
In the reign of Hadrian, Salvius Julianus gave a new form
to the prætorian law by the Perpetual Edict, which was
approved of by the senate, A.D. 131. This was long regarded
as a standard work, and was commented on by Ulpian, Paulus, and other eminent lawyers. Some modern authors have
endeavoured to collect the scattered fragments of the Edict,
and arrange them according to their primitive order.[1]

Imperial
constitu-
tions.

As the imperial constitutions were the last, so they also
became the only source of written law, public and private.
The most ancient constitutions in Justinian's Code go no
farther back than the reign of Hadrian. But there are
several imperial ordinances of a prior date mentioned in
the Institutes and Digest.[2]

The term constitution is used in a general sense to indicate all the acts of the prince; but in the Institutes they are
divided into three principal branches—edicts, rescripts, and
decrees.[3] The edicts were general laws. The rescripts were
the answers of the emperor to those who consulted him,
either as public functionaries or as private persons. The
decrees were the judgments given by the emperor in lawsuits
brought before him as supreme magistrate, either in the first
instance or by way of appeal. As the rescripts and decrees
were from their nature confined to particular cases, they had
not the force of general laws ; but they were sometimes collected by lawyers, and founded on as precedents for the
determination of similar questions. Some constitutions by
the worst emperors, such as Nero, Domitian, Commodus, and
Caracalla, are remarkable for their prudence and wisdom,
which is to be attributed solely to the laudable custom of
making laws with the advice of the most famous civilians in
the council of state, called Auditorium Principis. Whatever
may have been their original character, all the constitutions

---

[1] See Fragmenta Edicti Perpetui,
in the Pandectæ Justinianiæ, by Pothier, t. i. p. 176.

[2] Ortolan, Hist. de la Legislation
Romaine, t. i. p. 264.

[3] I. 1. 2. 6.

inserted in the Theodosian Code, and in the Code of Justinian, became general laws for the whole empire.[1]

Among the civilians who flourished between the reign of Hadrian and the death of Alexander Severus, we find the distinguished names of Pomponius, Cervidius Scævola, Gaius, Papinian, Ulpian, Paulus; and the brilliant series of classical jurists ends with Modestinus. These men were "the great lights of jurisprudence for all time." *Celebrated juriscon- sults after Hadrian.*

During this golden age of Roman jurisprudence, many law books were written—commentaries on the Twelve Tables, on the Perpetual Edict, the Laws of the People, and the Decrees of the Senate; elaborate works on the general body of the law called Digests, or Libri Juris Civilis; elementary books, under such titles as Institutiones, Regulæ, Sententiæ, and the like; notes or commentaries on the writings of the earlier lawyers; and a great mass of treatises on special subjects in every department of the law. Some idea may be formed of the extent and variety of these works from their titles, as given in the Pandects. Time has robbed us of these valuable contributions to legal science, with the exception of a few isolated works and the fragments which have been preserved by the compilers of the Digest. *Writings of the juriscon- sults.*

Some legal treatises which have reached us nearly in their original form, have acquired great celebrity, and are regarded as classics by those engaged in the study of the Roman law. Of these the most precious are the Institutes of Gaius, who flourished under Marcus Aurelius, about A.D. 169. For a long time this work was only known to us from an imperfect epitome in the Breviarium of Alaric. But in 1816, Niebuhr found in the library of Verona a palimpsest which contained the Epistles of St Jerome; and beneath the writing he discovered the manuscript of Gaius. His discovery was verified by Savigny, and the care of deciphering the palimpsest was *Institutes of Gaius.*

[1] There has been much controversy as to the meaning of the *lex regia* mentioned in the Institutes as conferring legislative power on the Roman emperors. It seems now to be generally understood that these expressions mean no more than the imperial prerogatives, which were conferred by law on each emperor at his election. Ortolan, Institutes, t. i. p. 265. De Fresquet, Droit Rom., t. i. p. 80.

intrusted to Professor Goeschen, of Berlin, who was assisted
by Becker and Holweg. These Institutes of Gaius, which
were published under the title 'Gaii Institutionum Commentarii IV.,' are of inestimable value in what may be termed
the classical study of the Roman law. They have thrown
new light on some important branches of law previously involved in much obscurity, and particularly on the forms of
judicial procedure; and they are of immense use in explaining and illustrating the Institutes of Justinian, which are
mainly founded on this long-lost work of Gaius.

Fragmenta Ulpiani. By the side of Gaius we may place the 'Fragments of
Ulpian,' which were preserved in a single manuscript, forming part of the library of the Vatican, entitled, 'Tituli ex
Corpore Ulpiani,' but now usually called 'Ulpiani Fragmenta.' This little treatise, which was probably taken from
the 'Liber Singularis Regularum,' is written with admirable
perspicuity, and contains valuable information upon a variety
of subjects. Next to Papinian, Ulpian holds the first rank
as a Roman jurisconsult, and his works have contributed
more to the Digest than those of any other author.

'Receptæ Sententiæ' of Paulus. Another work deserving of notice is the 'Receptæ Sententiæ' of Julius Paulus, who was a contemporary of Ulpian.
In the Breviarium of Alaric we find an extract from this
valuable work, 'Pauli Sententiarum Libri quinque;' but
doubts exist as to the purity of the text transmitted to us.[1]
Some other works of less importance will be found in the
edition of the 'Corpus Juris Romani Antejustinianei,' lately
published at Bonn.

Schoool of law at Berytus. Towards the beginning of the third century, we find a
special school of law established at Berytus, in Phœnicia,
which acquired great celebrity, and was long a distinguished
rival of two other schools afterwards formed at Rome and
Constantinople.

Decline of law after Alexander Severus. After the death of Alexander Severus, A.D. 235, the Roman

[1] Reference may here be made to
a useful work by Dr Gneist, entitled
'Institutionum et Regularum Juris
Romani Syntagma, exhibens Gai et
Justiniani Institutionum synopsin,
Ulpiani librum singularem regula-
rum, Pauli sententiarum delectum,'
8vo, Lips., 1858.

empire, formerly so powerful, but already much enfeebled, showed manifest symptoms of rapid decay. Ulpian had lost his life in a vain endeavour to restrain the unbridled licence of the prætorian guards, who had usurped the power of electing and dethroning emperors at their pleasure. Government was transformed into a military despotism ; confusion and anarchy prevailed everywhere ; property was not secure, and life was of no value. Amid the distractions of the succeeding times, jurisprudence, like every other branch of knowledge, declined ; and the organisation of Roman government, being left to depend on the accidental character of one man, could never be relied on even to secure the first necessities of civilised life.

When Christianity first appeared in the Roman world, the law could not fail to be affected by the struggle which was for some time maintained between the Pagan element and the Christian element. In 300 years after the death of Christ, we come to the reign of Constantine, which was signalised by the establishment of Christianity as the religion of the state ; the removal of the seat of government from Rome to Constantinople ; and a new organisation of the empire by the separation of the civil administration from the military power which had formerly been united. *Political changes under Constantine.*

At this epoch a great change is perceptible in Roman law. If the emperor was Christian, the empire was still half Pagan. Neglected in worship, Paganism long pervaded society, and lived in the manners of the people. The development of Christianity in Roman life led to great ameliorations in the law, and brought it more into harmony with modern civilisation ; but it is much to be regretted that the intolerant spirit of some of the Christian emperors led to many ordinances, as absurd as they were cruel, against heretics, apostates, and all those who did not belong to the orthodox church.

After Constantine there were two senates, one at Rome and the other at Constantinople, both without any real power. They were municipal councils rather than political bodies. Despotism was established without disguise ; and the ancient magistrates were replaced by imperial functionaries.

New titles of nobility introduced. The simplicity of the early Roman titles was no longer suitable for the state and splendour of the Byzantine Court. Already Diocletian had assumed the diadem and robed himself in purple and gold; and Constantine, following out the same policy, established a titled nobility, who were to stand between the throne and the people. A few of the most intimate councillors of the sovereign were called Patricians; and the titles Count and Duke, which became so common in later ages, now appeared for the first time in the Roman world. The diversity of these honorary distinctions was very great. The princes of the imperial family were *Nobilissimi.* The principal officers and magistrates were divided into five classes, according to a regular gradation of rank and office :—1. The *Illustres;* 2. The *Spectabiles;* 3. The *Clarissimi;* 4. The *Perfectissimi;* and, 5. The *Egregii.* On this subject some curious information will be found in a sort of almanac or court guide of the fifth century, under the title 'Notitia Dignitatum Orientis et Occidentis,' which contains a description of all the territories of the Roman empire, and all the public functionaries employed in every department of the administration.[1]

Ordinances on the works of certain jurists. If the lawyers who flourished from Trajan to Alexander Severus had no successors, the elaborate works they left behind them were of inestimable value in guiding the decisions of the judges, towards the close of the period we are now considering. Constantine ordained the works of Papinian and the Sentences of Paul to be received as authorities in the legal tribunals; but he declared the notes which Paul and Ulpian had written upon Papinian to be of no value. By a remarkable ordinance of Theodosius II. and Valentinian III., in the year 426, the works of five civilians, Gaius, Papinian, Paul, Ulpian, and Modestinus, were established as standard authorities in the courts of law; if they differed, a majority was decisive, but if their opinions were equally divided, a casting vote was given to Papinian, who was considered the first jurisconsult of antiquity, and of whom Cujas has said—"There never was so great a lawyer before, nor ever will be after

[1] See the edition published by Böcking, at Bonn, in 1839.

him." The notes of Paul and Ulpian on Papinian were again declared to .be of no weight, there being strong reasons for believing that his commentators affected to differ from him in order to disparage his memory and gain the favour of Caracalla, who had put him to death. However distinguished these selected jurists might be in their own age, they soon fell two or three centuries behind the times; and at a later period, Justinian repealed the law of citations, by restoring to the judges the full liberty of deciding suits according to their own judgment, without being trammelled by the opinions of any lawyers, however eminent.

On the death of the first Theodosius, A.D. 395, the Roman empire was divided between his two sons,—the provinces of the East being allotted to Arcadius, those of the West to Honorius; and the two parts were never reunited, except for a short time under Justinian. Notwithstanding this division, however, the two parts were still considered as forming one empire; the laws were promulgated in the names of the two emperors, and frequently it is only by the town from which they are dated that we can discover the emperor from whom they emanated.[1] *Division of Roman empire, A.D. 395.*

As the constitutions of the emperors became numerous, they were collected in two works called the Gregorian and Hermogenian Codes. These codes were framed by private individuals, probably under Constantine; but considerable obscurity hangs over their date and contents, as a few fragments only have reached us, which will be found in the 'Corpus Juris Antejustinianeum' of Haenel. *Gregorian and Hermogenian Codes.*

A more important collection was made under the authority of Theodosius II., who ordered certain lawyers, under the direction of Antiochus, to collect and arrange the constitutions from Constantine to his own time. This new collection, called the Theodosian Code, was promulgated as law in the Eastern empire, A.D. 438, and in the same year it was adopted in the Western empire by Valentinian III. It embraces a selection of the edicts and rescripts from A.D. 312 to 438, a period of 126 years, during which sixteen emperors *Theodosian Code, A.D. 438.*

[1] Maynz, Droit Romain, t. i. p. 149.

succeeded to the throne. The work is divided into sixteen books, and the laws which compose each title are arranged in chronological order. Unfortunately, the first five books and the beginning of the sixth have reached us only in a mutilated shape, as epitomised in the 'Breviarium' of Alaric; but some parts of the lost books have been recently recovered by Clossius at Milan, and the Abbé Peyron at Turin.[1]

The Theodosian Code had much more success in the West than the East, where it was soon superseded by Justinian's legislation. In the West it was held in high esteem by the various tribes who overran the Roman empire.

In the seventeenth century the Theodosian Code was enriched by the valuable commentary of James Godefroy, a civilian of great learning and research, who devoted thirty years of his life to this immense work, which was published after his death in 1665.[2]

Gibbon the historian says: "Among the books which I purchased, the Theodosian Code, with the commentary of James Godefroy, must be gratefully remembered. I used it (and much I used it) as a work of history rather than of jurisprudence; but in every light it may be considered as a full and capacious repository of the political state of the empire in the fourth and fifth centuries."[3]

From the Theodosian Code to the time of Justinian we find only a few novels or new constitutions by Theodosius, Valentinian, Marcian, Majorianus, and Anthemius. These are usually printed as a sort of supplement at the end of the Theodosian Code.

Fall of Western empire, A.D. 476. After having been repeatedly invaded by the barbarians, the Western empire was at last destroyed by Odoacer, king of the Heruli, in the year 476. This event marks the fall of the Roman empire of the West. Odoacer, in his turn, was dethroned by Theodoric, the founder of the kingdom of the Ostrogoths in Italy.

---

[1] Codicis Theodosiani Fragmenta inedita, ab Amadeo Peyron. Turin, 1824.

[2] James Godefroy, who was profes-

sor of law at Geneva, died there on 24th June 1652.

[3] Gibbon's Memoirs, p. 213, 8vo.

According to the common reckoning, the reigns of the ancient kings extended to 244 years, the republic endured 478 years, and the Roman empire of the West 507 years; making altogether a period of 1229 years from the foundation of Rome.[1]

[1] The Græco-Roman empire of the East continued to subsist for nearly a thousand years longer, till Constantinople was captured by the Turks in 1453.

CHAPTER II.

Justinian's reform of jurisprudence.

THE reign of Justinian, which extended from A.D. 527 to 565, though not unimportant in other respects, is chiefly remarkable for his great reform of jurisprudence. " In the space of ten centuries," says Gibbon, " the infinite variety of laws and legal opinions had filled many thousand volumes, which no fortune could purchase and no capacity could digest. Books could not easily be found; and the judges, poor in the midst of riches, were reduced to the exercise of their illiterate discretion."[1] Justinian resolved to remedy this state of things, and he conceived the happy idea of recasting the ancient legislation and making it the basis of his own, by uniting into one body all the rules of law, whatever might have been their origin.

Code of imperial constitutions.

In the year 528 Justinian appointed ten jurisconsults, among whom was Tribonian, to select and arrange the imperial constitutions that were still in force, with large discretionary powers to retrench what was obsolete or objectionable, and to make such changes as might appear to them to be necessary to adapt these laws to the existing state of society. The first edition of the Code was completed in fourteen months, and published in April 529.

This Code, however, did not remain long in use. After the publication of the Pandects, Justinian in 534 appointed a new commission of four jurists, under the direction of Tribonian, to revise the Code and place it more in harmony

[1] Gibbon's History, ch. 44.

with the Digest. This was rendered necessary, chiefly in consequence of numerous constitutions issued by the emperor after the year 529, the most important of which were fifty remarkable decisions given by Justinian to settle a series of practical controversies among the ancient lawyers, which had greatly embarrassed the commissioners engaged in the preparation of the Pandects. The new code, called, on account of this revision, 'Codex repetitæ prælectionis,' has alone come down to us, and was published with the force of law in the year 534.

. The Code is divided into twelve books, each book into titles, and each title is composed of a number of imperial constitutions, some entire, and others mutilated, arranged in chronological order. Different matters are treated separately, and the order observed in the successive titles corresponds with the Perpetual Edict. The constitutions bear the names of the emperors by whom they were made, and their dates. Plan of the revised Code.

As the Code comprises the constitutions of the emperors from Hadrian to Justinian, its literary character is far from being uniform. While the laws of Hadrian, and his early successors at Rome, are framed with elegance and precision, those published by the later emperors at Constantinople are often so diffuse that it is difficult to catch their true meaning; and in point of prolixity, Justinian himself is one of the greatest offenders, though the excellence of his matter generally makes up for his deficiencies in form. It must also be observed that many of the constitutions in the Code have been altered by the compilers, so as to discredit it in a historical point of view. This appears from a comparison of Justinian's collection with the Theodosian Code, and is strongly animadverted upon in the commentary of Godefroy.

After the publication of the first edition of the Code, Justinian, in December 530, authorised Tribonian, with the aid of sixteen commissioners, to prepare a collection of extracts from the writings of the most eminent Roman jurists, so as to form a body of law for the government of the empire, suited to the wants of the age. Full power was given to this legislative commission to select what only was useful, to omit what was The Pandects, A.D. 533.

antiquated or superfluous, to avoid contradictions, and to
make such alterations or corrections on the original works as
they might think expedient. Ten years were allowed by the
emperor for this immense work; but it was completed in
three years. It was published, under the title of Digest or
Pandects, on the 16th December 533, and declared to have
the force of law from the 30th of that month.

Extracts
from thirty-
nine jurists.
All the juridical literature of former times was laid under
contribution by Tribonian and his colleagues. Selections
from the works of thirty-nine of the ablest lawyers, scattered
over two thousand separate treatises, were collected in one
volume; and care has been taken to inform posterity, that
three millions of lines were abridged and reduced, in these
extracts, to the modest number of one hundred and fifty
thousand. Among the selected jurists, only three names belonged to the age of the republic; the civilians who flourished
under the first emperors are seldom appealed to; so that most
of the writers whose works have contributed to the Pandects
A.D. 131 to
A.D. 235.
lived within a period of about a hundred years, from the
Perpetual Edict of Hadrian to the death of Alexander Severus.
More than a third of the whole Pandects is from Ulpian, who
is the largest contributor; next to him, the principal writers,
grouped according to the extent of the extracts taken from .
their works, are Paulus, Papinian, Salvius Julianus, Pomponius, Q. Cervidius Scævola, and Gaius.

Great liberties were used with the original works by the
compilers of the Pandects. This was a necessary consequence
of the instructions given to them by Justinian, to make the
collection consistent and suited to the new system of manners, religion, and government. So the extracts are not
always trustworthy; much has been retrenched on purpose,
much added, much changed, in order to produce a harmonious whole. These interpolations are usually ascribed to
Tribonian, who presided over the commission, and are called
Emblemata Triboniani.

Division of
books and
titles.
According to the plan which Justinian prescribed, the
Digest is divided into fifty books. Each book, with the exception of the 30th, 31st, and 32d, is divided into titles, the

total number of which differs in various editions from 427 to
440. Each title, bearing a rubric to indicate its contents, is
subdivided into sections, consisting of extracts from different works relating to the matter specified in the title. The
articles so collected are sometimes termed laws; but as that
expression is not quite accurate, they are now generally called
fragments. Each fragment bears the name of the author and
the title of the work from which it is taken, and is usually
divided into paragraphs, which are all numbered except the
first one called *principium*. The Digest contains at the close
two instructive titles, one " De verborum significatione," and
the other " De regulis juris."

The method which the compilers of the Pandects followed
in arranging the fragments under each title, is the subject of
a learned essay by Bluhme, an ingenious German civilian.[1]

The order of the Digest has been often severely criticised,
and not without reason. Fault has been found with the form
of the extracts, and the mode in which they are ranged under
the different titles. A great number of the laws appear to
be misplaced, and to this disorder is attributed the difficulty
of understanding them. Though the variety of subjects embraced by the Digest is immense, it has no pretensions to
scientific arrangement. It is a vast cyclopedia of heterogene-
ous law badly arranged; everything is there, but everything
is not in its proper place. Yet, with all its imperfections, the
Digest is the collection in which the principles of the Roman
law are most fully developed; and it has been justly described by Sir William Jones as " a most valuable mine of
judicial knowledge."

When Justinian published the Digest, he prohibited the
works of the ancient jurists from being used for the future,
either in the academies or in courts of law; and, in order to
prevent new controversies, all commentaries on the Pandects
were strictly forbidden.

By order of Justinian, an elementary work on law, called The Institutes, A.D.
the Institutes, was composed by two professors, Theophilus 533.

---

[1] On this point see Zeitschrift of   p. 278; De Fresquet, Droit Rom.,
Savigny, t. iv. p. 257; Themis, t. iii.   t. i. p. 28.

and Dorotheus, under the direction of Tribonian. It was published at the close of the year 533, and received the force of law at the same time as the Pandects. This work, which was intended for the use of students, was chiefly founded on the Institutes of Gaius, but the topics were retouched, so as to place them in harmony with the changes which the law had undergone.

The Institutes of Justinian consist of four books, each of which is divided into titles; and the total number of titles is ninety-nine. This abridgment is limited almost exclusively to matters of private law, which is considered under the three-fold division of persons, things, and actions; but at the close of the fourth book there is a title on "judicia publica," a subject omitted by Gaius. Theophilus, one of the compilers of the Institutes, wrote a Greek paraphrase upon them.

No law-book has been so much admired for its method and elegant precision, and none has been so frequently printed, translated, imitated, and commented on, as the Institutes of Justinian. In 1701 a work was published by a learned professor with this remarkable title, ' On the deplorable multitude of commentaries on the Institutes.'[1] And even in our day the tide has not yet turned, for hardly a year passes without adding some volumes to the camel's load.[2]

Novels of Justinian.

Justinian's legislation did not terminate with the publication of the Revised Code in 534. In the subsequent years of his reign, from A.D. 535 to 565, the emperor issued many ordinances, which made important changes on the law,

[1] And. Homberg, De multitudine nimia commentatorum in institutiones juris. Helmstadt, 1701, in 4to.

[2] Vinnius, who was professor at Leyden about the middle of the seventeenth century, published an excellent commentary on the Institutes, which was a favourite book of Pothier. Among recent works, three may be mentioned which de-serve the attention of the student —Les Institutes nouvellement expliquées, by M. Ducarroy, 3 vols. 8vo, 1822 - 27; Explication Historique des Institutes, by M. Ortolan 3 vols. 8vo, 6th edition, 1857; and the Translation of Justinian's Institutes, with Notes, by Sandars, 1 vol. 8vo, 1853.

though their number became less after the death of Tribonian in 545. These new constitutions are written partly in Greek and partly in Latin, in a style somewhat obscure. They are called Novellæ Constitutiones, or, more shortly, Novels. They were officially published some time after Justinian's death; the whole number of Novellæ is 168, of which 154 are ascribed to that emperor, and the rest to his successors, or to prætorian prefects.

A considerable part of this collection relates to matters of private law; and the 118th and 127th Novels merit particular attention, as containing the admirable rules of intestate succession devised by Justinian.

Shortly after Justinian's death, Julian, a professor of law at Constantinople, published a Latin abridgment of 125 Novels, under the title 'Epitome Novellarum.' Another Latin translation of the Novels afterwards appeared, called 'Corpus Authenticum;' and this was the collection which the Glossatores adopted, as having the authority of law.

It was the object of Justinian to comprise in the Code and the Pandects a complete body of law; and Savigny has remarked that these two works "ought properly to be considered as the completion of Justinian's design. The Institutes cannot be viewed as a third work independent of both; it serves as a sort of introduction to them, or as a manual. Lastly, the Novellæ are single and subsequent additions and alterations; and it is merely an accidental circumstance that a third edition of the Code was not made at the end of Justinian's reign, which would have comprised the Novellæ that had a permanent application."[1]

The Roman law, as received in Europe, consists only of what is called the Corpus Juris Civilis—that is, according to the modern arrangement, of the Institutes, the Pandects, the Code, and the Novels—and that in the form which was given to this body of law in the celebrated school of Bologna. According to Savigny, "It was in that form that the Roman law became the common law of Europe; and when, four

Corpus Juris Civilis.

---

[1] Savigny, Geschichte des Röm. Rechts in Mittelalter, vol. i. p. 14.

centuries later, other sources came to be added to it, the Corpus Juris of the school of Bologna had been so universally received, and so long established as the basis of practice, that the new discoveries remained in the domain of science, and served only for the theory of law. For the same reason the Antejustinian law is excluded from practice." Besides, even with reference to the sources generally recognised, it is conceded that the public law has no application in our days, and that there are many matters of private law, such as those relating to slavery and stipulation, which are entirely rejected in modern times.[1]

Antinomies or contradictions.

Where contradictions occur in different parts of the Corpus Juris, we must bear in mind that the new law takes precedence of the more ancient. The Novels have higher authority than the Institutes, the Pandects, and the Code; and among the Novels themselves the last in date are preferred to the earlier ones. The Revised Code prevails over the Institutes and the Pandects, because it is more recent. If there be a discrepancy between the Institutes and the Pandects, it is not easy to solve the difficulty, as they both received the force of law on the same day. No general rule can be laid down; each case must be considered with reference to its own particular circumstances; and a similar course must be followed when contradictions are found between passages occurring in the same part of Justinian's Collection.[2]

Mode of citing Roman law.

The mode of citing the Institutes, the Pandects, and the Code, anciently in use, consisted of reciting the first words of the rubric of the title, as well as of the law and the paragraph. This rendered it necessary to consult the index to Justinian's Collection, which comprehends upwards of twelve hundred titles. In modern times, the manners of citing are very various; but in this country we generally adopt what Gibbon calls " the simple and rational method of numbering the book, the title, and the law." Instead of the term *law*, some writers think it more correct to use the

---

[1] Savigny, Droit Romain, vol. i. p. 68.

[2] Mackeldey, § 77, p. 47. Maynz, vol. i. p. 176, note.

word *fragment* in reference to the Pandects, and *constitution* in reference to the Code.

As to the Novels, they were cited by the Glossatores under the name of Authenticæ, or by the abbreviation Auth. In modern times they are usually distinguished by their number and chapter, thus,—Nov. 118, ch. 1.

On the merits of Justinian's Collection the most opposite opinions have been expressed. By some it has been denounced as a vast unshapely mass of legal lumber, which has long ceased to have any practical utility. By others it is extolled as the most beautiful monument raised by the genius of man. One enthusiast has carried his idolatry so far as to declare that, with the single exception of the Holy Scriptures, there is no work comparable to the Corpus Juris. On both sides of this controversy there has been much exaggeration, and the truth will probably be found to lie between these two extremes. Even the most ardent admirers of Justinian's compilation admit its great faults and imperfections ; and, after the lapse of thirteen centuries, it can excite no surprise that a large portion of it is now wholly inapplicable to the exigencies of modern society. But, with all these drawbacks, this great body of jurisprudence, viewed as a system of private law, has unquestionably exercised the most beneficial influence, both on moral and political science, and has introduced more just and liberal ideas concerning the nature of civil government, and the administration of justice, in all the nations of modern Europe, which rose on the ruins of the Roman empire.

[marginal note: Opinions on Justinian's works.]

CHAPTER III.

Destiny in the East.

Greek translations. IN the Eastern empire the Institutes, Pandects, and Code of Justinian, were translated into Greek. Most of the Novels had been originally issued in that language. These translations, with abridgments and commentaries in Greek, were soon preferred in the East to the originals.

. The emperors of Constantinople published a great number of ordinances which modified the law of Justinian; and then a series of official works appeared in the Greek language, which, without formally abrogating the authority of the Corpus Juris, gradually led to its disuse.

The Basilica. In 867 the Emperor Basilius the Macedonian began to form a new collection in Greek, containing extracts from the Institutes, the Digest, the Code, and the Novels of Justinian, arranged consecutively according to the subjects discussed, with the imperial constitutions of later date, and even upon some points drawing back upon the earlier and purer sources of the Roman law. This work, which consisted of sixty books, divided into titles, was completed by his son Leo the Philosopher, who reigned from A.D. 886 to 911, and was published by him under the title of 'Basilica.' A new edition was issued by Constantine Porphyrogenitus, about A.D. 945.

The 'Basilica,' which maintained their authority till the overthrow of the Eastern empire, have not reached us entire. In 1647 Fabrot published them at Paris, with a Latin version

Thirty-six books are given complete, and seven incomplete, with some extracts from the remaining books. Four of the deficient books were afterwards discovered and published, with a translation, in Meerman's 'Thesaurus Juris Civilis et Canonici.'

The 'Basilica,' written in Greek, and the works of the By- Works of
zantine jurists, among which may be mentioned the 'Promp- jurists.
tuarium' of Constantine Harmenopulus, a judge of Thessal-
onica, who died at Constantinople in 1382, are of great use
in explaining the books of Justinian; for which purpose they
have been largely drawn upon by the famous Cujas, who was
the founder of the historical school of Roman jurisprudence
in France in the sixteenth century.[1]

Destiny in the West.

The Western empire had been dismembered before the
reign of Justinian, and his law-books were at first only destined for his subjects in the East. They were published when
the dominion of the Goths continued in Italy.

From A.D. 415, the Visigoths founded a kingdom in South- Legal
ern Gaul. About the middle of the same century, the Bur- codes in
the West.
gundians formed a kingdom on the banks of the Rhone.
Odoacer, after having overturned the Empire of the West in
476, was himself defeated in 493 by the Ostrogoths, who
became masters of Italy.

For these three kingdoms three legal codes appeared. First
in date was the Edict of Theodoric (' Edictum Theodorici'),
published in 500 for the kingdom of the Ostrogoths. It contains extracts from the sources of the Roman law, very freely
handled; it is short and very incomplete. After Narses had
reconquered Italy in 553, the Edict of Théodoric was replaced
by Justinian's legislation.

The ' Lex Romana Visigothorum,' commonly called ' Breviarium Alaricianum,' which Alaric II. composed in 506 for
the Romans of the kingdom of the Visigoths, contains extracts

---

[1] Haubold, Manuale Basilicorum, t. 9, p. 321. Mortreuil, Histoire du
Lips. 1819. Themis, t. 7, p. 165, and Droit Byzantin, 3 vols., 1847.

from the Theodosian Code, and the Novels annexed to it; from the two works of Gaius and Paulus; from the Gregorian and Hermogenian Codes; and from the Responses of Papinian. Alaric's code was in force in Spain till the middle of the seventh century. In France the same laws were followed under the kings of the first race, in the provinces conquered from the Visigoths.

Of these collections the shortest and most insignificant is that which was compiled for the Burgundians, after the year 517, 'Lex Romana Burgundiorum,' long known by the name of 'Papianus.' This name was given to it by an error of Cujas, which he afterwards corrected, *Papianus* being a contraction for *Papinianus*, some of whose responses are given in the collection. After the fall of the kingdom of the Burgundians in 536, the Breviarium came into use.[1]

By the victories of Belisarius and Narses, Justinian recovered, for a time, Italy and Africa; and, by an edict in 554, he ordered his laws to be observed in the conquered territories. But these laws did not then penetrate beyond Italy into Gaul or Spain, where such of the inhabitants as lived under Roman law were governed by the codes of the Germanic conquerors, who had adopted a considerable part of the Theodosian Code, and other sources of Roman law, such as they subsisted in the Western empire at the time of its dissolution. After a short interval, the Lombards obtained possession of the greater part of Italy: and the emperors of the East lost what remained to them—the Exarchate of Ravenna—in 752.

Roman law never wholly unknown. The researches of Savigny have disproved the popular story, which had already been discredited by Muratori and other writers, that the Roman law had remained for centuries buried in oblivion, till it was suddenly revived, and spread over Europe, by the discovery of the Florentine copy of the Pandects, at the sack of Amalfi, in 1135. There can be no doubt that the Roman law, such as it subsisted in the Western empire at the time of its dismemberment, never lost its authority, but was received in the new Gothic, Lombard, and Carlovingian kingdoms as the rule of those who by birth and

[1] Maynz, § 85.

choice submitted to it. Besides, the works of Justinian, and particularly the Pandects, were known and studied in different parts of Europe long before the siege of Amalfi. In the countries of the West, Justinian's compilation seems to have superseded the Theodosian Code, at some period not quite fixed between the ninth and the eleventh century; and Peter of Valence, in a law-book published by him in the eleventh century, made use of the Institutes, the Pandects, the Code, and the Translation of the Novels by Julian.[1]

Revival of Roman Law in Europe.

The revival of the Roman law as a science in Europe, cor- School of Bologna, A.D. 1120. responded with the rise of the Italian cities. " To Italy, the cradle of the Roman law," says Lerminier, " was reserved the honour of being the theatre of its scientific revival."[2] Irnerius was the founder of the school of law at Bologna, where he gave lectures about the year 1120. The early jurists of Bologna chiefly confined themselves to writing *glosses*, which were short notes explaining what was ambiguous or obscure in the original texts. These glosses were collected and recast by Accursius of Florence, whose work has been severely criticised by some authors, who do not make sufficient allowance for the ignorance inevitable to the age in which he wrote.

From the famous school of Bologna, the knowledge of Roman law spread rapidly over Europe. The absurdities which prevailed at that time in the administration of justice, may be conceived from the authentic monuments which remain of the ancient barbarian laws ; and nothing tended more to recommend the study of the Roman law, than the extreme imperfection of that jurisprudence which preceded it among all the European nations.[3] Vacarius, a Lombard, went to England, and delivered a course of lectures at Oxford, so early as 1149. He wrote a work intended for poor students, consisting of extracts literally taken from the

---

[1] Lerminier, Histoire du Droit, p. 462.
[2] Ibid., p. 33.
[3] See Hume's History of England, vol. iii. p. 300.

C

Pandects and parts of the Code, with this title : ' Liber ex universo enucleato jure excerptus, et pauperibus præsertim destinatus.' King Stephen interdicted Vacarius from teaching the Roman law in England, and ordained all manuscripts on that subject to be destroyed; but this edict had little effect, and the study of the civil law was promoted by the clergy, who engrossed all the learning of the times, and filled the most important offices in the kingdom.

Scholastic jurists.   To the Glossatores succeeded the Scholastic lawyers, who figured from the thirteenth to the end of the fifteenth century, and among whom Odofredus, Bartolus, and Baldus are conspicuous. They are sometimes called Bartolists, and are charged with sacrificing the authority of the original texts of the Roman law to the private opinions of the commentators; their tiresome prolixity, idle subtleties, and barbarous style, have now almost condemned their works to total oblivion.

During four centuries the cultivation of the science of law in Europe was chiefly confined to the schools of Italy, where jurisprudence flourished by the side of literature and poetry. Dante was born five years after the death of Accursius ; Petrarch and Boccaccio were contemporaries of Bartolus ; and when the Greeks were driven from Constantinople, some noble exiles repaired to Italy, where they diffused a taste for polite literature as well as for history and antiquities, and, by raising the standard of learning, greatly improved jurisprudence. Angelus Politanus, who died in 1494, takes high rank as one who powerfully contributed to unite classical literature with the study of law.

French school in sixteenth century.   In the sixteenth century, the science of theoretical law passed from Italy to France. On the invitation of Francis I., Andrew Alciat of Milan went to Bourges, where he delivered lectures on Roman law, and attracted great crowds of students. He was one of the first who combined the study of law with polite learning and the knowledge of antiquities. Bayle describes Alciat as a tall burly man, of a restless disposition, very fond of money and good living, and says he died of a surfeit at Pavia in 1550.[1]

[1] See Bayle's Dict. Hist., voce *Alciat.*

About the year 1550, Cujas, better known, perhaps, under his Latin name Cujacius, became professor at Bourges, the principal scene of his labours, where he acquired great renown and founded the historical school of jurisprudence. Though his writings are voluminous from the great variety of subjects embraced by them, they are not diffuse; on the contrary, he combined the art of lucid explanation with great brevity. His famous Paratitla on the Digest contains a brief exposition of every title in order, with little additional matter; and his great rival, Hotman, prized this little book so highly, that he advised his son to carry it constantly about with him. Among all the interpreters of Roman law who have appeared in modern Europe, Cujas is generally acknowledged to hold the first rank. His works make an epoch in jurisprudence; and we are told that, in the public schools of Germany, such was his renown, that when his name was mentioned every one took off his hat.[1] Cujas, who was a native of Toulouse, died at Bourges in 1590.[2]

Doneau, a professor of Bourges, who was strongly opposed to Cujas, wrote independent treatises on Roman law in vigorous Latin. In 1567, Francis Hotman published his 'Anti-Tribonianus,' to mortify Cujas, and please the Chancellor de l'Hôpital. In this work Hotman declares war against the whole Roman law. Not only does he malign Justinian and Tribonian, but he has no admiration to spare even for the classical jurists, such as Papinian, Paul, and Ulpian. The learned and acute author of this curious book is the father of the Anti-Romanists. He recommended that a new code of laws should be framed, taking whatever was valuable in the Roman system, and adding whatever from other sources might appear worthy of adoption. These opinions were favourably received by many lawyers in France; and this party had so much influence, that, by the ordinance of Blois in 1579, the University of Paris was forbidden to give lectures on civil law. This was not strictly regarded; and, in a century after-

'Anti-Tribonianus' of Hotman.

[1] Biog. Univ. Hallam's Literature of Europe, vol. ii. p. 72.
[2] For a list of his principal works,

see Lerminier, Hist. du Droit, p. 48, note.

wards, the lectures were resumed, on account of the uncertainty which the neglect of the Roman law was said to have occasioned.[1]

In order that the French law might receive in the sixteenth century the same impulse as the Roman law did from Cujas, Charles Dumoulin appeared.   He was an advocate of the Parliament of Paris, and was esteemed, at his death in 1566, the most learned man of his time in the civil and customary law of France.   In his commentaries on the customs of Paris, Dumoulin combined so admirably the Roman law with that of France, that all who have come after him have followed him as their master; he paved the way for the works of Pothier; and he may be said to hold the same place as a jurist in France, as Sir Edward Coke does in England, and Lord Stair in Scotland.

School of the Netherlands.
In Spain and the Netherlands, the Roman law was cultivated with great success, particularly after the sixteenth century.   A school was formed in the Netherlands, which, if it did not surpass, at least deserves to be placed alongside of the French school of the sixteenth and seventeenth centuries. Among other able civilians, Holland may be justly proud of such men as Grotius, Van Leeuwen, Vinnius, Huber, Voet, Schulting, Noodt, and Bynkershoek; and so high was the reputation of her professors, that for a considerable time they acquired pre-eminence over the French, and attracted large crowds of students to Leyden and Utrecht, in place of Bourges and Toulouse.

In the seventeenth and eighteenth centuries, the Roman law was discussed, improved, and illustrated by many able writers besides those already mentioned, such as the Godefroys, Domat, Gravina, Heineccius, Bach, and Pothier.

Heineccius and Bach.
In threading his way through the labyrinths of Roman law, Gibbon acknowledges that he found an able guide in Heineccius, a German professor, who died at Halle in 1741. Heineccius enjoyed great authority as an elegant writer on all that was known on this subject in his time; he wrote a history of Roman law and German law. His Roman Antiquities,

---

[1] Hallam's Literature, vol. ii. p. 75.

particularly in the new edition brought out by Haubold, have been much admired, and are considered by many as his best work.   As to his elementary treatises on the Institutes and the Pandects, they are written in a concise and perspicuous style, and were long adopted as text-books in some of the principal universities of Europe; but they have now lost much of their value by the labours and discoveries of the historical school.   Bach, another German civilian, who died in 1758, was, before the advent of the historical school, the best historian of the Roman law.

Rapid and imperfect as this sketch must necessarily be, it would be unpardonable to pass over Pothier.   He died in 1772, before the French Revolution, after writing those celebrated works on French jurisprudence which brought it to the highest perfection it ever attained before the formation of the Codes.   But his laurels were not confined to one field of glory.   For it was reserved to Pothier to realise the magnificent project of Leibnitz, which was to reform the Roman law of Justinian, by reducing it to systematic order, without destroying the purity of the original texts.[1]

About the middle of the eighteenth century Pothier published his great work, entitled 'Pandectæ Justinianeæ in novum ordinem digestæ.'   Sensible of the great imperfections of Justinian's collection in point of arrangement, Pothier resolved to throw light over this chaos of Roman law, and to do for it what Tribonian and his associates ought to have done—that is to say, to collect together the texts which were scattered through these immense books, to elucidate these texts one by the other, and that solely by the manner in which they were placed and connected; in a word, by substituting order for confusion, to render almost useless the innumerable commentaries under which the buried texts had groaned for ages.   Nothing could exceed the boldness of this

Pothier's Pandects.

---

[1] This merit has been erroneously ascribed by Mr Hallam (Literature of Europe, vol. iii. p. 447) to Domat, who published in 1689 his 'Loix Civiles dans leur Ordre Naturel,'—a book which had great success in its day, particularly in France.   But it did not carry into effect the project of Leibnitz, being a systematic treatise in the French language, and not a rearrangement of the laws of Justinian.

design; it seemed to surpass the resources of any single man, and to require time exceeding the ordinary duration of human life. And how was this herculean task accomplished? After twelve years of continuous labour, Pothier produced a work written in Latin, in which he preserved the ancient division of the books and titles of the Pandects, but re-arranged the texts under each title according to their natural order, so that each title forms a complete treatise on the subject indicated in the rubric. Immediately after the exposition of the subject are placed the texts containing definitions and general principles. Methodical divisions and subdivisions facilitate the classification and understanding of the other texts. The ancient law is explained and illustrated, and great care is taken to show how far its provisions have been confirmed, interpreted, modified, or repealed by the Institutes, the Code, and the Novels. Antinomies are either reconciled or explained, and obscure texts are elucidated in notes of remarkable clearness and brevity. Whatever is the work of the author, the transitions by which he has so skilfully connected the laws so as to show their relation to each other, the notes, equally learned and concise, with which he has illustrated them, are all clearly distinguished by being printed in italics, and by this ingenious device the texts are presented in their original purity.

Of the utility of this work of Pothier to the students of Roman law it is impossible to speak too highly, though the method followed is diametrically opposed to that of his countryman Cujas. In explaining the Roman law to his scholars, Cujas, like a literary antiquarian, reunited all the extracts from the same jurisconsult which are scattered in the Digest; it was not, properly speaking, the Pandects he made them read—it was Ulpian, Paul, Papinian. On the other hand, Pothier in his Pandects has dealt with his subject like a practical lawyer—he has preserved the same distribution and the same sequence of books and of titles; but he has changed the order of the laws ranged under these titles, and combined in one view all that relates to the same matter. For this reason, whoever wishes thoroughly to understand the topic discussed under any particular title of the Digest, should carefully peruse all the texts under that head in Pothier's Pandects, where he will find brought together in one view, not only what is scattered under different titles of the Digest, but what relates to the same matter in the Institutes, the Code, and the Novels.

To Roman jurisprudence, it must be confessed, Britain *Civilians in Britain.* has contributed very little. Arthur Duck, an Englishman, acquired some reputation for a succinct treatise in Latin, on the use and authority of the civil law in different countries in Europe. The 'Elementa Jurisprudentiæ' of Dr Richard Zouch, published at Oxford in 1629, and reprinted by the Elzevirs at Leyden, is an excellent epitome of the leading doctrines of the Roman law. 'Wood's Institutes' have long been thought antiquated. Without undervaluing the learning and research of Dr Taylor, his 'Elements of the Civil Law' are very imperfect, the subjects discussed being of very limited extent, while the bulk of the book is swelled by numerous digressions and long quotations from Greek and Roman authors. Dr Browne's 'View of the Civil Law' contains some interesting comparisons between the Roman system and the English law, and, though not free from inaccuracies, is a work of considerable merit. In the 44th chapter of his History, Gibbon has given a rapid and masterly sketch of the Roman jurisprudence—a wonderful effort of genius, to which it would be difficult to find a parallel in the writings of the professed civilians. Hugo translated this celebrated chapter into German in 1789, and Warnkoenig published a French version of it, with notes, in 1821. Within the last few years a considerable number of works on Roman law have issued from the English press. Of these the most remarkable is an elaborate treatise in four volumes published by Dr Colquhoun, formerly a pupil of Thibaut, and now a judge in the Ionian Islands.

That the Roman law exercised considerable influence on the law of England cannot be doubted; for Bracton, and other early writers, who contributed much to the formation of the English law, borrowed many rules and principles from the civilians. Though the old English common lawyers showed great aversion to the Roman law, the Crown and the Church were generally arrayed in its favour. Everywhere the churchmen combined the study of the civil law with their own canons, and degrees in both laws were given in the universities. The English system of equity and the ecclesiastical law have been formed more or less extensively on the Roman law, or on the Roman through the Canon law. On the other hand, the English people, jealous of their national freedom, had a rooted dislike to the public law of the Romans, which set no limits to the royal prerogative, and placed the prince beyond the control of any other power ; and therefore, when at various times attempts were made in Parliament to introduce changes founded on the Roman law, these innovations were strenuously resisted by the English barons, from a natural apprehension that they might prove injurious to the liberties of the subject.[1] In every free country there are good grounds for rejecting the public law of the Romans, as being suitable only for an absolute government ; but this circumstance does not derogate from the excellence of their private law, the value of which is acknowledged by the most eminent English jurists. Mr Austin observes : " The importance of securing the existence of a body of lawyers with a somewhat extensive knowledge of the civil law is not to be disputed. Questions arise incidentally in all our tribunals on systems of foreign law, which are mainly founded on the civil. The law obtaining in some of our colonies is principally derived from the same original ; and questions arising directly out of colonial law are brought before the Privy Council by way of appeal."[2]

In Scotland the Roman law was much more favourably received than it was in England. From the close alliance that so long subsisted with France, Scotland borrowed many of its institutions from that country, besides importing a large portion of Roman jurisprudence to make up the deficiencies of a municipal law, long crude and imperfect, and which

[1] Dr Hurd's Moral and Political Dialogues, vol. ii. p. 194-209.

[2] Austin's Lectures on Jurisprudence, vol. iii. p. 367.

had made little progress as a national system till some time after the establishment of the Court of Session in 1532. King James V. instituted that court, as Sir George Mackenzie informs us, after the model of the Parliament of Paris ; and, by its original constitution, the ordinary judges were composed of seven churchmen and seven laymen, with a president. Properly speaking, the teaching of the civil law commenced in Scotland at the Reformation, in 1560. Previous to that era, it was a common practice for young men destined for the legal profession, upon finishing their course of education in Scotland, to go abroad and prosecute their studies in civil law at one or more of the universities on the Continent; and this practice continued to a considerable extent with those who wished to attain proficiency in this department of jurisprudence, long after chairs for teaching it had been established in the Scottish universities. In Scotland a knowledge of the Roman law has always been regarded as the best introduction to the study of the municipal law. No person can be admitted a member of the Faculty of Advocates without undergoing an examination in both laws. The judges of the Supreme Court are usually selected from that body ; and by an express article of the Treaty of Union, no one, not an advocate, can be appointed a judge of the Court of Session without passing an examination in Roman law. All the best writers on the law of Scotland, such as Stair, Bankton, Erskine, and Bell, were able civilians ; and though they have not produced separate treatises on the subject, their works abound with admirable illustrations of the Roman law, evincing great learning and research, and a familiar acquaintance with the writings of the Continental jurists.

Since the close of the eighteenth century a new historical school has sprung up in Germany, where the study of Roman jurisprudence has been prosecuted with extraordinary ardour and success. By the discovery of some ancient works, disclosing new sources of information, something like the enthusiasm of the sixteenth century has been rekindled. The Institutes of Gaius, the new constitutions of the Theodosian Code, the 'Fragmenta Vaticana,' the 'Republic' of Cicero, the

Historical school of Germany.

Letters of Fronto and Marcus Aurelius, the 'Rhetoric' of
Julius Victor, the fragments of Symmachus, of Dionysius of
Halicarnassus, of Lydus on Magistrates, have opened up a
rich mine for the investigation of the modern German jurists.
Facts formerly unknown have been revealed; ancient errors
traditionally received have been exploded; and Roman law,
as a science, has in many respects assumed a new aspect.
To this department of knowledge the writings of Hugo, Haubold, Thibaut, Niebuhr, and Savigny have given a wonderful
impulse.   In 1811 M. Niebuhr published the first edition
of his 'Roman History;' but he afterwards saw reason to
modify many of his views.   Frederick Charles von Savigny,
professor of law at Berlin, who died in October 1861, in the
83d year of his age, stood at the head of the historical school
of Germany.   Besides a treatise on Possession, published in
1803, he is the author of two celebrated works—first, the
'History of the Roman Law during the Middle Ages,' and,
secondly, the 'System of actual Roman Law,' both being distinguished by great erudition and learning.   To Charles de
Vangerow, professor of Roman law at Heidelberg, we are
indebted for an admirable treatise on the Pandects ('Lehrbuch
der Pandecten,' 3 vols., 6th edition, 1855); this contains a
clear exposition and probably the best solutions of the controversies on the civil law which have engaged the attention
of modern jurists.   Nor, among other eminent German civilians in our day, must we omit to mention Mackeldey, Marezoll, and Warnkoenig, who are the authors of excellent elementary works on Roman law, which we have found extremely
useful in guiding our researches.

In some countries of Europe, and particularly in France
and Germany, the publication of new civil codes has superseded to a considerable extent the practical application of the
Roman law; but this circumstance has not proved so injurious to the study of that law as was often predicted by the
adversaries of the historical school.   For, as Marezoll has
justly remarked, the Roman law not only possesses a universal scientific value, which it can never lose, but preserves
also indirectly a practical value, in this sense, that it forms

the basis of the new civil codes of different states, besides furnishing an inexhaustible store of general principles for the decision of questions constantly occurring in daily practice which are not settled by statute, precedent, or usage. In giving judgment in Acton *v.* Blundell, Chief-Justice Tindal observed: " The Roman law forms no rule binding in itself on the subjects of those realms; but in deciding a case upon principle, where no direct authority can be cited from our books, it affords no small evidence of the soundness of the conclusion at which we have arrived, if it prove to be supported by that law—the fruit of the researches of the most learned men, the collective wisdom of ages, and the groundwork of the municipal law of most of the countries of Europe." [1]

[1] 12 Meeson and Welsby, p. 324.

ON JURISPRUDENCE AND THE PRINCIPAL DIVISIONS OF LAW.

THE object of this chapter is to take a cursory glance at jurisprudence as a science, and to make some general observations on the principal divisions of law which form the subject of a course of legal education. In some Continental universities, chairs are set apart for this general instruction, as forming the best introduction to the study of law in any of its special departments.

Jurisprudence defined.

Jurisprudence, in its literal sense, means knowledge of law. Ulpian, who entertained very lofty ideas of his favourite study, defined jurisprudence to be the knowledge of things divine and human, and the science of right and wrong.[1] According to modern notions, jurisprudence is the science or philosophy of positive law—that is, law established in an independent political community by the authority of its supreme government. By positive law jurists understand a collection of rules, to which men living in civil society are subjected in such a manner that they may, in case of need, be constrained to observe them by the application of force. General jurisprudence investigates the principles which are common to various systems of positive law, apart from the local, partial, and accidental peculiarities of each ; while particular jurisprudence treats of the law of a determinate nation, such as France or England.[2] By French writers, jurisprudence is sometimes used in a technical sense to denote law

[1] "Jurisprudentia est divinarum atque humanarum rerum notitia, justi atque injusti scientia."—I. 1. 1. 1.

[2] Austin, Lectures on Jurisprudence, vol. iii. p. 349 et seq.

founded on judicial decisions, or on the writings of lawyers ; and in popular language it is frequently employed with us as synonymous with law.

Natural justice or equity consists in doing what is right in the circumstances of each particular case. Legal justice means acting in conformity with positive law. *Justice natural and legal.*

Justice was defined by Ulpian to be a constant and uniform disposition of mind to render to every one his due.[1] Judicial tribunals, however, without diving into the motives of men, only take cognisance of their external actions, which in a legal sense are accounted just or unjust, according as they are or are not in conformity with positive law.

As the science of ethics embraces the whole range of moral duties, its province is evidently much wider than that of jurisprudence, which treats only of those duties that can be enforced by external law. To explain these distinctions, writers on ethics affirm that what is enjoined by jurisprudence is of perfect obligation, and what is enjoined by morality is of imperfect obligation—that is, that we may or may not do what our conscience dictates, but that we can be compelled to do what positive law directs. *Relations of positive law and morality.*

Experience shows that the number of actions which are commonly withdrawn from the free will of the individual, and regulated by state legislation, is exceedingly various, being sometimes more and sometimes less, so that no limits can be assigned to the domain of law. Of positive moral rules, some are laws properly so called, being transcribed into the civil law, and adopted by it; while others are merely rules imposed by opinion, and not imperative, the obligation to observe them resting only upon the conscience.

The divine law, morality, and positive law, are related to each other in various ways; and it has been observed, that " there are cases wherein they agree, wherein they disagree without conflicting, and wherein they disagree and conflict."[2]

When Hobbes affirms that " no law can be unjust"—an

---

[1] " Justitia est constans et perpe-tua voluntas jus suum cuique tribu-endi."— I. 1. 1. pr.

[2] Austin, Province of Jurispru-dence Determined, p. 17.

assertion which may appear to many a startling paradox—he means, that no positive law is *legally unjust;* and this is quite correct. For, according to the explanation already given, the measure or test of *legal justice and injustice* is positive law. But, although an act may be just, as tried by a given law, the law itself may be unjust, as measured by a different standard, such as the divine law, or positive morality.

"Though it signifies conformity or nonconformity to any determinate law, the term *justice* or *injustice* sometimes denotes emphatically conformity or nonconformity to the ultimate measure or test—namely, the Law of God. This is the meaning annexed to justice, when law and justice are opposed."[1]

Principal divisions of law. Before entering upon the special subject of Roman law, it may be useful to give a short explanation of the principal divisions of law. These may be considered under the following heads: 1. The Divine Positive Law; 2. Natural Law; 3. The Positive Law of Independent States; and, 4. The Law of Nations, or International Law. The divine law, though of vast importance to all men, is the province of the theologian; natural law is a branch of practical morality; the positive law of different states is the proper study of professional lawyers; and the modern law of nations, which regulates their mutual relations, is an object of the most lively interest, not only to jurists and publicists, but to statesmen and politicians of every class throughout the world

I.—OF DIVINE POSITIVE LAW.

Divine positive law. The positive law of God is that which concerns the duties of religion, being the principles regarding faith and manners revealed in the Holy Scriptures. The precepts derived from revelation are called the divine positive law, as distinguished from the divine natural law, which is composed of principles recognised by reason alone, without the aid of revelation.

Though it may be possible for us, by the use of our reason,

[1] Austin, note, p. 276 *et seq.*

to discover the natural difference between good and bad actions, or between virtue and vice, divine revelation is of infinitely more value than any moral system framed by ethical writers, not only in making known to us the rule of duty, but in establishing our obligations to observe it. For the voice of revelation is the most authoritative and authentic declaration of the will of God. Besides instructing the ignorant and the careless, it will help "to teach the rule of duty even to those who are the most diligent inquirers; because, as the knowledge of God is infinitely superior to our own, His declarations about the nature and consequence of our actions will be a surer guide to us than our own experience and reasonings can be."[1]

II.—OF NATURAL LAW.

Natural law, the existence of which has sometimes been contested, has been a fertile subject of controversy. The idea which the Romans attached to the *jus naturale* is singularly vague and uncertain. By Ulpian it is described as the law which nature has taught all living creatures, so as to be common to men and beasts;[2] but this notion has been generally condemned, the law of nature in a proper sense being peculiar to rational beings. Sometimes it is used as equivalent to equity, and sometimes it is represented as synonymous with the *jus gentium.*[3] In a very striking passage of his work, 'De Republica,' Cicero has given us his views of natural law, declaring God to be its author, and its duties to be of unchangeable obligation. "It is not," therefore," says he, "one law in Rome and another in Athens, one to-day and another to-morrow; but it is ever the same, exerting its obligatory force over all nations and throughout all ages."[4] *Roman notions of natural law.*

There is some difference in the theories of writers on the law of nature. Chancellor Kent, following very nearly the *Opinions of Grotius and other writers.*

---

[1] Rutherforth, Institutes of Natural Law, vol. i. p. 21.
[2] D. 1. 1. 3.

[3] Gaius, D. 1. 1. 9. I. 1. 2. 1.
[4] Cicero de Republica, lib. iii. 23.

definition of Grotius, says: "By the law of nature, I under-stand those fit and just rules of conduct which the Creator has prescribed to man as a dependent and social being, and which are to be ascertained from the deductions of right reason, though they may be more precisely known and more explicitly declared by divine revelation."[1] This law is said to be written on the heart of every man by the finger of God, so that no one can pretend ignorance of it, and being essen-tially just, its authority is the same at all times and in all places.

Many writers, like Dr Paley, consider natural law as equi-valent to moral science, which embraces our duties to God, to our neighbours, and to ourselves.[2] Others apply the term natural law exclusively to the rules prescribed to man by right reason in his conduct to his fellow-men.[3] A third class use this term in a still more restricted sense, to denote the theory of that part of our duties to our fellow-men which is capable of being enforced.

In discussing the question whether natural law is the same as the moral law, or, if they differ, in what the difference con-sists, M. Serrigny observes: "The *moral law*, taken in a large sense, appears to me to embrace all the rules of conduct pre-scribed to man by his reason either towards himself or to-wards God. *Natural law*, equally in a large sense, is often taken for the collection of the rules of conduct prescribed to man by right reason; but, in a restricted sense, it relates exclusively to that branch of the same rules of conduct by man to his fellow-creatures, which oblige him in a stricter manner, and which may furnish matter for an actual law in favour of others against him. In other words, *natural law* embraces that part of the duties of man towards his fellow-creatures which may be sanctioned by written law; while the *moral law*, besides the duties of man towards himself

[1] Wightman, 4 Johns, Ch. R., 343. Cited in Story's Conflict of Laws, p. 208, note.
[2] Paley's Moral Philosophy, book i. chap. i. p. 1.
[3] "Le droit naturel, c'est la partie de la morale qui embrasse tous les devoirs des hommes les uns envers les autres." — De Fresquet, Traité Elementaire de Droit Romain, t. i. p. 11.

and towards God, comprehends that part of his duties towards others, which do not oblige him in a legal sense, and do not become matter for the sanction of the civil law." [1]

Among early writers, natural law was more a system of morals than a theory of law. It is only recently that an attempt has been made, chiefly by German philosophers, to separate natural law from morality, by distinguishing human duties into those the performance of which may be compelled by external force, and those which must be left entirely to the conscience of the individual. On the relation of natural law to positive there is great want of precision among the German writers, and they leave undecided the question, whether the law of nature should be regarded merely as a branch of morality, or whether its principles should be practically applied in judicial tribunals.[2] As moral law leaves everything to conscience, it is generally considered that a judge can only enforce moral duties when they are also recognised by positive law.[3]

There are common rules of justice dictated by reason and founded on the rational nature of man, which are not peculiar to any one nation, but are universally recognised; and although these rules would be morally binding on men living in a social state independently of human institutions, yet a great part of the civil law is taken up in confirming and enforcing them. Where the law of nature absolutely commands or forbids, it is immutable and of universal obligation, so that, although it may be confirmed, it cannot be controlled by human laws without a manifest violation of the divine will. There are many things, however, which, as moral agents, we are at perfect liberty to do or not to do, without infringing our moral duties; so that a wide field is left open for the operation of what is called the law of the land.

[1] Serrigny, Traité du Droit Public des Français, t. i. p. 92.

[2] Falck, Encyclopédie Juridique, traduite de l'Allemand par C. A.

Pellat, p. 113.

[3] Lindley's Introduction to Study of Jurisprudence, p. 9.

III.—OF THE POSITIVE LAW OF INDEPENDENT STATES.

Positive law, when applied to a determinate nation, such
as France, Spain, or England, is the collection of rules of
civil conduct prescribed and enforced by the supreme power
in the state. Differences in climate, locality, wealth, commerce, civilisation, manners and customs, and an infinite
variety of external circumstances and relations, lead to an
endless diversity of laws among different nations.[1]

Diversities
of law in
different
states.

For the same reasons the law of the same people under-
goes constant changes, independently of the action of the
legislative power. Nor can this instability be justly regarded as a reproach. For it is impossible to imagine a
body of positive law equally fitted for all times and circumstances; and experience shows that the symmetry of a sound
philosophical system of jurisprudence can only be maintained
by adapting it from time to time to the progress and common feelings of the people.

Many
positive
rules
arbitrary.

In every civilised state there are numerous rules of positive
law which are purely arbitrary, and admit of being repealed
or altered without doing injustice to any one. Thus the
form of solemnising marriage, the number of witnesses required for a testament, the proper age for legal majority, the
term of years necessary for prescription, the procedure to be
observed in courts of law, and a multitude of other things,
are all left indifferent by the law of nature, and are fixed by
mere arbitrary regulations, which are different in different
states, and may be changed at any time on grounds of public
convenience.

Nothing, however, is indifferent, when positive law has
once enjoined or prohibited it. If the authority of the law-
giver be sufficient, the law must be respected in small things
as well as in great, without regard to its wisdom or importance; and, if required, the whole power of the state may be

---

[1] Pascal has expressed himself
with bitter irony on the diversities
of law in different countries :—
" Plaisante justice qu'une rivière
ou une montagne borne : verité en
deça des Pyrenées, erreur au dela."
—Pensées, part i. art. vi. § 8.

employed to enforce obedience. For " laws are mere nullities without the force necessary to support them ; " and if the breach of any one law, however trivial, were tolerated, it would demoralise the people, by diminishing the habit of respect for other laws of vital importance to the public welfare.

Apart from the element of force, obedience to the just _{Moral} laws of our country is generally acknowledged to be a moral _{obligation of positive} duty binding on the conscience. This conclusion is rested _{law.} not only on the deductions of reason, but on Scriptural grounds ; and Jeremy Taylor, in a learned dissertation on the subject, declares this doctrine to be " certain as an article of faith, and as necessary as any rule of manners." No doubt, if the laws of man are directly at variance with the declared will of God, the last must be obeyed as of paramount authority, whatever penalty may thereby be incurred. But no man is wiser than the law, and it must always be presumed, till the contrary be proved, that the human law is just, and not opposed to the divine law ; so that disobedience is presumptively wrong in morals, and the responsibility, in case of error, lies on him who disobeys.[1]

The best contrived laws being intended for general use, it _{Imperfections in} is impossible to shape them so correctly as to suit all the _{all legal} variety of cases that may happen ; and there are many ways _{systems.} in which men may injure one another without the civil law affording any means of redress. So imperfect, indeed, is the civil law, that, in attempting to do justice, it sometimes puts it in the power of a man to take exorbitant advantages contrary to conscience.

Against these imperfections there is no appeal except to the conscience. And here we are reminded of the three general precepts mentioned by Justinian—to live uprightly to hurt nobody, and to render to every one his due.[2] These maxims breathe a fine spirit of morality, and are evidently for the common advantage of men in their social relations ; yet

---

[1] See Black. Com., vol. i. p. 58, Coleridge's Note.

[2] "Juris præcepta sunt hæc : hon- este vivere, alterum non lædere, suum cuique tribuere."—I. 1. 1. 1.

with all their excellence, they fall greatly short of the golden rule of the Gospel: " All things whatsoever ye would that men should do to you, do ye even so to them " (Mat. vii. 12).

The general security of private rights and of civil life, requires adherence to fixed rules and prior decisions by courts of law, and this occasionally leads to hardship in particular cases ; but this particular hardship, after all, is a lesser evil than the general uncertainty and confusion that would spring up everywhere, were the discretion of judges left entirely unfettered by positive rules.[1]

Positive law written and unwritten.

The positive law of every country may be divided, after the example of the Romans, into written and unwritten. Written or statutory law is enacted by the express authority of the supreme power, and is always reduced into writing. Unwritten or customary law is that which has not been promulgated by the legislature in a written form, but derives its binding power from long usage.[2]

All laws may be abrogated in whole or in part by other laws, and this may be done either expressly, by the repeal of the old law, or tacitly, when the new law contains provisions contrary to those of the former one ; for, whenever a contradiction arises between a new and an old law, the new one has the preference : *Jus posterius derogat priori.*

Unwritten laws, though at first established by usage, may be repealed or altered by an express act of the legislature. They may likewise be abrogated by long disuse ; for as they are founded merely on custom, long and uninterrupted disuse affords evidence that they are no longer in force.

Sometimes written laws are said to become obsolete, if they have not for any considerable time been put in execution, so that what they enjoin has been long neglected, or

---

[1] Lord Camden has drawn a very alarming picture of the dangers that would result from allowing too great scope to judicial discretion. "The discretion of a judge is the law of tyrants ; it is always unknown ; it is different in different men ; it is casual, and depends upon constitu- tion, temper, passion. In the best, it is oftentimes caprice ; in the worst, it is every vice, folly, and passion to which human nature is liable." See also Lord Eldin's re- marks, in 1 Bligh, 23, 24.

[2] I. 1. 2. 9.

what they forbid has been long practised with impunity. But, in principle, no written law can be abrogated by disuse. Nevertheless it was a maxim of the Roman jurists, that as laws may be established by long custom, so they may likewise be abrogated by desuetude or contrary usage.[1] In Scotland this doctrine has been adopted and applied even to statutes. For it has been determined that Scotch Acts of Parliament passed before the Union in 1707, may lose their force and become ineffectual by contrary practice, without any express repeal. The law of England follows a different rule, which is, that every statute, however ancient, continues in force till repealed by another statute. A striking illustration of the application of this rule occurred in the well-known case of Ashford v. Thornton, in 1818, where the Court of King's Bench, in an appeal of murder, sustained trial by battle.[2] After this decision, which sanctioned judicial combat in the nineteenth century, an Act was passed repealing the law respecting appeals of murder and wager of battle.

Another distinction originated with the Roman jurists, who divided positive law into public and private. Public law is that which treats of the constitution of the state, and the relations existing between the government and the individual members of the community. Private law (sometimes called civil law) is that which treats of the relations of these individual members *inter se*.[3] Public and private law.

Public law is sometimes distinguished into political or constitutional and administrative. Under the first head the constitution of the state is considered. Under the second the general administration is traced, including the judicial organisation, military and naval establishments, finance and other departments under the charge of public officers employed by the government. By most of the modern jurists criminal law is treated as a part of public law. It is an

---

[1] I. 1. 2. 11. D. 1. 3. 32. 1.

[2] Barn and Ald., p. 405. In his work on the origin and progress of French legislation (Paris, 1816, note, p. 305), M. Bernardi pointed ont this strange anomaly, and observed, "Il n'est pas possible de porter plus loin le respect pour les anciens usages."

[3] "Publicum jus est quod ad statum rei Romanæ spectat ; privatum, quod ad singulorum utilitatem."— I. 1. 1. 4.

established rule, that the public law cannot be controlled or altered at the will of individuals, by private agreements.[1]

Though the division of law into public and private has been almost universally adopted by the Continental jurists, it is not to be found in the institutional treatises of English law. Mr Austin contends, that the portion of law usually called public law should be classed under the law of persons, distinguishing between private conditions and political conditions. This is the course followed both by Sir Matthew Hale and by Blackstone. In the first book of his 'Commentaries,' Blackstone treats of the rights and duties of persons, not only as private individuals, but also in their public relations, so as to comprehend a portion of what is called public law. Political persons include all those who share the sovereign power, ministers of state, judges, magistrates, and all other public functionaries; while private persons include chiefly the conditions of husband and wife, parent and child, master and servant, guardian and ward.

As to the political constitutions of separate communities, they belong to the public law of each state. This is exclusively municipal in its character, and essentially distinct from that system of jurisprudence which regulates the *mutual* relations subsisting between independent states.[2]

Division of private law according to subjects.

Nothing has given rise to more difficulty among jurists than the proper division of private law with reference to its subjects. Justinian, in his Institutes, has treated of the law of persons, the law of things, and the law of actions. This system, though often criticised, has its advantages, not the least of which is, that it has been so often followed that it has become familiar to lawyers in all parts of the world.

[1] "Jus publicum privatorum pactis mutari non potest."—Papinian, D. 2. 14. 38. See also Code Civil, art. 6.

[2] It may not be uninteresting to notice here some of the most remarkable fundamental acts regarding constitutional law. These are, for Great Britain, the Great Charter of 1215, the Bill of Rights of 1688, and the Reform Bill of 1832; for the United States, the Constitution voted by Congress in 1787; for Germany, the Federal Pact of 1815; for Spain, the Constitution promulgated at Madrid on 23d May 1845; and for France, the different Constitutions established from 1791 till that of 14th January 1852.

But some jurists are of opinion that the entire body of private law should be divided into *two* categories—the law of persons, and the law of things ; actions, which are the means the law affords to make our rights effectual, being considered under the different matters to which they relate. In his 'Analysis of the Law,' Sir Matthew Hale says, that, in order to render the subject more simple and intelligible, the law of things should precede the law of persons ; and this plan, which is approved of by Mr Austin, has been followed by some eminent jurists, and is the order of the Prussian Code. On the other hand, many writers have followed in the wake of Justinian, by treating the law of persons before the law of things — such as Blackstone, Sir George Mackenzie, Erskine, and Pothier in his collected works ; and this is the order of the Code Napoleon.

Equity, in its true and genuine meaning, is synonymous with natural justice ; and to this the judge must have recourse where the laws are silent, and there is nothing else to guide his decision.[1]

In the English system of jurisprudence there is a division into common law and equity. But equity, as understood by English lawyers, is that portion of law which is exclusively administered by the courts of Chancery, as contradistinguished from that portion of law which is exclusively administered by the courts of common law. "The separation of law and equity," says Lord Brougham, "is the other great peculiarity of English jurisprudence. Originally it probably was devised in order to mitigate the rigour of the positive law ; but the discretion thus vested in courts of equity has for many ages been exercised according to rules as technical as those of the unwritten jurisprudence which guides the common-law courts. It is a more correct description of the courts of equity to say that they deal with questions of law different from those which the courts of common law deal with." [2]

The division of the two jurisdictions proceeds on no very intelligible grounds, and leads to many anomalies. Until

English system of equity.

[1] Stair, 1. 1. 16. Portalis, Discours Préliminaire du Projet de Code Civil.   [2] British Constitution, p. 353.

recently the courts of common law could award damages, but could not compel the execution of contracts ; while the courts of equity could compel the execution of contracts, but could not give damages for their breach. If a suitor, therefore, wished to recover damages for breach of a contract, or for the commission of some wrong, or for some failure of duty, he had recourse to a court of common law. On the other hand, if his object was to enforce specific performance of a contract, or to bring a trustee to an account, or to recover a legacy from an executor, or to obtain an injunction, then his recourse was to a court of equity.[1] By recent acts, courts of common law are empowered to order delivery of specific goods contracted to be sold, or chattels illegally detained, without giving the defendant the option of retaining them on paying the damages assessed ; and, in all cases of breach of contract or other injury which they have jurisdiction to entertain, to grant injunctions against the repetition or continuance of such breach of contract or other injury ; and, on the other hand, courts of equity are authorised, if they think fit, in certain cases, " to award damages to the party injured, either in addition to, or in substitution for, such injunction or specific performance." [2] But, notwithstanding these improvements, many evils still attend this double system of judicature, which occasions great expense and delay to litigants, who are frequently obliged to appeal to two tribunals to obtain redress for a single wrong, or to settle one and the same dispute.

In Scotland there is no division into courts of law and equity, both these jurisdictions being combined and exercised by the same courts, according to the system which is understood to be universal on the continent of Europe.

IV.—OF THE LAW OF NATIONS, OR INTERNATIONAL LAW.

By the law of nations (*jus inter gentes*) we understand those rules which define the rights and prescribe the duties

---

[1] Paterson's Compendium of English and Scotch Law, p. 361.

[2] Common Law Procedure Act, 1854 (17 & 18 Vict., c. 125), s. 78, 79, and 82 ; 19 & 20 Vict., c. 97, s. 2 ; 21 & 22 Vict., c. 27, s. 2.

of independent states in their intercourse with each other.[1]
Before entering upon this subject, a short explanation may
be given of a branch of jurisprudence sometimes called
private international law, which has acquired great importance in modern times.

Private international law has for its object the conflicts Private
between the positive laws of different nations, and regulates national
disputes between private persons who may be members of law.
the same state or of different states.

This system of law deals with cases which come before the
ordinary judicial tribunals. It determines before the court
of what country a particular suit should be brought, and by
the law of what country it should be decided. Conflicts of
law arise not only from diversities in the jurisprudence of
different nations, but from different systems of law prevailing
in different parts of the same kingdom, of which no better
example can be given than the British empire, which, though
united under one allegiance, is governed by different laws in
England and Scotland, and in various colonies and depen-
dencies of the United Kingdom.

It is a fundamental principle that every nation possesses
and exercises exclusive sovereignty and jurisdiction in its
own territory. Hence the laws of every state affect and bind
all property, movable and immovable, within its territory,
and all persons resident within it, whether natural-born subjects or aliens. On the other hand, no nation by its laws
can directly bind or affect property beyond its territory, or
persons not resident within it, whether they have been born
within it or not. Cases frequently occur, however, where,
by the comity of nations, one independent state will give
effect to the laws and judicial acts of another, so far as this
can be done without prejudice to its own laws and to the
fundamental and distinctive principles of its own internal
policy. A familiar example of this is afforded by contracts
entered into in a foreign country and intended to be performed there, which our courts are in the practice of enforcing according to the law of the place in which they were

[1] Kent's Com., vol. i. p. 1.

made, provided that law is not repugnant to our own institutions or to good morals.[1]

Public international law. Public international law designates the true law of nations which governs the mutual relations of independent states in their conduct towards each other. It is founded partly on the principles of natural law, which are binding on nations as moral persons as well as on individuals, and partly on a system of positive institutions fixed by public treaties and conventions, and the long-established customs of civilised states.

According to Grotius, this system of law derives its authority from the common consent of nations, or at least of a considerable number of them. Yet it may fairly be questioned whether the law by which nations profess to be governed in their mutual relations can be treated as a positive law of human institution, or regarded as law otherwise than in a figurative sense, because it is deficient in those sanctions which are inseparable from the positive law of every distinct state. First, independent states acknowledge no human superior invested with cosmopolitan authority to make positive laws between nation and nation as such; and as no nation can legislate for another, so no given number of nations has power to make laws to bind the rest, at least with respect to things left indifferent by the law of nature. Next, as there is no accepted tribunal to settle disputes between nations, the rules of international law are not judicially administered, and there is no supreme executive authority to enforce them.

If all the states of Europe were to concur in framing a general code of international law, which should be binding on them all, and form themselves into a confederacy to enforce it, this might be regarded as a positive law of nations for Europe. But nothing of this sort has ever been attempted. The nearest approach to such international legislation is the

[1] See Dr Story's Conflict of Laws, 5th ed., Boston, 1857; Westlake's Private International Law, or the Conflict of Laws, with principal reference to English practice, London, 1858; Traité du Droit International Privé, par M. Fœlix, 3d ed., revue par Charles Demangeat, Paris, 1856.*

* The most important work on this subject is Savigny's Treatise on Private International Law, translated by Guthrie, Edinburgh, 1869.

general regulations introduced into treaties by the great
powers of Europe, which are binding on the contracting
parties, but not on the states that decline to accede to them.

To settle disputes between nations on the principles of justice, rather than leave them to the blind arbitrament of war,
is the primary object of the European law of nations. When
war has broken out, it regulates the rights and duties of
belligerents, and the conduct of neutrals.

As the weak side of the law of nations is the want of a
supreme executive power to enforce it, small states are exposed to great disadvantages in disputes with their more
powerful neighbours. But the modern political system of
Europe for the preservation of the balance of power forms a
strong barrier against unjust aggression. When the power of
one great state can be balanced, or kept in check, by that of
another, the independence of smaller states is in some degree
secured against both ; for neither of the great powers will
allow its rival to add to its strength by the conquest of the
smaller states.

Between all distinct states nature has established a perfect *Pacific*
equality of rights, and they are entitled to enjoy independence *nations.*
rights of
and security of territory. It is a consequence of the liberty
and independence of nations that all have a right to be governed as they think proper. That no state, unless authorised
by treaty stipulations, is entitled to interfere in the internal
concerns of another, is a general rule of the law of nations ;
but, in practice, it has been departed from in some extreme
cases. Contests upon the question who shall be the responsible ministers of the Crown, and by what principles of administration the country shall be governed, are questions
purely domestic in their bearing, with which foreign powers
are not entitled to interfere. For this reason the British Government protested against the intervention of France with
the affairs of Spain in 1822, which led to the overthrow of
the Spanish constitution. On the other hand, questions of
disputed succession have always been deemed matters which
might justly be considered as involving the political interests
of foreign states ; and in such questions, wherever arising,

the powers of Europe have, from time to time, according as their interests impelled them, held themselves at liberty to take an active part. To oppose the union of the two crowns of France and Spain on the same head in 1700 was considered essential for the security of the other European states. So, by the quadruple treaty in 1834, Britain and France united with Spain and Portugal in expelling from the Peninsula the two Infantes, Don Carlos and Don Miguel. "Although it is certainly laid down by writers on the law of nations that, when civil war is regularly established in a country, and when the nation is divided into conflicting armies and opposing camps, the two parties in such a war may be dealt with by other powers as if they were two separate communities, and such other powers may take part with one side or the other, according to their sympathies and interests, just as they might in a war between separate and independent nations ; yet the cases in which such interference is justifiable are rare, and it is better and safer in general to leave each nation to decide for itself upon questions which relate to its own internal organisation and interests."[1]

Rights of war.

The law of nations allows independent states to vindicate their rights and redress their injuries by having recourse to war, when all amicable means of obtaining satisfaction have failed.[2] War is defined by Vattel as "that state in which we prosecute our right by force."[3] Unfortunately too many wars have been undertaken, without a shadow of right, for conquest and other unwarrantable purposes. But war has been described as an interruption of all pacific relations, and a general contention by force authorised by sovereign powers.[4] It was long the custom to make a declaration of war to the enemy before commencing hostilities. But since the peace of Versailles in 1763 such declarations have been discontinued, and the existing usage is for the state which commences the war to publish a manifesto, announcing the fact within its own territories.[5] According to Dr Wheaton, the modern rule is,

---

[1] Lord Palmerston's Despatch, 5th April 1847—Parliamentary Papers.
[2] Martens, Précis, t. ii. p, 203.
[3] Vattel, t. ii. p. 1.
[4] Manning, p. 96.
[5] 1 Kent, 54.

that neither the property of the enemy within the belligerent state, nor the debts due to his subjects, are confiscated on the breaking out of war, though the right to enforce payment of debts may be suspended till peace is declared.[1]

One nation may lawfully assist another in a just war; and whatever makes a war just, in respect of the principal nation, will make it just also in respect of its allies.

In civil war the vanquished are sometimes denied the treatment of lawful enemies, and punished as rebels. But this is irregular, because all publicists are agreed that the laws of war, as they are called, are the same in civil as in foreign warfare.[2] *Civil war.*

According to the principle laid down by Vattel, no greater injuries should be inflicted upon an enemy in time of war than are absolutely necessary to obtain the end of the war. If humanity is still shocked at the slaughter of men, the burning of ships, the pillage of towns, the devastation of provinces, and the havoc and misery to which the people on both sides are exposed, it is consoling to reflect that, great as these inevitable horrors are, the usages of modern nations have imposed restraints upon the unlimited violence which marked ancient warfare. Secret assassination, the use of poison in weapons, food, and wells, and all atrocities of a similar nature, are now universally condemned as contrary to the law of nations. Anciently prisoners became the slaves of the conquerors. In the days of chivalry, it was customary to demand ransom for the liberation of prisoners. Among all Christian powers they are now released, either during the war, under agreements, called *cartels*, or at the end of the war, without ransom on either side.[3] *Rules of war.*

---

[1] 2 Wheaton, 18.

[2] Mr Hallam says: "The line is not easily drawn in abstract reasoning between the treason that is justly punished, and the social schism which is beyond the proper boundaries of law ; but the civil war of England seems fairly to fall within the latter description."—Constitutional Hist., vol. ii. p. 82. The same thing may be said of the long war carried on by Spain against the united provinces of the Netherlands from 1566; of the war by Great Britain against her American colonies from 1774 ; and of the war now pending between the Federal Government and the Confederate States of America.[*]

[3] Manning, p. 157.

[*] Ended April 1865.

Some writers have stated it to be a general rule, when hostilities are carried on by land in the territory of the enemy, that " private property is exempt from confiscation, with the exception of such as may become booty in special cases when taken from enemies in the field or in besieged towns, and of military contributions levied upon the inhabitants of the hostile territory."[1] But this practice has not been always uniformly observed. When hostile armies are in an enemy's country, they too frequently take everything they want, and destroy what they do not want, for the mere purpose of destruction; and in the necessary operations of war, immense damage is done for which no compensation is given by the depredators, to say nothing of the military contributions which are raised from the inhabitants in the places occupied by force of arms. Besides, even though some governments may hesitate to adopt such a violent policy, it must not be forgotten that the real ground for the general immunity now more frequently accorded to private property on the enemy's soil · is, that it could not be touched without surrounding the invading army with more danger than it would otherwise have to encounter by humane and judicious treatment.

In modern times, old people, women, and children, and all those subjects who take no part in hostilities, are generally exempted from violence. Again, the commission of actual hostilities, excepting in case of self-defence, is only allowed to those who are authorised by the sovereign power; and all private persons who carry on war without such authority, in place of being entitled to the privileges of enemies, are liable to be treated as pirates or marauders. Even when a contest at sea has commenced in self-defence, maritime prizes made by uncommissioned captors do not belong to them, but to the Crown under the droits of Admiralty.[2] The case is different when letters of marque are issued, commissioning the owners of private vessels to seize the ships and cargoes of the enemy.[3]

In a report made to Geo. II. in 1753 by Sir George Lee,

---

[1] Wheaton's International Law, p. 420. Tudor's Select Maritime Cases, p. 804.

[2] Manning, p. 153.

[3] Ibid., pp. 106, 107.

Dr Paul, Sir Dudley Ryder, and Mr Murray (afterwards Lord Mansfield), we find the following statement as to the maritime rights of belligerents :—

"When two nations are at war, they have a right to make Maritime rights. prizes of the ships, goods, and effects of each other on the high seas. Whatever is property of the enemy may be acquired by capture at sea; but the property of a friend cannot be taken, provided he observes his neutrality.

" Hence the law of nations has established—

"(1.) That the goods of an enemy on board the ship of a friend may be taken.

"(2.) That the lawful goods of a friend on board the ship of an enemy ought to be restored.

"(3.) That contraband goods going to the enemy, though the property of a friend, may be taken as prize ; because supplying the enemy with what enables him better to carry on the war is a departure from neutrality." [1]

Formerly, in the case of ships and goods taken at sea, undisputed possession for twenty-four hours was deemed sufficient to constitute a prize the property of the captor. The rule now firmly established in Britain, France, and the United States, and generally followed elsewhere, is, that the title does not pass until the validity of the capture has been declared by a prize court of the state to which the captor belongs.[2] Under peculiar circumstances our Court of Admiralty will condemn a prize which has been taken into a neutral port, and allow it to be sold there.[3]

In case of unjust decisions, the government of the injured party may demand redress. The British Government paid an indemnity to Prussia in 1752, for cases in which injustice had been done by our tribunals.[4]

By the law of *postliminium*, persons or property revert to

---

[1] Collectanea Juridica, vol. i. p. 129-66. The principles in this report were adopted by Lord Stowell and Sir John Nicholl in a paper addressed by them to Mr Jay, the American minister in London, in Sept. 1794. See 1 More's Stair, Notes, p. 152.

[2] Manning, p. 382. Wheaton, vol. ii. p. 95-111. 4 Rob. 55.

[3] Tudor's Select Maritime Cases, p. 825.

[4] Manning, p. 383.

their original state when recaptured from the enemy by their countrymen. In this country, property captured at sea, and afterwards recaptured, is restored to the original owners, upon payment of salvage, however long it may have been possessed by the enemy, and whether it had been regularly condemned or not. As the law of *postliminium* only exists during war, peace extinguishes all right to claim captured property, whether condemned in a prize court or not.[1]

Though the law of nations be the general rule, yet it may be varied or departed from by mutual agreement; and where an alteration or exception is introduced by convention, that is the law between the parties to the treaty. So it is competent by agreement to declare the goods of an enemy on board the ship of a friend to be free.

That a belligerent is entitled to seize an enemy's goods on board a neutral vessel was long an established principle of the law of nations, and is said to go back as far as the middle ages, though it has been repeatedly called in question in more recent times.[2] On this subject a dispute arose between Great Britain and Prussia in 1752, when a memorial from the Prussian minister elicited the celebrated report of the English jurists already noticed. During the war which followed the French Revolution, the controversy was revived, and the northern powers of Europe and the United States joined France in maintaining that free ships make free goods, excepting contraband; that nothing is contraband but arms and military stores; and that a convoy precluded neutral ships from being searched.[3] But Britain uniformly resisted these pretensions as contrary to the law of nations.

Declaration of Paris, 16th April 1856. By the declaration of 16th April 1856, the Congress of Paris, held after the Crimean war, adopted four principles of international law. 1. Privateering is and remains abolished. 2. The neutral flag cover's the enemy's merchandise, with the exception of contraband of war. 3. Neutral merchandise,

[1] Manning, p. 143.
[2] Grotius, lib. iii. c. vi. § 26. Hautefeuille, t. iii. p. 223. Martens, Précis, t. ii. p. 319.
[3] Thiers, Hist. du Consulat et de l'Empire, t. ii. p. 102. North American Review, vol. xxvi. p. 211.

with the exception of contraband of war, is not liable to seizure under an enemy's flag. 4. Blockades, in order to be binding, must be effective ; that is to say, must be maintained by a force really sufficient to prevent approach to an enemy's coast.[1] This declaration was signed by the plenipotentiaries of the seven powers who attended the Congress, and it was accepted by nearly all the states of the world. But the United States of America, Spain, and Mexico, refused their assent, because they objected to the abolition of privateering.[2] So far as these powers are concerned, therefore, privateering —that is, the employment of private cruisers commissioned by the state—still remains a perfectly legitimate mode of warfare.[3] Britain and the other powers who acceded to the declaration are bound to discontinue the practice in hostilities with each other. But if we should have the misfortune to go to war with the United States, we should not be bound to abstain from privateering, unless the United States should enter into a similar and corresponding engagement with us.

As to the other three articles in the declaration of Paris, the only new point conceded by Britain was that the neutral flag covers the enemy's goods, except contraband. This was the doctrine of the United States and every other maritime power except Britain ; and if we had persisted in maintaining the opposite doctrine, and had gone to war, we should inevitably have run the risk of adding to our difficulties by another armed neutrality, so that it was deemed good policy to make that concession. On general principles the effects of neutrals on board an enemy's ships are exempt from seizure ;[4] and this principle is confirmed by the third article of the declaration. With regard to the fourth article, as to blockades, there is much force in the criticism of Mr Marcy, the American Secretary, who says, in his despatch of 28th

[1] Martens, Précis, t. ii. p. 269.
[2] Official Report to the French Emperor in Moniteur of July 1858. ·
[3] Prussia and the United States of America engaged, in 1785, if war should break out between them, not to grant letters of marque ; but this article was suppressed in their treaty of 1799. See Martens, Précis, t. ii. p. 268, note.
[4] 2 Wheaton, 162. 1 Kent, 120.

E

July 1856, "This rule has not for a long time been regarded
as uncertain," and " merely reiterates a general undisputed
maxim of maritime law."

To constitute a violation of blockade, according to Lord
Stowell, " three things must be proved : 1st, The existence of
an actual blockade ; 2d, The knowledge of the person supposed to have offended ; and, 3d, Some act of violation,
either by going in or by coming out, with a cargo laden
after the commencement of blockade."[1]

A neutral vessel is not permitted to trade with a port
blockaded by one of the belligerent powers, whatever may be
the nature of the trade, and although the cargo may not be
contraband.   The object is to exclude the blockaded place
from all commerce, whether outwards or inwards.   Hence,
neither the subjects nor allies of the state establishing the
blockade can be allowed to infringe it.[2]   If a vessel has
entered a blockaded port before the blockade, she is entitled
to come out again with the cargo she took in, or in ballast,
or with cargo loaded before notice of the blockade.   A ship
should also be restored if the breach of blockade has
been occasioned by unavoidable necessity, as where she has
been compelled to enter the blockaded port by stress of
weather.[3]

Law of
blockade.

A mere declaration of a blockade will avail nothing ; it
must be maintained by a naval force adequate to prevent
vessels from leaving or entering the port.   Besides, notice
of the existence of the blockade should be made to neutrals ;
and such notice may be given on the spot, where the master
is ignorant of it.   After a blockade is established, any attempt
to enter or quit the port is punished by the seizure and condemnation of the offending ship or cargo, and sometimes of
both ; and the offence is not considered discharged until the
end of the return voyage.[4]

The Berlin decree of November 1806, and the Milan decree
of December 1807, declared the whole British dominions
in a state of blockade, and all vessels, of whatever country,

[1] 16 Rob. 93.
[2] 10 Moore, p. 6. 637.
[3] Tudor, p. 767. Fortuna, 56 Rob. 27.
[4] Manning, pp. 328, 329.

trading to them, liable to be captured by the ships of France. There can be no question as to the invalidity of these decrees according to the law of nations. The British Government retaliated by issuing Orders in Council, declaring France and all its tributary states to be in a state of blockade. These orders, which tried to establish a "paper-blockade," whether there was a force present to support it or not, were equally illegal; because no violation of international law by one belligerent power could justify the other in pursuing a similar course, especially where the policy adopted on both sides was a flagrant infringement of the rights of neutral nations.

The freedom of commerce, to which neutral states are entitled, does not extend to contraband of war; but, according to the principles laid down in the declaration of Paris, of April 1856, it may now be said that "a ship at sea is part of the soil of the country to which it belongs," with the single exception implied in the right of a belligerent to search for contraband. What constitutes contraband is not precisely settled; the limits are not absolutely the same for all powers, and variations occur in particular treaties; but, speaking generally, belligerents have a right to treat as contraband, and to capture, all munitions of war and other articles directly auxiliary to warlike purposes.[1] The neutral carrier engages in a contraband trade when he conveys official despatches from a person in the service of the enemy to the enemy's possessions; but it has been decided that it is not illegal for a neutral vessel to carry despatches from the enemy to his ambassador or his consul in a neutral country.[2] The penalty of carrying contraband is confiscation of the illegal cargo, and generally condemnation of the ship itself. Even the innocent part of the cargo will be forfeited, if it belong to the same owner as the contraband.

To sell arms, military stores, or other articles of contra-

Law of contraband.

---

[1] Martens, Précis, t. ii. p. 316. Hautefeuille, Droits et Devoirs des Nations Neutres, t. ii. p. 337. The Jonge Margaretha, 1 Rob. 189.

[2] The Caroline, 6 Rob. 465. The Madison, Edw. 224. Polson, Law of Nations, p. 63.

band, to the agents of a belligerent power in a neutral country, is not prohibited by international law. Transportation of such goods to the enemy's country is necessary to constitute the offence against the law of nations. This is clearly explained by Chancellor Kent, and is supported by American decisions as well as other authorities.[1]

Affair of the Trent.

The affair of the Trent, West Indian mail, gave rise to an important question of maritime law deeply affecting the rights of neutrals. In November 1861, Captain Wilkes, of the American war-steamer San Jacinto, after firing a round shot and a shell, boarded the English mail-packet Trent, in Old Bahama Channel, on its passage from Havannah to Southampton, and carried off by force Messrs Mason and Slidell, two commissioners from the Confederate States, who were taken on board as passengers bound for England. The commissioners were conveyed to America, and committed to prison; but, after a formal requisition by Britain, declaring the capture to be illegal, they were surrendered by the Federal Government.

The seizure of the commissioners was attempted to be justified by American writers on two grounds : 1st, That the commissioners were contraband of war, and that in carrying them the Trent was liable to condemnation for having committed a breach of neutrality ; 2d, That, at all events, Captain Wilkes was entitled to seize the commissioners either as enemies or as rebels. Both these propositions are plainly untenable.

As to the first point, nothing is known to international law as contraband, unless what is *going to an enemy's port.* Unless, therefore, it could be pretended that the real destination of the Trent was to an enemy's port, and not to an English port, the very definition of contraband precludes the application of the term to any goods or passengers on board that vessel. The Trent was not bound to a place belonging to either of the belligerents. It was carrying its cargo and passengers from one neutral country to another neutral country.

---

[1] Kent's Com., vol. i. p. 142. Wheaton, Hist. of International   Law, p. 312. Ortolan, Regles Internationales, vol. ii. p. 156-9.

Official despatches from an enemy sent by a neutral ship *to a neutral country* are not contraband ; and Messrs Mason and Slidell could not be so considered on the pretext that they were the bearers of such despatches. Neither were they military men actually in the service of the enemy, so as to fall under the category of persons who are sometimes liable to be captured under the stipulations found in particular treaties.

As to the second point, the capture of the commissioners by forcibly carrying them off from a neutral ship cannot be justified, whether they be viewed as enemies or rebels. For the seizure of the persons of belligerents, on the analogy of the seizure of enemy's goods, is wholly new to international law, and this doctrine is not sanctioned by any precedents. A neutral territory must not be violated for the purposes of war. A ship at sea is part of the territory of the country to which it belongs ; and, setting aside contraband, the flag covers both goods and passengers. According to this view, which has always been most vigorously maintained by the United States, the commissioners were under the protection of the British flag, and the Federal Government had no jurisdiction over them either as enemies or as rebels.

In an able despatch by the French Government to the Cabinet of Washington, M. Thouvenel declared that the seizure of the commissioners in a neutral ship, trading from a neutral port to a neutral port, was not only contrary to the law of nations, but a direct contravention of the principles which the United States had up to that time invariably avowed and acted upon. Russia, Austria, and Prussia officially intimated their concurrence in that opinion.

To argue the matter on the legal points in opposition to the disinterested and well-reasoned despatch of the French minister was a hopeless task. In an elaborate state-paper, Mr Seward, the American Secretary of State, professed to rest the surrender of the commissioners upon a mere technicality—that there had been no formal condemnation of the Trent by a prize-court ; but, apart from this point of form, the seizure was indefensible on the merits as a flagrant violation of the law of nations; and if the principle was not so frankly acknowledged by Mr Seward as it ought to have been, some allowance must be made for a statesman who was trammelled by the report of his colleague, Mr Welles, the Secretary of the Navy, approving of Captain Wilkes's conduct, and still more by the necessity of adopting a policy directly contrary to the whole current of popular opinion in the Northern States.

Neutral territory.

No hostile operations can be carried on, and no capture can be made by a belligerent, within the limits of neutral territory, whether it be land or water. All acts of violence are forbidden, not only in ports and harbours, but also within such distance from the shore as is acknowledged by the custom of nations to be within the jurisdiction of a neutral state. Formerly a country was generally considered to extend from the coast for three miles to seaward, or as far as cannon-shot could reach: but as the range of warlike missiles has increased, the neutral territory will probably be held extended. It is the duty of the government whose dignity is infringed to insist that all prizes taken within the prescribed limits shall be restored to their rightful owners, provided they apply, as they ought to do, for immediate protection. Some neutral states have been in use to issue regulations, that when a ship belonging to a belligerent has left one of their ports, no vessel belonging to the other belligerent shall be allowed to leave that port till after an interval of twenty-four hours.[1]

Public treaties.

Treaties between one nation and another are usually negotiated and signed by plenipotentiaries; but in modern practice such treaties are not held to be binding till they are ratified by the signature and seal of the sovereign of each country.

When a treaty is not intended to be made public, it is called a secret treaty; and sometimes a few articles which are added to the principal treaty remain secret. Besides the general treaty of Paris of 30th March 1856, to which Russia was a party, a separate triple convention was entered into,

---

[1] Manning, p. 387.

whereby Britain, France, and Austria agreed to guarantee
the integrity of Turkey, and declared that any infringement
of its territory by Russia should be regarded by each and all
of the contracting powers as a *casus belli.* This convention
was probably intended to be kept secret; but, Count Orloff
having contrived to procure a copy of it in Paris, the British
Government laid it before Parliament along with the other
official documents.

Treaties cease to be obligatory: 1st, When the state
which has contracted them loses its independence, or comes
to be dissolved; 2d, When it voluntarily changes its constitution, and the treaty becomes inapplicable from altered circumstances; 3d, When war has broken out between the
contracting powers; but in this last instance articles framed
for the case of rupture are excepted.[1]

Accordingly, it has been customary in treaties of peace to
renew and confirm prior treaties, which have manifestly been
broken or revoked by the recurrence of war. So the important treaties of Westphalia and Utrecht have been repeatedly
renewed or confirmed in treaties of peace or commerce subsequently entered into between the same powers.[2]

In modern times there are four classes of diplomatic
agents, who take rank in the following order: 1st, Ambas-
sadors, the only ministers who are understood to represent
the persons of their sovereigns, and are addressed by the title
of Excellency; 2d, Envoys and Ministers Plenipotentiary,
accredited to sovereigns; 3d, Resident Ministers; 4th,
Chargés d'affaires, who are merely agents accredited to the
Foreign Office.[3] Consuls, though a most useful class of
public functionaries in commercial affairs, are not usually
classed among diplomatists.

By the Convention of Vienna of 19th March 1815, diplomatic agents rank among themselves in each class according
to the priority in date of the official intimation of their arrival
at a particular court, reserving the precedence granted to the

Classification of diplomatic agents.

---

[1] Martens, Précis, Paris, 1858, t. i. p. 167.
[2] Ibid., t. i. p. 181.
[3] Martens, Précis, t. ii. pp. 50 and 99.

Papal Nuncio in Catholic states.[1]   To avoid unseemly disputes about precedence among nations, the principle of alter-
nation has been frequently adopted. · At the Congress of
Vienna all treaties and public acts were signed in the alpha-
betical order which the French language assigns to the different nations.

[1] Martens, Précis, t. ii. p. 98.

EXPOSITION

OF

THE ROMAN LAW

WITH COMPARATIVE VIEWS

OF THE

LAWS OF FRANCE, ENGLAND, & SCOTLAND

ARRANGEMENT OF THE SUBJECTS.

I. OF THE LAW OF PERSONS.

II. OF THE LAW RELATING TO REAL RIGHTS.

III. OF THE LAW OF OBLIGATIONS.

IV. OF THE LAWS OF SUCCESSION.

V. OF ACTIONS AND PROCEDURE.

VI. OF CRIMINAL LAW AND PROCEDURE.

PART I.

OF THE LAW OF PERSONS.

CHAPTER I.

OF PERSONS IN GENERAL.

WHILE the Roman jurists of the classical period, who were deeply imbued with the Stoic philosophy, acknowledge that all men are equal by the law of nature, they are careful to distinguish the great differences which exist among the different classes of men, both as regards social condition and civil capacity.

In a strict legal sense, a *person* is one clothed with a certain status, and capable of enjoying civil rights. So a slave, being incapable of civil rights, was accounted by the Romans not a person but a thing, though this distinction was not always rigidly adhered to.[1] They used the term *status* or *caput* to describe civil capacity, which varied in different individuals, and depended on the existence of certain qualities determined partly by public and partly by private law.

(margin: Person and status.)

By the Roman jurists men are considered under three divisions : 1st, Freemen and slaves ; 2d, Citizens and foreigners ; 3d, Men who are independent (*sui juris*), and

---

[1] D. 1. 5. 3. Gaius.   Here *personæ* are said to be divided into freemen and slaves.

those who are *alieni juris,*—that is, subjected to the power of another—such as children under the power of their father, and slaves under the power of their master.[1] The *manus,* by which a married woman was subjected to the power of her husband, as if she had been a daughter, not a wife, and the *mancipatio,* by which a free citizen fell under the power of another, though of common occurrence under the ancient law of Rome, had entirely disappeared before the time of Justinian.

Marriage is considered in the Institutes in relation to the paternal power, because it is from the procreation of children, in a regular marriage, that the paternal power usually and most naturally takes its origin. Guardianship is an institution for the care of those who are not under paternal power, but are considered unfit to protect their own interests. Hence the doctrine of tutory and curatory is dealt with as an appendage to the theory of paternal power.[2]

Juridical persons.

As the rights of natural persons may be said to die with them, corporations were established by the Romans for the advancement of religion, learning, and commerce, and even for social and convivial purposes, such as our English clubs, when it was thought for the public advantage to have particular rights preserved entire for an indefinite period, in place of allowing them to fall with the lives of the members of which the body corporate might at any time be composed. These corporations, though consisting of numerous individuals, are treated in law as forming a unity, or single person, capable of enjoying rights. Of this description are universities, chapters of churches, town-councils, and a vast number of societies, religious and secular, which constitute artificial persons in law, each of them having its own proper goods, rights, and immunities, and enjoying what Blackstone calls "a kind of legal immortality."[3]

[1] I. 1. 3. D. 1. 5, De statu hominum.
[2] Marezoll, § 81.
[3] Marezoll, § 69. Maynz, Droit Romain, § 109. Black. Com., book 1, ch. 18.

CHAPTER II.

OF THE CIVIL CAPACITY OF PERSONS.

ALL persons are capable of enjoying civil rights, but not all Differences in legal capacity. in the same degree. Individuals differ from each other in their natural and social qualities, from sex, birth, age, state of mind, and a variety of other circumstances, which are made the grounds of peculiar privileges or disabilities. Some of the most important of these distinctions may here be noticed.

The Roman law has given more extensive privileges to Sex. men than to women, not so much as encroachments on the freedom, as from indulgence for the weakness, of the female sex. At Rome women could not act as magistrates, judges, or advocates; they were incapable of all public civil employments;[1] they were long under a kind of perpetual guardianship; they were not permitted to be sureties for any one; and it was only under the later emperors that they were allowed to be guardians to their own children or grandchildren. Sometimes the punishments inflicted upon women were less severe than upon men.[2]

A child is held to be born alive, if it has breathed after Birth. having been separated from the body of the mother. Some of the ancient lawyers insisted that it was necessary that the child should have been heard to cry; but Justinian rejected that opinion in accordance with the views of the Sabinians.[3] By a legal fiction a child *in utero*, so far as regards its patri-

---

[1] D. 50. 17. 2.   [2] N. 134, ch. 9.   [3] C. 6. 29. 3.

monial interests, was considered in the same light as if it had been born—*Nasciturus pro jam nato habetur, quando de ejus commodo agitur.*[1] If, therefore, any one died leaving a widow with child, a share was reserved in the division of the succession for the coming infant.

Birth gives rise to the distinction between lawful children and bastards. A lawful child is one procreated by husband and wife united in lawful marriage; a bastard was the offspring of unlawful intercourse. Strictly speaking, natural children were those born of a concubine.[2] As concubinage was a legal institution at Rome, they were regarded with more favour than other illegitimate children, called *spurii* or *vulgo quæsiti.* As a general rule, lawful children follow the condition of the father; bastards follow the condition of the mother. All illegitimate children are *sui juris,* because the law admits no relationship between them and their father, but it recognises them as relations of their mother.

Age. Age has a most important effect on legal capacity. In the case of minors, the period of incapacity terminates at a limit conventionally fixed. Full age in the Roman law was twenty-five; all below that age were minors. There was a subdivision of minors into adults, or those who had attained puberty, and pupils — that is, males under fourteen, and females under twelve. All children below seven years of age were called infants.[3]

Pupils could not contract marriage or make a testament. This double incapacity was absolute, and nothing could remove it. As to other acts of civil life, pupils, though *sui juris,* could not contract obligations or alienate property; and the intervention of a tutor was required to give validity to necessary acts of administration. By the ancient law of Rome a minor *pubes* had full power to dispose of his property; but as he was liable to be imposed upon, he had the privilege of restitution under the edict of the prætor, on proof of lesion,

[1] D. 1. 5. 7.

[2] Though this is the correct meaning of "natural children," the expression is sometimes used to denote the children procreated of a lawful marriage, in contradistinction to adopted children.

[3] C. 6. 30. 18.

and a curator might be appointed to protect his interests. As the legal restraints of minority were sometimes attended with inconvenience, men above twenty, and women above eighteen, might obtain from the emperor the privilege called *venia ætatis*, which placed them on the same footing as if they had attained majority, but subject to some restrictions on the power of alienation.

Full age is fixed in France[1] and in this country at twenty-one. In England children under twenty-one cannot make a will of real or personal estate. In Scotland a minor *pubes* can make a will of personal estate; but he cannot make a testamentary disposition of real estate, even with the consent of his guardians.

At Rome, persons who reached an advanced age were relieved from certain public functions and duties. Thus men above seventy might decline to accept the office of tutor.

Unsoundness of body seldom affects the legal capacity of persons. Unsoundness of mind has more important consequences. Absolute incapacity may arise from madness or mental derangement. The law of the Twelve Tables deprived insane persons of the administration of their property, and placed them under curatory. All such persons are considered to have no will of their own, and consequently they are incapable of coming under any obligation, or doing any act which can be legally binding on them. But when mental derangement is of a fluctuating character, deeds done during a lucid interval are sustained.[2] State of mind.

Apart from these peculiarities, and others of a similar nature which affect the legal capacity of persons, civil status among the Romans had reference chiefly to three things— liberty, citizenship, and family. The *status libertatis* consisted of being a freeman, and not a slave. If a freeman was also a Roman citizen, he enjoyed the *status civitatis*. Upon this quality depended not only the enjoyment of political rights, but the capacity of participating in the *jus civile*. Finally, the *status familiæ* consisted in a citizen belonging to a particular family, and being capable of enjoying certain Civil status.

---

[1] Code Civil, art. 488.   Maynz, § 106.

rights in which the members of that family, in their quality of agnates, could alone take part.[1]

If an existing status came to be lost or changed, the person suffered what was called a *capitis diminutio*, which extinguished either entirely or to some extent his former legal capacity. There are three changes of state or condition attended with different consequences, called *maxima, media,* and *minima.* The greatest involves the loss of liberty, citizenship, and family; and this happened when a Roman citizen was taken prisoner in war, or condemned to slavery for his crimes. But a citizen who was captured by the enemy, on returning from captivity, was restored to all his civil rights *jure postliminii.*

The next change of state consisted of the loss of citizenship and family rights, without any forfeiture of personal liberty; and this occurred when a citizen became a member of another state, was forbidden the use of fire and water, so as to be forced to quit the Roman territory, or was sentenced to deportation under the empire.

Finally, when a person ceased to belong to a particular family, without losing his liberty or citizenship, he was said to suffer the least change of state—as, for instance, where one *sui juris* came under the power of another by arrogation, or a son who had been under the *patria potestas* was legally emancipated by his father.[2]

[1] Marezoll, § 67.   [2] I. 1. 16.   D. 4. 5.

81

CHAPTER III.

OF CITIZENS AND FOREIGNERS.

I.—ROMAN LAW.

In the early period of the Roman state, not only were Roman citizens. foreigners not admitted to the rights of citizens, but even the plebeians were for a considerable time deprived of many of the privileges which the patricians enjoyed. Savigny[1] has observed :—" In the free republic there were two classes of Roman citizens, one that had and another that had not a share in the sovereign power. That which peculiarly distinguished the higher class, was the right to vote in a tribe and the capacity of enjoying magistracies." According to this view, those who had the suffrage at public elections and access to the honours of the state, were full citizens — *cives optimo jure;* while those who had the civil rights of Romans without enjoying those political privileges, were citizens of an inferior class.

Citizenship, in its full sense, embraced both political and civil rights. Under the first aspect, it comprehended particularly the right of voting in the comitia, and the capacity of enjoying magistracies, *jus suffragii et honorum.* Political rights, however, were not held to constitute the essence of citizenship, as these were not enjoyed by many of the free-born subjects of Rome, such as the *ærarii,* and those who were inscribed on the tables of the Cærites. What essentially distinguished the Roman citizen was the enjoyment of the civil

[1] Geschichte des Röm. Rechts im Mittelalter, c. 2. p. 22.

F

rights of *connubium* and *commercium*. In virtue of the *connubium*, the citizen could contract a valid marriage according to the *jus civile*, and acquire the rights resulting from it, and particularly the paternal power and the civil relationship called agnation, which was long necessary to enable him to succeed to the property of persons who died intestate. In virtue of the *commercium*, he could acquire and dispose of property of all kinds, according to the forms and with the peculiar privileges of the Roman law.

By the Porcian law, " De capite et tergo civium," B.C. 256, a Roman citizen could not be scourged or put to death without trial before the centuries, so that his person was in a manner sacred (Liv. x. 9). Of this we have a remarkable example in the history of St Paul, who asks the centurion, " Is it lawful for you to scourge a man that is a Roman, and uncondemned ? When the centurion heard that, he went and told the chief captain, saying, Take heed what thou doest; for this man is a Roman."—Acts, xxii. 25, 26.   To evade the Porcian law a subtle fiction was introduced, whereby a condemned criminal became at the moment of his sentence the slave of punishment, *servus pœnœ*, and so ceased to be regarded as a Roman citizen.

Position of foreigners.   Foreigners, *peregrini*, had neither political nor civil rights. They could not acquire rights under the *jus civile*, nor invoke the protection which it afforded to citizens. They were allowed only the benefit of what was called the *jus gentium*, or the natural principles of equity, which are common to all nations. Their marriages were valid, but did not produce the same effects as a Roman marriage. They could contract obligations and acquire property, but they were deprived of the absolute and efficacious protection guaranteed by the *jus quiritium*. Originally, indeed, the foreigner could obtain no protection at Rome, unless he was placed under the patronage of a citizen. But in proportion as the intercourse with foreigners increased, a more liberal policy was adopted ; and towards the end of the fifth century of Rome, a special tribunal was established for administering justice to foreigners.   Sometimes the *connubium* or the *commercium* was granted to foreigners ; but these were exceptional measures, contrary to the common law.

Originally the Romans divided free persons into citizens and foreigners, *cives et peregrini;* but towards the close of the republic an intermediate class of persons sprang up, with limited citizenship, under the name of *Latini*, who enjoyed the *commercium* without the rights resulting from *connubium.*

During the flourishing period of the republic, when the Roman territory had been greatly extended by conquests, treaties, and alliances, a crowd of new subjects and allies aspired to participate in the privileges of citizenship, to which great value was attached.   The refusal to concede these led to the social war (B.C. 90), at the close of which the Roman citizenship was conferred, not only on the inhabitants of Latium, but on all Italy.   After this change the term *jus Latii* was used by the jurists to describe an artificial class of persons occupying an intermediate position between citizens and foreigners, in so far as they enjoyed *commercium* without *connubium.*   Hence the division into *cives, Latini*, and *peregrini*, subsisted for a long time. *Citizenship extended to all Italy.* *Jus Latii.*

When the free republic degenerated into a pure monarchy, citizenship lost many of its attractions for private persons. The acquisition of civil rights became more and more easy. The *jus Latii* was given to whole countries at once, of which the grant to Spain by Vespasian may be cited as an instance.   Even the citizenship, which had been conquered by the Italian allies at the price of their blood, was lavished with extreme levity.   Some emperors made the concession a source of revenue; and Marcus Aurelius, it is said, granted it to any one who asked it.   Finally, Caracalla bestowed the citizenship on all the free subjects of the Roman empire.   In taking that course the emperor was not guided by liberal ideas, but solely by motives of avarice; for by that expedient he subjected all the subjects of the empire to a tax of five per cent upon succession (*vicesima hæreditatum*), which was only exigible from Roman citizens.[1] *Citizenship made general under Caracalla.*

---

[1] Caracalla raised this tax to 10 per cent; but it was reduced to its former rate by his successor.   Dion Cassius, 77. 9.   Maynz, § 54.

Here we may briefly explain how the right of citizenship was acquired, and how it was lost.

How citizenship acquired.

Citizenship was acquired—1st, By birth. In a lawful marriage the child followed the condition of the father, and became a citizen, if the father was so at the time of conception. If the child was not the issue of *justæ nuptiæ*, it followed the condition of the mother at the time of its birth. 2d, By manumission, according to the formalities prescribed by law, the slave of a Roman citizen became a citizen. This rule was modified by the laws Ælia Sentia and Junia Norbana, according to which, in certain cases, the freedman acquired the status of a foreigner, *peregrinus dedititius*, or of a Latin, *Latinus Junianus*. Justinian restored the ancient principle, according to which every slave, regularly enfranchised, became in full right a Roman citizen. 3d, The right of citizenship was often granted as a favour, either to a whole community or to an individual, by the people or the senate during the republic, and by the reigning prince during the empire; and this was equivalent to what the moderns call naturalisation.

How lost.

Citizenship was lost—1st, By the loss of liberty—as, for instance, when a Roman became a prisoner of war; 2d, By renouncing the character of Roman citizen, which took place when any one was admitted a citizen of another state; 3d, By a sentence of deportation or exile, as a punishment for crime.[1]

Personal distinctions —nobles.

Birth and fortune are the two great sources of rank and personal distinction. The original aristocracy of Rome were the patricians, who were descended from the most ancient and illustrious families. When the plebeians became eligible to all the high offices of state, the two orders were put on the same footing as to political capacity. Every citizen, whether patrician or plebeian, who won his way to a curule magistracy, from that of ædile upwards, acquired personal distinction, which was transmitted to his descendants, who formed a class called *nobiles*, or men known, to distinguish them from the *ignobiles*, or people who were not known. "The charac-

[1] Marezoll, § 74.

ter of nobility," says Dr Middleton, "was wholly derived from the curule magistracies which any family had borne; and those which could boast of the greatest number were always accounted the noblest, so that many plebeians surpassed the patricians themselves in the point of nobility."[1]

As a class, the nobles had no legal privileges beyond the heraldic distinction, established by usage, of setting up the *imagines majorum*—that is, waxen masks or busts of departed ancestors who had borne a curule office. These *imagines,* with the names and honours of the deceased inscribed, were kept in the atrium. On festive days the waxen masks received fresh crowns of laurel, and at great funerals were brought out by men resembling the deceased in size and figure, who joined in the solemn procession, and the whole race of ancestors swept along in front of the corpse, represented by living individuals in proper costume.[2] A plebeian who first attained a curule office and became the founder of a noble family, was called by the Romans a *novus homo,* or new man; and we find this term applied to Cicero. Such a person could have no images of himself or his ancestors, because they were not made till after the death of the first member of the family who had enjoyed the dignity of a curule magistrate.

We have already noticed the numerous titles of nobility which sprung up during the Lower empire, and from which some of the titles now in use, such as Duke and Count, were derived. *Titles of honour under Constantine.*

An unsullied reputation was necessary to enable a Roman citizen to exercise his rights to their full extent.[3] Civil honour was entirely extinguished by the loss of liberty or citizenship—as, for instance, by being forbidden the use of fire and water. Without losing liberty or citizenship, the Roman citizen might be deprived of particular rights for *Civil honour.*

[1] Middleton's Cicero, vol. i. p. 123, note.

[2] Becker's Gallus, translated by Metcalfe, p. 512.

[3] " *Existimatio* est dignitatis illæsæ status, legibus ac moribus comprobatus, qui ex delicto nostro auctoritate legum aut minuitur, aut consumitur."—D. 50. 13. 5. 1.

ignominy. Persons convicted of certain crimes, and those who followed disreputable employments, were by law declared infamous, and were placed under important civil restrictions. They were deprived of political rights, having neither the suffrage nor access to public honours, and they laboured under various incapacities even in their private rights. Infamy resulted from condemnation in a *judicium publicum*, from being convicted of certain offences, such as robbery, theft, perjury, or fraud; from appearing on a public stage as an actor or gladiator; from ignominious expulsion from the army; from gaining a living by aiding in prostitution and other disreputable occupations; and from a variety of acts involving gross moral turpitude.[1]

It was in the power of the censors, in superintending public morality, to deprive senators of their dignity, to remove knights from the equestrian order, and even to strip a citizen of all his political rights by classing him among the *ærarii*. The censors could also put a *nota censoria* opposite a man's name in the roll of citizens; and this might be done upon their own responsibility, without special inquiry, though they generally acted in accordance with public opinion. The *nota censoria* produced no effect except during the magistracy of the censor who imposed it. In this respect it differed essentially from infamy, which was perpetual, unless the stigma was removed by the prerogative of the people or the emperor.[2]

Religion as affecting civil rights. Originally, when the Romans all followed the same pagan worship, religion could occasion no difference in the enjoyment of civil rights. Under the Christian emperors, heretics and apostates, as well as pagans and Jews, were subjected to vexatious restrictions, particularly as regards their capacity to succeed to property and to make a will. Only orthodox Christians, who recognised the decisions of the four œcumenical councils, had the full enjoyment of civil rights.[3]

[1] D. 3. 2. C. 2. 12.   [3] Marezoll, § 77. Maynz, § 106.
[2] Maynz, § 105.

II.—FRENCH LAW OF CIVIL RIGHTS.

In France, prior to 1789, there were many Frenchmen who *Before 1789 no equality of civil rights.* did not enjoy civil rights, or only did so imperfectly and unequally. Serfs were numerous; native-born Jews were considered as foreigners; persons devoted to a religious life were supposed to be civilly dead; Protestants were incapable of holding any public office. The rights of other Frenchmen varied according to the order to which they belonged—to the clergy, the nobility, the army, the law, finance, or any other public department whatever. That portion of the community called the *tiers état* or *roturiers,* supported vexatious burdens from which the clergy and nobility were wholly free, without participating in the prerogatives of these privileged orders. To be born or domiciled in the country of the written law, where the Roman jurisprudence prevailed, or in the country of customary law, in which province differed from province, and county from county, in the nature of its usages, was another fertile source of discord in the enjoyment of civil rights. Property was governed as variously as persons. Inequality ruled the soil as well as individuals, and pervaded the whole operations of social life.

Privileged castes and exclusive rights received their death-blow at the Revolution. The law of 24th December 1789 raised all Frenchmen who were not Catholics to the rank of citizens; that of 15th March 1790 emancipated the serfs; that of 27th September 1791 nationalised the Jews. Shortly afterwards persons devoted to religion as monks or nuns were restored to the rights and duties of civil life.[1] Finally, *Equality of civil rights under Code.* equality of civil rights was established among all Frenchmen by the Civil Code, which declares—1st, "The exercise of civil rights is independent of the quality of citizen, which can only be acquired and maintained in conformity with constitutional law." 2d, "Every Frenchman will enjoy civil rights."[2]

[1] Pailliet, Manuel du Droit Français, 8th ed., p. 8, note.

[2] Code Civil, art. 7, 8.

Who are held French subjects.

In France, lawful children, wherever born, are held to be members of that state to which their fathers belong at the time of their birth, but may choose, if they prefer it, the nationality of their place of birth. A child born in France of foreign parents may, within one year after he has attained majority, claim to be a Frenchman; if he is not then in France, he must declare his intention to reside there, and he must fix his domicile there within one year after such declaration.[1]

Some states have adopted the principle of complete reciprocity, by treating foreigners in the same manner as their subjects are treated in the country to which these foreigners belong.[*] Other states regard certain rights as absolutely inherent in the quality of citizens, so as to exclude foreigners from their enjoyment. Thus Britain does not permit foreigners to acquire real property for a longer term than twenty-one years.

Rights of foreigners in France.

In France a foreigner enjoys the same civil rights as those which are allowed to Frenchmen by the treaties of the nation to which the foreigner belongs. Moreover, a foreigner who has obtained permission from the sovereign to establish his domicile in France, will, so long as he resides there, enjoy all civil rights.[2] The *droit d'aubaine*, or right of succeeding to the effects of a deceased alien, formerly claimed by the crown of France, was finally abrogated by the law of 14th July 1819, so that foreigners are now placed on the same footing in respect to succession as native Frenchmen. A foreigner

---

[1] Code Civil, art. 9, 10.

[*] The principle of reciprocity cannot be invoked by foreigners in France in criminal matters. Although a Frenchman tried in England for crime may demand a jury, one-half of whom are his own countrymen, an Englishman in France has no such privilege, 24th April 1816. Sirey 16. 2. 144. Foreigners in France have copyright in their literary works; they may obtain patents for inventions; they cannot be tutors to Frenchmen; nor hold public offices in France; nor discharge any ecclesiastical function without permission of the Government; nor be admitted to exercise the profession of advocate; nor publish a journal in France; and foreigners, whether in France or not, cannot complain of the fraudulent use by Frenchmen of their trade-marks. Les Codes Annotés de Sirey, vol. i. p. 59, *seq.*, ed. 1867, par P. Gilbert.

[2] Code Civil, art. 11, 13.

can buy and hold land in France without any permission from the crown or legislature.[1]

III.—BRITISH LAW ON SUBJECTS AND ALIENS.

By our law, all persons born in the British dominions— *Who are held British subjects.* that is, either within the United Kingdom or the territories thereto belonging — whether their parents be natives or foreigners, are held to be natural-born subjects of Britain. Further, all children born abroad, whose fathers or grand-fathers by the father's side were natural-born subjects, are now deemed to be natural-born subjects themselves, unless the ancestors of such children at the time of their birth were attainted of treason, or were liable for the penalties of treason. Every person born of a British mother abroad may hold real or personal estates in this country; and if an alien woman marry a natural-born subject, or person naturalised, she becomes *ipso facto* naturalised.[2]

An alien who is the subject of a friendly state may take *Rights of foreigners in Britain.* and hold every species of personal property, except chattels real and British shipping, as fully and effectually as natural-born subjects. The subject of a friendly state may also, for the purpose of residence or occupation, either by himself or his servants, hold lands, houses, or tenements for any term not exceeding twenty-one years.[3]

The right of asylum accorded to political refugees is not incompatible with the surrender of criminals. Upon this principle Britain has entered into extradition treaties with France and the United States of America for mutually delivering up to justice persons charged with murder, piracy, arson, or forgery, committed within the jurisdiction of either of the contracting states.[4]

Formerly naturalisation could not be obtained in this

---

[1] Pailliet, Manuel du Droit Français, 8th ed., p. 10.

[2] Stephen's Com. on Laws of England, 4th ed., vol. ii. p. 413. 7 & 8 Vict. c. 66, s. 3, 16.

[3] 7 & 8 Vict. c. 66, s. 4, 5.

[4] Treaty with France, 1843, confirmed by 6 & 7 Vict. c. 75. Treaty with United States, 1842, confirmed by 6 & 7 Vict. c. 76. Phillimore, International Law, vol. i. p. 427.

Naturalisation, how obtained.

country except by Act of Parliament.   But now, under the Act 7 & 8 Vict. c. 66, s. 8, naturalisation is conferred by the certificate of one of the Secretaries of State, and the oath of allegiance taken thereupon.   The granting of this certificate is discretionary, and it must except the capacity of becoming a member of the Privy Council or of either House of Parliament, and may except any other rights and capacities belonging to a British subject.

As naturalisation involves the acquisition of a new national character, it ought to be accompanied with the loss of the old.   In principle, no one should be a citizen of two nations at the same time, because, in the event of a war arising between them, he would be involved in conflicting duties by a divided allegiance.   Yet, with singular inconsistency, some of the states which readily admit foreigners as citizens, strenuously insist on the perpetual allegiance of their own subjects.

Discordant views as to allegiance.

In Britain, as well as in America, allegiance is regarded as a perpetual obligation, or at least one that cannot be renounced or dissolved without the mutual consent of sovereign and subject.[1]   We have already shown that an opposite doctrine of a national character, freely chosen by the person, was recognised by the Roman law ; and the same principle is adopted in the French Civil Code, which declares the character of a French subject to be lost by naturalisation in a foreign country, by accepting public employment from a foreign government without the sanction of the sovereign of France, and by every establishment made in a foreign country without the intention of returning, in which light, however, no establishments for commercial purposes are to be regarded.[2]   Similar regulations exist in other Continental states.

[1] Westlake's Private International Law, p. 21.   2 Kent's Commentaries on American Law, 10th ed., p. 10.   [2] Code Civil, art. 17.

CHAPTER IV.

OF SLAVERY.

IN this country, labour, being voluntary, rests upon contract, and the master's authority over the servant extends no farther than the terms of the contract permit. For this reason slavery possesses for us only a sort of historical interest; but it enters so deeply into the public and private life of the Romans, that some brief notice of it may not be without its use.

In principle, the Roman jurists acknowledge that all men are originally free by natural law; and they ascribe the power of masters over their slaves entirely to the law and general custom of nations. Slavery is accordingly defined, " constitutio juris gentium, qua quis, dominio alieno, contra naturam, subjicitur."[1]

Among the Romans slavery had its origin chiefly in three ways. 1st, Prisoners of war were considered the absolute property of the captors, and were either retained for the service of the State and employed in public works, or were sold by auction, *sub corona*, as part of the plunder. 2d, All the children of a female slave followed the condition of their mother, and belonged to her master, according to the principle applicable to the offspring of the lower animals,—*Partus sequitur ventrem.* Slaves born in the house of the master were called *vernæ*, as opposed to those acquired by purchase or otherwise. 3d, By judicial sentence Roman citizens might be condemned to slavery as a punishment for heinous offences, like the galley-slaves of modern times.[2]

How slavery arose.

[1] D. 1. 5. 4.   I. 1. 3. 2.   [2] Marezoll, § 71.

According to strict rule a Roman could not be the slave of another Roman. For, although by the Twelve Tables an insolvent debtor might be made over to his creditor, the law required that the debtor should be sold abroad or *trans Tiberim*. However, if a free man above twenty allowed himself to be sold as a slave by an accomplice, in order to share the price, he forfeited his liberty as a penalty for the fraud. A free woman who cohabited with a slave was liable to be reduced to slavery under the senatus-consultum Claudianum, but this law was repealed by Justinian.[1]

Condition of slaves at Rome.

In the earlier ages of the republic the number of slaves was small, but after the Roman conquests had extended beyond Italy, the influx of captives became very great, and slaves were sold by dealers in the public market. A large portion of the wealth of the Romans consisted of slaves, among whom many were artisans, whose labour yielded a highly profitable return. All slaves were under the power of their master. He had absolute control over their actions, their industry, and their labour; whatever they acquired belonged to him; and he could transfer them, like his goods and chattels, by sale, gift, or legacy to any one he pleased. They had no political or civil rights, and were in most respects considered in law as things rather than as persons. If they were sometimes allowed to retain a portion of their gains as a *peculium*, this was regarded as a favour rather than a right.

During the republic, and for a considerable time under the empire, the master had the absolute power of life and death over his slaves. Historians and poets make us acquainted with the dark side of slave life, and draw a lamentable picture of the cruel treatment to which this unhappy class were exposed. The Roman slaves were despised by rich and poor, and when they grew old, were sometimes left to die of starvation. The jaded voluptuary whose property they were, could scourge, brand, or torture them at pleasure; and even in the Augustan age we read of Vedius Pollio having ordered one of his domestics, who had broken a crystal goblet, to be

[1] C. 7. 24.

cast into his fish-pond to feed his lampreys.　Female slaves were often barbarously punished by their mistresses from mere caprice, or for the most venial mistakes in arranging the mysteries of the toilet.　Ulpian informs us that a Roman damsel called Umbricia was banished for five years by the Emperor Hadrian for atrocious cruelty to her female slaves.[1]

By a constitution of Antoninus Pius, mentioned in the Institutes, a master who wilfully put his slave to death was declared to be guilty of murder.　The same emperor issued a rescript to protect slaves from cruelty and oppression, directing the governors of provinces to inquire into the complaints of all slaves who took refuge in temples or at the statues of the emperor, which were placed in all the principal towns, and if it appeared that they had been treated with unreasonable severity, to order them to be sold, so that they might never return again to the same master.[2]　By these and similar measures the condition of slaves was in some degree ameliorated; but the master still retained a power of correction over them, which was substantially unlimited, and led to great abuses.　For, even if the slave died in consequence of the chastisement inflicted on him, the master had no prosecution to dread, unless it appeared that he intended to kill.[3]

Between slaves and free men we find, in the Roman empire, a class of persons who occupied an intermediate position; these are the *coloni*, sometimes called **adscriptitii** or *servi terræ*—that is, serfs who were attached to the soil for the purpose of cultivation, and were transferred along with the land when it was sold.　Some authors, such as Savigny, are of opinion that this institution goes no farther back than the reign of Diocletian, though they admit traces of it existed at an earlier period.　But other writers think serfs are of more ancient origin.

These serfs could contract marriage, and were regarded in law as persons capable of enjoying certain rights.　But in other respects their condition strongly resembled that of ordinary slaves.　Their master had the power of chastisement, and they could not dispose of their effects without his

Coloni or serfs.

[1] D. 1. 6. 2.　[2] I. 1. 8. 2.　[3] Collatio Legum Mosaicarum, tit. 3, c. 2.

consent. Originally the *colonus* was so strictly attached to the land that he could not be separated from it by enfranchisement; but afterwards this rigour disappeared.[1]

How slavery was terminated. Masters were entitled to give liberty to their slaves by manumission. In ancient times this was usually done in three ways. 1st, By the *census*, or putting the slave's name on the censor's roll. 2d, By the *vindicta* or lictor's rod, a ceremony performed in presence of the prætor. And, 3d, By the master in his testament conferring freedom on his slave. Some other less solemn forms of emancipation were afterwards introduced by the Roman emperors, such as *in ecclesiis, inter amicos, per epistolam, per convivium.*[2] At first the power of enfranchisement, being founded on the master's right of property, was absolutely unlimited; it was subsequently restrained by the laws Ælia Sentia and Furia Caninia, and indirectly by the law Julia Norbana; but, in order to afford every encouragement to freedom, these laws were repealed by Justinian.

Effects of manumission. Originally, all freedmen emancipated according to the proper forms became Roman citizens, though they were naturally looked down upon as inferiors by those who had no taint of servile blood. Under Augustus there were three classes of freedmen. 1st, Those who had the full rights of citizens. 2d, The Latini Juniani, who had only the privileges which the Latins enjoyed before the social war. And, 3d, the *dedititii*, who had only an inferior degree of liberty conferred on them, subject to various incapacities, one of which was that they were for ever debarred from attaining the rank of Roman citizens. All these distinctions among freedmen were swept away by the bold innovations of Justinian.

Gold ring. The privilege of wearing a gold ring, which was at first reserved to the equestrian order, was extended to all classes of *ingenui* or free-born subjects. If any one who was free at his birth was reduced to slavery and afterwards recovered his liberty, he did not cease to be considered *ingenuus.* But a freedman, if born a slave, had no right to wear the gold ring,

[1] De Fresquet, vol. i. p. 110-112,   [2] I. 1. 5. 2.   Ulp. 1. 7-9.
Du Colonat.

to which great importance was attached, unless he obtained the rank of free-born by special grant from the emperor.[1] At length, when all freedmen without distinction became Roman citizens, Justinian conferred on them the right of wearing the gold ring, which till then had been the distinguishing symbol of a man who had been free at his birth.[2]

After emancipation, the master, as patron, retained certain rights over his freedman. The freedman was required to pay a certain degree of respect, and to perform certain services, to his patron. Thus, if the patron was reduced to poverty, the freedman was bound to support him according to his abilities. On the other hand, the patron who failed to support his freedman when poor, was deprived of the rights of patronage. When a freedman died intestate, without heirs, his former master, as patron, succeeded to his effects. *Relations with the patron after manumission.*

The ancient condition of villenage in England expired about the commencement of the seventeenth century, and no other form of slavery was recognised by law, though a different rule prevailed in the colonies. In the case of James Somerset, the negro who was brought before the Court of King's Bench by *habeas corpus* in 1772, it was decided that a slave could not be carried out of the country back to the colonies by his master.[3] A similar question arose in Scotland, in the case of Knight v. Wedderburn, in 1778, where it was declared that the negro was in all respects free.[4] Strange to say, notwithstanding these decisions, the colliers and salters in Scotland remained in a condition resembling that of slaves till near the close of the last century. They were bound to continue their service during their lives, were fixed to their place of employment, and sold with the works to which they belonged.[5] In 1775 an Act was passed for their relief; but it was found to be

[1] "Ingenuus est qui statim ut natus est liber est." "Libertini sunt qui ex justa servitute manumissi sunt."—I. lib. 1, tit. 4 and 5. "Aureus annulus insigne ingenuitatis. Hoc jus libertini impetrabunt a principe."—Pandectæ Justinianeæ, auctore Pothier, vol. v. p. 18.
[2] N. 78, ch. 1.
[3] State Trials, xx. 1.
[4] Mor. Dict., p. 14, 545.
[5] Bankton, 1. 2. 82. Cockburn's Memorials, p. 76. Chambers's Domestic Annals of Scotland, iii. 453.

practically inoperative, in consequence of the ignorance and degradation of this class of work-people, and because enfranchisement could only be obtained by a decree in the Sheriff Court. It was not till 1799 that their freedom was established, so as to relieve the soil of Britain from the reproach of slavery.[1]

Slavery in modern times.

In modern times, slavery is still maintained in Asia, Africa, and some parts of America. But in Europe it gradually disappeared, in its most obnoxious form, with the progress of Christianity. What is called *serfdom*, however, subsisted in the various countries of Europe, not only during the middle ages, but down to a comparatively recent period; and it is only in our day that measures have been taken to emancipate many millions of serfs in the Russian dominions. After the discovery of America, the Spaniards and other European states revived the practice of slavery, by purchasing and transporting African negroes to be employed in their colonies. Great Britain was the first among European powers to declare the slave-trade illegal, in 1807; and in 1834, after some judicious preparatory regulations, all the slaves in her colonies were declared free, while twenty millions sterling were voted by Parliament as compensation to the slave-owners.[2] France followed the same course in regard to her colonies, by a law which came into force in 1848, full indemnity having been allowed to the masters.[3]

[1] 15 G. III. c. 28; 39 Geo. III. c. 56. May's Constitutional History of England, vol. ii. p. 284.

[2] Act 3 & 4 Will. IV. c. 73.

[3] Bouillet, Dict. des Sciences, des Lettres, et des Arts, *voce* Esclavage.

CHAPTER V.

OF MARRIAGE.

I.—ROMAN LAW.

Sect. 1.—Constitution of Marriage.

MARRIAGE is a contract by which a man and a woman enter Nature of marriage. into a mutual engagement, in the form prescribed by law, to live together as husband and wife, during the remainder of their lives. According to Modestinus—" Nuptiæ sunt conjunctio maris et fœminæ et consortium omnis vitæ, divini et humani juris communicatio." [1]

The words " consortium omnis vitæ " must not be extended to the property of the spouses ; for each preserved his or her patrimony distinct, unless where the wife was *in manu* of the husband.

Among the Romans, marriage was distinguished into *matri-* Justum and non-justum. *monium justum* and *non justum.* The first occurred when both parties had the capacity to enter into a lawful marriage, carrying along with it the paternal power, and other civil rights; and originally this was strictly confined to Roman citizens, or those to whom the *jus connubii* was conceded.[2] The *matrimonium non justum,* on the other hand, in which connubium was wanting, as in the case of marriage between *Latini,* or foreigners, or between Romans and foreigners, though an equally valid and binding marriage, did not confer the *patria potestas,* and other important civil rights.

In ancient times, equality of condition was required in

---

[1] D. 23. 2. 1.   [2] Ulp. 5. 4-5.

marriage, so that both patricians and plebeians married only amongst their own class, and freedmen were prohibited from marrying the freeborn. By the lex Canuleia, A.U.C. 309, connubium was authorised between patricians and plebeians; and by the lex Julia, A.U.C. 757, between freedmen and the freeborn, subject to certain restrictions as regards alliances with families of senatorial rank, which were afterwards removed by Justinian, who allowed senators to marry whom they pleased.[1] Actual marriage was the privilege of the free alone; the union of slaves was called *contubernium*.

Marriage with or without manus. Though certain forms were necessary to bring the wife *in manu mariti*, these were not essential to the validity of marriage itself; and the wife did not pass under the power of her husband, unless she expressly consented to do so. A lawful marriage could, therefore, be entered into in two ways—either with *conventio in manum*, or without it. By the first form, the wife passed out of her own family into that of her husband, who acquired all her property, and exercised over her a kind of *patria potestas* as if she had been his daughter. According to the other form, the woman remained in the power of her father or tutor, and retained the free disposition of her own property.

Three ancient forms. There were three modes of contracting marriage with *manus*, called *confarreatio, coemptio,* and *usus. Confarreatio* was a solemn religious ceremony, before ten witnesses, in which an ox was sacrificed, and a cake of wheaten bread was divided by the priest between the man and woman as an emblem of the *consortium vitæ,* or life in common. *Coemptio* was a sort of symbolical purchase of the wife by the husband, *per æs et libram,* in presence of five witnesses and the balance-holder. *Usus* was founded on prescription, by the woman cohabiting with the man as her husband for a whole year, without having been absent from his house for three whole nights following each other.[2] In later times the *conventio in manum* was found inconvenient by the Roman women, and these three ancient forms of marriage fell into disuse. Confarreation shared the

---

[1] N. 117, ch. 6.
[2] Gai. 1. 109.-113. Becker's Gal-   lus, translated by Metcalfe, p. 158 *et seq.*

fate of the old Pagan worship to which it belonged. Coemption, though more frequent, and still in use in the time of Gaius, gradually disappeared. Under the new system, marriage without *manus* became the ordinary rule of the common law, so that married women could dispose of their property without the authority of their husbands, and arrived at a degree of liberty unknown to most systems of legislation, and contrasting very strongly with the heavy disabilities imposed on wives by the common law of England and Scotland.

At Rome, marriage was sometimes preceded by espousals, *sponsalia*, being a mutual promise to marry at a future period; but this was not essential, and could not be enforced by one of the affianced persons against the other, so as to compel marriage.[1] Sponsalia.

By the Roman law marriage was contracted by the simple consent of the parties. As a general rule no writing of any kind was necessary; but when the spouses were of unequal condition, it became customary to draw up a marriage-contract, in order to rebut the presumption of concubinage. At first, Justinian dispensed with any written contract as unnecessary; but he afterwards required this form to be observed in the marriages of the great dignitaries of the empire and persons of illustrious rank.[2] How marriage is contracted.

According to the general opinion, marriage is completed by consent alone—*consensus facit nuptias;* but some writers, such as Ortolan, think the marriage is not perfected till after the wife has been delivered over to the husband, which is usually manifested by the *deductio in domum mariti.* According to this theory, marriage is viewed as a real contract completed by tradition.[3]

As regards physical capacity for marriage, the Romans fixed puberty at fourteen years of age for males, and twelve for females. All below these ages were pupils, and could not marry. Absolute impotency was generally considered a disqualification. Under Justinian's constitution, however, old age was no bar to matrimony. Polygamy was not permitted Impediments to marriage.

---

[1] C. 5. 1. 1.

[2] N. 74, ch. 4. . N. 117, ch. 4.

[3] Ortolan, Institutes, vol. ii. p. 80.

by the Romans, so that a subsisting marriage incapacitated any one from entering into a second marriage.

Relationship.
Relationship within certain degrees, either of consanguinity or affinity, rendered the parties incapable of contracting marriage. Ascendants and descendants to the most remote degree could not marry; and this rule applied to relations by adoption, even after the tie was dissolved. In the collateral line, marriage was prohibited between brothers and sisters, including persons so related by adoption while it subsisted, and also in the special case where one of the parties stood *in loco parentis* to the other, as uncle and niece, aunt and nephew. For, although the Emperor Claudius was authorised by the Senate to marry his niece Agrippina, and this example was followed by some Romans, the practice was suppressed by Constantine.[1] Marriage between cousins - german, which had for some time been prohibited, was declared lawful by Arcadius and Honorius.[2]

Degrees prohibited in consanguinity were also prohibited in affinity, which is the connection arising from marriage between one of the married persons and the blood relations of the other. Under Constantine, who abrogated the ancient law, marriage was prohibited with the widow of a deceased brother and the sister of a deceased wife.[3]

These rules as to forbidden degrees have been substantially adopted both in England and Scotland, except that we do not recognise adoption. In the Code Napoleon (articles 161, 162, and 163) the prohibitions are thus expressed:—

" In the direct line marriage is prohibited between all ascendants and descendants, whether lawful or natural, and persons connected by affinity in the same line.

" In the collateral line marriage is prohibited between the brother and sister, whether lawful or natural, and persons connected by affinity in the same degree.

" Marriage is also prohibited between uncle and niece, aunt and nephew."

Some marriages were prohibited by the Romans on grounds of public policy. So governors of provinces were not allowed

[1] Cod. Theod., 3. 12. 2.   [2] C. 5. 4. 19.   [3] Cod. Theod., 3. 12. 2.

to take wives from the territory under their administration ;
guardians could not marry their wards or give them in marriage to their children ; and in the later period of the empire,
Christians were not permitted to marry Jews.

By the Roman law the consent of the father, or *paterfa-* Father's
milias, was indispensable to the marriage of children under consent, when
power ; but neither the consent of the mother nor that of the necessary.
guardian was required. Farther, the tacit consent of the
father was sufficient.

In early times celibacy was considered censurable by the Celibacy at
Romans. This view passed away in the general degeneracy of Rome.
manners at Rome, especially after the civil wars at the close
of the republic, when the conduct of women of rank rendered
marriage exceedingly distasteful to the men. To counteract
these evils, Cæsar encouraged marriage by rewards. Augustus went still further, by passing the famous law Julia et
Papia Poppæa, containing some severe regulations against
celibacy, while solid favours were bestowed on those who had
a certain number of children. Little benefit resulted from
these laws, which operated very unequally and sometimes
oppressively, and they " were frequently defeated by the
emperors themselves, who were in use to give the *jus trium
liberorum* to persons who had no children, and even to some
who were not married."[1] Constantine abolished the penalties
of celibacy.

Under Augustus, concubinage—the permanent cohabita- Concubin-
tion of an unmarried man with an unmarried woman—was age.
authorised by law. The man who had a lawful wife could
not take a concubine ; neither was any man permitted to take
as a concubine the wife of another man, or to have more than
one concubine at the same time.[2] A breach of these regulations was always condemned, and fell under the head of
stuprum. In later times the concubine was called *amica*.
Between persons of unequal rank concubinage was not uncommon ; and sometimes it was resorted to by widowers who
had already lawful children and did not wish to contract

[1] Becker's Gallus, translated by   [2] Paul. 2. 20.
Metcalfe, p. 177.

another legal marriage, as in the cases of Vespasian, Antoninus Pius, and M. Aurelius.

As regards the father, the children born in concubinage were not under his power, and were not entitled to succeed as children by a legal marriage ; but they had an acknowledged father, and could demand support from him, besides exercising other rights. As regards the mother, their rights of succession were as extensive as those of her lawful children.

Under the Christian emperors concubinage was not favoured ; but it subsisted as a legal institution in the time of Justinian.[1]   At last Leo the Philosopher, Emperor of the East, in A.D. 887, abrogated the laws which permitted concubinage as being contrary to religion and public decency. " Why," said he, " should you prefer a muddy pool, when you can drink at a purer fountain ?"[2]   The existence of this custom, however, was long prolonged in the West among the Franks, Lombards, and Germans; and it is notorious that the clergy for some time gave themselves up to it without restraint.[3]

Sect. 2.—Effects of Roman Marriage.

Effect on persons of spouses.

As a general rule resulting from the *consortium vitæ*, the wife followed the domicile of the husband, and was entitled to protection and support from him. She took his name and rank, and retained them even after his death, so long as she did not enter into a second marriage.[4]

All the children born of a lawful marriage fell under the paternal power of the husband, who was always presumed to be the father, unless the contrary was established by certain proof.[5] A child was held to be conceived during the marriage, if it was born not more than ten months after its dissolution.[6]

Effect on property.

With regard to the property of the spouses, we have already

[1] D. 25. 7. C. 5. 26.
[2] Leon. Const. 91.   Ortolan, Institutes, vol. ii. p. 102, note.
[3] Ducange, *voce* Concubina. Tropong, De l'Influence du Christianisme sur le Droit Civil des Romains, p. 247.
[4] Mackeldey, § 550.
[5] D. 1. 6. 6.
[6] D. 38. 16. 3. § 11.

explained that, in early times, when marriage was entered into with the *conventio in manum,* the wife became entirely under the power of her husband, and all her property devolved on him. But at a later period, when the *conventio* was abandoned, marriage had no effect in rendering the property of the spouses common ; on the contrary, each was entitled to preserve what was his or her own, and to dispose of it at pleasure. If, therefore, the wife was *sui juris,* and had a private fortune, she retained it as her own property, entirely separated from that of her husband.

At the celebration of the wedding a contract of marriage was frequently entered into, to regulate the pecuniary rights of the spouses. In early times these contracts were unknown, and were unnecessary in the marriage with *manus;* but when the *manus* had become obsolete, the want of such agreements was felt.

It was considered to be the duty of the father to give to his daughter a marriage-portion or dowry, in proportion to his means. Such dowry was called *dos profectitia.* When the marriage-portion was given by the wife from her own property, or by any third person, it was called *dos adventitia.* However, the constitution of a *dos* was not essential to the validity of marriage ; it was one of those things which were regulated by special convention. The husband had the sole management of the *dos,* and the fruits of it, during the marriage ; and he could even exercise over it all acts of ownership, so far as it consisted of movables, but he could not alienate or encumber any part of it which was immovable, or invested in land, even with his wife's consent. As a general rule, the husband's right to the *dos* ceased on the dissolution of the marriage. According to the last state of the Roman law, when the marriage was dissolved the marriage-portion was restored to the wife or her heirs, and, exceptionally, to the wife's father (*profectitia dos*), or to the third person who had made the advance, when this had been done under an express reservation that it should return to him (*receptitia dos*). A different course might be adopted by special convention, as it might be stipulated in the marriage-contract that

Dos or dowry.

the husband should retain the *dos*, if the marriage was dissolved by the wife predeceasing him.[1]

All the property of the wife not comprehended in the dowry was called paraphernal (*parapherna*); the wife remained proprietor of it, and the husband had no rights over it, beyond those which she might relinquish in his favour.[2]

Donatio propter nuptias.

The *donatio propter nuptias* was a provision made by the husband for the wife, to be enjoyed by her by way of jointure, in the event of her surviving him. While the marriage subsisted the husband had the management of the whole fund, and applied the funds or profits to support the burdens of matrimony. If the marriage was dissolved by the death of the husband, the donation *propter nuptias* fell to the wife; but if she predeceased him, it was retained by the husband as his own absolute property.[3]

In certain circumstances marriage gave rise to reciprocal rights of succession between the spouses, as will be seen when we come to treat of the law of succession.

Donations between husband and wife.

To preserve the marriage relation in its purity, neither husband nor wife, as a general rule, could make a gift of anything to each other during the marriage. Under Septimius Severus the strictness of the law as to these donations was relaxed, and they became valid if the donor died first without having revoked them. There were also exceptions to the general rule. Some donations between husband and wife were, from their nature, valid and irrevocable, such as remuneratory grants, or those made with a view to a divorce; and a woman could make gifts to her husband in order to qualify him for certain honours.[4]

How far marriage a religious ceremony.

The Abbé Fleury states that marriage was considered by the earliest Fathers of the Christian Church an ecclesiastical as well as a civil ceremony. But other eminent writers take a different view, and contend that the authorities cited by Fleury do not support his assertion. Among the Romans marriage was purely a civil contract, and so it remained in the time of Justinian. The Emperor Leo the Philosopher,

[1] Marezoll, § 165.
[2] C. 5. 14.
[3] I. 2. 7. 3. C. 5. 3.
[4] D. 24. 1. C. 5. 16. Mackeldey, § 566.

A.D. 886, appears to have been the first who declared ecclesiastical benediction necessary to marriage; but his constitution was in force only in the Eastern empire. Among the early barbarian codes no mention is made of this ceremony; and in the history of Gregory of Tours marriage is treated as a civil contract.

In most countries the marriage ceremony is now performed in presence of a clergyman, and accompanied with the nuptial benediction, or other religious observances. The religious forms, however, are not essential to the validity of marriage, any further than may have been rendered necessary by the positive institutions of any particular State; for it belongs to the secular power alone to determine what forms, if any, shall be required in addition to the consent of the parties, in order to constitute a valid marriage. Blackstone observes, " The intervention of a priest to solemnise this contract is merely *juris positivi*, and not *juris naturalis aut divini.*" [1]

Before the decree of the Council of Trent, in November 1563, which declared that after that date all marriages not contracted in presence of a priest and two or three witnesses should be void, private marriages without the intervention of the clergy were recognised throughout Christendom. This famous decree is stigmatised by Pothier as a clerical usurpation, which never had any authority in France. Fifty-six prelates voted against it. Maillard, the Dean of the Sorbonne, we are told, declared that it was beyond the power of the Church, as well as unsound in principle, the first marriage between Adam and Eve, which was the pattern for all others, having been contracted privately without witnesses.[2]

Decree of Council of Trent, 1563.

II.—FRENCH LAW OF MARRIAGE.

By the Code Napoleon marriage in France requires to be celebrated before a civil officer of the domicile of one of the

How marriage contracted in France.

---

[1] Black. Com., book 1, ch. 15. On this point see Principal Lee's Lectures on the History of the Church of Scotland, vol. i. p. 248, note.

[2] Father Paul's History of the Council of Trent, book 7. Pothier, Traité de Mariage, part 4, c. 1, § 4.

contracting parties, in presence of four witnesses, after certain
public notices have been given ; and a formal instrument,
called *acte de mariage*, is drawn up in evidence of the contract.[1] This is usually followed by a religious ceremony to
consecrate the union of the spouses, but that is not required
to validate the marriage ; and any minister of public worship
who proceeds to the religious ceremony before the civil
marriage, is liable to severe punishment under the penal
code.[2] In this country we adopt the same age of consent
to marriage as the Roman law—that is, fourteen for males
and twelve for females ; but in France a man under eighteen
and a woman under fifteen cannot. marry,—at least they
cannot do so without a dispensation from the Crown for grave
reasons. A son under twenty-five, and a daughter under
twenty-one, cannot marry without the consent of their
parents, or the survivor of them ;' but in case of difference
the father's consent is sufficient. If the parents are dead, or
cannot consent, the grandfather and grandmother take their
place ; and failing all these, the consent of a family council
must be obtained. When the son and daughter are above
the ages specified, they may marry without any of the fore-
going consents, provided they previously make certain re-
spectful applications to their parents, according to prescribed
forms.[3] Children have no legal right to demand a marriage-
portion, or other establishment in life, from their father or
mother.[4]

Marriage-
contracts.
It is usual in France, before marriage, to make a contract
to regulate the respective rights and interests of the future
spouses ; and if such a contract exists, it requires to be mentioned in the *acte de mariage*, under the law of 18th July
1850. The contract may contain special conventions, or
may declare in a general manner that the parties understand
their marriage to proceed either upon the principle of the
communion of goods, or upon the principle of dotation (sous
le régime de la communauté, ou sous le régime dotal). In
the first case, under the communion of goods, the rights of

[1] Code Civil, art. 75, 76, 165.   [3] Code Civil, art. 144-151.
[2] Code Penal, art. 199, 200.   [4] Ibid., art. 204.

the spouses and their heirs will be governed by the regulations in book 3, title 5, chapter 2, of the Civil Code, beginning with article 1390. In the second case, under the principle of dotation, their rights will be governed by the regulations in chapter 3 of the same book and title commencing with article 1540.

The rules of the French law regarding the constitution of marriage will be found in the first book of the Civil Code, art. 63-76, and art. 144-228; and the legal effects of marriage, as affecting the property of the spouses, are treated very fully under the head "Contract of Marriage," in the third book of the Civil Code, art. 1387-1581. *Rules of Civil Code.*

III.—ENGLISH LAW OF MARRIAGE.

Sect. 1.—Constitution of Marriage in England.

In the celebrated case of Dalrymple,[1] Lord Stowell expressed an opinion that, prior to the Marriage Act of George II., marriage, by the law of England, was constituted by consent *de præsenti*, without the presence of a clergyman, or any religious ceremony. But that opinion was overruled by the judgment of the House of Lords, in Queen v. Millis, in 1844, where it was decided that, after the decree of the Council of Trent, the ecclesiastical law of England required the presence of a clergyman to marriage.[2] *After Council of Trent, presence of clergymen required.*

In England, the formalities of marriage are now regulated by the Marriage Acts, which allow marriage to be solemnised either with a religious ceremony or without it. The Act of 4 Geo. IV. c. 76 adhered to the principle of the common law, that marriages taking place in England must be solemnised between all persons (whatever their religious belief) by a minister in holy orders, and according to the rites of the Established Church, the only exceptions being in favour of Jews and Quakers, whose usages were left undisturbed. This principle having been found to operate harshly against Dissenters, the Act 6 and 7 Will. IV. c. 85 (since amended in *English Marriage Acts.*

---

[1] 2 Hagg. C. R. 54, and Dodson's Report.   [2] 10 Cl. and Fin., p. 534.

sundry points of detail) introduced new regulations, whereby marriages may now be celebrated in England, after due notice and certificate issued; either in a registered place of worship, and in the presence of some registrar of the district and of two witnesses, or at the office of the superintendent-registrar, and in his presence, and in the presence of some registrar of the district and of two witnesses, upon making the declaration and using the form of words prescribed.

By these Acts, marriage cannot be constituted, in England, by mere consent alone, however clearly expressed, before witnesses. There must be some previous notice, or proclamation of banns, or licence. Either a clergyman of the Established Church or the registrar of the district must be present, with witnesses, at the ceremony or mutual declaration respectively; and the marriage must be in an authorised place, and at authorised hours.

Where marriage must be celebrated. It will thus be observed, that in England the marriage ceremony must take place in a church, or, after due notice and certificate, in a licensed chapel or building, or in the registrar's office.

Ceremony. When the marriage takes place in a church or chapel of the Church of England, the service must be performed by the officiating minister, according to the rites of that Church, in presence of two or more witnesses. If the marriage is solemnised in a registered dissenting chapel, there may be superadded to the civil contract whatever religious ceremony the parties may think fit to adopt. But if the parties contract marriage in a registrar's office, the mutual declaration and exchange of matrimonial consent completes the civil contract, and no religious ceremony is used at such marriage.[1]

The Archbishop of Canterbury is authorised to grant special licences to marry at any convenient time or place. In all other cases, marriage in England cannot take place in a private house, and must be celebrated with open doors in canonical hours—that is, between 8 and 12 in the forenoon.

Marriage of minors. If the person proposing to marry is a minor, and not a widow or widower, the consent of the father of such person,

[1] 19 & 20 Vict. c. 119, s. 12. Paterson's Compendium, p. 287.

if living, must be obtained. If the father is dead, the consent of a guardian is required; and if there be no guardian, the consent of the mother, if unmarried; if there be no mother unmarried, then the consent of a guardian appointed by the Court of Chancery; and in some cases of disability, or where consent is unreasonably withheld, relief may be obtained by petition to the Lord Chancellor. Formerly a marriage might be declared void by reason of the want of consent by parents or guardians, but this rule was found to be productive of mischief; and, under the existing law, if a minor succeed in getting the marriage ceremony performed, the marriage is not accounted void by reason of the non-consent of parents and guardians.[1] All marriages, whether taking place under 4 Geo. IV. c. 76, or 6 and 7 Will. IV. c. 85, are required by law to be registered.

These Acts do not extend to any marriage contracted by British subjects out of England. A marriage entered into in Scotland or in a foreign country, if made in such form as is deemed sufficient in the place where it is contracted, will be considered valid by the law of England; and even the Gretna Green marriages were recognised by the English courts, though the parties eloped to Scotland on purpose to evade the laws of marriage in their own country. Marriages out of England.

It is a general rule, whatever inconveniences may sometimes attend it, that a marriage duly solemnised in any country according to its own law, ought to be recognised as binding in point of form all over the world. But there is a distinction between marriage rites and the legal capacity of marrying; for the form of the ceremony depends on the place where the marriage is solemnised, while the legal capacity of persons to marry is determined by the country of their domicile. This principle was established by the judgment of the House of Lords in Brook v. Brook. The parties were domiciled in England, where marriage with a deceased wife's sister is prohibited, and they were married at the Danish port of Altona, where the law permitted them to marry. This marriage was declared invalid, and the grounds of decision

---

[1] 6 & 7 Will. IV. c. 85, s. 25. Addison on Contracts, 5th ed., p. 756.

were, that all persons domiciled in England can marry only those whom the law of England allows them to marry; and that, by getting the ceremony performed at Altona, or elsewhere, they might vary the form but could not enlarge the capacity to marry.

Sect. 2.—*Effects of English Marriage.*

Wife's power to sue.

Generally speaking, a wife cannot sue in a court of law without her husband being joined with her. She can sue, however, as a *femme sole*, when judicially separated from him.

Effects on property of spouses.

By the common law of England, the husband acquires all the personal property belonging to the wife at the time of the marriage, or which may accrue to her during its subsistence, except her paraphernalia, and such property as may be settled for her separate use. He is also entitled to all her chattels real, or leasehold interests, and to her *choses in action*—such as debts due to the wife on bond or otherwise; but these are so far an exception that they do not in general become the husband's until he reduces them into possession. If he dies before this is done, they remain to the wife; and if she dies before this is done, they form part of her estate. The husband is also entitled to the management, and to the rents and profits, of the wife's freehold estates during the marriage. After his wife's death, he may enjoy for his life lands of the wife of which they were seised in her right for an estate of inheritance, if issue of the marriage is born capable of inheriting the property.

When the husband requires the intervention of a court of equity to obtain the benefit of any of his wife's property—as, for instance, to recover a legacy left to her—and when no other adequate provision has been made for her, the court will order part of such property to be settled upon the wife for her separate use.[1]

Rights of wife on husband's death.

As to the rights of property acquired by the wife on her husband's death, the law of England allows them to stand on

[1] Paterson's Compendium, p. 297.

a very precarious footing. Dower is the widow's life-estate in one-third of the husband's real estate, and was at one time a very valuable provision, but it has now dwindled into insignificance. Under the Act 3 and 4 Will. IV., which applies to all marriages contracted after 1st January 1834, dower cannot be claimed, 1st, Where the estate of the husband has been disposed of by him either in his lifetime or by will. 2d, A simple device of real estate subject to dower by the husband to the wife will bar the dower, unless a contrary intention be expressed. And, 3d, Any declaration by the husband, either by deed or will, that the wife shall not have dower, is sufficient to defeat her claim.

If the husband happen to die intestate, the statute of distributions (22 and 23 Car. II. c. 10) gives to the widow one-third of his personal property when he leaves issue living, and one-half when there is none; but this is a mere chance or hope of succession, which may be defeated at any time by the husband's will.

IV.—SCOTTISH LAW OF MARRIAGE.

Sect. 1.—*Constitution of Marriage in Scotland.*

In Scotland marriage is a civil contract, constituted by the mutual consent of the parties. The consent to marriage must be to a present act; a promise or engagement to marry at a future period, however formal, where no sexual intercourse has followed upon it, may be retracted, though the person retracting may be liable in damages for breach of promise. To the marriage of minors the consent of parents or guardians is not necessary. *Marriage contracted by mutual consent.*

The law of Scotland recognises four different modes by which marriage may be constituted. 1st, A public or regular marriage celebrated by a minister after proclamation of banns. 2d, The deliberate exchange of matrimonial consent by words *de præsenti*, without the nuptial benediction or *concubitus*. 3d, Promise of marriage followed by copula, at least when declared a marriage by an action of declarator in the Court of Session.   4th, Cohabitation as man and wife, and being held and reputed as married persons.[1]

Public or regular marriage. A public or regular marriage is one celebrated by a clergyman, in presence of two or more witnesses, after due proclamation of banns according to the rules of the Church.   All marriages entered into in any other form are clandestine or irregular ; but if the matrimonial consent has been seriously and deliberately interposed, they are equally effectual with regular marriages, though they expose all concerned in them to certain statutory penalties, which, however, are seldom if ever enforced in modern times.

By the 4 and 5 Will. IV. c. 28, regular marriages may be solemnised by the clergy of any religious persuasion, after due proclamation of banns in the parish churches of both parties.   The privilege was previously confined to ministers of the Established Church of Scotland and Episcopal clergymen who had taken the oaths to government.   Among Presbyterians these regular marriages are usually solemnised, not in a church, but at the private house where the woman resides ; but the place of celebration is a matter of indifference in point of law.   The question of mutual acceptance as husband and wife is put by the minister and answered by the parties : he then declares them married persons in presence of the witnesses, and the ceremony is closed by the nuptial benediction.   The registration of marriages in Scotland is regulated chiefly by 17 and 18 Vict. c. 80, and 18 Vict. c. 29.

Irregular marriages. As to irregular marriages, and the evidence by which they may be established, we cannot do better than lay before our readers a short exposition of the law in the words of Lord Moncreiff, whose authority in consistorial questions is justly entitled to the greatest weight :—

" The governing rule of law is unquestionably that marriage is constituted by the consent of the parties alone ; and that upon legal and satisfactory evidence that such mutual consent has been seriously and deliberately interposed, the court will declare such marriage, though it should be clear that no formal ceremony or celebration has taken place.

[1] Fraser, Personal and Domestic Relations, vol. i. p. 112.

" Proof of celebration *in facie ecclesiæ* is, of course, the Declaration before witnesses. first and best mode. Proof of a formal, serious, and deliber- ate declaration of consent before witnesses, if the court be satisfied that such declaration was made with the true intention of entering into marriage, is another settled mode of proving the constitution of marriage, as in the cases of Macadam, Dalrymple, and many other cases. Written de- Written acknowledgments. clarations or acknowledgments of marriage given and accepted, if there be no doubt of the reality of the purpose, are effectual to the same end, as in the case of Edmonstone against Cochrane, Honeyman, and other cases. Legal proof Promise cum copula. of a promise of marriage, followed by that intercourse which generally attends marriage, is held to prove the mutual consent required, on a presumption that at the moment of consummation, that which was before a promise only, became a present consent to marriage. Some lawyers have doubted whether this last mode of proving marriage does not differ from the others in this point, that it requires to be established by declarator in the lifetime of the parties. Without attempting to resolve this point, it is a settled rule of law that the promise must be proved either by the writing or by the oath of the party by whom it is said to have been given. Finally, the present consent necessary to constitute marriage may be effectually, and, in the Lord Ordinary's opinion, Cohabitation, and habit and repute. most satisfactorily constituted by a long or continued course of open cohabitation of the parties in the avowed characters of husband and wife, in which mode of proof regard must be had in the first place to what in general constitutes the cohabitation of persons bearing the relation of husband and wife, and then to the habit and repute, the reputation in which the parties have been held by their friends and connections, and the community in which they live. When such a cohabitation for a length of time, with the distinct character affixed to it by the open acts and conduct of both parties, is proved by credible and consistent evidence, no more satisfactory proof can be required that the present consent to marriage has been given in the face of all the world. But it is evident, from the very nature of the thing, that this mode of proving the consent necessarily supposes that there was no secrecy in it; that the parties did truly dwell together in the common meaning of the term cohabitation, and that they consorted with one another, not in the mode proper to a state of concubinage or illicit intercourse, but in the manner and with all the ordinary qualities of the marriage state in Christian nations.[1]

It has been a question amongst lawyers in Scotland, whether promise followed by *copula* is itself marriage, or is only a ground on which marriage may be constituted by a declarator in the Court of Session in the lifetime of the parties. This point, which may come to be of great importance as affecting the legitimacy of children, if raised after the death of either of the parents, does not appear to have been judicially decided. But, in a case which came before him in 1843, Lord Moncreiff expressed an opinion, that a promise *cum copula* does not constitute marriage without a declarator in the consistorial court; and that if no such declarator be brought in the lifetime of both parents, the marriage can never be established afterwards.[2]

Gretna Green marriages. To put an end to runaway marriages by English persons at Gretna Green and elsewhere in Scotland, which had become very common, it was enacted, by 19 and 20 Vict. c. 96, that, "after the 31st December 1856, no irregular marriage contracted in Scotland by declaration, acknowledgment, or ceremony shall be valid, unless one of the parties had at the date thereof his or her usual place of residence there, or had lived in Scotland for twenty-one days next preceding such marriage."

Declarator of putting to silence. In Scotland a process called a declarator of putting to silence may be brought in order to set aside a groundless claim of marriage. On the other hand, where a marriage which has actually taken place is denied by one of the parties, the other, by raising an action of declarator in the Court

---

[1] Lord Moncreiff, in Lowrie v. Mercer, 28th May 1840, 2 D. and B. 960, 961.

See also, on this point, Fraser's Personal and Domestic Relations, vol. i. p. 164.

[2] Brown v. Burns, 30th June, 1843.

of Session, may have the marriage declared, with all its consequent rights and privileges.

Sect. 2.—*Effects of Scottish Marriage.*

After marriage the husband becomes the curator or guar- Powers of
dian of his wife, and should be joined with her in deeds and married
women.
law proceedings to which she is a party. The wife is the
proper agent in all that relates to her separate estate, but the
husband's consent is generally required to validate deeds
granted by her. Thus she may exercise over her heritable
property, with the husband's consent, all the acts of administration competent to any other proprietor. Generally
speaking, the personal obligations of a married woman are
ineffectual, but they are binding if they are *in rem versum*
of the wife, or have special reference to her own property, or
have been granted by her while carrying on trade on her own
account, her husband being abroad, or when she is judicially
separated from her husband.[1] A married woman, without
her husband's consent, may validly execute a settlement, or
dispose of her separate estate by any deed which is not to
take effect till her own death.

By the common law of Scotland, marriage transfers to the Effect on
husband all the personal property of the wife at the time of spouses.
property of
the marriage, or which may accrue to her during its subsistence, with the exception of personal bonds bearing interest,
and the *paraphernalia*, which are limited to her clothes,
jewels, and ornaments of dress. The wife remains proprietor
of her lands or real estate ; but the husband is entitled to
the administration, and to the whole yearly rents and profits,
during the marriage. It is commonly said that the property
so acquired by the husband in right of his wife falls under
the communion of goods, as if there was a common fund for
behoof of both spouses ; but, as the husband has the absolute
power of use and disposal under the *jus mariti*, the goods

---

[1] Churnside, 11th July 1789, M. and D. 149. 24 & 25 Vict. c. 86,
6082. Orme, 30th Nov. 1833, 12 S. s. 6.

nominally in communion are in reality his property.[1] After the wife's death, if there has been a living child born of the marriage, and the wife has left no heir to her heritage by a former marriage, the surviving husband has a liferent right to the rents and profits of her heritable estate, which is called the courtesy. The rights of the spouses at common law may be modified by settlements before marriage, under which the husband's right of administration and *jus mariti* may be renounced in regard to the whole or any part of the wife's property ; and in any gift or bequest by a stranger to a married woman, the property may be specially destined for her separate use.

By the Act 24 and 25 Vict. c. 86, " to amend the law regarding conjugal rights in Scotland," some important changes have been introduced as to the proprietary rights of married women.

Equitable provision to wife.

First, when a married woman succeeds to property, or acquires right to it by any other means than the exercise of her own industry, the husband, or his creditors, or any one claiming through him, shall not be entitled to such property except on the condition of making therefrom a reasonable provision for the support and maintenance of the wife, if such a claim be made on her behalf ; and in the event of dispute as to the amount of the provision to be made, the matter shall be determined by the Court of Session. The wife's claim for such provision, however, must be made before the husband or his assignees shall have obtained possession of the property, and before his creditors shall have attached it by completed diligence.[2]

After separation, wife's funds her own.

Secondly, " after a decree of separation *a mensa et toro*, obtained at the instance of the wife, all property which she may acquire, or which may come to or devolve upon her, shall be held and considered as property belonging to her, in reference to which the *jus mariti* and husband's right of administration are excluded, and such property may be disposed of by her in all respects as if she were unmarried, and on her decease the same shall, in case she shall die intestate, pass to

---

[1] Shearer, 18th Nov. 1842.   [2] Sect. 16.

her heirs and representatives in like manner as if her husband had been then dead;" "and the wife shall, while so separate, be capable of entering into obligations, and be liable for wrongs and injuries, and be capable of suing and being sued, as if she were not married." The husband is not liable for the acts or obligations of the wife during the separation under such decree; but if he has been decerned to pay aliment to her, and has failed to do so, he will remain liable for necessaries supplied for her use.[1]

And may act and sue as if single.

Thirdly, when a wife has been deserted by her husband she may apply by petition to any Lord Ordinary of the Court of Session, or, in the time of vacation, to the Lord Ordinary on the Bills, for an order to protect property which she has acquired or may acquire by her own industry, or which she has succeeded to or may succeed to after such desertion, against her husband, or his creditors, or any one claiming through him. If any such order of protection be made and intimated, "the property of the wife as aforesaid shall belong to her as if she were unmarried;" and the order of protection "shall have the effect of a decree of separation *a mensa et toro*, in regard to the property, rights, and obligations of the husband and of the wife, and in regard to the wife's capacity to sue and be sued." This protection, however, does not extend to any property of which the husband or his assignees shall have obtained lawful possession, or which his creditors shall have attached by completed diligence before the date of the petition.[2]

Deserted wife entitled to order of protection.

Before the Statute 18 Vict. c. 23, when a wife predeceased her husband her next of kin or other representatives had right to a share of the goods in communion, extending to one-half when there was no issue, and one-third when there was such issue; but as the enforcement of that claim was found to be highly injurious to the interests of the surviving husband and his family, it was abrogated by the 6th section of that Act, which provides that, on a wife predeceasing her husband, her representatives shall have no right to any share of the goods in communion.

[1] Sect. 6.   [2] Sect. 1-5.

Rights of wife on husband's death.

On the death of the husband, the surviving wife, if she has no conventional provision, has a right to the *terce*, which is a liferent of a third of the heritable property in which the husband died infeft, including burgage subjects.[1] She is also entitled to the *jus relictæ*, which is a share of the free movable estate, or goods in communion, amounting to one-half where there are no children of the marriage, or where the husband has left no children by a former marriage, and to one-third only where there are children. The widow's legal provisions of *terce* and *jus relictæ*, unless barred by antenuptial settlements, or discharged by the acceptance of conventional provisions in lieu of them, must receive effect, and are not liable to be defeated arbitrarily at the pleasure of the husband, as the corresponding rights of the widow to dower, and a share of the movables, may be in England.

Proprietary powers of married women.

While the Roman law allowed great freedom to married women as regards their proprietary powers, the law in modern times lays them under severe restrictions. " The Code Napoleon," it has been observed, " is much influenced by the principles of the Roman law as regards the powers of married women; but the Scottish law goes in the very opposite direction. The systems which are least indulgent to married women, are invariably those which have followed the canon law. The English common law, as well as the Scottish, is very harsh in the proprietary incapacities it imposes on married women, and the doctrines of both are largely borrowed from the canonists." [2] Though recent legislation has materially improved the position of wives, it must still be acknowledged that much remains to be done to soften the rigour of the common law as to conjugal relations in both ends of the island, and more particularly in England.

[1] 1681, c. 10. 24 & 25 Vict. c. 86, s. 12.   [2] See H. S. Maine, Ancient Law, pp. 159, 160.

CHAPTER VI.

I.—ROMAN LAW.

A ROMAN marriage was dissolved by the death of one of the spouses, and by divorce in the lifetime of the parties.

Divorce existed in all ages at Rome. In the earliest times it was probably little used; but it is difficult to accept as true the traditional story told by Aulus Gellius, that Calvisius Ruga was the first who divorced his wife, in the 523d year after the building of Rome. *Divorce always existed at Rome.*

Divorce, in the Roman law, was the dissolution of a lawful marriage in the lifetime of the spouses, by the will of both or of one of them. In this matter the Romans proceeded on the notion that, as marriage was a free union founded on mutual consent, it might be terminated at any time by either of the parties. Even the *conventio in manum*, whatever effect it may have had in ancient times, did not, in the age of Gaius, limit the wife's freedom to seek divorce.[1] Under the new law no such impediment could exist, so that the declaration of divorce was equally competent to both spouses; and originally this liberty was only restrained by sentiments of morality and by public opinion, without any legal prohibitions.

During a long period divorce was not abused by the Romans; but at the close of the republic and the commencement of the empire, when the corruption of manners at Rome became general, divorce prevailed to a frightful extent. *Very common at close of republic.*

[1] Gai. 1. 137.

Marriage was thoughtlessly entered upon and dissolved at pleasure. Sylla, Cæsar, Pompey, Cicero, and Antony put away their wives, and Augustus and his successor did not scruple to follow their example. At the same period divorces on the woman's part were extremely common. Seneca notices this laxity of manners; and Juvenal (6 Sat. 20) gives a remarkable instance of a Roman matron who is said to have gone the round of eight husbands in five years.

Imperial laws to restrain practice. To check this deplorable corruption, laws were passed inflicting severe penalties on those whose bad conduct led to divorce; and there are imperial constitutions pointing out what should be deemed just causes of divorce. These penalties are directed not only against the spouse whose misconduct furnished a just occasion for divorce, or who spontaneously repudiated without just cause, but also against both spouses, when, without sufficient lawful motives, they dissolved their union by common accord, *bona gratia.* Yet, notwithstanding these penal enactments, divorce was in all cases left entirely to the free-will of the spouses.

No judicial sentence required. Among the Romans divorce did not require the sentence of a judge, and no judicial proceedings were necessary. It was considered a private act, though some distinct notice or declaration of intention was usual. At one period it became the practice for one of the spouses to intimate the divorce to the other in an epistolary form, by means of a freedman, in presence of seven witnesses, all Roman citizens above the age of puberty; and this was no doubt intended to preserve clear evidence of a transaction which was attended with such important consequences on the civil rights of the parties concerned.

When the marriage was dissolved by the death of the husband or by divorce, the wife was bound to wait a year before entering into a new marriage. In violating that prohibition a woman incurred infamy, besides being subject to other penalties.[1]

---

[1] C. 5. 17. 8 and 9. N. 22, ch. 16, pr. Mackeldy, § 573. Compare with Code Civil, art. 228.

II.—FRENCH LAW.

In modern times there has been much difference of opinion among lawyers and theologians as to the lawfulness of dissolving marriage by divorce. Some of the early fathers of the Church allowed divorce in the case of adultery, as the Greek Church does to this day; but the Church of Rome adopted the views of St Augustine, and the Council of Trent declared that marriage was a sacrament and indissoluble. Hence the canonists only allowed a separation from bed and board even in the case of adultery.

Before the Revolution the law of France adopted the principle which holds marriage to be indissoluble. Pothier says, emphatically, that "no power can break a marriage when it has been once validly contracted; for God himself having formed the bond of matrimony, no human power can dissolve it."[1] *Divorce allowed after Revolution.*

The law of 20th September 1792 permitted divorce in France, and this was afterwards confirmed by the Civil Code (art. 229-231), which authorised divorce on the following grounds: 1st, Adultery by the wife, or by the husband if he kept a concubine in the common dwelling-house; 2d, Outrageous conduct or ill-usage by either of the spouses; 3d, Condemnation to an infamous punishment; and, 4th, In a certain limited class of cases by mutual consent, but only upon the conditions and under the restrictions specified, which are of the most stringent character. After the restoration of the Bourbons, divorce was abolished by the law of 8th May 1816, judicial separation for just causes assigned being still retained. In 1830 and 1848 attempts were made to re-establish divorce in France, but without success.[2] *Grounds of Divorce under Code Civil.* *Divorce abolished in 1816.*

[1] Pothier, Traité du Contrat de Mariage, part 6, ch. 1, art. 3.
[2] Pailliet, Manuel de Droit Français, 8th ed., p. 69. Bouillet, Dict. des Sciences, *voce* Divorce.

III.—ENGLISH LAW.

Prior to 1858 no divorce allowed.

At the Reformation the Protestants rejected the Popish tenet that marriage was a sacrament and indissoluble. In some Protestant countries, however, the ecclesiastical courts clung to the old canon law of Europe ; and, down to a recent period, the law of England did not allow a marriage once validly contracted to be rescinded by divorce. Where there was no canonical disability, nothing short of an Act of Parliament could authorise divorce *a vinculo matrimonii;* but private Acts were occasionally obtained by persons of rank and condition, who could afford the expense, to dissolve marriages for adultery on the part of the wife, and for adultery accompanied by aggravated circumstances on the part of the husband.[1] So deeply rooted was this principle in the law of England, that in Lolly's case, where the parties were married in England and divorced in Scotland, and the husband subsequently married in England, he was tried and convicted there for bigamy, the conviction being affirmed by the unanimous opinion of the common-law judges. The English courts, however, recognised separation, or (as it was termed) divorce *a mensa et toro*, for certain conjugal wrongs, such as adultery and cruelty.

Divorce now sanctioned under statute.

Divorce is now sanctioned in England by the Act 20 and 21 Vict. c. 85, which came into operation in January 1858 ; and since that time the court established for the trial of matrimonial causes has not been idle.

A husband may obtain from this court a divorce on the ground of adultery committed by the wife. Generally the adulterer must be made a party to the suit ; and the court may order him to pay damages and also the costs, or may dismiss him from the suit ; but it is no longer competent for the husband to sue the adulterer in a separate action for damages.[2]

Neither of the spouses can obtain a divorce on the ground of mere desertion by the other, however long continued.

[1] Dr Harris's Justinian's Institutes, p. 30, note.

[2] 20 & 21 Vict. c. 85 ; 21 & 22 Vict. c. 108.

As to the wife, a divorce cannot be obtained by her on the ground of the husband's adultery alone ; but she may obtain a divorce if the husband has been guilty of incestuous adultery ; or of bigamy with adultery ; or of adultery coupled with gross cruelty, or with other aggravated circumstances ; or of adultery, coupled with desertion for two years without reasonable cause.[1]

If the petitioner has been accessory to, or has connived at, the adultery, or has condoned it, or if the petition is presented or prosecuted by collusion, no decree of divorce can be granted. Farther, the court is not bound to grant such decree if the petitioner has been guilty of adultery during the marriage, or guilty of unreasonable delay in the petition, or of cruelty to the other party, or of desertion or wilful separation from the other party before the adultery and without reasonable excuse, or guilty of such wilful neglect or misconduct as has conduced to the adultery.[2]

After the decree of divorce has become final, the parties are at liberty to marry again, as if the previous marriage had been dissolved by death.[3] *

From the same court, either the husband or the wife may obtain a judicial separation, formerly called a divorce *a mensa et toro*, on the ground of adultery, or cruelty, or desertion without cause for two years and upwards.[4] After a decree of judicial separation the wife is considered as a *femme sole* in regard to all property she may subsequently acquire, or which may come to or devolve upon her, and she can sue or be sued as if she were unmarried ; and, on the other hand, the husband is not liable for her debts, except for necessaries supplied to her when he fails to pay the alimony decreed to her by the court.[5]

Judicial separation.

[1] 20 & 21 Vict. c. 85, s. 27.
[2] Ibid. s. 30, 31.
[3] Ibid. s. 57.
* See as to Appeals, 31 & 32 Vict.
c. 77.
[4] 20 & 21 Vict. c. 85, s. 16.
[5] Ibid. s. 25, 26.

IV.—SCOTTISH LAW.

Divorce for adultery and wilful desertion.   By the law of Scotland a divorce may be obtained by the husband or the wife on the ground of adultery, or of wilful desertion for four years together without just cause, after adopting the forms of the Act 1573, c. 55, so far as these are still required.[1]

Husband and wife have equal rights.   In suing for a divorce in Scotland the wife has precisely the same rights as the husband. If she can prove adultery or wilful desertion for four years by the husband, that entitles her to take proceedings for a divorce, in the same manner as adultery or wilful desertion on her part entitles him to a similar remedy.

The action of divorce proceeds before the Court of Session, and the right to institute it is personal to the husband or the wife. As a preliminary the pursuer is required to make oath that the suit is not collusive. In this and all consistorial actions the summons must be served upon the defender personally when he is not resident in Scotland ; yet, upon evidence to the satisfaction of the Court that the defender cannot be found, edictal citation will be held sufficient ; but in every case where the citation is edictal the summons must be served on the children of the marriage, if any, and on one or more of the next of kin of the defender, exclusive of their children, when the children and next of kin are known and resident within the United Kingdom ; and such children and next of kin, whether cited or so resident or not, may appear and state defences to the action.[2]

When the husband sues for divorce on the ground of adultery, he may cite the alleged adulterer as a co-defender, and the Court may order him to pay the whole or any part of the costs, or may dismiss him from the action, as may seem just.[3]

[1] Ersk. 1. 6. 43. Fraser, Per. and Dom. Relations, vol. i. p. 652 et seq.

By the 24 & 25 Vict. c. 86, s. 11, it seems to have been intended to abolish the forms of the Act 1573 ; but the clause is not happily expressed.

[2] 24 & 25 Vict. c. 86, s. 10.
[3] Ibid. s. 7.

In the case of adultery, divorce is barred by condonation or forgiveness, as well as by collusion or connivance. Recrimination cannot be pleaded as a defence to exclude the suit; but it may be stated in a counter-action, as the mutual guilt may affect the patrimonial interests of the parties.[1]

The legal effect of divorce on the ground of wilful desertion under the Act 1573, c. 55, is, that the offending husband is bound to restore the tocher (*dos*), and to pay or implement to the wife all her provisions, legal or conventional; and the offending wife forfeits her terce, and all that would have come to her had the marriage been dissolved by the predecease of the husband. By analogy the same consequences have been extended to the case of divorce for adultery, with this exception, that it appears to have been decided, upon very questionable grounds, that the offending husband in the case of adultery is not bound to restore the tocher.[2] *Effects of divorce.*

After divorce both parties are at liberty to marry again; but the Act 1600, c. 20, annuls any marriage contracted between the adulterer and the person with whom he or she is declared by the sentence of divorce to have committed the offence.

---

[1] Fraser, Per. and Dom. Relations, vol. i. p. 666-672.

[2] Justice, 13th Jan. 1761, M. p. 334. Fraser, vi. p. 691. Ersk. 1. 6. 48.

CHAPTER VII.

OF THE LEGITIMATION OF NATURAL CHILDREN.

Distinction as to lawful children. APART from the effect of legitimation, the Roman law only considered those children lawful at their birth who were begotten in marriage. It is a peculiarity of the English law that it does not concern itself with the conception, but considers a child legitimate who is born of parents married before the time of his birth, though they were unmarried when he was begotten.[1]

Legitimation by subsequent marriage. The legitimation of children *per subsequens matrimonium* originated in a constitution of Constantine, which has not reached us, though its tenor is given in a law of the Emperor Zeno, who renewed it.[2] The import of it was, that persons who had been living in a state of concubinage, which was then a known condition of society not condemned by Roman customs, might, by entering into marriage, render the children born in that state legitimate, provided the woman was *ingenua*, or free-born, and the man had not already children of a lawful wife. The general object of this law probably was to encourage persons who had been living in concubinage to enter into marriage. Justinian extended the law of Constantine, by declaring that children born in concubinage should be legitimate generally, and whether the father had legitimate children by a lawful wife or not ; and he removed the distinction as to the quality of the woman as being *ingenua* or *libertina*. The children so legitimated were subjected to the paternal power, and entitled to all the rights of lawful children.[3]

Applied only to children born in concubinage. By the Roman law the privilege of legitimation *per subsequens matrimonium* was strictly confined to the children of a concubine, and did not extend to any other description of bastards.

---

[1] Stephen's Com. on the Law of England, 4th ed., vol. ii. p. 289.

[2] C. 5. 27. 5.
[3] I. 1. 10. 13.   C. 5. 27. 10.

Another kind of legitimation, *per oblationem curiæ*, was Two other kinds of legitimation. introduced by Theodosius II., A.D. 443. As the duties of a decurio were very onerous, and accompanied with risk, a natural son who undertook the office was thereby rendered legitimate. A natural daughter who married a decurio had the same privilege. Finally, Justinian added a third species of legitimation, *per rescriptum principis*, when the emperor declared natural children legitimate upon the requisition of the father in certain special circumstances ; as, for instance, when marriage with the concubine had become impossible, and there were no lawful children,—or when the father, who had from some fortuitous cause been prevented from legitimating his natural children in his lifetime, declared in his testament that they should succeed to him as lawful children and heirs *ab intestato*.[1]

The doctrine of legitimation by subsequent marriage is Extended to bastards by canon law. said to have been established in the canon law by two constitutions of Pope Alexander III., preserved in the decretals of Gregory.[2] The canon law was more indulgent than the Roman law, in granting the privilege of legitimacy not merely to the offspring of concubinage, but to children begotten in fornication, when their parents were afterwards married, provided the father and mother were capable of contracting marriage at the date of the sexual intercourse.

Legitimation by subsequent marriage was never acknow Legitimation rejected by English law. ledged by the law of England. When the clergy struggled to introduce the rule of the canon law, it was indignantly rejected by the famous statute of Merton, the English barons declaring with one voice, " quod nolunt leges Angliæ mutare quæ huc usque usitatæ sunt et approbatæ." [3] From the earliest period the English law has considered a child born before marriage (*ante natus*) as illegitimate. And it has been decided, that even where the child is born and the parents are subsequently married in a foreign country, the law of which allows legitimation by subsequent marriage, he is nevertheless incapable of inheriting land in England.[4]

---

[1] N. 74, ch. 1, 2.   N. 89, ch. 9, 10.   Mackeldey, § 587.

[2] Decretal, 4. 17. 1 and 6.

[3] Statute of Merton, 20 Henry III.

Dr Harris's Justinian's Institutes, p. 31, note.

[4] Doe *v.* Vardill, 5 Barn and Cress., 438. 6 Bing. N. C. 385.

French law admits it, On the other hand, the rule of the canon law, which allowed the legitimation of all bastards, provided they were not the offspring of an incestuous or adulterous connection, has been followed both in France* and Scotland, not by authority of the decretals, but in consequence of the equity and expediency of the rule itself. By the Civil Code (art. 331-333) it is declared : 1. " Children born out of wedlock, other than those born of an incestuous or adulterine intercourse, may be legitimated by the subsequent marriage of their father and mother, provided the children have been legally acknowledged before marriage, or in the act of celebration itself. 2. Legitimation may take place even in favour of deceased children who have left descendants, and in that case it operates in favour of these descendants. 3. Children legitimated by subsequent marriage shall have the same rights as if they had been born of that marriage."

By the law of France, marriage makes the children of an illicit connection legitimate, although one of the spouses had, after the connection and the birth of the children, contracted a marriage with another person, and the parents had only married after the dissolution of that marriage. As the child legitimated is considered to be born of the marriage which has made him legitimate, he cannot participate in a succession

---

* The French law seems to be settled on a point in regard to which the law of Scotland is doubtful; and even the Roman law, as to it, is a matter of controversy. By the law of France, a child *conceived* in adultery cannot be legitimated even though at its birth the parents were free to marry (23d May 1838, Le Havre, Recueil General, par MM. Villeneuve et Carrette, 40, 2, 463; Merlin Rep. v. Legitimation, sect. 2, § 2, Nos. 6 et 7). As regards the Roman law, Voet (xxv. 7, 7 *seq.*) and others say that legitimation can take place; while Pothier maintains the contrary (Tr. de Mar, Par. 5, c. 2, No. 415). The views of Scottish lawyers are stated by Bankton, i. 5, 54, and Erskine, 1, 6, 49 and 52, and per Lord Chancellor in Monro,
1 Rob. Ap. Ca., 492. The French law also differs from the Roman, canon, and Scottish laws in requiring that the children shall be recognised as children of the married parties, by them, before the marriage, or at the act of celebration. After the marriage, any acknowledgment or recognition of them is unavailing (15th May 1816, Douai, Sirey, 16, 2, 337). This rule bars those inquiries which have occurred in Scottish practice— always difficult and expensive—as to whether a person claiming the benefit of legitimation is, *de facto*, the child of the two individuals whose child he alleges himself to be.—See Innes *v.* Innes, 20th Feb. 1837, 2 S. and M'L. Ap. Ca., 444.

which has opened before that marriage, though subsequent
to his birth. For the same reason he cannot claim any preference, in respect of mere priority of birth, in any question of
succession with the children of the intermediate marriage.[1]

In Kerr v. Martin, which was elaborately discussed in the *And the law of Scotland.*
Court of Session, the question was raised, whether a marriage
by either of the parents with a third person, after the birth
of a natural child, formed a bar to legitimation by the subsequent marriage of the parents. Though the judges were
divided in opinion, the Court, by a majority, decided that
the child was legitimate, and that no mid-impediment was
created by the intervening marriage.[2]

In Scotland legitimation by subsequent marriage confers
upon a bastard the rights of a lawful child. Besides being
entitled to legitim, he succeeds under a destination to lawful
children. In any question with the children born of the
bastard's parents in lawful wedlock, he has the same civil
rights, as regards succession and otherwise, as he would have
enjoyed had he been born in lawful marriage. But where
there is lawful issue of an intermediate marriage by one of
the parents with a third person, a child legitimated by a
second marriage seems only a lawful child of the family as
becoming so by the second marriage, and therefore it is
thought he can claim no preference in respect of primogeniture or priority of birth, which would have the effect of
defeating or prejudicing the rights of succession of the children of the first marriage arising at their birth. According
to this view, if the father had a natural son, and after this
a lawful son by a marriage with a third person, and then
entered into a second marriage with the mother of the bastard,
the lawful son by the first marriage would be entitled to the
Scotch heritage *ab intestato,* and could not be deprived of
that right by the legitimation of the natural son arising from
the *second* marriage.[3]

[1] Paillict, Manuel de Droit Français, 8th ed., p. 84.
[2] Kerr v. Martin, 1840, 2 D. B. M.
p. 750. See also Shedden, 1854, 1

Macq. App. Ca. 535.
[3] See Fraser, Per. and Dom. Relations, vol. ii. p. 18.

CHAPTER VIII.

OF ADOPTION.

AMONG the Romans the relation of father and child arose either from marriage or from adoption.

Adoption of two kinds. There were two kinds of adoption—*adoptio*, strictly so called, and *adrogatio*. The first was the ceremony by which a person who was in the power of his parent, whether child or grandchild, was transferred to the power of the person adopting him. In ancient times the person to be adopted was emancipated *per æs et libram*, and surrendered to the adoptive father by the legal form called *in jure cessio*. Afterwards adoption was effected under the authority of a magistrate having jurisdiction for the purpose—such as, for instance, the prætor at Rome or a governor in the provinces.

Adrogatio defined. When the person to be adopted was *sui juris*, and not in the power of his parent, the ceremony of adoption was called *adrogatio*. Originally this could only be accomplished by a vote of the people in the *Comitia curiata*, but under the empire the authority of an imperial rescript was required. If pupils were adopted in this form, the adoptive father was bound to give security to restore their property, if they died within puberty, to their lawful heirs, and to make such restitution to themselves if they were emancipated upon just grounds.[1]

Conditions of adoption. Every man, whether married or not, could adopt, provided he had the capacity to contract marriage. In ancient times this privilege was denied to women, because they could have

[1] I. 1. 11.   D. 1. 7.   C. 8. 48.

no one under their power; but the law was altered about
the period of Diocletian, and women were allowed to adopt
in order to console them for the loss of their children : they
could thus attach to themselves children who were not
under their power, but who acquired certain rights to their
succession.[1]

No person could adopt one who was older than himself,
"for adoption imitates nature, and it seems unnatural that
a son should be older than his father."[2] It was, therefore,
required that the adopter should be older than the person
adopted by full puberty, that is, eighteen years.[3] Under the
republic, patricians who wished to become tribunes of the
people caused themselves to be adopted by plebeians ; of
which we have an example in the case of Clodius, the enemy
of Cicero, who was adopted by a plebeian younger than
himself, in direct violation of the law as laid down in the
Institutes.

A person having no child could, by the Roman law, adopt
a grandchild ; but one having a son was not permitted to
adopt a grandson without the son's consent. In common
adoption only one person passed under the power of the
adoptive father ; but if a person having children in his
power gave himself in arrogation, both he as a son and his
children as grandchildren became subject to the power of the
adopter. Augustus did not adopt Tiberius, who succeeded
him in the empire, till Tiberius had adopted his nephew
Germanicus ; and the effect of this was, that Tiberius became
the son, and Germanicus the grandson of Augustus at the
same time.

At the close of the republic, a usage was introduced of
declaring in a testament that the testator considered a certain
citizen as his son. The person so indicated, after obtaining a
confirmation of this declaration by a plebiscite, had the right
of succession to the deceased : this, however, was not a proper
case of adoption, but rather a particular mode of nominating
an heir.

By the ancient civil law adoption created the relation of

[1] I. 1. 11. 10.   [2] I. 1. 11. 4. D. 1. 7. 40. 1.   [3] Ibid.

father and son for all practical purposes, just as if the adopted
son were born of the blood of the adoptive father in lawful
marriage. The adopted child quitted entirely his own family
and entered the family of his adopter, passing under the
paternal power of his new father, and acquiring the capacity
to inherit through him. An adopted child added to his own
name that of his adopter, modifying it by the termination
ianus. A Scipio adopted by Emilius was called *Scipio
Emilianus*.[1] Public honours were not changed by adoption,
so that a senator adopted by a plebeian remained a senator.

In practice, serious inconveniences were found to arise from
forcing the adopted child to leave his natural family, for, if
he was afterwards emancipated by the adoptive father, he
could have no right of succession in the character of agnate
to either family. To obviate this difficulty, Justinian made a
distinction between the case of adoption by a stranger and
adoption by an ascendant, such as a grandfather. When the
father of a family gave his son in adoption to a stranger,
there was no dissolution of the paternal power, and the
adoptive father did not acquire it, though the adopted child
had a right to succeed to the adopter *ab intestato ;* but if the
child was given in adoption to its grandfather, or other direct
ascendant, after its father had been emancipated, the civil
consequences of adoption were maintained, and the child
passed under the power of the adopter. In the first case, the
adopted person remained a member of his natural family,
while he also acquired the rights of succession *ab intestato* to
the adopter. In the second case, it was presumed that affec-
tion springing from the ties of blood would influence the ascendant to refrain from emancipating the adopted child, so as
to prejudice his rights of succession, apart from the protection otherwise given by the new law introduced by the
prætorian edicts and the constitutions of the emperors.[2]
According to the rigour of the ancient law, a son under power
might be given in adoption without his consent ; but under
the new legislation the son had a right to object.[3]

Adoption was extremely common at Rome, and was con-

---

[1] De Fresquet, vol. i. p. 144.   [2] I. 1. 11. 2.   [3] Marezoll, § 179.

sidered a very useful institution. Many powerful patrician ^{Adoption} families, on the verge of extinction by the failure of children, ^{common at Rome.} were revived by adoption; but it was always considered more honourable to be the actual father of children born in lawful marriage than to have recourse to fictitious paternity. Julius Cæsar, by his testament, which was confirmed after his death by a *lex curiata*, adopted his great-nephew, Octavius, who assumed the name of Cæsar Octavianus, and was afterwards better known as the Emperor Augustus. Some of the Roman emperors, who had no male children, appointed their successors to the purple by adoption; and if their choice was not always fortunate, as in the instances of Tiberius and Nero, yet it must be acknowledged that Rome was indebted to this custom for a series of princes unequalled in history—Nerva, Trajan, Hadrian, and Marcus Aurelius.

In France the usage of adoption was lost after the first ^{Adoption in France.} race of kings: it disappeared, not only in the customary provinces, but also in the provinces governed by the written law. Re-established in 1792, adoption is now sanctioned by the Civil Code. Adoption, however, is only permitted to persons of either sex above the age of fifty, having neither children nor other lawful descendants, and being at least fifteen years older than the individual adopted. No married person can adopt without the consent of the other spouse. The privilege can only be exercised in favour of one who has been an object of the adopter's care for at least six years during minority, or of one who has saved the life of the adopter in battle, from fire, or from drowning. In the latter case the only restriction respecting the age of the parties is, that the adopter shall be older than the adopted, and shall have attained his majority. In no case can adoption take place before the majority of the person proposed to be adopted.

The form of adoption consists of a declaration of consent by the parties before a justice of the peace for the place where the adopter resides, after which the transaction requires to be approved of by the tribunal of first instance. After adoption, the adopted person retains all his rights as a member of his natural family. He acquires no right of succession to the property of any relation of the adopter ; but in regard to the property of the adopter himself, he has precisely the same rights as a child born in marriage, even although there should be other children born in marriage after his adoption. The adopted takes the name of the adopter in addition to his own.   No marriage can take place between the adopter and the adopted or his descendants, and in certain other cases specified.[1]

No adoption in Britain.   The practice of adoption, which is better suited to some states of society than to others, still prevails among Eastern nations.   It has never been recognised as a legal institution in England or Scotland.

[1] Code Civil, art. 343-360.

CHAPTER IX.

I.—ROMAN LAW.

No one acquainted with Roman institutions can doubt the truth of Justinian's observation, that "the power which we have over our children is peculiar to the citizens of Rome ; for there is no other people who have the same power over their children which we have over ours." [1]

As developed at Rome, the *patria potestas*, though well fitted to maintain discipline and obedience, bears the impress of a rude age. "It cannot be disputed," says Becker, "that the arbitrary power which the Roman father had over his children was a flagrant injustice, for the child was held in an unnatural state of dependence on his father, so as to be almost entirely deprived of personal freedom. The radical error of the Roman system was, in extending the power which nature imposes as a duty on a parent, of guiding and protecting a child during infancy, to a most unnatural control of his person and property, continuing during his entire existence." [2]

The *patria potestas* was the power which a Roman father had over his lawful children, and also over his grandchildren or other descendants by a son, who were under his dependence. The father must be *sui juris* at the birth of the children, in order to acquire paternal power ; for if he be under the power of another, his children will fall under the dependence of the same ascendant, and the paternal power will only

Nature of paternal power.

---

[1] I. 1. 9. 2.   [2] Becker's Gallus, translated by Metcalfe, p. 178.

accrue to the father on the ascendant's death. Grandchildren born of a daughter are in a different position from grandchildren born of a son, being under the power, not of any ascendant on the mother's side, but of their own father, or father's father, as head of the family.

Paternal power was acquired naturally by the birth of children in a lawful marriage, and civilly by legitimation and adoption.

Effects on person and property of children.
In ancient times the father had the power of life and death over his children (*jus vitœ et necis*). Plutarch says Brutus condemned his sons to death, without judicial forms, not as consul, but as father. The father could sell his children as slaves under an express law of the Twelve Tables, and he could change their personal condition by transferring them to another family by adoption. Under the republic the abuses of paternal authority were checked by the censors ; and in later times the emperors interfered to reduce the father's powers within reasonable limits. The power of life and death was taken from the father and given to the magistrate. Alexander Severus limited the right of the father to simple correction ; and Constantine declared the father who should kill his son to be guilty of murder, A.D. 318.[1]

A revolting practice prevailed under the empire, of killing or exposing new-born children, in consequence of the parents being unable to support them. Diocletian and Maximinian took away the power of selling free-born children as slaves, but made an exception of newly-born infants when the parents were in extreme misery.[2] In later times a father could not give his son or daughter to another by adoption without the child's consent.

By the ancient law, the son, who was in the power of his father, could not acquire property for himself; all his acquisitions, like those of a slave, belonged to his father. As a consequence of this doctrine, children under power could not make a testament, as they had nothing to bequeath. In the progress of Roman civilisation this rigour was relaxed. Frequently the father of a family gave a portion of his pro-

[1] C. 4. 17.   [2] C. 4. 43. 2.

perty to his son to administer or trade upon, and this was Different kinds of peculium. called *peculium*. Moreover, under the new law, the son under power might acquire property of his own in various ways, independently of his father. Under Augustus and his successors, the son acquired as his own property whatever he gained in military service, including all gifts and successions from his comrades in arms. This was called *peculium castrense.*

Under Constantine, about three centuries later, the son was entitled to any property acquired by him in offices of the court, in exercising the profession of an advocate, acting as assessor, or discharging other civil functions. All acquisitions of this kind were called *peculium quasi castrense.*

As regards the *peculium castrense* and *quasi castrense*, the absolute property belonged to the son, with full power to dispose of it by deeds *inter vivos* or *mortis causa*, without any control on the part of the father.

When the son received from his father a particular fund for the purposes of administration, it was called in the new law *peculium profcctitium*, and, as a general rule, this remained the property of the father; but the son retained this fund when he ceased to be under power by his nomination to a high office in the state, or when his father emancipated him without withdrawing the *peculium.*

All property which the children inherited from the mother or received from strangers, and all acquisitions not coming from the father, and not falling under the description of *castrense* or *quasi castrense*, are called *peculium adventitium.* By the law of Justinian, all such acquisitions belonged in property to the children; but, while the paternal power subsisted, the father had the enjoyment of a life interest in the produce; and, if the son was emancipated, the father retained the usufruct of one-half of the *peculium adventitium* during his life. "Even this," it has been remarked, "the utmost relaxation of the Roman *patria potestas*, left it far ampler and severer than any analogous institution of the modern world."[1]

---

[1] Maine, Ancient Law, p. 143. See Mackeldey, § 590 *et seq.*, as to the different kinds of *peculium.*

No one but a Roman citizen could exercise the domestic despotism of the *patria potestas,* which affected all the relations of private life.   One redeeming feature of this institution, however, was, that it was never allowed to influence the public law ; for a son under power was in all public affairs as independent as his father, and was equally entitled to vote at the popular elections, and aspire to the honours of the state, to act as a magistrate, or command an army in the field.   In later times, when the son was promoted to the consular dignity, and other high offices of state, he ceased to be under paternal power, irrespective of the will of his father, but retained his rights of succession.[1]

Public rights not affected by paternal power.

Notion of the Roman family. The Roman family, as it existed in ancient times, was a collection of individuals recognising the power of a single chief. Whoever was under this power was within the family, and this applied to all persons brought under power by adoption.   Whoever was freed from this power by emancipation or change of status, though he might be a child or descendant of the common ancestor, ceased to belong to the family.   All who were connected by the tie of the paternal power, or who would have been so if the common author had been alive, had between them the relationship called *agnation,* which alone, by the ancient civil law, gave the rights of family and of succession.

Agnates and cognates. Cognates, in a general sense, are those relations who derive their common descent from the same pair of married persons, whether the descent be traced through males or females. When opposed to *agnates,* the term *cognates* has usually a more restricted signification.   Agnates are the members of the ancient Roman family, such as we have described it. There is agnation between two persons when one is under the paternal power of the other, or both are under the same power, or would have been so but for a natural cause, such as the death of the father of the family.   The agnates comprehend only those who trace their connection exclusively through males, leaving out the descendants of women. Daughters under power are agnates of their father, and suc-

[1] N. 81, ch. 2. Ortolan, Institutes, vol. ii. p. 125, 126.

ceed to him in the same way as sons. But when a daughter
married, and had issue, her children fell under the *patria
potestas*, not of her father, but of her husband, and were thus
lost to her family. The sister is agnate of her brother, when
both are born of the same father. There is no agnation
between a mother and her children under a marriage without
manus. As the paternal power was the foundation of agnation, emancipation broke this civil relationship. When the
potestas ceased kinship ceased; so that, by the ancient civil
law (afterwards corrected in more enlightened times), emancipated children, though descendants in the direct line, were
excluded from the succession of their father.[1]

Mr Erskine thus explains the meaning of the terms *agnate*
and *cognate*, as used in the law of Scotland:—" Agnates, in
the sense of the Roman law, were persons related to each
other through males only. The relation of cognates was
connected by the interposition of one or more females. Thus,
a brother's son is his uncle's agnate, in the language of the
Romans, because the propinquity is connected wholly by
males; a sister's son is his cognate, because a female is interposed in that relation. But in our law language, all kinsmen by the father are agnates, though females should inter-
vene; and those by the mother cognates. Justinian abolished
so entirely the distinction of the old Roman law between
agnates and cognates, that he admitted, both to the legal succession and to the office of tutor-at-law, not only kinsmen by
the father, though a female had been interposed in that relation, but even those by the mother.—Nov. 118, c. 4, 5."[2]

Paternal power came to an end by the death of the father How
or the son, or when either of them suffered the *capitis*
diminutio maxima or *media*, the nature of which has already
been explained. In the case of a daughter, it ceased when
she entered into marriage with the *conventio in manum*, or
became a vestal virgin.[3]

By adoption, the paternal power might be transferred to
another, and it might be extinguished by emancipation. The
ancient form of emancipation consisted of three fictitious

------

[1] Maynz, § 102.   [2] Ersk. 1. 7. 4.   [3] Aulus Gellius, i. 12. Ulp. 10. 5.

sales, *per œs et libram*, followed by manumission. Subsequently emancipation was effected either by an imperial rescript, or by a formal declaration before a magistrate, with the consent of both father and child. In the time of Justinian the child could not be emancipated against his will.[1]

The person emancipated became *sui juris;* he quitted the family to which he formerly belonged, and, as a general rule, he lost the rights of agnation. These rights, however, might be preserved to the child by express reservation, when emancipation was effected by an imperial rescript.[2]

Lawful children, who had no separate means to supply their wants, had a right to aliment from their parents. This obligation was imposed in the first instance on the father and mother, and, failing them, on the grandfathers. It was reciprocal, however, the children being bound to maintain their parents when in want.

Illegitimate children were treated as if they had no father, and originally the mother alone was bound to support them. Justinian gave to natural children (*liberis naturalibus*) a right to demand aliment from their father.[3]

II.—FRENCH LAW.

In modern systems of jurisprudence the power of the father over the child is recognised to a greater or less extent, but in none of them is it carried so far as it was in the Roman law. According to the French law, as laid down in the Civil Code, marriage imposes on the parents the obligation of maintaining their children; and children are bound to support their father and mother, and other ascendants, when they are in want.[4] At every age the child owes honour and respect to the father and mother, and remains under their authority till majority or emancipation. The father alone exercises this power during the marriage. A child cannot quit the paternal

Reciprocal obligations to support.

[1] N. 89, ch. 11.
[2] Mackeldey, § 593-599.
[3] N. 89, ch. 12, 13. Mackeldey
§ 574, 575.
[4] Code Civil, art. 203-205.

residence without the permission of the father, before majority or emancipation, except for enrolment in the army at
eighteen years of age.[1]

Majority is fixed at twenty-one years. A minor is emancipated by marriage. At fifteen years of age he may be
emancipated by his father, or, if the father be dead, by his
mother, by a simple declaration before a magistrate. *Powers of father till majority or emancipation.*

For grave misconduct by his children, the father has strong
means of correction. If the child be under sixteen years of
age, the father may obtain a warrant to arrest and detain
him in prison for a period not exceeding a month. When
the child is above sixteen, and has not been emancipated or
attained majority, the father, on proper cause being shown
to the satisfaction of the magistrate, may obtain an order for
imprisoning the child for a period not exceeding six months.[2]

The father, during the marriage, and the surviving parent
after its dissolution, is entitled to the usufruct of any property belonging to their children till they reach eighteen, or
are emancipated, subject to the burdens of maintenance and
education ; but this right does not extend to what the children may acquire by their separate labour or industry, or
what may be gifted or bequeathed to them under an express
condition, excluding the interference of the parents.[3]

III.—ENGLISH LAW.

By the law of England, a father is, generally speaking,
guardian to his lawful children in minority ; " and it is understood that, though this right ceases, in some instances, and
for some purposes, at fourteen, he is always entitled, in his
paternal capacity, to the control of their persons until the
age of twenty-one, or until their marriage."[4] It belongs to
the father to direct the education of his children, and he
has the power of moderate chastisement. When the child *Father guardian to minor children.*

---

[1] Code Civil, art. 371-374.
[2] Ibid. art. 375-383.
[3] Ibid. art. 384-387.

[4] Stephen's Com. on the Laws of
England, 4th ed., vol. ii. p. 299.

has real estate, the father, as guardian, may receive the rents, subject to liability to account for them on the child attaining full age.   But the legal power of the father over the persons or property of his children extends not, in any case, beyond the age of twenty-one ; and, to some effects, marriage before that age operates as a species of emancipation, at least in the case of daughters.   By deed or will the father may appoint a guardian to such of his children as shall be unmarried at his death until they reach twenty-one.   The mother has no legal power over the child in the father's lifetime, and cannot, like the father, appoint a guardian ; but after the father's death she seems entitled to stand in his place as regards the right to the custody of the child.

His power to appoint guardian.

However plain the moral duty may be, it is said that, by the common law of England, there is no obligation on parents to maintain their children, or on children to maintain their parents.   But the statute law, in its provisions relating to the poor, makes it compulsory upon all parents who are able to do so, to provide a maintenance for their children, of whatever age, when in poverty, and unable, through infancy, disease, or accident, to support themselves ; and a reciprocal obligation is imposed on children to support their indigent parents who, from old age or infirmity, are disabled from earning a livelihood.[1]

Testamentary power of the father.

Another striking peculiarity in the law of England, which differs in this respect from the Roman law, as well as from · the law of France and Scotland, is that, as a general rule, a father can devise and bequeath his whole estate, real and personal, by will, to strangers, so as to exclude his wife and children from succeeding to any part of the property left by him at his death.   If the father die intestate, his real estate will· be inherited by the eldest or only son as heir, or, if there be no son, by the daughters as co-heiresses ; and all the children as well as the widow, if any, will take a share in the personal estate, under the statute of distributions.[2]

In the county of Kent, land descends by the custom of

[1] See Stephen's Com., 4th ed., vol.   p. 279, 296.
ii. p. 296.   Paterson's Compendium,   [2] Paterson's Compendium, p. 280.

"Gavelkind" to all the sons equally. And in some places the custom of "Borough English" holds, by which land descends to the *youngest* son on the death of his father.[1]

The law of England draws a distinction between the powers of a father over lawful children and his powers over bastards. He is entitled to the custody of lawful children. But the mother of a bastard is preferred to its custody, and is bound to maintain it if she has the means of doing so. If the mother be not of sufficient ability, the law gives her the means of compelling the father of the bastard to provide a fund for its maintenance by proceedings before the justices.[2]

Illegitimate children.

IV.—SCOTTISH LAW.

In Scotland, the father, under the name of administrator-in-law, is tutor and curator of his children. The father's right of administration extends over all the property belonging to the children, except where an estate has been left to them by a stranger, and placed by him under different management. As a general rule, this right ceases on the children reaching majority. According to Erskine, the father's administration is restricted to such of his children as continue in family with him; and, as to this question, a child is held to continue in his father's family, though he should reside elsewhere, if he earns not his livelihood by his own industry and labour independently of any aid from the father. But it has been contended that as the marriage of a son, during minority, does not infringe on the powers of ordinary curators, the same principle should apply to the father's powers as administrator-in-law. However this may be, it is quite settled that the father's right of administration comes to an end by the marriage of a daughter during minority, because the husband becomes the guardian of his wife.[3] By the Statute 1696, c. 8, the father may, by will or

Father administrator-in-law to minor children.

---

[1] Black. Com., book 2, ch. 6.
[2] 7 & 8 Vict. c. 101, amended by 8 & 9 Vict. c. 10.
[3] Ersk. 1. 6. 54. 55. Fraser, Per. and Dom. Relations, vol. ii. p. 154.

deed, not executed on deathbed, appoint tutors and curators to his children.

Power of
father over
minor
pubes.
While the children are in pupilarity, the father has a general control over their persons. He may fix their place of residence, direct their education, and how they are to be employed, and inflict reasonable chastisement for misconduct. It is difficult, however, to define with precision the limits of the *patria potestas* in the case of children who have reached puberty, and are under twenty-one years of age, and upon this point the authorities are conflicting. Some writers think the father may compel his child to reside with him, and to labour for him, at least till majority; while others contend that a child, after pupilarity, cannot be restrained from leaving his father's house, and living wherever he pleases.[1] It would be dangerous to hold that a girl at the age of twelve, and a boy at fourteen, are entitled to choose their own residence, and do as they please, without paternal control. In the recent case of Harvey, it was observed [2]—" The Court have no desire to give countenance to a doctrine which should enable any girl, on attaining the age of twelve, if possessed of independent fortune, to desert the paternal mansion, and fix her own present residence, and thereby, probably, her future fate and course of life, in defiance of all parental control." Still, it must be acknowledged, the father's authority over the persons of children in puberty is very limited as compared with the same authority during their pupilage, and, in a great variety of circumstances, it may be wholly lost. According to Stair, the father's power to compel his children to remain in his family, and employ their services for his use, may be lost, not only by the children's marriage, or by their being allowed to engage in an independent trade or occupation, but also by the parent's dealing unreasonably with them, and refusing to maintain or settle them suitably to their condition ; " or if the father countenance or allow the children to live by themselves, and to manage their

[1] Fraser, Per. and Dom. Relations, vol. ii. p. 27. More's Stair, vol. i. p. 31, 32, notes.　　　[2] Harvey, 15th June 1860, 22 Sess. Ca. 1208.

own affairs apart, from whence his tacit consent to their emancipation may be inferred."[1]

At common law the father is liable for the aliment of his lawful children, including clothing and necessaries. Failing the father, by death or otherwise, the mother is next liable; then the paternal grandfather and great-grandfather in their order. On the other hand, children who have the means of doing so, are bound to aliment their parents when they become unable to provide for themselves. In all cases the aliment, so far as it can be enforced by law, is strictly limited to what is necessary for reasonable support.[2] *Reciprocal obligations to support.*

A bastard is not under paternal power, and a father cannot appoint a guardian to him by will. By the law of Scotland, both the mother and the father are liable to support the bastard; so that, when the paternity is established, the mother's claim against the father resolves into a claim of rateable contribution or relief.[3] *Illegitimate children.*

---

[1] Stair, 1. 5. 13.   [3] Fraser, vol. ii. p. 48, 49.
[2] Fraser, vol. ii. p. 34.

CHAPTER X.

OF TUTORS AND CURATORS.

I.—ROMAN LAW.

FULL age, by the Roman law, was twenty-five years complete, both for males and females; while the laws of France, England, and Scotland all fix majority at twenty-one. Minors, in an extensive sense, include all under age; and their guardians are either tutors or curators.

Guardianship defined.

Tutory is the right to govern the person, and administer the estate, of a pupil. Curatory is the right to manage the estate, either of a minor who has reached puberty, with his concurrence, or of a person of full age who, from insanity or defect of judgment, is incapable of acting for himself.

Sect. 1.—Tutors.

Originally two classes of persons were placed under tutory,—pupils, on account of their age—and women, on account of their sex. There is hardly any trace of the *tutela mulierum* in Justinian's legislation, but the discovery of the Institutes of Gaius has thrown some light on the subject.[1]

Ancient tutory of women.

According to the ancient Roman law, a woman was placed through her whole life under the tutory of agnates when she ceased to be under paternal power, and was not *in manu mariti*. The origin of this kind of tutory was to protect the property of women, and prevent it from being withdrawn from the lawful succession of agnates. For this reason the

[1] Gai. 1. § 190 *et seq.*

nearest male relations were appointed tutors. They had no right of administration, properly so called, but only the power of preventing the woman from alienating her property, or undertaking any important obligation, without their authority.

Though the tutory of women was rigidly enforced in ancient times, it lost by degrees its primitive character. By the law Papia Poppæa, the privilege of children released many married women from this inconvenient superintendence. A law of Claudius delivered free-born women from the lawful tutory of agnates; but a tutor-dative was still required to validate the principal acts of women in civil life. Finally, many ingenious expedients were devised to withdraw women from their legal tutors who were found to be troublesome, and allow them to choose more complaisant guardians, who left them at liberty to do whatever they liked. Vestiges of this degenerate tutory, which had become an idle form, remained as late as Diocletian; but under the emperors who succeeded him it entirely disappeared.[1]

Pupils who were *sui juris*, and no longer under the paternal power, were placed under the guardianship of a tutor. No one could fill that office but a Roman citizen of the full age of twenty-five. As a general rule, females could not be tutors; but under the new law an exception was made in favour of the mother and grandmother of the pupil. *(side note: Tutory of pupils.)*

Guardianship was considered a *munus publicum*, so that persons appointed tutors or curators were bound to act, unless they could plead exemption under certain excuses allowed by law. Persons holding high offices in the state, clergymen and professors, men employed in the army or absent on the public service, those who had a certain number of lawful children still living (three at Rome, four in Italy, and five in the provinces), and those who were upwards of seventy years of age, were, among others, excused from this duty.[2] Debtors and creditors of minors were prohibited from acting as their tutors or curators.[3]

[1] Marezoll, § 189.   [2] I. 1. 25.   [3] C. 5. 34. 8. N. 94.

Three kinds of tutors. There are three kinds of tutors in the Roman law — a testamentary tutor, a tutor-at-law, and a tutor-dative.

Testamentary tutor. A testamentary tutor is one named by a father in his testament to his lawful children, and is preferred to every other tutor. From the confidence reposed in the father's choice, such a tutor is not obliged to find security for the faithful discharge of his office.

Tutor-at-law. If there was no nomination by the father, or if, from any cause, it became inoperative, a tutor-at-law was entitled to act. This sort of tutory devolved by the ancient Roman law on the nearest agnate, or agnates, where there were two or more equally near to the pupil, because they were entitled to the legal succession. By the law of Justinian, the distinction between agnates and cognates was abolished, both as regards legal succession and the office of tutor-at-law; and the mother or grandmother of the pupil was appointed tutor-at-law, even preferably to the agnates.[1]

Any person who emancipated his child or other descendant below the age of puberty became his tutor-at-law. As patrons were entitled to the legal succession of their freedmen who died intestate and without issue, they also became tutors-at-law to children who were enfranchised in pupilarity; and those rights of patrons descended to their children.

Tutor-dative. On the failure both of tutors-testamentary and tutors-at-law, certain magistrates had the right to appoint a tutor-dative.

Powers and duties of tutors. The powers of the tutor extend generally over the person as well as the property of the pupil. To take proper care of the pupil's person and education is the tutor's first duty.

If the pupil be an infant—that is, under seven years of age —he has in law no will of his own, and the tutor must act alone without the direct intervention of the pupil. But if the pupil be above seven years of age, he was considered to have a will of his own, though it was imperfect; so that, in contracting obligations, it required to be completed by the intervention of the tutor as a consenting party. In such

[1] N. 118, ch. 4, 5.

cases the tutor appears to have had the option either of acting alone for the pupil, or of giving his consent to transactions entered into by the pupil.[1]

Pupils may better their condition, but cannot make it worse, without the authority of their tutors. Where there are mutual obligations arising from sales, leases, or other engagements, a person of full age who transacts with a pupil is bound by the contract, but the pupil is not bound unless the tutor has authorised it.[2]

No pupil could take up an inheritance without the authority of his tutor; for, although this may be profitable, it is sometimes attended with loss, when the debts of the deceased proprietor exceed the value of the inheritance.[3]

A tutor must manage the estates of the pupil like a good father of a family, and he will be liable for loss occasioned by bad management. He is entitled to recover debts, levy rents and interest, and he may sell the movable property, if this appear to be proper or necessary; but he cannot sell immovable subjects, such as lands or houses, except in a case of necessity, and then only after full inquiry under judicial authority. It is the tutor's duty to employ the pupil's funds profitably; and being a trustee, he cannot acquire any portion of the estate, or do any act connected with it for his own personal benefit.[4]

Tutory expires—1st, By the pupil reaching puberty; 2d, By the death either of the tutor or pupil; 3d, By the pupil before puberty changing his condition, so as to be no longer *sui juris*—as, for instance, from deportation or slavery, or from that species of adoption called *adrogatio*—because no one can be under tutory who is not *sui juris*; and, 4th, By supervening disqualification or removal of the tutor.[5]

Termination of tutory.

---

[1] I. 3. 19. 9. Mackeldey, § 611.
Marezoll, § 186.
[2] I. 1. 21. pr.

[3] I. 1. 21.
[4] Mackeldey, § 628.
[5] I. 1. 22.

Sect. 2.—Curators.

Curators of different kinds.
A curator is a person appointed to aid a minor *pubes* who is *sui juris*, in the administration of his property till he reaches majority. The term is also applied to the guardian of a lunatic, who is necessarily intrusted with power over the person as well as the property. Generally speaking, persons competent for the office of tutory may be appointed curators ; but the mother and grandmother, though they might be tutors, were not qualified to act as curators to their children or grandchildren.[1] The tutor of a pupil, on the expiry of the tutory, was not bound to accept the curatory of the same person.[2]

Curators to minors.
A father, in his testament, might name a curator to his children, but the nomination required to be confirmed by the magistrate. If no person was named in the testament, the magistrate appointed the curator, having regard to the claims of the nearest relations to the office.[3]

A minor *pubes* who is *sui juris* has power to administer his property, and to perform many acts in civil life, without requiring the consent of a curator. But when he wishes to sell or burden his property, or do certain things of more than ordinary importance, the deed is not valid without the curator's consent. Even when the curator has given his consent so as to render the act binding on the minor in strict law, he is entitled to be restored against it on proof of lesion or injury. A minor, after fourteen, is himself the principal party in all transactions regarding his affairs, and the curator merely consents to what is done.

A curator is responsible like a tutor, being liable to render an account of his management, and subjected to similar actions.

The curatory of minors expires by their arrival at legal majority, being twenty-five years complete, or by their obtaining before that period a dispensation of age—*venia ætatis*—by a rescript from the emperor.[4]

[1] Mackeldey, § 617.
[2] I. 1. 25. 18.
[3] I. 1. 23. 1.
[4] C. 2. 45. 2.　I. 1. 23. pr.

By the Twelve Tables the curatory of persons who were **Curators to insane persons.** insane, or incapable of managing their affairs, whatever might be their age, was devolved on the nearest agnates. If there were no such relations, or if from any cause they were disqualified, curators were appointed after due inquiry by the magistrate.[1] Though the guardianship of insane persons be generally treated of under curatory, yet it seems rather to correspond with tutory; for the curator to a lunatic has the charge of the person as well as of the estate of his ward; and the latter being incapable of consent, the curator must transact all business in his own name.

Curators were sometimes named to a minor for a special **Curators ad litem.** purpose. Thus, if the minor was engaged in a lawsuit with his guardians, or, having no guardians, with strangers, a curator *ad litem* was given to him by the judge, to aid in the prosecution or defence.[2]

A minor is indulged with four years, after he reaches ma- **Restitution of minors.** jority, to obtain restitution against all deeds granted, either by himself, if he had no curators, or if he had curators, with their consent, which he can show to be prejudicial or injurious to him. When loss arises from some accidental cause, and is not inherent in the original transaction, no redress is given. The lesion or injury must be considerable, and it is estimated as at the date of the transaction itself, not of the challenge. After the *quadriennium utile* has expired, no action can be raised. Minors may bar themselves from claiming restitution by confirming or homologating the deed after majority, as by paying interest.[3]

This doctrine as to the restitution of minors is followed in Scotland. Mere revocation within the *quadriennium utile*, however, is not sufficient. The deeds against which the minor is entitled to be restored must also be challenged by an action of reduction in the Court of Session within that term.[4]

[1] I. 1. 23. 3, 4.
[2] I. 1. 23. 2.
[3] D. 4. 4. C. 2. 22.
[4] Ersk. 1. 7. 34. Stewart, 20 Dec. 1860, 23 D. 187.

II.—FRENCH LAW.

Guardians in France.

By the French law the office of guardian to children not emancipated belongs to the father, then to the mother, if she be the last survivor, and, failing them, to the male ascendants, calling first the paternal grandfather and then the maternal grandfather. Guardians may be appointed by the longest liver of the parents, whether father or mother, by testament; and the persons so chosen are preferred to ascendants. Failing all these, a family council may name a person to act as guardians to children in minority.[1] Whoever is chosen guardian is bound to act, unless he can plead a lawful ground of exemption. The Civil Code (art. 427-449) indicates the grounds of dispensation, incapacity, and exclusion. Women are incapable of acting as guardians, except the mother and ascendants.

Their powers and duties.

In France the guardian takes care of the person of the minor, and represents him in all civil acts. He also administers the property of his ward; but he has no power to alienate or impledge immovables without the express authority of a family council, and then only on grounds of absolute necessity or evident advantage, and after judicial sanction has been obtained. A guardian who has grave reasons to be dissatisfied with the behaviour of the minor, may bring a complaint before the family council, and obtain their authority for procuring his detention in a house of correction.[2] Guardianship terminates by the majority of the minor, and even before that age, by his contracting a lawful marriage, which operates as emancipation, and puts an end to the power both of parents and guardians.[3]

[1] Code Civil, art. 389 et seq.
[2] Ibid. art. 450-468.

[3] Pothier, Traité des Personnes, tit. 6. sec. 4, art. 5.

III.—ENGLISH LAW.

According to the technical phraseology of the law of Eng- Guardians in England.
land, an infant is a person under twenty-one years of age;
in the Roman law this term was only applied to pupils under
seven.   In England a father is the guardian of his children
during minority, and he may, by deed or will, appoint a
guardian to act after his death.   Failing such nomination,
the mother becomes guardian;* but though she should survive her husband, she has no power of appointment by will
or otherwise.

When a minor has no guardian, the Court of Chancery has Wards of Chancery.
the power of appointing one. If a suit be depending respecting the minor or his estate, the minor becomes a ward of
Court.   When this occurs, the minor is not allowed to marry
without the leave of the Court; and any one marrying a
female ward clandestinely, may be committed to prison for
contempt.[1]

IV.—SCOTTISH LAW.

By the law of Scotland the father can, by deed executed Guardians named by father.
in *liege poustie* (that is, not on deathbed), appoint tutors and
curators to his children.   Any person who is of full age may
be so named, except a married woman, who, being herself
under the curatory of her husband, cannot act as a guardian
for others during the subsistence of her marriage.   The
guardians appointed by the father have precedence over all
others.[2]

If no tutor be nominated by the father, the next male Tutor-at-law, or factor loco tutoris.
agnate of twenty-five years of age, who is heir-at-law, is
entitled to the office of tutor-at-law for the management of
the pupil's estate ; but his person is intrusted to the mother,
or to the nearest cognate.[3]   On the failure both of tutors-

---

* To the person only, not to property.

[1] Stephen's Com. on Laws of England, 4th ed., p. 315-317. Paterson's
Compendium, p. 270.

[2] Act 1696, c. 8. Fraser, Per. and
Dom. Relations, p. 76 and p. 185.
Ersk. 1. 7. 12.

[3] Ersk. 1. 7. 7.

nominate and tutors-at-law, the Court of Session may appoint a tutor-dative,[1] or a *factor loco tutoris*. The powers of a *factor loco tutoris* are similar to those of a tutor; but the factor may be superseded at any time by the service of a tutor-at-law.

Curators chosen by minors. A minor *pubes*, whose father has not named curators, may either take the management of his estate upon himself, or he may put himself under the direction of curators, who are chosen by him at the sight of the Court, by citing his next of kin in an action, and adopting the course prescribed by the Act 1555, c. 35.[2]

Powers and duties of guardians. There is a distinction between the offices of tutor and curator: a tutor is vested with the management both of the person and the estate of his pupil; while a curator's sole concern is with the estate; and this has given rise to the maxim, *Tutor datur personæ, curator rei*. The tutor acts alone, the pupil having, strictly speaking, no person in law; while the minor *pubes*, on the other hand, is the principal party in all transactions regarding his affairs, and the curator merely consents along with him. A deed signed by a pupil is null; and a deed signed by a curator alone would be equally ineffectual against the ward. Where a minor who has curators duly appointed to him acts without their concurrence, his deeds are, *ipso jure*, null; but where the minor having no curators, or, having curators, with their consent, executes deeds to his injury, these subsist, unless they are reduced on the ground of minority and lesion.[3]

Decennial prescription. By the Statute 1696, c. 9, a decennial prescription was introduced of all accounts between tutors and curators and their wards, so that any claims competent to the one against the other, if not pursued within ten years after the majority of the minors, or within ten years after their death, should they die in minority, are for ever excluded.

---

[1] 19 & 20 Vict. c. 56, s. 19.   [3] More's Stair, vol. i. p. 46, notes.
[2] Fraser, vol. ii. p. 188.

CHAPTER XI.

I.—ROMAN LAW.

A CORPORATION consists of a number of individuals united Nature of corporations. by public authority in such a manner that they and their successors constitute but one person in law, with rights and liabilities distinct from those of its individual members. Cities, colleges, hospitals, scientific and trading associations, and societies for other public purposes, may be so incorporated.

Among the Romans every corporation was constituted by How constituted. a law, by a decree of the senate, or by an imperial constitution. Three members at least were necessary to form the corporation, but its existence might be continued by one; and it subsisted as an abstract legal person though all its original members were changed.[1]

The powers and privileges of corporations vary according Corporate powers and privileges. to the nature of their original constitution. They are generally authorised to hold property, and to sue and be sued, in the corporate name; to choose syndics or other office-bearers to manage the business of the body; to elect new members from time to time; and to make by-laws for the administration of their own affairs, so far as not contrary to the law of the land or their own special constitution. There must always be some person authorised to represent the corporation in its external relations.[2]

[1] D. 3. 4. D. 47. 22. D. 50. 16. 55.

[2] Valuable information on corporations will be found in Savigny, System des heutigen Römischen Rechts, vol. ii. § 86 et seq.

All corporate property and effects belong to the corporate body as a separate person in law, and not to the particular members of which it is composed ; and the same principle applies to debts due to the corporation. On the other hand, the individual members are not answerable either in their persons or property for the corporate debts, so that if there are no corporate effects against which execution can be directed, the creditors of the corporation must go unpaid : "Si quid universitati debetur, singulis non debetur; nec quod debet universitas, singuli debent."—D. 3. 4. 7. 1.

Voting at corporate meetings. The mode of voting at general meetings of the corporate body depends, in the first place, on the original constitution; and when it makes no provision regarding this matter, the will of the majority, at a corporate assembly duly constituted, is the will of the corporation, and binds the minority as well as those who are absent. Some writers on the Roman law are of opinion, that when the constitution lays down no rule, the decision of the majority is only binding when two-thirds of the members are present at the meeting; but the texts on which they rely refer only to the *curiæ* in the Roman *municipia*, and are not sufficient to establish any general rule applicable to all corporate bodies.[1] The principle adopted in England, when the act of incorporation contains nothing to the contrary, is, " that a corporation acts by the majority, or that the will of the majority is the will of the corporation, and binds the minority. Hence the act of the major part of such corporators as are present at a meeting of the corporators corporately assembled, is, in general, the act of the whole corporation."[2] But if the act of incorporation, or the special constitution, fix what shall be necessary to constitute a corporate assembly, whether as regards the number of members present or otherwise, this must be strictly attended to. Of this we have a good illustration in the English Municipal Corporations Act (5 & 6 Will. IV. c. 76, s. 69), which provides that all questions relating to general business shall be decided by a majority of the members present at any regular

---

[1] Maynz, § 108. Mackeldey, § 148 and note.

[2] Grant on Corporations, p. 68. Att. Gen. v. Davy, 2 Ak. 212.

meeting, provided the whole number present be not less than *one-third part of the whole council.*

A corporation may come to an end by the expiry of the term fixed by the constitution, when it is established for a limited period; by the death of all the members, when it has for its object the personal interests of the individuals composing it; and by any act of the legislature declaring it dissolved. *How a corporation may terminate.*

What becomes of the property of a dissolved corporation, is a question which has led to some discussion. No positive rule can be laid down on this subject, and it may receive different solutions according to the object for which the corporation was established. Where it was instituted solely for the public benefit, such property is usually appropriated by the state.[1]

Besides the corporations where several individuals are united into one body, and which in England are called corporations aggregate, the Romans recognised another class of artificial persons as capable of rights and obligations, bearing some resemblance to the corporation sole of the English law. Of this description were the state itself; the prince, in so far as he was regarded as the depositary of sovereign power; every public office, considered with reference to the rights and duties attached to it; the public treasury or fisc; and, finally, the inheritance of a deceased person (*hæreditas jacens*), so long as it was not taken up by any one as heir. *Special corporate bodies.*

The public treasury, as distinguished from the private fortune of the prince, was called the *fisc*,[2] and was always considered in law as an ideal person. To the fisc belonged not only all the ordinary and extraordinary revenues of the state, including all property and effects which had no owner (*bona vacantia*), but many other prerogatives and privileges which need not be enumerated here. In disputes between the subject and the fisc, it was a general rule, in all cases of doubt, to decide against the fisc.[3] *The public treasury.*

---

[1] Mackeldey, § 148.

[2] The treasury of the Roman people was called *ærarium*, that of the prince, *fiscus*, which put an end to the first by absorbing it.

[3] D. 49. 14. 10. Compare, however, N. 161, ch. 2, and Edict. Justin. 4, c. 2, s. 1.

In England corporations may be created by Act of Parliament or royal charter, and some exist by prescription.

Aggregate or sole. By the law of England corporations are divided into aggregate and sole. Corporations aggregate consist of a number of persons united into one society, so as to keep up a perpetual succession of members—such as the mayor, aldermen, and burgesses for the local administration of a borough, the head and fellows of a college, and the dean and chapter of a cathedral church. Corporations sole consist of one person only, and his successors in some particular station, who are incorporated by law, so as to preserve the powers and rights which belong to the office in perpetuity; and of this the sovereign, a bishop, or a parson—each in his official capacity —may be taken as an example.[1] The idea of a corporation sole has been claimed as peculiar to English law, but the novelty consists only in the name; and it has been justly remarked that, "as so little of the law of corporations in general applies to corporations sole, it might have been better to have given them some other denomination.[2]

Common seal. All contracts of importance entered into by English corporations must be made under the common seal of the body corporate, and in the corporate name; but trifling matters of business, and ordinary contracts of constant recurrence, such as the hiring of servants and the like, are binding on the corporation without the employment of their common seal.[3]

Corporation creditor cannot sue individuals. By the common law of England the creditor of a corporation can have no remedy except upon the funds or property of the corporation, there being no right under a judgment against a corporation to sue out execution against the individuals who are members of it. Under the Acts of Parliament incorporating railway companies, the capital stock and

---

[1] Stephen's Com., 4th ed., vol. iii. p. 125.
[2] Dr Wooddeson, Vin. Lect., vol. i p. 471, 472.
[3] Addison on Contracts, 5th ed., 701-707. Smith's Compendium of Mercantile Law, 6th ed., p. 113.

property of the corporation are alone liable for the debts and
engagements of the company, the personal liability of the
shareholders being limited to the amount of their shares not
paid up. Companies may be incorporated for a variety of
purposes under the Joint Stock Companies Act of 1862,
either with or without limited liability.[1] Where the liability
of the members is unlimited, they are liable to the same
extent as if the company had not been incorporated. But
the liability of the members may be limited either to the
amount, if any, unpaid on the shares respectively held by
them, or to such amount as the members may respectively
undertake to contribute to the assets of the company in the
event of its being wound up.[2]

Trading corporations may be dissolved on their bankruptcy
under the Joint Stock Companies Act.

III.—SCOTTISH LAW.

The corporation law of Scotland has a general resemblance
to that of England, both being originally derived from the
civil law, and modified by rules to suit the form of government and state of society in each of these countries; but in
some details and matters of form the law of Scotland has
peculiarities which distinguish it from that of England.

In Scotland the charters of most royal burghs confer upon Seals of
them a power of constituting subordinate corporations by a cause.
seal of cause; that is, a writ in the form of a charter issued
under the burgh seal. A seal of cause so issued erects the
grantees into a corporation, and gives them power to sue and
be sued, with every other privilege necessarily incident to a
corporate body, whether expressed in the grant or not; such
as the power of electing officers, imposing fines, making by-
laws, and the like. Similar powers have been exercised by
lords of regality and barony, who had authority under their
rights from the crown to erect corporations within their

---

[1] 25 & 26 Vict. c. 89, s. 6.*
[2] Ibid. s. 7-10. Smith's Mercantile Law, 6th ed., p. 111.
* Amended by 30 and 31 Vict. c. 131.

Corporate rights by prescription.

burghs of regality and barony. Even where no charter or seal of cause can be produced, the prescriptive possession and exercise of corporate rights has been sustained as sufficient. But where no charter exists, or where it contains no specific directions, the managers or office-bearers should obtain the sanction of a general meeting of the members before granting any deeds of importance, taking care to enter the resolution in the minutes of the corporation:[1]

[1] Ersk. 1. 7. 64.   Glasgow Surgeons—House of Lords, 7th August 1840, 1 Rob. Ap. 307.

PART II.

OF THE LAW RELATING TO REAL RIGHTS.

CHAPTER I.

OF THE DIVISION OF THINGS.

NATURAL philosophy considers things according to their physical properties; law regards them as the objects of rights. In legal phraseology the word *res* or *thing* comprehends not only material objects, but also the actions of man; and, in general, everything that can be the object of a right.[1] Notion of things.

All things, whether susceptible of property by man or not, are distinguished into corporeal and incorporeal.[2] Corporeal things are those material objects which may be seen and felt —as a house, a field, a horse, or the like. Incorporeal things are those which cannot be handled or perceived by the senses, but are created by law; they are more properly rights enjoyed in respect to things than things themselves, such as rights of inheritance, servitudes, obligations. Corporeal and incorporeal.

There are certain objects over which we can exercise no exclusive right; these are called *res extra commercium.* For some things are naturally common to all mankind, some are public, some belong to a particular city or corporation, and some are the property of none; but most things are the private property of individuals, by whom they are acquired in various ways.[3] Things not in commerce.

[1] Maynz, § 112.   [2] I. 2. 2.   [3] I. 2. 1. pr.

L

Things common to all.

Those things which are by nature incapable of appropriation are called common—such as the air, the light, the ocean; none of which can become the property of any one, though their use be common to all. So no nation has an exclusive right to the open sea so as to debar others from using it for navigation and fishing. But the parts of the sea near the coast being, in some degree, susceptible of property, and of great importance to the safety of the country, are held by the modern law of nations to be comprehended within the territory of the state to which the coast belongs. To what distance a nation may extend its rights over the sea by which it is surrounded is a problem which has been a fruitful source of controversy, and is not easily determined. By most publicists the whole space of sea within cannon-shot of the coast is considered a part of the territory of the state; and for that reason a vessel captured within range of the cannon of a neutral fortress is not a lawful prize. During the war between Spain and Holland, James I. caused a line to be drawn as a maritime boundary at a certain distance from the British coast, and declared that he would not suffer the armed vessels of either of the belligerent powers to approach within these limits either in pursuit of an enemy or for observing the ships that might enter or sail out of British ports.[1]

Things public.

Things public are those which belong to the sovereign power of the state, but the use of which is common to all its subjects as well as to strangers to whom the privilege may be communicated, such as navigable rivers, highways, harbours, and the like. In countries where the feudal law prevails, those things which the Romans accounted public are held to be vested in the crown in trust for the people. The shore of the sea is the tract of land covered by the greatest winter flood, *quatenus hibernus fluctus maximus excurrit*.[2] Though the sea-shore is classed among things common by Justinian,[3] it belongs more properly to the state which possesses the coast, and this was the opinion of Celsus.[4] No one was allowed to make any erections on the sea-shore

---

[1] Vattel, vol. i. p. 115.   [3] I. 2. 1. 1.
[2] I. 2. 1. 3.   [4] D. 43. 8. 3.

without the authority of the prætor, and this was refused when the privilege claimed interfered with the navigation, public use, or private utility.[1] The public had a right to use the banks of navigable rivers, so that a qualified ownership in the soil of such banks was all that could be acquired by private persons.

When property belonged to a particular city or corporation, it was distinguished as *res universitatis.* Of this description were theatres, stadia, and forums. *Corporation property.:*

Things sacred, religious, and holy, were exempted from commerce, and held to be the property of no one. Temples, churches, altar-pieces, communion-cups, and whatever was consecrated according to the forms prescribed by law, were held *sacred,* and could not be applied to profane uses. According to Papinian, even the ground on which a temple had stood continued sacred after the edifice had been destroyed.[2] Among the epistles of Pliny the younger, we find one addressed to the Emperor Trajan, inquiring whether an ancient temple in Nicomedia, dedicated to the mother of the gods, but not formally consecrated, could be removed consistently with the ceremonies of religion to make way for a new forum. To this Trajan replied, that the temple might be removed without scruple, notwithstanding the dedication, because it had not been legally consecrated, " for the ground of a foreign city is not capable of receiving that kind of consecration which is observed by our laws." [3] *Things sacred or religious.*

Every place where a dead body was buried became *religious,* and exempted from commerce; but this exemption ceased if the body was disinterred and removed to another spot. By the Twelve Tables no burial was permitted within the precincts of Rome, and Hadrian extended this prohibition to all the cities of the empire.

The walls and gates of a city were accounted *holy* because any one who violated them was punished with death.[4]

Though not made the basis of any precise classification in the Roman law, corporeal things in most modern systems are *Things movable and immovable.*

---

[1] D. 41. 1. 50.　D. 43. 8. 3 and 4.　　[3] Pliny, x. Ep. 58, 59.
[2] I. 2. 1. 8.　　　　　　　　　　　　　　[4] I. 1. 1. 10.

divided into movables and immovables. Movables consist of money, goods, and every kind of property except land and things attached to land, which are called immovables. As movables, from their nature, may be transported from one place to another, they are held to follow the person of the owner, and to be governed by the law of his domicile. On the other hand, immovable subjects, such as land and houses, being inseparably connected with a particular territory from which they cannot be removed, are governed by the law of the place where they happen to be situated.

Description of real rights. The most absolute power which the law gives us over a thing is called the right of property—*dominium*. This is a real right in a thing which is our own—*jus in re propria*. There are other real rights in things belonging to another, which are called *jura in re aliena*. Of these the Roman law, in its last stage of development, admitted four kinds: servitudes, *emphyteusis*, *superficies*, and pledge. Among these rights, *emphyteusis* and *superficies*, the nature of which will be afterwards explained, bear the closest resemblance to property.[1]

[1] Maynz, § 162.

CHAPTER II.

PROPERTY is a right to the absolute use, enjoyment, and dis- Nature of property. posal of a thing, without any restraint, except what is im- posed on the owner by law or paction.[1] Thus the unlimited proprietor of a house may use it as a place of residence, or let it to another and draw the rents, or dispose of it by sale, or gift, or even destroy it, if he choose to do so.

Not only lands and movable goods, such as horses, plate, money, and the like, but also incorporeal things, are con- sidered in law as objects of property. The word *bona* was used by the Romans to express all kinds of property, and, generally, all that a man was in any way entitled to.[2] While the essence of property consists in dealing with a thing as one's own, the powers of the proprietor may be absolute and unlimited, or may be subject to limitations arising either from the terms of his own title or from rights created in favour of other persons, by mortgages, servitudes, and otherwise.

As a general rule, the property of the soil carries along with it the property of everything above and below it ; *cujus est solum, ejus est a cælo usque ad centrum.* Sometimes, however, the soil belongs to one person and the mineral estate to another.

The real right which belongs to a proprietor, or to the Jus in re and jus ad rem. holder of a mortgage or pledge, is called a *jus in re.* When there is only a personal right to a thing to be enforced by an action, the legal ownership belonging to another, this per- sonal claim is called a *jus ad rem.* A *jus in re* implies a

[1] Code Civil, art. 544.　　　　[2] D. 50. 16. 49.

complete acquisition—a *jus ad rem* is a mere right to acquire
a thing. The difference is nearly the same as that between
property and obligation. These terms are not Roman, having
been borrowed from the Canonists.[1] To the uninitiated this
distinction may appear trivial; but it enters deeply into
legal discussions, and sometimes helps the solution of difficult problems.

Originally the Romans recognised only one kind of property, which was called *dominium ex jure Quiritium*. This
property could only be acquired by certain forms called *acquisitiones civiles*. As to the acquisition of particular things,
the general rule is thus stated by Ulpian,—"Singularum
rerum dominium nobis adquiritur mancipatione, traditione,
usucapione, in jure cessione, adjudicatione, lege."[2] But the
distinction between the *civiles et naturales acquisitiones*, so
important before Justinian, lost all practical interest under
the new Roman law.[3]

Res mancipi et nec mancipi. By the ancient civil law things were divided into *res
mancipi* and *res nec mancipi*, and traces of this distinction
continued to a late period in the empire. According to
Ulpian, *res mancipi* comprehended lands or houses in Italy,
predial servitudes thereto attached, slaves, and ordinary
beasts of burden, such as horses, mules, asses, oxen, but not
elephants or camels; while all other things, taken separately
and not as a *universitas*, were *res nec mancipi*.[4] The
property of the first class of things could only be acquired
by certain solemn forms, either by *mancipatio*,[5] which was
a sort of imaginary sale *per æs et libram*, in presence of
five witnesses and a balance-holder, or by a formal ceremony before the magistrate, called *in jure cessio*.[6] If these
forms were not observed, the property of *res mancipi* was
not transferred; they were only held to be *in bonis* of the
acquirer, till his possession had been continued long enough
to fortify his right by prescription. All other things called
nec mancipi admitted of being transferred by simple tradition.

[1] Dr Taylor's Elements of the Civil Law, p. 53. Ortolan, Institutes, vol. i. p. 458. Maynz, § 162.
[2] Ulp. 19. 2.
[3] Marezoll, § 89-92.
[4] Ulp. 9. 1.
[5] Gai. 1. 119.
[6] Gai. 2. 24.

This trait of Roman manners is brought out in some scenes of the comedies of . Plautus. A good-natured fellow buys slaves without observing the forms of *mancipatio*, and thinks he has made a capital bargain, when an accomplice of the seller appears and claims the slaves as his own, so that the buyer is cheated out of the price. To check these frauds, the prætor allowed the buyer to plead the *exceptio rei venditæ et traditæ*, not only against the seller, but all other persons who derived right from him. These distinctions between *res mancipi* and *nec mancipi*, which had fallen into disuse before Justinian's time, were formally suppressed by him.[1]

The territory of Italy enjoyed the privilege of Roman property, and was free from the land-tax. This was called the *jus Italicum*. In the conquered provinces the land was possessed by the inhabitants, subject to payment of the land-tax, from which Italy remained exempt till the third century of the Christian era. Under the emperors the *jus Italicum* was given to some colonial settlements out of Italy.[2]

Jus Italicum.

[1] C. 7. 25.   [2] Maynz, § 32.

CHAPTER III.

THE acquisition of property is either original or derivative. An original acquisition applies to things which have never previously been the property of any one, or which, at least, were not so immediately before the acquisition. A derivative acquisition arises when a person enters into the right of property which had pre-existed in another, and derives the thing from him. In this class of cases there is always a loss of property by the former owner, who makes it over to the new proprietor.

Acquisition by occupancy.

Among the original modes of acquiring property, occupancy is the most natural. It consists of taking possession of things which have no owner, with a view to their appropriation. The Romans applied the rule *res nullius cedit occupanti*, not only to things which had never before been appropriated, but also to those which, though previously acquired, had ceased to belong to any one. There are different kinds of occupancy, according to the different classes of things without an owner.

Wild animals.

All wild animals, whether beasts, birds, or fish, fall under this rule, so that even when they are caught by a trespasser on another man's land they belong to the taker, unless they are expressly declared to be forfeited by some penal law.[1] Deer in a forest, rabbits in a warren, fish in a pond, or other wild animals in the keeping or possession of the first holder, cannot be appropriated by another, unless they regain their liberty, in which case they are free to be again acquired by

[1] I. 2. 1. 12.

occupancy. Tame or domesticated creatures, such as horses, sheep, poultry, and the like, remain the property of their owners, though strayed or not confined. The same rule prevails in regard to such wild animals already appropriated as are in the habit of returning to their owners, such as pigeons, hawks in pursuit of game, or bees swarming while pursued by their owners.[1]

Justinian was of opinion that a wild beast does not belong to the person who wounds it, and that the property cannot otherwise be obtained than by actually taking it; " because many accidents frequently happen which prevent the capture."[2] In whale-fishing particular rules are established in this country. Where a fish is harpooned with the line attached, or so entangled in the line as to continue in the power or management of the striker, it is a fast fish, and belongs to the striker. But where, without any interference by another, the line breaks, or is not in management, the fish is considered loose, and liable to be captured by any one.[3]

By the law of nature the chase is free to all men; but the civil law of most nations has imposed restrictions, more or less severe, on this natural liberty. Game-laws are said to be as old as the days of Solon. Among the Romans any one could kill game on his own land or that of another; but every proprietor had the right to prevent strangers from entering upon his ground for the purposes of sport. In 1789 the ancient game-laws of France, which were very oppressive, were repealed; and under the present system every man who possesses landed property may sport on it at stated times, after obtaining a licence or *permis de chasse;* but no one can sport on another's land without his permission, and if he does so he is liable to an action for damages and to pay fines, both to the proprietor and the commune. A law on the police of the chase was passed on 3d May 1844, and an ordinance of 5th May 1845 regulates the details.[4] In this country the

[1] I. 2. 1. 14 and 15.
[2] I. 2. 1. 13. Vinnius Com. h. t.
[3] Bell's Pr. 5th ed. § 1289. The King's Advocate v. Rankine, 1677, Mor. Dict. p. 11,930.

[4] 2 Black. Com. p. 414, note by Coleridge. Bouillet, Dict. Universel des Sciences, des Lettres, et des Arts, *voce* Chasse.

game-laws are the subject of special statutes. Any person who purchases a certificate or licence may kill game on his own land, or on the land of any other person, with his permission.

Inanimate objects. According to the Roman law, inanimate objects, having no owner, such as pearls, shells, or precious stones on the sea-shore, belong to the finder.[1] Treasure-trove is gold or silver hidden in the ground, the owner being unknown. Such treasure naturally belongs to the finder; but the laws or customs of any country may ordain otherwise. The Roman law on this subject varied at different periods. By Hadrian's constitution, which is referred to in the Institutes, when treasure was found by any one on his own ground it became his property; but if it was accidentally discovered by a person on the ground of another, one half belonged to the finder and the other half to the landowner.[2] This rule is adopted in the modern French Code.[3] In Britain and some other countries, treasure-trove belongs to the Crown.

Derelicts are things wilfully abandoned by the owner, with an intention to leave them for ever, and they might be appropriated under the Roman law by any one who found them. Things lost by negligence or chance, or thrown away by necessity—as, for instance, goods thrown into the sea in a storm for lightening the ship—were not considered derelicts, but continued the property of the owners.[4]

Prize of war. Among the Romans occupancy extended both to the goods and persons of enemies captured in war. Immovable property seized in war appears to have been left to the disposal of the state; and even in regard to movables captured from the enemy, the rule as to their belonging to the first occupant was modified by the discipline of the army, and the regulations regarding booty taken by the troops in common.[5]

In the French Civil Code the general rule laid down is, that things which have no owner belong to the state.[6] In

---

[1] I. 2. 1. 18.
[2] I. 2. 1. 39.
[3] Code Civil, art. 716.
[4] I. 2. 1. 46 and 47.

[5] Ortolan, Institutes, vol. ii. p. 264.
[6] Code Civil, art. 713.

this country it is an established maxim that all lands in the kingdom, to which no title can be shown by a subject, belong to the Crown. And even in regard to those things already appropriated, but lost or abandoned as waif or stray goods, we follow the rule, *quod nullius est fit domini regis.*

Another mode of acquiring property is by accession, whereby the principal thing draws after it the property of the accessory. Thus the natural or industrial fruits of land, civil fruits—such as the rents of houses, or the interest of money, and the increase of animals—all belong to the proprietor of the principal subject by right of accession. A house or other building, though erected with materials and at the expense of another, belongs to the owner of the ground on which it is built—*solo cedit quod solo inedificatur;* but indemnity should be given for such expenditure when made in good faith. On the same principle, trees and shrubs taking root in your ground, though planted by a stranger, become yours.[1] Lands gained from the sea or a river, either by alluvion from the washing up of sand and earth, or by the water gradually and imperceptibly receding, accrue by natural accession to the owner of the estate which receives the addition; but property is not changed by a temporary inundation. And when, in consequence of a sudden flood in a river, a considerable portion of land clearly distinguishable is forcibly carried off from one estate and added to another, either on the opposite side or lower down the stream, the ground so severed still remains the property of the original owner, provided he asserts his right to it in proper time.[2]

When a new island rises in the sea, the Roman law gives it to the first occupant,[3] but our law gives it to the Crown;[4] and the same principle applies with us to the case of an island rising in a public river. Labeo says, "insula quoque, quæ in flumine publico nata est, publica esse debet."[5] But the Romans established the rule, that if an island rise in the middle of a river, it belongs in common to those who

Acquisition by accession.

---

[1] I. 2. 1. 30-32.
[2] I. 2. 1. 20 and 21.
[3] I. 2. 1. 22.

[4] 2 Black. Com., book 2, ch. 16.
[5] D. 41. 1. 65. 4.

have lands on each side thereof; but if it be nearer to one
bank than the other, it belongs only to him who is proprietor
of the nearest shore.[1] This regulation has been adopted in
the modern French Code, so far as regards private rivers,
not navigable or floatable; but when an island springs up in
a public river it is held to belong to the state, if there is no
title or prescription to the contrary.[2]

In applying the law of accession to movables, some perplex-
ing questions arise when the workmanship is performed by
one person and the materials belong to another, or when two
movable things, belonging to different owners, are blended
or incorporated.   When a new subject or species is formed

Specifica-
tion.

from materials belonging to another, as flour from corn, wine
from grapes, or the like, the operation is called by the commentators specification.   In such cases the general rule is,
that if the new species can be again reduced to the matter of
which it was made, as plate into bullion, the law considers
the former subject as still existing, so that the property may
be claimed by the owner in its altered state; but when the
substance is wholly changed, so that it can never be restored
to its former condition, as in the case of bread from corn or
wine from grapes, the property belongs to the workman,
under the obligation to give satisfaction for the value of the
materials to the owner.   A painting drawn on another man's
board or canvas belonged to the painter, in consideration of
the excellence of his art; "for it would be ridiculous," says
Justinian, "that a work by Apelles or Parrhasius should
go as an accession to a miserable tablet."[3]   With some inconsistency, however, this favour was not extended to what was
written on another man's paper or parchment, which went,
not to the writer, but to the owner of the materials.[4]   It has
been observed that this doctrine had no reference to literary
property, considered as the result of study or of genius, but
merely to the property of the writing, as such, at a time when
printing was unknown.[5]

[1] I. 2. 1. 22.
[2] Code Civil, art. 560, 561.
[3] I. 2. 1. 34.

[4] "Cujus diversitatis vix idonea
ratio redditur."—Gai. 2. 78.
[5] Ortolan, Institutes, vol. ii. p. 293.

When two things are mixed with the consent of the pro- Commix-
prietors, the whole becomes common property, whether a new ^{tion.}
species is formed or not, and whether they admit of separation or not. If things of the same sort are mixed without
the consent of the proprietors and admit of separation, as in
the case of two flocks of cattle or sheep, the property remains
distinct. But when the things so mixed cannot again be
separated, as for instance two casks of wine, the whole becomes common property, the different qualities of the wines
before they were blended being taken into account in the
division of the price. All such questions should be determined as far as possible upon the principles of natural
equity.[1]

Among the derivative modes of acquiring property, are Tradition.
gift, exchange, contract, succession, or other just title, followed
by possession of the thing.[2] In short, it is of the essence of
property that the owner of a thing should have the right to
transfer it to another by giving up possession to him. But
it is an established principle of the Roman law, which in
this respect differs from some modern systems, that property
is not transferred from one person to another by mere convention without tradition. Two things are required for the
transference of property:—1st, The consent of the former
owner to transfer the thing upon some just ground—as gift,
sale, exchange, or the like; and, 2dly, The actual delivery
of the thing, in pursuance of that intention, to the person
who is to acquire it; or, if it was previously in his possession, it must be left with him in the view of his becoming
proprietor.[3]

The French law recognises the general doctrine that property may be transferred from one person to another by the
sole effect of convention.[4] But this principle is not consist-

---

[1] I. 2. 1. 28. Code Civil, art. 565
et seq.
[2] I. 2. 1. 40.
[3] "Nunquam nuda traditio trans-
fert dominium, sed ita, si venditio,
aut aliqua justa causa præcesserit,
propter quam traditio sequeretur."

—Paulus, D. 41. 2. 31. pr.
"Traditionibus et usucapionibus
dominia rerum, non nudis pactis
transferuntur."—C. 2. 3. 20. Diocletian.

[4] Code Civil, art. 711, 1138, 1583.

ently carried out as regards movables. For possession of movables is declared to be equivalent to a title, though, if they have been lost or stolen, the owner may recover them from any one in whose hands they are found within three years.[1]

[1] Code Civil, art. 2279. " En fait de meubles la possession vaut titre." Maynz, Droit Romain, vol. i. p. 462.

CHAPTER IV.

OF POSSESSION.

POSSESSION, the badge of property, is attended with impor- tant consequences in law. Thus, in movables the law presumes the property to be in the possessor till positive evidence is produced to the contrary. Again, if a person has obtained possession by fair and justifiable means, he is entitled to continue it till the question of property be finally decided; and if he has been dispossessed by stealth or violence, he has a right to be summarily restored to the possession of the subject without waiting till the issue of the cause.

Possession may be taken either upon a good or a bad title, and therefore it does not necessarily give a right to the fruits. In this respect the law distinguishes between a *bona fide* possessor, who, though not the true proprietor, conscientiously believes himself to be so on probable grounds, and a *mala fide* possessor, who knows, or ought to know, that he is not the rightful owner of the subject possessed by him.

By the Roman law a *bona fide* possessor was entitled to the fruits of the subject reaped and consumed by him, while he had reason to think his own title good.[1] It has been much-debated among commentators whether, besides gathering the fruits, they required to be consumed in order to secure the *bona fide* possessor; and the prevailing opinion among the best authorities is, that consumption was necessary to produce this effect, unless the possessor had acquired a prescriptive right to the fruits as movables.[2] By the

[1] I. 2. 1. 35. [2] De Fresquet, vol. i. p. 261. Marezoll, § 97, p. 261, note.

custom of Scotland, however, perception alone without consumption secures the possessor. As to a *mala fide* possessor,
it has never been doubted that he is obliged to restore to the
proprietor all the intermediate fruits from the time of his
entering into possession, whatever their nature may be, and
whether they have been consumed or not.[1]

All fruits, whether natural or industrial, might be acquired
by the *bona fide* possessor; and civil fruits, as the rents of
houses, are in the same situation as the rents of lands. Some
writers, however, such as Lord Bankton, hold that this doctrine is not to be received in regard to the interest of bonds
or other investments.[2] But no reason has been assigned for
this opinion which would not equally apply to other subjects not yielding natural fruits; and although the theory
receives some support from a text of Pomponius,[3] this is
more than counterbalanced by the authority of Ulpian, who
says, " Usuræ vicem fructuum obtinent et merito non debent
a fructibus separari." [4]

[1] I. 2. 1. 35.
[2] Contrast Bankton, 1. 8. 19, with
Erskine, 2. 1. 26. See also Nisbit,
10th July 1707, Mor. Dict., p 1768.
[3] D. 50. 16. 121.
[4] D. 22. 1. 34.

CHAPTER V.

PROPERTY, though naturally unlimited, is susceptible of im- General
portant restrictions. By servitudes the proprietor is either character of
servitudes.
restrained from the full use of his property, or is obliged to
suffer another to do something upon it. The Romans divided
servitudes into predial and personal, according as the right
was granted in favour of an estate or a person.[1] Predial servitudes are granted in favour of the proprietor of a particular
estate as such—*prædium servit prædio.* Personal servitudes
arise when the use of a thing is granted as a real right to
a particular individual other than the proprietor—*prædium
servit personæ.*

As a servitude is a sort of dismemberment of the right of
property, it is never presumed, and the person claiming it
must prove its existence and extent. No one can have a
servitude on his own property—*nulli res sua servit.*[2] The
object of a servitude is either to suffer something to be
done by another, or not to do something, and never consists in doing anything—*servitus in faciendo consistere non
potest.*[3]

The proprietor of the subject burdened can do nothing to
obstruct the use of the servitude, or to render it more inconvenient ; and, on the other hand, he who has the right of
servitude must exercise it in the manner least burdensome
to the servient tenement.

Predial servitudes were numerous. They imply the exist-

[1] D. 8. 1. 1.   [2] D. 8. 2. 26.   [3] D. 8. 1. 15. 1.

M

ence of two immovable subjects—the one enjoying the right is called the dominant tenement; and the other, bearing the burden, is called the servient tenement. Originally predial servitudes were confined to lands in Italy—a restriction which disappeared under the new Roman law.[1]

Predial servitudes are divided into rural and urban—the former relating to lands, vineyards, gardens, or the like, wherever situated; and the latter to houses and buildings, whether in town or country. The chief rural servitudes of the Romans were *iter, actus, via, aquæductus, aquæhaustus,* and *jus pascendi pecoris. Iter* was a right to pass over the property of another, either on foot or horseback, or in a litter. *Actus* was a right to use a road for carriages, and for driving cattle and other beasts of burden. *Via* was the most complete right of passage, comprehending not only the two first, but also the right of using the road for all sorts of carriages, and for dragging stones, wood, and building materials. In our law, and in most modern systems, the servitude of passage is of three degrees; foot-road, horse-road, and cart or carriage road. This kind of servitude imposes no obligation on the owner of the servient property to maintain the road ; but the dominant proprietor has a right to do so at his own expense.

Aquæductus is a servitude to conduct water by canals, conduits, or pipes, through another's ground. The dominant proprietor must maintain the aqueduct in proper order, and is entitled to reasonable access for that purpose. *Aquæhaustus* is a right to water cattle at a stream, pond, or well in another's ground. There is also a privilege of drawing water from another's fountain for domestic use; and both imply a right of passage, so far as necessary to exercise the servitude.

Pasturage (*jus pascendi pecoris*) is the right to pasture cattle or sheep on another's ground, the nature and extent of the burden being generally fixed either by the deed of constitution or by usage. If there be no special agreement as to the extent of the right, it can only be exercised for the number of beasts attached to the dominant property.[2] Finally,

Marginal note: Rural servitudes.

---

[1] Marezoll, § 105.   [2] I. 2. 3. 2

there are many other servitudes which give the right to take from the servient property stones, lime, sand, chalk, props for vines, and the like.[1]

Some of the chief urban servitudes of the Romans may now be noticed. The servitude of support (*oncris ferendi*) gives a right to rest the whole or part of a building on the house-wall or property of another. It was incumbent on the owner of the servient property to keep it in repair, so as to make it sufficient to bear the burden.[2] This appears to be an exception to the general rule already mentioned, that servitudes are purely passive as regards the servient proprietor.[3] By the custom of Scotland there is no such obligation to repair in a servitude of support, without a special contract to that effect.[4] The *jus tigni immittendi* is the right of fixing a joist or beam in a neighbour's wall. Urban servitudes.

No proprietor can build his house so as to throw the rain-water falling from the roof upon another's ground, unless he has the benefit of a servitude, which was called *stillicidii vel fluminis recipiendi servitus*. The word *stillicidium* means rain in drops; when the water is collected in a flowing body, it is termed *flumen*. On grounds of public convenience, the old Roman law obliged proprietors in building to keep at a certain distance within their own property.

By the servitudes *altius non tollendi et non officiendi luminibus vel prospectui*, proprietors were restrained from raising their houses or other buildings beyond a certain height, or from constructing them in such a manner as to hurt the light or prospect of the dominant tenement. Where no such restrictions are constituted, a proprietor, in the common case, may erect buildings on his own ground to any height he pleases, whatever injury this may occasion to his neighbours.[5]

Servitudes were established in the Roman law by convention, by testament, and by prescription.[6] They were extinguished, 1st, By renunciation; 2d, By the dominant and ser- How acquired and lost.

---

[1] I. 2. 3. 2.   D. 8. 3. De Servitutibus Prædiorum Rusticorum.
[2] D. 8. 5. 6.
[3] D. 8. 1. 15. 1.

[4] Ersk. 2. 9. 8.
[5] D. 8. 2. De Servitutibus Prædiorum Rusticorum.
[6] I. 2. 4. 4.

vient tenements coming to belong to the same person, which was called consolidation or confusion ; 3d, By circumstances emerging which rendered the servitude no longer available— as, for instance, by the extinction either of the dominant or servient tenement; but if a building to which a servitude belonged was pulled down and rebuilt *de recenti*, the servitude revived ;[1] 4th, Positive servitudes were lost, *non utendo*, by the dominant proprietor neglecting to use the right for the term of the negative prescription—that is, for ten years, if the parties were present in the same province, and twenty years, if they were absent.[2]

Modern law of servitudes. The servitudes of the French law are regulated by the Code Civil, book 2, title 4, "Des Servitudes ou Services Fonciers," art. 637 to 710. The Scottish law of servitudes is based substantially on the Roman system, with this difference, that the period of prescription is the full term of forty years.[3]

The easements of the English correspond in some respects with the servitudes of the Roman law. By the Statute 2 & 3 William IV. cap. 71, forty years' enjoyment of any way or other easement, or of any watercourse, or of the use of any water, and twenty years' "uninterrupted access and use of any light to and for any dwelling-house" or other building, now constitute an absolute right in the occupier, unless in either case he enjoys "by some consent or agreement expressly given or made for that purpose by deed or writing."[4]

---

[1] D. 8. 2. 20. 2.
[2] D. 8. 2. 6.   Hein. Inst. § 413.
[3] Ersk. 2. 9.

[4] Lord St Leonards's Treatise on New Statutes relating to Property, 2d ed., p. 162-165.

CHAPTER VI.

OF USUFRUCT, USE, AND HABITATION.

UNDER personal servitudes the Romans classed three rights —usufruct, use, and habitation. Of these usufruct is the most important, the other two being of little practical value in modern systems of law.

Usufruct is a right of using a thing belonging to another, and enjoying its fruits or profits, without impairing its substance. This right might be conferred by contract or testament, either for the life of the grantee or for a fixed period. The objects of usufruct may be land, houses, slaves, beasts of burden, and other things.[1] A proper usufruct relates only to such things as can be restored entire when the right expires, and not to such things as wine or other fungibles which perish in the use. Nevertheless, by a *senatus consultum*, of uncertain date, ascribed by Hugo to the reign of Augustus, and by other writers to that of Tiberius, a *quasi* usufruct might be established in regard to things which are consumed in the use, upon security being given by the usufructuary to restore, on the expiry of his right, as much in quantity and value as he had received, or to pay an equivalent in money.[2] *Nuda proprietas* is the term used to denote the reserved right of property in opposition to usufruct.

The usufructuary is entitled to all the fruits of the subject, both natural and civil. His title to the fruits of land, however, does not accrue till they are reaped; and if he die before this, no right passes to his representatives.[3] He is en-

Nature of usufruct.

Rights and obligations of usufructuary.

---

[1] I. 2. 4. pr. § 2.   [2] D. 7. 5. 7.   [3] I. 2. 1. 36.

titled to the increase of animals, but not of slaves ; and for
this exception Ulpian assigns the reason, that slaves are given
in usufruct with a view to their labour alone, and not to
their offspring. Justinian accounts for this by considerations
drawn from the dignity of human nature—a theory evidently
derived from the Stoic school of philosophy, but not easily
reconciled with a system of law that permitted slaves to be
sold and bequeathed like the beasts of the field.[1]

The usufructuary may either possess the subject himself,
or let it to another ; and he may cede the exercise of his
right either onerously or gratuitously. He is bound, however, to manage the property like a good husbandman, to
execute all proper and necessary repairs, and to defray
the ordinary annual burdens. It is his duty to replace
vines or fruit-trees that have fallen into decay or been
destroyed by accident ; and in the case of cattle or sheep
he should keep up the usual number of the herd or
flock. To guard against threatened waste or encroachment,
he may be compelled to give security to restore the subject
in the same condition in which it stood at the time of his
entry.[2]

Expiry of right.

Usufruct is terminated in the Roman law by the natural
or civil death of the usufructuary, or the expiry of the period
for which the right is granted ; by consolidation where the
usufruct and the property come to be united in one person ;
by the total destruction of the subject ; and by non-use for
ten years when the parties are present in the same province,
and twenty years when they are absent.[3]

Usus defined.

Usus in the Roman law was a right to use a thing belonging to another without wasting its substance, and without
being entitled to the produce or fruits beyond what was necessary to supply the daily wants and necessaries of the user
and his family. There was thus much less benefit or emolu-
ment in the use of a thing than in the usufruct. Besides,
the user could only exercise his right personally, and could
not let, sell, or give it away to another.

[1] I. 2. 1. 37.
[2] D. 7. 9. 1.
[3] Inst. 2. 4. 3. Ortolan, Institutes,
vol. ii. p. 344.

Usus was constituted and terminated in the same way as usufruct.[1]

Habitatio was a right to reside gratuitously in a house be- Habitatio. longing to another. In its origin it was probably a personal privilege; but Justinian permitted the grantee either to live in the house, or to let it as a place of residence to another.[2]

Under this head may be noticed the *operæ servorum*, which Operæ servorum. was a personal right to the services of slaves belonging to another.[3] When such a legacy was left, the right did not terminate by the death of the legatee, but passed to his heirs, who enjoyed it during the life of the slave. Of the like nature is the right to the labour of animals, *operæ animalium*.[4]

[1] I. 2. 5. pr. and 1 & 2. [3] D. 7. 7.
[2] I. 2. 5. 5. [4] D. 7. 9. 5. 3. Maynz, § 217.

CHAPTER VII.

OF EMPHYTEUSIS AND SUPERFICIES.

Nature of emphyteusis. *EMPHYTEUSIS* in the Roman law is a contract, whereby a proprietor, without abandoning the property, gives over to another a real right to land, generally in perpetuity, in consideration of a certain annual return in money or produce. The word *emphyteusis* was used from the second century of the Christian era; but rights more or less analogous existed from a much earlier period. In its origin this contract was a sort of *perpetual lease ;* in progress of time, when the rights it conferred grew more important, it became a question whether it should not be regarded as a sale ; and at last it was declared, by a law of the Emperor Zeno, that it should be considered neither a sale nor a lease, but a particular contract to be regulated by its own provisions.[1] According to Sir Thomas Craig and other writers, this right bore a strong resemblance to the feu-right well known in the law of Scotland ; but Maynz contends that it did not confer what is commonly called the *dominium utile* or a right of property, and says the Romans were always careful to distinguish between the *emphyteuta* and the *dominus.*[2]

How constituted. *Emphyteusis* might be established by convention or by testament. According to Maynz, there is no express authority for holding that this right could be acquired by prescription.[3]

Rights and obligations of grantee. Though the rights conferred by the emphyteutical grant fell short in theory of absolute property, they were very

[1] I. 3. 25. 3.
[2] Maynz, § 232.
[3] Maynz, § 236. See, however, Mackeldey, § 333.

nearly the same in substance, and they were more extensive than usufruct. Not only was the grantee entitled to possess the lands and reap the fruits, under the burden of the annual payment, but he could make changes in the substance by reclaiming waste lands, building, planting, and other operations, provided he did not deteriorate the subject. He could sell his right, and it descended to his heirs. In case of a sale the proprietor had the privilege of pre-emption, if he was desirous to purchase the subject on his own account, and willing to pay the price offered for it; and for every alienation to a stranger he was entitled to exact a fine called *laudemium*, which was fixed by Justinian at the fiftieth part of the price or value of the lands. The right was forfeited and returned to the proprietor by the grantee deteriorating the subject, or neglecting to pay the annual duty for two years in the case of church property, and for three years in other cases.[1]

The right might be extinguished also by consent of parties, *Expiry of grant.* the total destruction of the subject, the expiry of the term when the grant was constituted for a time, and by the death of the grantee without leaving lawful heirs.[2]

Another real right, which bears a strong analogy to *emphy-* *Nature of superficies.* *teusis*, was called *superficies*. By this a landed proprietor conceded to another person an area of ground for erecting a building upon it, without parting with the ownership of the soil. The property of the building remained with the proprietor of the land, but the grantee acquired a real right to the full possession and enjoyment of the edifice, either for a definite period or in perpetuity, and this right was transferable during life, and descendible to heirs. It was regulated by contract, and the right might be granted either for a price or an annual payment.[3] In many respects this *jus superficiarium* bears a strong resemblance to the long building leases granted by landholders in England, in consideration of a rent, and under reservation of the ownership of the soil.

---

[1] C. 4. 66. 2. N. 7. 3. § 2.
[2] Ortolan, Institutes, vol. iii. p. 292 *et seq.* Maynz, § 232-237.
[3] D. 43. 8. De Superficiebus. Ortolan, vol. iii. p. 295. Maynz, § 238.

CHAPTER VIII.

OF PRESCRIPTION.

I.—ROMAN LAW.

PRESCRIPTION gives an unchallengeable title to property by continuous possession for a certain time under the conditions determined by law. It is also a mode of extinguishing claims which are not prosecuted within the time fixed by law. Hence rights are both acquired and lost by prescription.

General nature of prescription.

According to Modestinus, *usucapio* is the acquisition of property by continuous possession for the period defined by law.[1] The *præscriptio longi temporis*, on the other hand, was an exception which barred the remedy of the former owner against the possessor. When a person who had been in possession for the prescriptive period afterwards lost it, he was allowed by the prætorian law an *actio utilis* to vindicate his right. In the time of Justinian the *usucapio* and the *præscriptio longi temporis* were blended, and new rules were introduced. By modern jurists the term prescription is used in a general sense, so as to apply either where lapse of time extinguishes the right of the former owner and transfers it to the possessor, or where it merely bars the remedy of the former owner against the possessor.

Prescription in Justinian's time.

In the earliest period of the Roman law, a prescriptive title to movables was acquired by possession for one year,

[1] "Usucapio est adjectio dominii per continuationem possessionis temporis lege definiti."—D. 41. 3. 3. Modestinus.

and to immovables by possession for two years.[1] These periods were afterwards extended in the time of Justinian to three years' undisturbed possession in the case of movables, and in the case of immovables to ten years when the parties were present, that is, domiciled in the same province, and twenty years when they were absent, that is, living in different provinces, and this without any reference to the local situation of the subject.[2] But a title to the thing possessed could only be acquired in this manner by one who obtained possession in good faith and under a sale, gift, or other just means of acquiring property. It was necessary that the possession should be peaceable and uninterrupted for the period required by law, and on a title as proprietor ; but in order to complete prescription, any one could add to his own possession that of his author. When the parties resided in the same province during a part of the ten years, but not for the full period, the deficiency was made up by computing two years' absence as equivalent to one year's presence.[3]

Undisturbed possession for thirty years in general gave a good defence by way of exception, even when the possessor had come in under no title, or when, having an ostensible title, the thing belonged to a class excepted from ordinary prescription. But when both these conditions of ordinary prescription were awanting, the Roman law still allowed effect to be given to the extraordinary prescription of forty years.[4]

Prescription of 30 and 40 years.

Prescription may be interrupted by any deed whereby the proprietor or creditor exercises his right. Natural interruption takes place when the possessor is deprived of the possession of the subject by the true proprietor. Civil interruption arises from judicial proceedings brought by the owner to vindicate his right before the full time defined by law is completed. Interruption has the effect to cut off the course of prescription, so that the person prescribing cannot avail himself of his previous possession, but must begin a new course from the date of interruption. The operation of pre-

Effect of interruptions.

---

[1] I. 2. 6. pr.
[2] I. 2. 6. pr. C. 7. 33. 12.
[3] N. 119, ch. 8.
[4] Mackeldey, § 295.   Maynz, § 198.

Prescription suspended during minority. scription is suspended during the minority of the person entitled to challenge ; but it is not an interruption so as to break the course of prescription, though in computing the prescriptive period the years of minority must of course be deducted.

When prescription begins to run. Prescription, as a mode of extinguishing obligations, only begins to run from the time that the right or debt can be sued on or demanded judicially, because till then there is properly no cause of action. Therefore when a bond or other debt falls due at a fixed term, prescription does not begin to run till that date. When the debt depends on a condition, prescription does not run till the condition is fulfilled, nor on an obligation of warranty till eviction has taken place.

Things not in commerce. Things exempted from commerce are incapable of prescription. By the Roman law things stolen or possessed by violence were considered so far *extra commercium* that they could not be acquired by the ordinary prescription even by a *bona fide* possessor; but this and all other grounds of challenge seem to have been excluded by the prescription *longissimi temporis.*[1]

II.—FRENCH LAW.

French law of prescription. In the modern French code there are two general rules of prescription very similar to those which prevailed in the Roman law. 1st, He who acquires in good faith and upon an ostensible title an immovable subject, prescribes the property of it in ten years, if the true owner live in the territory of the royal court within which the subject is situated, and in twenty years if he is domiciled elsewhere.[2] It is sufficient if good faith exist at the commencement of the acquisition, and, as this is always presumed, he who alleges' bad faith must prove it. A title defective in form cannot serve as a basis for this prescription of ten or twenty years.[3] 2d, All real and personal actions are barred by the lapse of thirty years, and this prescription may be pleaded by a party

[1] I. 2. 6.   D. 41. 3.   C. 7. 33.   [3] Code Civil, art. 2267-2269.
[2] Code Civil, art. 2265.

without producing any title, and without being exposed to any exception founded on bad faith.[1] Shorter prescriptions are established by the French law for particular claims, varying according to their nature from five years to six months.[2]

III.—ENGLISH LAW.

In England the Act 3 & 4 Will. IV. c. 27, introduced some important changes, limiting the time within which actions can be brought concerning real property. The old statutes of limitation barred the remedy, but did not extinguish the right; but, under the 34th section of that Act, when the remedy is barred by time, the right and title of the person in any land, rent, or advowson whose remedy is taken away are extinguished. By the 2d section of the same statute it is enacted, that no person shall bring an action to recover any land or rent but within twenty years after the right to bring such action has first accrued to the claimant or some person through whom he claims. Thus, under ordinary circumstances, twenty years form the regular bar; but there is an exception in the case of disabilities arising from infancy or minority, coverture, unsoundness of mind, or absence beyond seas. For, if any one to whom the right accrues is under any of these disabilities, then such person or any one claiming through him may, notwithstanding the lapse of twenty years, bring an action to recover land or rent within ten years after the time at which the person to whom the right first accrued ceased to be under disability or died; but, even in the case of disability or a succession of disabilities, not more than forty years are allowed after the right first accrued. Lord St Leonards attempted to prevail on Parliament to shorten this period of limitation, but without success.[3]

It has already been explained that twenty years' enjoyment

English law of prescription or limitation.

Act 3 & 4 W. IV. c. 27.

---

[1] Code Civil, art. 2262.
[2] Ibid. liv. iii. sect. 4, art. 2271 *et seq.*
[3] Sec. 16, 17, 18. Lord St Leon- ards's Practical Treatise on New Statutes relating to Property, p. 8, 17, 70, and 82.

of light, and forty years' enjoyment in the case of other ease-ments or servitudes, create an absolute right, unless there shall be some consent or agreement by deed or writing.[1]

The principal statutes limiting the time within which actions or suits may be brought in England, are 3 & 4 Will. IV. c. 27 and c. 42, and 21 Jac. I. c. 16. The most import-ant statutory limitations are stated by Mr Lindley to be as follows :—

"Forty years ; the extreme limit for the recovery of land or rent by any person other than a corporation sole.

"Twenty years ; the limit for the same under ordinary circumstances ; and also for the redemption of mortgages ; and for the recovery of legacies, and of rent (upon an inden-ture of demise), and of money charged on land, and the limit for actions and suits on specialties.

"Six years ; the limit for the recovery of arrears of dower, rent, interest of money charged on land ; personal actions not otherwise limited.

"Four years ; the limit for actions of assault, battery, false imprisonment.

"Two years ; the limit for actions for words of themselves defamatory ; penalties, damages, or sums given by statute to the party aggrieved.

"The time begins to run from the moment the right to sue accrues to a person within the realm, of full age, of sound mind, out of prison, and, if a woman, unmarried."[2]

Formerly, absence beyond seas, or imprisonment, had the effect of extending the period of limitation ; but by the 19 & 20 Vict. c. 97, s. 10, it is enacted that no person shall be entitled to any time within which to commence an action or suit beyond the period fixed by these statutes, by reason only of his being absent beyond seas, or in imprisonment, at the time the cause of action or suit accrued. Absence beyond sea of any of several joint defendants formerly prevented the

---

[1] 2 & 3 Will. IV. c. 71, s. 2 and 3. St Leonards's Treatise, p. 165.

[2] Lindley's Introduction to the Study of Jurisprudence, 1855, App. p. 112, 113. See also Addison on Contracts, 5th ed. 1862, p. 1000 et seq.

statutes from running as against those who were resident in England. But this has been altered by the eleventh section of the same statute.[1]

IV.—SCOTTISH LAW.

In Scotland, the long positive prescription was introduced by the Act 1617, c. 12, for the protection of land rights. It declares that possession for forty years, on charter and sasine, or (where there is no charter) on sasines, one or more continued and standing together, shall render the title secure against all challenge, even though it flowed *a non domino*. By the long negative prescription, which rests on the same statute and two prior acts, all real and personal claims, founded on contracts, or obligations of any kind, are extinguished, unless prosecuted within forty years from the time when the cause of action arises.[2] *Long prescription.*

These prescriptions may be legally interrupted, and they do not run against minors. Neither does the long negative prescription operate against one who is under any legal incapacity to sue—*contra non valentem agere non currit prescriptio*.[3] *Bona fides* is not required by one who pleads either the positive or negative prescription of forty years.[4] In the negative prescription, the creditor's neglecting to insist on his claim for so long a time is construed as an abandonment of it, and is equivalent to a discharge; so that an offer to prove the subsistence of the debt by the debtor's oath after the forty years, would be of no avail.[5]

Besides this long prescription, there are several shorter prescriptions applicable to mercantile and other claims, the effect of which generally is, not to extinguish the obligation, or even to cut off the remedy by action, but to limit the mode of proof, so that claims which might be proved by parole, or other legal evidence, within the years of prescription, can only be established, after that period has elapsed, *Shorter prescriptions.*

---

[1] Addison, p. 1001, 1002.
[2] Ersk. 3. 7. 8.
[3] Stair, 2. 12. 27. Ersk. 3. 7. 37.
[4] Ersk. 3. 7. 15.
[5] Ibid.

by the writing or oath on reference of the debtor. The duration of cautionary obligations, executed in a certain form, is
limited to seven years, by 1695, c. 5 ; but the statute does not
extend to a letter of guarantee in a mercantile transaction.
Bills of exchange and promissory-notes cannot be enforced
by action after six years from the time when they became
exigible ; but the debts they represent, if still due, may be
proved by the writ or oath of the debtor.[1] All single transactions regarding movables or sums of money which the law
allows to be proved by witnesses—such as sale, location, and
other contracts, to the constitution of which writing is not
essential—prescribe in five years after making the bargain,
unless the creditor shall prove the subsistence of the debt by
the writ or oath of the debtor.[2]

Actions for house-rents, board, servants' wages, merchants'
accounts, and the like debts, prescribe in three years, unless the creditor prove the subsistence of the debt claimed
by the debtor's writ or oath.[3] In current accounts the
triennial prescription runs, not upon each article separately,
but only from the last article. House-rents and servants'
wages prescribe from year to year, each year's rent or wages
running a separate course of prescription from the last day
of payment.

V.—INTERNATIONAL LAW.

Conflict of laws as regards prescription. As the rules of prescription are of an arbitrary character,
and vary very much in different countries, there has been
much discussion among writers on international law upon
the question, Whether the prescription of the place where
the contract is made, or the prescription of the place where
the action is brought, when they happen to differ, should
Immovable property. prevail. It is settled, that all questions of prescription concerning land, or other immovable property, must be govern-
ed by the law of the place where the property is situated.
And, as real actions regarding such property require gener-

---

[1] 12 Geo. III. c. 72, s. 37, made perpetual by 23 Geo. III. c. 18, s. 55.
[2] 1669, c. 9. Ersk. 3. 7. 20.
[3] 1579, c. 83. Ersk. 3. 7. 17.

ally to be brought in the place where it is situated, the *lex rei sitæ* and the *lex fori* usually concur in this class of cases.[1]

As to actions founded on personal contracts or obligations, it has been determined that prescriptions which do not affect the right or obligation, but only the mode of enforcing it by limiting the time for suing, or the kind of proof competent, are governed by the *lex fori*. Thus, an obligation, called a cash-credit bond, which had been entered into in Scotland, where the plaintiffs carried on business, and the defendant resided, having been sued upon in England, after six years from its date, the Court of King's Bench held that the case fell within the English sexennial limitation applicable to simple contract, and that the obligation was not kept in force for forty years, the term of prescription applying to it by Scotch law.[2] So when bills, accepted in France, were sued upon in Scotland after the lapse of six years, the House of Lords held that they fell within the Scotch sexennial limitation, although judicial proceedings had been adopted in France (which was the place of acceptance, and assumed to be the *locus solutionis*) sufficient to interrupt the French prescription.[3]

But it is necessary carefully to distinguish between a foreign prescription which extinguishes the right, and one which merely strikes at the remedy.   For, if the *lex loci contractus* makes the obligation wholly void after a certain time, and if the parties have resided within the jurisdiction during the whole of that period, the right will not revive on the defendant's removal to another country, where a similar prescription does not exist.[4]

Personal obligations.

[1] Story's Conflict of Laws, § 581. Ersk. 3. 7. 49.

[2] British Linen Company *v.* Drummond, 1830, 10 Barn. and Cress., 903.

[3] Don *v.* Lippman, 1837, 1 Clark and Fin.; p. 1.

[4] Story's Conflict of Laws, § 582. Dickson's Law of Evidence, vol. i. p. 298.

PART III.

OF THE LAW OF OBLIGATIONS.

CHAPTER I.

OF OBLIGATIONS IN GENERAL.

I.—ROMAN LAW.

Nature of obligations. A LEGAL obligation is an engagement to make some payment, or to do or not to do some act, conferring on the person in whose favour the engagement is made a right by law to exact performance of it.[1]

Natural and civil. Obligations are sometimes divided into natural and civil. A natural obligation exists, where one person is bound to another by the law of nature, though he cannot be compelled by a civil action to the performance; but such an engagement may receive effect by way of exception, for if the debtor has fulfilled the obligation, he cannot demand restitution on the ground that the debt was not due, or paid in error.[2] In this class of cases, too, a cautionary obligation may be effectually interposed.[3] Civil obligations are those which are accounted perfect, and may be enforced by an action. There are always at least two persons interested, one the creditor and the other the debtor; and the obligation only confers on

------

[1] I. 3. 14. pr. Code Civil, art. 1101.

[2] D. 12. 6. 19.

[3] D. 20. 1. 5.

the creditor a right purely personal against the particular
debtor.

By convention is meant an agreement between two or Convention
more persons regarding a matter in which they are interested, defined.
—"*Est autem pactio duorum pluriumve in idem placitum
consensus.*"[1] If the engagement be on one side the convention is unilateral; it is bilateral if there be reciprocal engagements undertaken by both parties.

Among the Romans the term *contractus* was reserved for Contracts.
those conventions which were specially recognised as obligatory, and fortified by action under the ancient civil law. All
other conventions were called *pacta*, even after some of them
had been rendered obligatory, so as to found an action, either
by authority of the prætor, or under the more recent law of
the emperors—such as the *pacta legitima, pacta prætoria*, and
pacta adjecta.[2] A *nudum pactum*, or simple promise, was so Nudum
called, because it did not found an action, though it might pactum.
sometimes give rise to an exception.[3]

Any one may grant an obligation, or contract for himself, Requisites
if not declared incapable by law; but no man can contract of obliga-
for another without power from him to do so. tions.

Every contract must have a lawful object; it must neither
be prohibited by law nor contrary to public policy or good
morals. No one can bind himself to do what is naturally
impossible. An impossible condition is not only null in
itself, but renders null the convention which depends upon
it—*impossibilium nulla obligatio est.*[4] Bracton holds that if
a man, being at Oxford, engage to pay money the same day
in London, he shall be discharged of his contract, as he
undertakes a physical impossibility; but in these days of
rapid transmission by railways and electric telegraphs this
illustration cannot be admitted, though the general doctrine
is sound.

As the consent of the contracting parties is indispensable,

[1] D. 2. 14. 2.
[2] Ortolan, Institutes, vol. iii. p. 136.
[3] "Nuda pactio obligationem non parit, sed parit exceptionem."—Ulpian, D. 2. 14. 7. 4.
[4] D. 50. 17. 185. Code Civil, art. 1172.

no contract will be effectual if it has been made under essential error—*non videntur qui errant consentire.*[1] Neither will a contract be sustained, when it is proved to have been procured by fraud or extorted by violence. When fraud is pleaded as a ground of nullity, it must be of such a nature as to have induced the party to enter into the contract—*fraus dans causam contractui.* Labeo describes *dolus malus*— "omnis calliditas, fallacia, machinatio ad circumveniendum, fallendum, decipiendum alterum adhibita;"—and this definition is approved of by Ulpian.[2] To invalidate a contract, violence must be of such a nature as to alarm a mind of reasonable firmness, regard being always had to the age, sex, and condition of the person. When fraud or deception is combined with constraint, a less degree of violence may suffice to show that there was no real consent to bind the bargain.

In mutual contracts the engagements are reciprocal, and one who fails to perform his part cannot insist on implement from the other. There are contracts, however, which may be declared null by one of the contracting parties, although they are binding irrevocably on the other; as, for instance, when a person of full age enters into an agreement with a minor, it may be annulled by the latter when it is to his disadvantage, but it subsists against the person of full age when the minor does not demand relief.

Obligations pure or conditional. Where an obligation is entered into without a term, it must be performed immediately, or without delay. If a day, which must arrive, is fixed for the performance, a proper debt arises from the date of the obligation, but the execution is suspended till the term specified; in this case the debt is due but not payable, or, as it is technically expressed by the civilians, *dies cedit sed non venit.* When an obligation is entered into under a condition, the occurrence of which is uncertain, there is no proper debt, but only the hope of a debt, till the condition be fulfilled—*dies nec cedit nec venit, nisi exstiterit conditio.* Where there is a proper alternative obligation to do one of two things, the debtor has the right of elec-

---

[1] D. 50. 17. 116. 2.   [2] D. 4. 3. 1. 2.

tion, unless the contrary be stipulated, so that upon fulfilling either alternative he will be discharged.

In treating of the general properties of conventional obli- *Material contents of obligations.* gations, Pothier and other jurists distinguish between the essence, the nature, and the accidents of contracts. Those things are of the essence of the contract without which it could not subsist. For instance, there can be no sale without a thing to be sold and a price ; consequently these things are essential to the contract of sale. Things are of the nature of the contract which are included in it by the operation of law without being expressed. Thus, when a thing is sold, it is at the risk of the purchaser as soon as the contract is completed, before delivery, so that, if it perish without the fault of the seller, the loss falls on the purchaser ; and this flows from the nature of the contract of sale. Those things are accidental to a contract which form no part of it unless they are expressed. For example, if the seller agrees to keep the subject sold in repair for a certain time, or to accept payment of the price by instalments at distant dates, such conditions require to be specially expressed, seeing they do not flow from the nature of the contract itself.[1]

In considering the doctrine of responsibility for fault or *Theory of responsibility for fault.* neglect arising under the different contracts, a controversy has arisen among civilians which merits notice here. Until lately, the theory generally received—and adopted, among others, by Sir William Jones in his ‘Essay on Bailments’— was that the Roman law distinguished three degrees of fault, *culpa lata, levis, levissima ;* and the rules of responsibility were determined in the following manner. In contracts beneficial only to the owner, as mandate or deposit, good faith alone being required in the custodier, he was only held liable for *culpa lata,* or gross neglect. Next, where the benefit was reciprocal to the two parties, as in sale, hiring, or partnership, they were both held liable for *culpa levis,*—that is, for the care of a good father of a family, so as to be responsible for ordinary neglect. And, finally, where all the advantage was reaped by one of the parties, as in commodate, the

[1] Pothier, Traité des Obligations, part i. ch. i. art. 1, § 3.

slightest fault, *culpa levissima*, was held to subject him in a claim for indemnification. However plausible this theory may appear, it is now rejected by the most eminent Continental jurists, who maintain that it is not supported by the original texts of the Roman law, and is a pure invention of the commentators, contrary to equity. Already in the sixteenth century, Doneau had declared that the Roman law admitted only two degrees of fault; but his system, which was defective in other respects, found few partisans.[1] Lebrun, an advocate before the Parliament of Paris, broached the same doctrine; but his essay, published in 1764, besides being superficial, abounded with serious errors, and was disapproved of by Pothier. To M. Hasse, who published a dissertation on this subject in 1815, is ascribed the merit of having established the true Roman theory, and of having for ever extinguished the system of the three degrees of fault.[2] The substance of his argument is shortly given by Maynz in his 'Elements of Roman Law.' It is said the term *culpa levissima* occurs only once in the Corpus Juris in a fragment of Ulpian, and in that passage it has no technical signification; in particular, it is not opposed to *culpa lata* or *culpa levis*.[3] As *culpa levis* imports the want of care of a good father of a family—that is, of a man essentially attentive and careful—*culpa levissima* must mean the want of still greater care; but the Roman law nowhere requires a higher degree of diligence than that of a man essentially careful and attentive; and the original texts never mention anything but *culpa levis*, when it is intended to indicate an intermediate degree between an inevitable casualty and *culpa lata*, so that no place is left for *culpa levissima*. Finally, it is said that the theory of three degrees of fault is unjust in itself, as well as contrary to the fundamental principles of the Roman law, which distinguishes only between two cases,—that in which we derive no benefit from the contract, and that in which we derive benefit from it; that in the first we are generally liable

---

[1] Doneau, Com. Juris Civilis, lib. 16, cap, 6, 7.

[2] Die Culpa des Roemischen

[3] D. 9. 2. 44. pr. "In lege Aquilia et levissima culpa venit."

Rechts; Kiel, 1815.

only for gross neglect, while in the second we are liable for the care of a good father of a family.[1]

In general, *fault* or *culpa*, inferring responsibility for loss, consists either in a positive act done or in simple inaction. In the first place, every one is responsible for the consequences of his own fraud, even in the case of omission—*dolus semper præstatur*. Next, the Roman law distinguishes two degrees of fault—*culpa lata* and *culpa levis*. For the first every one is liable under all sorts of obligations, because *culpa lata æquiparatur dolo*, so that it is placed in the same category as fraud. But as regards the second, one is only answerable for *culpa levis* sometimes, and in virtue of certain obligations; and chiefly, but not exclusively, in virtue of those from which he. himself derived benefit. Under *culpa lata* is comprehended not only wrong caused wilfully and intentionally, but also wrong caused by simple imprudence or simple neglect, when it is *gross*. When any one is bound *præstare levem* or *omnem culpam*, he is liable for small blunders or mistakes, and he is not exempted from all responsibility, unless he has comported himself entirely as a good father of a family,—that is, in the same way as a prudent, careful, and attentive man is accustomed to conduct himself in like cases. But, in measuring the responsibility of a particular person, regard is sometimes had not so much to this general standard as to the habits of the individual, and there is required from him not absolutely the highest degree of care and attention, but only *talem diligentiam, qualem in suis rebus adhibere solet*.[2]

According to the view of those writers who maintain that the Roman law recognised only two degrees of fault—*culpa lata* and *culpa levis*—" there is no *culpa levissima*, as opposed to *culpa levis;* but the latter, as understood by the Romans, rather includes the former as understood by the moderns."[3]

As the subject is important, it may be useful here to lay before our readers the general rules of responsibility for fault

---

[1] Maynz, vol. ii. p. 15, § 260. 1
Bell's Com. 453.

[2] Marezoll, § 120.

[3] Lindley's Introduction to Study of Jurisprudence, p. 131. See also Appendix, p. 84.

as given by Maynz : 1st, If the debtor can derive no profit from the obligation, he is only liable for *culpa lata*. To this rule there is an exception in the case of a mandatory or *negotiorum gestor*, who is answerable for *culpa levis*. 2d, When the debtor derives advantage from the obligation, he is liable for *culpa levis*. To this there is an exception, where one obtains the use of a thing on a precarious title, as he is then only liable for *culpa lata*. 3d, When the two parties derive benefit from the obligation, as in sale, pledge, or partnership, they are both responsible for the consequences of *culpa levis ;* and this rule is said to be without exception. By special convention these general rules may, of course, be modified so as to extend or diminish the responsibility of the parties according to circumstances.[1]

Sources of obligations. Viewed with reference to their sources, obligations were divided by the Romans into those arising from, 1st, Express contracts ; 2d, Quasi contracts ; 3d, Delicts ; and, 4th, Quasi delicts. This division is imperfect ; for there are many instances of obligations which are not derived from any of these sources, being founded on the operation of a particular law, or on equity alone. But although this classification is incomplete, it is convenient to follow it, so far as it goes, in giving a succinct exposition of the Roman law of obligations.

Different classes of contracts. Contracts were divided by the Roman law into those which were perfected by the intervention of things, by solemn words, by writing, and by sole consent,—*re, verbis, literis, consensu.* These four kinds of contracts will be considered in the order in which they are treated in Justinian's Institutes.

II.—ENGLISH LAW.

Modern law of contracts. In the matter of contracts, the law of France, like that of Scotland, is substantially based on the Roman system. But there are some peculiarities in the English law of contracts, which may be here shortly noticed.

Peculiarities of English system. In the law of England contracts are classified under three heads : 1st, Contracts of record, such as judgments, cogno-

[1] Maynz, §. 259.

vits, and recognisances ; 2d, Contracts by specialty, or under seal; 3d, Simple contracts, or contracts not under seal, which may be either written or verbal.[1]

A judgment obtained in one of the superior courts of common law now binds the land of the debtor, if registered for the warning of purchasers at the office of the Court of Common Pleas.[2]* A specialty is distinguished from a simple contract in writing by sealing and delivery. A simple contract "is a contract either in writing not under seal, or verbal, or implied from the acts and conduct of the parties."[3]

In judgment debts and contracts under seal a consideration is implied. But it is essential to the validity of a simple contract that it should be founded on a sufficient consideration. For whether the agreement be verbal or in writing, it is a *nudum pactum*, and will not support an action, if a consideration be wanting. "The rule that a consideration is necessary to the validity of a contract applies to all contracts and agreements not under seal, with the exception of bills of exchange and negotiable notes, after they have been negotiated and passed into the hands of an innocent indorsee. The immediate parties to a bill or note, equally with parties to other contracts, are affected by the want of consideration; and it is only as to third persons who come to the possession of the paper in the usual course of trade, without notice of the original defect, that the want of consideration cannot be alleged."[4]

Simple contracts require consideration.

By the Act 19 & 20 Vict. c. 97, s. 3, it is declared that no promise in writing to answer for the debt, default, or miscarriage of another, shall be invalid, though the consideration does not appear in writing, or by necessary inference from a written document.

It has been observed that "contracts of record must be

---

[1] Broom's Com. on Common Law, p. 267.

[2] 1 & 2 Vict. c. 110. Broom's Com. p. 268.

* Such judgment does not now bind the land of the debtor, until such land shall have been actually delivered in execution by virtue of a writ of elegit or other lawful authority in pursuance of such judgment; 27 & 28 Vict. c. 112. § 1.

[3] Broom's Com. p. 308.

[4] Kent's Com. on American Law, 10th ed., vol. ii. p. 630.

Distinction between legal and equitable assets.

considered as of a higher nature than contracts of any other kind, and special as superior in efficacy to simple contracts."[1] In the administration of the legal assets of deceased persons in England, judgment creditors are ranked first, then creditors by specialty, and, lastly, creditors by simple contract. But, in the administration of equitable assets,[2] and the distribution of estates in bankruptcy, creditors have no priority or preference in respect merely of their claims resting on judgments and specialties, such claims being ranked in the same order with simple contracts. In Scotland there is no distinction between legal and equitable assets, and creditors are entitled to be ranked *pari passu* on the estates of their debtors, whether their claims be constituted by judgments or formal deeds, or rest on simple contract.[3]

III.—INTERNATIONAL LAW.

Lex loci contractus.

Generally speaking, the interpretation of personal contracts and their validity, as regards forms and solemnities, are governed by the law of the country where they are made, unless the intention of the parties to the contrary be clearly shown— *locus contractus regit actum.*[4] But if a contract be made in one country which is to be performed in another, parties are presumed to have in view the law of the place of performance, which in that case generally regulates the obligation and construction of the contract—*contraxisse unusquisque in eo loco intelligitur, in quo ut solveret se obligavit.*[5] If no place of performance is mentioned, or the contract may be indifferently performed anywhere, the *lex loci contractus* is usually held to be in the contemplation of the parties.[6]

Negotiable instruments.

Very important consequences arise from the application of the *lex loci contractus* to bills and other negotiable instruments used in commercial transactions. "It may be laid

---

[1] Broom's Com. p. 268.

[2] For an explanation of the distinction between *legal* and *equitable* assets, see Williams's Law of Executors, 5th ed., vol. ii. p. 1519.

[3] See the Second Report of the Mercantile Law Com. 1855, p. 27, and Ap. p. 133.

[4] Story's Conflict of Laws, § 242.

[5] D. 44. 7. 21. Story's Conflict of Laws, § 280.

[6] Ibid. § 282.

down as a general rule," says Chancellor Kent, "that negotiable paper of every kind is construed and governed, as to the obligation of the drawer or maker, by the law of the country where it was drawn or made; and, as to that of the acceptor, by the law of the country where he accepts; and, as to that of the indorsers, by the law of the country in which the paper was indorsed."[1]

In illustration of this rule, two adjudged cases may be referred to. In England an acceptance of a bill of exchange binds the acceptor to payment at all events. Not so by the law of Leghorn; for, if the acceptor has not sufficient effects of the drawer in his hands at the time of acceptance, and the drawer fails, the acceptance becomes void. An acceptance in Leghorn in these circumstances was accordingly found to import no obligation upon the acceptor.[2]

Again, though a blank indorsement of a promissory-note is valid by the law of England, it is not so in France, where certain formalities are required; and therefore such an indorsement in France will not entitle the holder to recover against the maker in an English court.[3] To some this doctrine may appear to be a departure from the rule that the law of the place of payment is to govern. But it is not so. For the drawer and indorsers of a bill of exchange only become bound on the failure of the drawee to reimburse the holder after due notice at the place where they entered into the contract.[4]

It is a general rule that whatever constitutes a good defence by the law of the place where the contract is made or is to be performed, is equally good in every other place where the question may be litigated. This proceeds upon the principle that the same law which creates the charge is to be regarded when it operates in discharge of the contract.[5]

[1] Kent's Practical Treatise on Commercial and Maritime Law, p. 378, note.
[2] Burrows v. Jemino, 2 Str. R. 733. Story, § 265.
[3] Trimbey v. Vignier, 1 Bing, New Cases, 151. Story, § 316 a.
[4] Story's Conflict of Laws, § 315.
[5] Ibid. § 331.

CHAPTER II.

OF REAL CONTRACTS.

WHAT the Romans described as obligations contracted *re*—by the intervention of things—are called by the moderns real contracts, because they are not perfected till something has passed from the one party to the other. Of this description are the contracts of loan, deposit, and pledge. Till the subject is actually lent, deposited, or pledged, it does not form the special contract of loan, deposit, or pledge.

Sect. 1.—*Contract of Loan.*

There are two sorts of loan—one of things that may be used without destroying them, and the other of things which are consumed by the use that is made of them. The first kind was called by the Romans *commodatum*, or loan for use; the second was called *mutuum*, or loan for consumption.

Commodate loan for use.   Commodate is a contract whereby the owner of a thing gives it in loan to another for a certain use without payment, upon condition that it shall be restored after the purpose is served. It is essential that the loan shall be gratuitous, for if anything were paid for the use, there would be a letting for hire. The lender remains proprietor of the thing lent, and the borrower is obliged to return the same identical thing which he has received, whether it be a horse, a carriage, or a book, and not another of the same kind.[1] If the article perish or be lost by accident, without any blame or

[1] I. 3. 15. 2.

neglect imputable to the borrower, the loss falls on the owner. In this way the Romans lent not only movable things, but also immovables, such as a house to dwell in.[1]

He who borrows a thing, gratuitously, for his own use, is obliged to take care of it, not only as he takes care of what is his own, but with all the exactness that is usually observed by a careful and diligent person. " In rebus commodatis talis diligentia præstanda est, qualem quisque diligentissimus pater familias suis rebus adhibet." [2]   Obligations of borrower.

The borrower can only use the thing for the purpose for which it was lent; he cannot allow another person to use it, nor keep it beyond the time agreed on, nor detain it as a set-off against any debt due to him by the lender. The loan may be either for a limited time or for a special occasion. When a thing is lent during pleasure, the loan is called *Precarium*. The borrower must restore the article in the same good plight in which he received it, subject only to such deterioration as may arise from reasonable use. He is bound to make good all injury which befalls the thing while it is in his possession, if the injury was caused by his fault, or was of such a nature that a careful person might have prevented it. Thus, if a man borrow a horse, and so maltreat the animal by over-riding it, or otherwise, as to cause its death or render it useless, he will be liable for its value to the owner. In some instances the borrower is held responsible for loss by inevitable accident, as when he has improperly detained the article borrowed beyond the time when he ought to have returned it; for the loss is then presumed to have arisen from his breach of duty. By the French law this is carried so far, that if the thing lent perish by an accident which the borrower could have guarded against by employing a similar thing belonging to himself; or if, not being able to save but one of the two things, as in a case of accidental fire, he has preferred his own, he is held responsible for the loss of the other to the lender.[3]

Mutuum is a gratuitous loan of things intended for con- Mutuum.

---

[1] I. 3. 15. 2.
[2] D. 13. 6. 1. pr.　I. 3. 15. 2.
[3] Code Civil, art. 1882.

sumption, which are usually estimated by number, weight, or measure, such as money, corn, wine, and the like, on condition that the borrower shall restore, not the same identical things, but as much of the same kind and quality.[1] From the nature of this contract, the property of the thing lent passes to the borrower, and if it perish from any cause, the loss falls on him. The lender becomes a mere creditor for the value; and this distinction is important in bankruptcy.

In the loan of corn, wine, and other articles of the like nature, the borrower must restore as much of the same kind and quality as he received, whether the price of the commodity has risen or fallen in the market. Should he fail to satisfy his obligation, he will be responsible to the lender for the value of the article, having regard to the time and place when it should have been delivered. The action under which the lender established his claim against the borrower was called *condictio certi*. By the Macedonian senatus-consultum, it was ordained, that any one who should lend money to a son under the power of his father, without the father's consent, should have no action for its recovery.

In a loan of money under *mutuum*, the borrower was not obliged to pay interest on the sum received. If it was intended that interest should be paid, a special engagement to that effect by the debtor was indispensable; and then interest became exigible, not under *mutuum*, but in virtue of express contract, by stipulation or otherwise.

Obligation to pay interest at Rome. By the Roman law interest was due *ex lege*, or by agreement. In contracts *bonæ fidei* interest was also due *ex mora*, where there was undue delay in paying the capital.[2] For, according to Ulpian, he pays less who pays late—*minus solvit qui tardius solvit*.[3] The capital sum was called *sors* or *caput*, and the interest *fœnus* or *usuræ*.

Among the Romans the legal rate of interest varied very much at different times. The Twelve Tables prohibited any

---

[1] I. 3. 15. pr.

[2] "In bonæ fidei contractibus ex mora usuræ debentur."—Marcianus,

D. 22. 1. 32. 2.

[3] D. 50. 17. 12. 1.

one from exacting more than the *unciarum fœnus*.[1] This expression has given rise to much controversy. The Roman pound (*as*) was frequently used in calculations to denote a unit or integral sum, and was divided into twelve parts or ounces; and it is now generally supposed that the *unciarum fœnus*, or uncial interest, was one-twelfth part of the capital for the year, that is 8⅓ per cent per annum. Niebuhr, however, is of opinion that this rate was introduced for the year of ten months; and if this theory be correct, then 8⅓ per cent for a year of ten months will be exactly 10 per cent for a year of twelve months.[2] Towards the close of the republic, the maximum rate of interest, called *usuræ centesimæ*, was 1 per cent per month, or 12 per cent per annum.[3] After many changes, Justinian at last regulated the rates of interest by a scale, which varied according to the condition of the creditors. Persons of illustrious rank could lend money at 4 per cent; ordinary persons at 6 per cent; merchants at 8 per cent; and for maritime risks, which were formerly unlimited, the interest was not to exceed 12 per cent.[4]

It was unlawful to charge interest upon interest, which was called *anatocismus*.[5]

Finally, if the interest was allowed to accumulate on a debt till it exceeded the capital, the surplus was not allowed to be charged.[6]

In this country the rate of interest has been usually regulated by law, and has varied at different times. A statute of the thirteenth year of Queen Elizabeth limited the rate of interest to 10 per cent per annum; a statute of James I. to 8 per cent per annum; a statute of Charles II., in 1660, to 6 per cent; and a statute of Queen Anne, in 1713, to 5 per cent. Mr Bentham pointed out the impolicy of these restrictions on the trade in money in his 'Defence of Usury,' published in the year 1787; but so deep-rooted was the prejudice against the rapacity of money-lenders, that more than

Interest in this country.

[1] Tac. Ann. vi. 16.
[2] Niebuhr, Röm. Geschichte, vol. ii. p. 431-439.
[3] Maynz, § 266.
[4] C. 4. 32. 26. § 1.
[5] C. 4. 32. 28.
[6] C. 4. 32. 27. § 1. Marezoll, § 121.

half a century elapsed before the system of restriction was abandoned. At length, after some experimental relaxation in the case of bills of exchange, the usury laws were finally repealed by the Statute 17 & 18 Vict. c. 90, passed in 1854. Where interest is payable upon any debt or sum of money by any rule of law, or upon any contract, express or implied, it is declared that the same rate of interest shall be recoverable as if the Act had not been passed.[1]

By the law of England, " interest is and always was payable where there has been a contract to that effect express or to be implied from circumstances, the usage of trade, or the mode of dealing between the parties, and also upon a bond, bill, or promissory note. In most other cases there was a considerable dispute upon the question of interest, and the leaning of the courts seemed, on the whole, against allowing it. However, by Statute 3 & 4 Will. IV. cap. 42, it is enacted, that upon all debts, or sums certain payable at a certain time or otherwise, the jury, on the trial of any issue or inquisition of damages, may, if they think fit, allow interest for the creditor at a rate not exceeding the current rate of interest from the time when such debts or sums certain were payable, if such debts or sums be payable by virtue of some written instrument at a certain time; or, if payable otherwise, then from the time when the demand of payment shall have been made in writing, so as such demand shall give notice to the debtor that interest will be claimed from the date of such demand until the time of payment ; provided that interest shall be payable in all cases in which it is now payable by law." [2]

In Scotland, interest is due *ex mora* as well as *ex pacto*. So, in many cases, an implied agreement to pay interest is held to arise from any undue delay in paying the principal sum ; but in regard to all claims or accounts upon which interest is not due, either by law or agreement, it has been said, no demand for interest can be made, till after they have been duly rendered and payment has been required.[3]

[1] Stat. s. 3.
[2] Smith's Mer. Law, 6th edition,　p. 545, 546.
[3] More's Stair, vol. i. p. 78, notes.

Sect. 2.—Deposit.

Deposit is a contract by which the owner places a thing *Nature and effects of deposit.* in charge of another to keep it gratuitously and restore it on demand. The property and the risk remain with the depositor, so that if the subject perish accidentally the loss falls on him. The depositary is bound to preserve the subject with reasonable care, and to exercise the same vigilance as he does in his own affairs. He is not entitled to make any use of the deposit, unless expressly or tacitly authorised to do so. As a general rule, he is liable only for gross neglect, because he derives no benefit from the transaction.[1] But he will be held responsible for ordinary neglect, if he come under a special undertaking for safe custody, or officiously propose to keep the subject without being asked to do so, or if he receive compensation for the deposit. In this last case the contract ceases to be a gratuitous deposit, and resolves into *locatio operarum.* The depositary is bound to restore the subject, with all its fruits and accessories. On the other hand, he is entitled to be reimbursed of all necessary charges. From the exuberant trust implied in deposit, the subject deposited cannot be retained as a set-off for any separate debt or claim due to the depositary by the owner.

Sufferers from fire, shipwreck, or other calamity, might be *Necessary deposit.* compelled by circumstances to leave their goods in the hands of persons wholly unknown to them, and this was called by the Romans *depositum miserabile.* In that class of cases the depositary who proved unfaithful to his trust was liable to be sued under a prætorian action for double the value of the articles embezzled.[2]

When a subject was placed in neutral custody to abide the *Sequestration.* issue of a lawsuit or reference for determining the right, this kind of deposit was called by the Romans sequestration. It might be either voluntary or judicial, and the condition of every such deposit was, that the subject should be delivered

[1] D. 13. 6. 5. 2. Ulpian.   [2] D. 4. 9. 1. § 1 and 3.

O

to the person who should be found to have the best right
to it.

Edict Nautæ, Caupones. By an edict of the Roman prætor, the policy of which has
been generally adopted in modern Europe, as well as by the
North American States, shipmasters, innkeepers, and stablers,
are responsible for the luggage and effects of travellers intrusted to their care, or brought into the ship, inn, or stable.
The edict is in these words :—" Nautæ, caupones, stabularii,
quod cujusque salvum fore receperint, nisi restituent, in eos
judicium dabo." [1] Under *nautæ* are comprehended carriers
by water ; but the principle has been extended in this country to land-carriers, whose responsibility is in some respects
more stringent than it appears to have been by the Roman
law. *Caupones* are the keepers of inns, where travellers are
accommodated with food and lodging. These inns abounded
at Rome, and along all the great roads of Italy, as appears
from Horace's description of his journey from Rome to
Brundusium (Sat. i. 5); and the persons who kept such
places of public entertainment were held in low estimation
among the Romans. " It is necessary," says Ulpian, in commenting on the edict, " to confide largely in the honesty of
such men ; and if they were not held very strictly to their
duty, they might yield to the temptation to commit a breach
of trust, and even enter into secret leagues with thieves." [2]

Rules of re-sponsibility under edict. On grounds of public policy, therefore, innkeepers were
held responsible for the loss or damage of goods deposited
with them by their guests, whether arising from the acts of
the servants of the inn or of strangers. When the goods are
stolen, either by one connected with the inn, or by some
other person who obtains access to the premises, the loss
must be made good to the owner ; for theft is no excuse, the
edict being intended to protect travellers both against negligence and dishonesty. But the innkeeper is not bound to
repair loss or damage occasioned by inevitable accident or
superior force, such as lightning, tempest, popular tumult,
piracy, robbery, or the like. An innkeeper was held not

---

[1] D. 4. 9. 1. pr. and § 1.   [2] Ibid.

liable for the value of horses placed in his stables, which were destroyed by an accidental fire; this, in the absence of any proof of negligence, being regarded as a *damnum fatale*.[1] The same principle seems to have been applied to a loss occasioned by robbers or housebreakers, who were convicted and transported.[2]   It was never doubted in Scotland, any more than in England, that the responsibility of innkeepers under the edict extends to theft.[3] Professor Bell thinks they are also liable for robbery [4]; but this seems questionable, as the Roman law makes a clear distinction between the case where goods are stolen clandestinely and where they are abstracted by overwhelming force.[5]   According to the French law, innkeepers are not responsible where the goods belonging to their guests are feloniously abstracted, either by an armed force, or any other superior force; but they are answerable, as in this country, for theft or damage, whether committed by the servants of the inn or by strangers.[6]

By the Act 26 & 27 Vict. c. 41, an innkeeper is not liable for loss or injury to goods or property brought by any guest to his inn beyond £30, except in the following cases: —1. Where the property consists of a horse or other live animal, or gear belonging thereto, or a carriage. 2. Where the property has been stolen, lost, or injured through the wilful act or neglect of the innkeeper or his servant. 3. Where the property has been expressly deposited for safe custody with such innkeeper. To entitle an innkeeper to the benefit of the Act, two things are required: 1st, He must not refuse to receive goods for safe custody; 2d, He must exhibit in the hall or entrance to his inn a printed copy of the first section of the Act.

A lodging-house keeper makes a contract with every man that comes, and stands in a different situation from an innkeeper, who is bound, without making any special contract, to provide lodging and entertainment at a reasonable price

---

[1] Macdonell, 15th Dec. 1809, F. C.
[2] Watling, 10th June 1825.
[3] Richmond *v.* Smith, 8 Barn. & Cres., 9. Kent *v.* Shuckard, 2 B. & Ad., 803. 1 Bell's Com., 470.
[4] 1 Bell's Com., p. 469.
[5] D. 4. 9. 3. 1. Kent's Com., 10th ed., vol. ii. p. 819.
[6] Code Civil, art. 1953.

to all comers, so far as his means of accommodation extend.
The edict, therefore, has been held not to extend to lodging-
house keepers.[1]

Sect. 3.—Pledge.

Nature of pledge.

Pledge is the delivery of a thing to a creditor as a security
for money due, on condition of his restoring it to the owner
after payment of the debt, and with a power of sale if the
debt should not be paid.   Hypothec is a security established
by law to the creditor upon a subject which continues in the
debtor's possession.[2]

Immovables, such as lands and houses, as well as corporeal
movables and other things, might be the subject of pledge by
the Roman law.   As the contract is for the benefit of both
parties, the creditor is bound to bestow ordinary care and
diligence in the preservation of the subject.   He is responsible for *culpa levis.*   As the pledge continues the debtor's
property, if it be lost from unavoidable accident, or perish
from intrinsic defect, the creditor is not answerable, and may,
notwithstanding, enforce payment of his debt.   But in such
a case it is not sufficient for the creditor to allege that the
pledge is lost; he must show how the loss occurred, and that
it was not in his power to prevent it.

The creditor, though in possession of the pledge, could not
use it, or take the profits of it, without a contract to that
effect.   He was bound to account for these profits, but he was
entitled to an allowance for all necessary expenses laid out

Pactum antichresis.

on the subject.   By the *pactum antichresis* the creditor was
allowed to take the profits in lieu of the interest on his debt.

Lex commissoria abolished.

It might be made a condition of the contract, by the *lex commissoria,* that the thing pledged should become the absolute
property of the creditor if the debt was not paid at the time
agreed on.   But as this condition was found to be a source of
great oppression and injustice, it was prohibited by a law of
Constantine, A.D. 326.[3]

[1] 1 Bell's Com., 469. Thompson
v. Lacy, 1819, 3 Barn. & Ald., 283.
[2] D. 20. 1.   C. 8. 14.
[3] C. 7. 35.

A thing might be pledged to several persons in succession, whose claims were to be satisfied according to their priority in time. To this rule there were some exceptions; for instance, where a subsequent creditor advanced money, which was applied to the preservation of the thing pledged, such as a ship, he was allowed a preference.[1] A similar principle is recognised in our law as to money lent on bottomry bonds.

The pledge covers the debt and interest, and all necessary expenses. When these are paid, the debtor is entitled to have the pledge restored to him. By the French Code the holder of a pledge has a right of retention for other debts due to him from the pledger, though not specifically charged on the subject pledged.[2] In England the creditor is not allowed to retain the pledge for any other debt than that for which it was given; and although it has been said that a different rule prevails in Scotland, this seems questionable under recent decisions.[3] *Pledge covers debt, interest, and costs.*

After the term of payment is passed the creditor has a right to sell the pledge, and retain his debt out of the produce of the sale. If there be a deficiency, he has a personal action to recover the balance from the debtor, and if there be a surplus the debtor is entitled to it. By the Roman law the power of sale was to be exercised pursuant to the terms of the contract, and this might be done without judicial authority. If there was no special agreement to regulate the matter, it was declared, by a constitution of Justinian, that the sale should not proceed till two years had elapsed from the date of the notice given to the debtor, or of a judicial sentence obtained against him.[4] In England, after default by the debtor in complying with his engagement, the creditor may sell without judicial process, upon giving reasonable *Power of sale.*

---

[1] D. 20. 4. 5.
[2] Code Civil, art. 2082.
[3] National Bank *v.* Forbes, 3d Dec. 1858, 21 Sess. Ca., 79—Observed: "If the title of possession be unlimited as a title of property, the party is entitled to retain till every debt due to him by the party demand-

ing delivery of the subject is paid. If his title be limited, he can retain only for the payment of that particular debt which is secured by his possession." — Lord Justice - Clerk Inglis.
[4] C. 8. 34. 3. Justinian.

notice to the debtor to redeem.[1] A judicial sentence is required to warrant the sale in Scotland, and the same rule is
followed in France.[2]

Expiry of pledge. A pledge is determined by the destruction of the subject,
by the payment of the debt, by the creditor releasing the
debtor, and in various other ways.

In connection with this subject, it may be observed that
the business of pawnbroking, one species of pledge, is in this
country placed under special regulations by the Acts 39 &
40 Geo. III. c. 99, and 9 & 10 Vict. c. 98.*

Tacit hypothecs. Tacit hypothecs were recognised by the Roman law to a
much greater extent than in modern times. Among other
instances the following may be mentioned :—1. The public
treasury had a preference by tacit hypothec over all the property of a person indebted to the Fisc. 2. If money was
lent for the repair of a house, the building was hypothecated
to the creditor for the debt. 3. The proprietor of a rural
subject had a tacit hypothec for his rent over the fruits belonging to the tenant : the landlord of a house or shop or
warehouse had a similar hypothec over the movables brought
into them by the tenant.[3]

Sect. 4.—Innominate Contracts.

Their different kinds. Before leaving the subject of real contracts, we require to
notice those called by modern jurists *innominate*, because
they have no special names. They are classed by Paulus
under four general heads : *Do ut des ; do ut facias ; facio
ut des ; facio ut facias.* It was essential that something
should be actually given or performed by one of the parties
in order to constitute an obligation against the other.

Exchange. One of the most important of these innominate contracts is
exchange (*permutatio*), which is perfected when one of the

---

[1] Story's Com. on the Law of Bailments, p. 206.
[2] 2 Bell's Com., 22.   Code Civil,
art. 2078.

* See also 25 and 26 Vict. c. 101,
s. 311 *et seq.*
[3] C. 20. 2. § 3, 4, 7.

parties has given a thing, in order that he who receives it may give another thing :—*Do ut des*.   In all such cases the person who performed his part had an option either to sue the other party for performance by an action *præscriptis verbis*, or to renounce the convention and recover back the thing given by him by the *Condictio causa data causa non secuta*.[1]

[1] D. 19. 5. 5. § 1 and 2.

CHAPTER III.

I.—ROMAN LAW.

Stipulations.

THE *verborum obligatio* of the Romans was contracted by uttering certain formal words of style, an interrogation being put by the one party and an answer being given by the other. These obligations were called stipulations, and were binding although without consideration. But a mere promise given without an interrogation was invalid as a *nudum pactum.* In stipulations the question and answer must exactly correspond, thus:—" Quinque aureos mihi dare spondes ? "— " Spondeo." " Promittis?"—" Promitto." "Dabis?"—" Dabo." " Facies ? "—" Faciam."

A stipulation might be absolute or conditional, and two or more persons might be concerned on either side of the contract. Where several persons bound themselves conjunctly and severally for the performance of the whole obligation, each was bound as if he had been sole debtor, and the creditor might sue whichever he pleased for the whole debt. The strict forms of stipulation were abolished by the Emperor Leo, so that a contract might be entered into by any words which clearly expressed the intention of the parties.[1]

Cautionary obligations.

Fidejussio was a contract by which a person bound himself as surety to fulfil the obligation of another, in case of the failure of the principal obligant. The obligation of the surety, which was usually entered into by stipulation, but might be reduced to writing, extended not only to the surety but to his

[1] I. 3. t. 16, 17, and 20.   D. 45. 1.   C. 8. 38 and 39.

heirs. A surety might be interposed in natural as well as in civil obligations, so that he was sometimes liable to be sued when the principal was not; but although the cautioner might be liable for less, he could not be bound for a greater sum than the principal. Where there are several sureties, each is liable *in solidum* to the creditor; but they are all equally liable in relief to each other.

Sureties by the Roman law are entitled to the benefit of discussion—that is, they may insist that the principal debtor should be first sued, unless the creditor can show that it would be useless to do so in consequence of insolvency or absence. They have an action to recover from the principal debtor whatever they have lawfully paid on his account. They may also require an assignation of the debt from the creditor to enable them to operate their relief against co-sureties for their shares.

By the Senatus-consultum Velleianum a cautionary obligation by a married woman was ineffectual. To this rule some exceptions were introduced before the time of Justinian, who ordained that such an obligation should be absolutely null, unless it was constituted by a public instrument signed by three witnesses.[1]

In Britain all cautionary obligations and guarantees must be in writing. Sureties are not entitled to the benefit of discussion, if there be no express stipulation to that effect in the instrument of caution. Any discharge by the creditor to one cautioner without the consent of the other sureties, operates as a discharge to all.[2]

The *obligatio literis*, in the Roman law, was a written acknowledgment of debt, and was chiefly used in the case of a loan of money, giving rise to an action called *condictio in chirographo*. The creditor could not sue upon the note within two years from its date, without being exposed to the *exceptio non numeratæ pecuniæ*, whereby he was bound to prove that the money was in fact paid to the debtor. But after the lapse of two years from the date of the obligation this plea was excluded.[3]

Obligations in writing.

[1] I. 3. 21.   D. 46. 1.   C. 8. 41.   [3] I. 3. 22.   C. 4. 30.
[2] See 19 & 20 Vict. c. 60, s. 6, 5, 9.

II.—ENGLISH AND SCOTTISH LAW.

English doctrine as to consideration.

It has already been explained that, by the law of England, a consideration is presumed when the contract is under seal, but as a general rule, a contract not under seal is incapable of being enforced by legal proceedings, unless it be supported by a consideration, according to the maxim of the civil law, "*Ex nudo pacto non oritur actio.*" Upon this subject Dr Browne observes :—"*Ex nudo pacto non oritur actio* is the rule of the civil law as well as of ours ; but the meaning of *nudum pactum* is very different in the two laws. With them a verbal agreement, if attended with a certain solemn form of words, and then called a stipulation, was valid, though without consideration, and not *nudum pactum.* With us, all verbal agreements without consideration are invalid and *nuda pacta.* With them agreements, though in writing, at least until ratified by time, did not import a consideration ; and even though they actually expressed one, it might be disputed during that time. With us deeds import a consideration ; but writings of a less solemn nature do not, unless negotiable at law and the interests of third persons concerned ; they may be evidence of the agreement or intent of the parties, but not conclusive evidence of sufficient consideration."[1]

As already mentioned, it is no longer necessary in England that the consideration for a written guarantee should appear in the writing.[2]

Does not hold in Scotland.

In Scotland it is not essential to the validity of an obligation that it should be granted for a valuable consideration, or indeed for any consideration whatever; the rule of the civil law, that no action arises from a naked paction, being rejected, and an obligation undertaken deliberately, though gratuitously, being binding. This is in conformity with the canon law, " by which every paction produceth action, *et omne verbum de ore fideli cadit in debitum.*"[3]

---

[1] Browne's View of the Civil Law, 1802, vol. i. p. 358, note.

[2] Act 19 & 20 Vict. c. 97 (1856), s. 3.

[3] Stair, 1. 10. 7.

CHAPTER IV.

OF CONTRACTS PERFECTED BY CONSENT ALONE.

CONTRACTS perfected by consent alone are usually classed under four heads: 1st, Sale; 2d, Location, or hiring; 3d, Partnership; and, 4th, Mandate. All these are considered contracts *bonæ fidei*, and will be considered in their order.

Consensual contracts.

Sect. 1.—Sale.

I. — ROMAN LAW.

Sale is a contract, by which one person becomes bound to deliver a subject to another, with the view of transferring the property in consideration of a money price. When one commodity is given in return for another, this constitutes exchange, not sale.[1]

Nature and form of contract.

By the Roman law all contracts of sale were good without writing, to whatever value they extended. Apart from the personal capacity to contract, three things were required for sale : a subject, a price, and the consent of the parties. Though consent alone was generally sufficient, yet if it was agreed by the parties that the contract should be reduced into writing, the sale was held to be incomplete, and either party was at liberty to resile till the writing was formally executed.[2]

All things adapted to commerce and susceptible of appropriation may be sold, unless the sale of them is prohibited by

What may be sold.

[1] I. 3. 23. 2.   [2] I. 3. 24. pr.

law. There may be a valid sale of a thing which is not in existence at the date of the contract, as the future produce of an estate; and even the chance of gain may be sold, such as the hope of a succession or the cast of a net.

Price.

The price must be certain, or capable of being ascertained; but it may be fixed by a reference to a third party.[1] When an article is sold and delivered, and nothing is said about the price, the fair value or market-rate, as fixed by custom, is understood to be in the view of the parties.

Læsio ultra dimidium.

When the price fell short of one-half of the value of the thing sold, the seller was entitled to rescind the contract, on the ground of lesion, unless the buyer consented to pay the deficiency in the price.[2] This doctrine proceeded on the erroneous notion that the price in sale should be equal to the value of the thing sold, in place of being the sum agreed upon between the parties, which ought always to be binding where no fraud or deceit is practised. Some writers have supposed that the buyer was equally entitled to rescind the contract when he suffered lesion beyond one-half of the price; but there is no authority for that doctrine.[3]

Warranty against faults.

By the Roman law the seller was held to be bound by the nature of the contract, and without any stipulation, to warrant the thing sold to be free from such defects as made it unfit for the use for which it was intended. When the subject did not answer this implied warranty, the sale might be set aside, and restitution of the price obtained. In such a case the ordinary remedy of the buyer was to rescind the contract by an *actio redhibitoria*, which required to be raised within six months from the date of the sale.[4]

Not only was the seller bound by the Roman law to warrant the thing sold against such faults as rendered it unfit for its proper use; but even where the defect complained of was of a slighter kind, so as merely to diminish the value, he was liable to repay as much of the price as exceeded what the buyer would have given, if he had known the defect. This obligation was enforced by the *actio quanti minoris*, which required to be brought within a year after the sale; but no

[1] I. 3. 23. 1.   [2] C. 4. 44. 2.   [3] Maynz, § 297.   [4] Ibid. § 296.

such proceeding is allowed in modern practice, being wholly inconsistent with the interests of commerce.

As a general rule, warranty against defects was implied in the Roman law; but it was in the power of the parties to derogate from this rule by special convention. So the seller could stipulate that he should not be held to warrant against any defects whatever, or any particular defects specified; and such clauses were valid where there was no fraud.

The seller was not bound to deliver the subject till the price was paid, unless the bargain was upon credit; and if payment was delayed after the term, interest was due. *Obligation of delivery.*

It was an established rule of the Roman law that the property of the thing sold was not transferred to the purchaser by the contract alone, without delivery actual or constructive. Where the same thing was sold by the owner to two different persons, and no delivery was given to either of them, the first purchaser was preferred in respect of the priority of his contract; but if the second purchaser obtained possession under a *bona fide* title, he was preferred to the first.

According to the Roman law, the property, or *jus in re*, is not transferred by the contract unless it be followed by tradition. By the French Code, immovables pass to the buyer by the so-called contract, which operates as a conveyance of the *jus in re*. But if the subject of the sale be movable, the property does not pass by the contract without tradition in a question with third parties: for a second purchaser, who has obtained possession under a *bona fide* title, is preferred to the first. This exception to the general principle is based on the free circulation of movables, which may pass on the same day through twenty different hands.[1]

As soon as the contract of sale is complete, all the risks of the thing sold (as well as the profits) pass to the purchaser, though it has not been delivered to him,—*Periculum rei venditæ nondum traditæ est emptoris*. But, in order to the risk passing to the buyer before delivery has been made to *Risk of things sold.*

---

[1] Rogron, Code Civil expliqué, art. 1141. Austin's Lectures on Jurisprudence, vol. iii. p. 206, 207.

him by the owner, the subject of the personal contract must be specific, and the price certain. In the case of commodities sold by weight, number, or measure, the contract is not complete till the goods are weighed, counted, or measured. Where the whole wheat in a particular granary, or all the wine in a particular cellar, is sold in the mass for a slump price, the risk passes to the buyer, because nothing remains to be done to complete the contract; but where any operation of weight, measurement, or the like, is necessary in order to ascertain the price, the quantity, or the particular parcel to be delivered, and to put it in a deliverable state, the contract is incomplete until such operation is performed. Considerable difficulty sometimes arises in the application of this rule.[1]

Exceptions to general rule.

The general rule, that the subject is at the risk of the buyer from the time of the sale, is subject to exceptions: 1st, When the loss has happened by the fault of the seller, by his improper delay in giving delivery, or by neglect of due care and diligence; 2d, When by special agreement the risk is laid on the seller.

Special conditions in sale.

Conditions might be annexed to sale for the benefit of the seller, such as the *pactum legis commissoriæ* and the *pactum de retrovendendo*. By the first it was agreed that, if the price was not paid within a certain time, the contract should become void, and the buyer be bound to restore the thing sold. By the second, the seller had a power of redeeming his property within a certain time, by paying back the price which he had received for it.

Warranty against eviction.

After delivery the seller was bound to warrant the title to the buyer, and to indemnify him for the loss, if the subject was evicted.[2]

How sale rescinded.

Sale might be rescinded in various ways: 1st, By the mutual consent of seller and buyer; 2d, By non-performance of some of the conditions agreed upon; and, 3d, By reason of fraud, force, error, and other grounds of nullity.

---

[1] D. 18. 1. 35. § 5 and 6. Hansen, 4th Feb. 1859, Sess. Ca., vol. xxi. p. 432.   [2] D. 21. 2.   C. 8. 45.

II.—ENGLISH AND SCOTTISH LAW.

Before leaving this subject, it may be proper to notice some distinctions between the English and Scottish law of sale.

In England, under the Statute of Frauds (29 Car. II. c. 3), no contract for the sale of goods, wares, or merchandise for the price of ten pounds or upwards, shall be good, except the buyer shall accept part of the goods so sold, and actually receive the same,—or give something in earnest to bind the bargain, or in part of payment,—or that some note or memorandum in writing of the said bargain be made and signed by the parties to be charged by such contract, or their agents thereunto lawfully authorised. Again, in England, the property in specific goods ready for delivery passes to the buyer on the making of the contract, and before delivery. In Scotland, a contract for the sale of goods (with the exception of ships) is effectual without writing; and may be proved by oral or other legal evidence. The property of goods sold does not pass to the buyer by the mere contract of sale, but remains with the seller, as in the Roman law, till the goods are delivered. *Statute of Frauds.* *Rule as to the passing of property.*

An important qualification of the Scottish doctrine of delivery, however, has been introduced by the Mercantile-Law Amendment Act, 19 & 20 Vict. c. 60, which enacts that, " Where goods have been sold, but the same have not been delivered to the purchaser, and have been allowed to remain in the custody of the seller, it shall not be competent for any creditor of such seller, after the date of such sale, to attach such goods as belonging to the seller by any diligence or process of law, including sequestration, to the effect of preventing the purchaser, or any one in his right, from enforcing delivery of the same ; and the right of the purchaser to demand delivery of such goods shall from and after the date of such sale be attachable by or transferable to the creditors of the purchaser."[1] Farther, the seller is now bound by the *Mercantile Law Amendment Act.*

[1] Sect. 1.

same Act to deliver the goods to a second or subsequent purchaser, on payment of the price or performance of the conditions of the original contract of sale, and is not entitled, in any question with a subsequent purchaser or others in his right, to retain the goods for any separate debt or obligation alleged to be due to such seller by the original purchaser.[1]

Warranty against defects. As to implied warranty in sales, the law of England is strongly opposed to it; and the general rule is stated to be that, "with regard to the soundness of the wares purchased, the vendor is not bound to answer, unless he expressly warrants them to be sound, or unless he knew them to be otherwise, and hath used any art to disguise them."[2] Another English writer, in treating of this point, observes:—"There is no implied warranty of quality in the sale of a chattel; but if goods are ordered of a tradesman for a particular purpose known to the vendor, there is a tacit engagement that the goods shall be fit for it, and correspond with the description."[3] On the other hand, the law of Scotland followed the Roman doctrine of implied warranty, till the matter was regulated by the Mercantile Law Amendment Act, which declares that, "Where goods shall, after the passing of this Act, be sold, the seller, if at the time of the sale he was without knowledge that the same were defective or of bad quality, shall not be held to have warranted their quality or sufficiency, but the goods, with all faults, shall be at the risk of the purchaser, unless the seller shall have given an express warranty of the quality or sufficiency of such goods, or unless the goods have been expressly sold for a specified and particular purpose, in which case the seller shall be considered, without such warranty, to warrant that the same are fit for such purpose."[4]

Stolen goods. In Scotland, no purchaser of stolen goods can acquire an absolute right to them against the true owner; but in England, a sale of stolen goods in open market gives the

---

[1] Sect. 2.

[2] Stephen's Com. on Laws of England, 4th ed., vol. ii. p. 75.

[3] Roscoe's Digest of the Law of Evidence, 10th ed., p. 332. Morley v. Attenborough, 3 Exch. 500.

[4] 19 & 20 Vict. c. 60, s. 5. See Young, 4th Dec. 1858, where this clause of the Act was held to apply to the sale of horses.

purchaser a good title, until the true owner has prosecuted the thief to conviction.[1]

Sect. 2.—Contract of Hiring.

This contract is of two kinds—the hiring of things and the hiring of work or service. The hiring of things is a contract by which one of the parties engages to give the use of a thing to the other for a limited time in consideration of a certain rent or hire. The hiring of work is a contract by which one of the parties engages to do something for another for a certain hire. In both cases the contract is perfected by consent, and bears a close affinity to sale.[2] *Nature of contract.*

1. *Hiring of Things.*—All sorts of things which are the subject of commerce, whether movable or immovable, may generally be let for hire. But things which are consumed in the use that is made of them, such as current money, coin, wine, and the like, though they may be sold, are not suitable for hiring. *Hiring of things.*

Leases of lands and houses are granted for a limited term agreed upon between the parties. Among the Romans the usual term for a lease of land was the *lustrum* of five years. If there was no stipulation to the contrary, the engagements formed by the contract passed to the representatives of both parties, and the lessee might sublet to another. *Leases of lands and houses.*

The principal obligations of the lessor are—1st, To put the lessee in possession of the subject; 2d, To deliver it in a proper state of repair, and to maintain it in such a condition that it may be fit for the purpose for which it is let; and, 3d, To guarantee the peaceable enjoyment to the lessee during the currency of the term agreed upon. The tenant of houses is called *inquilinus,* and the tenant of lands *colonus.*[3] *Obligations of lessor.*

There was this peculiarity in a lease of houses, that the lessee was bound to quit possession whenever the proprietor wanted the premises for his own occupation.[4] *Obligations of lessee.*

---

[1] 7 & 8 G. IV. c. 29, s. 57. Smith's Mer. Law, 6th ed., 486.
[2] L. 3. 25. D. 19. 2. C. 4. 65
and 70.
[3] Maynz, § 299.
[4] Ibid. § 300. C. 4. 65. 3.

P

As hiring only gave rise to a simple personal obligation, a purchaser of the subject let was not bound by the lease; he could eject the lessee, who could only claim indemnity from the lessor under the warranty. To obviate this result, it was usual to stipulate in a sale that the purchaser should be bound by the current leases.

Obligations of lessee. The lessee is bound to use the subject well, to put it to no other use than that for which it was let, to preserve it in good condition, and restore it at the end of the term. He is answerable for *culpa levis*, but not for loss occasioned by inevitable accidents.

The principal obligation of the lessee is to pay the rent or hire at the stipulated periods. The hire is generally fixed to be paid in current money, but when lands are let the rent may consist of a portion of the fruits or produce. The fruits of the ground are hypothecated to the proprietor for the rent of land, and there is a similar hypothec over the tenant's movables for the rent of houses. When two years' rents fall into arrear, the tenant may be ejected. The tenant of a farm is entitled to a remission of his rent if his whole crop is destroyed by an extraordinary and unforeseen accident, such as an inundation, or a hostile irruption in time of war; but if, during the remaining years of the lease, the loss so sustained is compensated by extraordinary fertility, the tenant is bound to pay the sum previously remitted.[1]

Tacit relocation. The contract of hiring usually terminated at the expiry of the stipulated term. If the tenant was allowed to continue in possession after the term, this was construed into a tacit renewal of the lease from year to year, or for such other period as might correspond with the nature of the subject let. All the ordinary conditions of the lease were held to be renewed in tacit relocation, but the obligation of a surety could not be extended in this manner. The contract also came to an end by the loss or destruction of the subject. And the lessee might be ejected before the lapse of the term, not only for non-payment of his rent, but also for damaging the premises or making a bad use of them in any way.

[1] Maynz, § 299, 300. D. 19. 2. 15. 2. Compare with French Civil Code, art. 1769, 1770.

Two rights, partaking in some degree of the nature of leases, but of a more permanent character, called Emphyteusis and Superficies, have already been noticed.

2. *Hiring of Work or Service.*—Most of the general principles which regulate the hiring of things apply to the hiring of work or service. To distinguish between hiring and sale, Justinian lays down this rule : If a workman furnish all the materials, as well as the work, for a certain price—as, for instance, if a silversmith should undertake to make a piece of plate and to supply the silver for a certain sum—this resolves into sale, not hiring ; but if silver be given to the artificer, and he is required to furnish the workmanship only, this is *locatio operis.*[1] When a builder contracts to erect a house on your ground and to furnish the materials, this also is location ; because the ground, which is the principal subject, belongs to you, and the building follows it as an accessory,—*ædificium solo cedit.*[2]

The person who undertakes to execute a piece of work must perform it in a proper manner and within the time agreed upon. He is bound to bestow upon it due care and skill ; and if, from negligence or ignorance, the work is defective or useless, he is liable in damages to his employer. No man should undertake a work which he is not fully qualified to perform. *Imperitia culpæ enumeratur.*

When a contractor undertakes a work *aversione*—that is, to be delivered as a whole after it is completed—the risk does not pass to the employer till it is finished and approved of. But when the work is to be performed by the piece, or by measurement as it advances, the risk of what is executed passes to the employer as soon as it is received and measured.[3]

As to the hiring of common labourers or servants, little need here be said. Their rights and obligations, and the kind and quantity of work to be required of them, involve many particulars, which, so far as not expressly fixed by contract, must be determined, in a great measure, by custom.

(margin note: Hiring of work or service.)

[1] I. 3. 25. 4.
[2] Pothier, Contrat du Louage,. part vii. c. i.
[3] D. 19. 2. 36. Florentinus.

Sect. 3.—Partnership.

I.—ROMAN LAW.

How part-
nership
constituted.   Partnership is a contract whereby two or more persons
agree to combine property or labour in a common stock for
the sake of sharing the gain.   There may be partnership in
one transaction as well as in a general business.   The contract is perfected by consent; and the capital contributed by
the partners may be equal or unequal, and may consist of
property or labour or both.   One of them may furnish money
and the other skill or labour alone.[1]

Rights of
partners.   If there be no express agreement on the matter, the shares
of profit and loss are divided among the partners equally, but
this is generally provided for by the contract.   One partner
may stipulate for two-thirds of the profit and to bear only
one-third of the loss, or even to participate in the profit and
to be entirely free from loss; and these stipulations will hold
good as between himself and the other partners, whatever
liability he may incur to strangers.   But an agreement that
one should take all the profit and the other bear all the loss,
which is called *societas leonina*, is invalid.   If profit has been
obtained in one branch of business and a loss has been
suffered in another, the whole transactions must be taken
into account in striking the balance of profit or loss.[2]

Liabilities
of partners.   A partner is bound to exercise the same care and diligence
in the business of the company as he does in his own private
affairs, and he is answerable to his copartners for loss arising
from negligence.   He is not liable for loss by fire or robbery
or other inevitable accidents.   The acts of one partner are
not binding on the rest, if he act without authority or beyond
the scope of the partnership; but where there is no such excess of power, his acts on account of the partnership bind the
whole partners for profit or loss.   A contract made by a
partner as an individual, and on his own account, cannot
affect the partnership.   So, if a partner admit another person

[1] I. 3. 25.   D. 17. 2.   C. 4. 37.   [2] I. 3. 25. 1, 2.

to participate in his share of the profits, this stranger does not become a member of the company in any question with the other partners, *nam socii mei socius, socius meus non est.*[1]

If one of the partners has advanced money, or entered into some engagement on account of the partnership, and for which it is bound to indemnify him, each of the partners must contribute to the indemnity in proportion to his share in the concern; and if any of them become insolvent, the solvent shareholders must make up the deficiency according to their respective interests.[2]

Partnership is dissolved by the expiry of the time for which Dissolution. the contract was made; by mutual consent of the parties; by one of the partners retiring, especially when no term is fixed, provided this is not done fraudulently or in a way to injure the others; and, lastly, by the death or bankruptcy of any of the partners.[3]

II.—FRENCH LAW.

The French law distinguishes three principal kinds of com- Different kinds of mercial partnerships. 1st, Partnership *en nom collectif* is partnership that which is carried on by two or more persons under a in France. social firm, each partner being liable for the whole engagements of the company. 2d, Partnership *en commandité* is that which is contracted between one or more partners whose responsibility is unlimited, and one or more persons who are merely money-lenders, and are not liable for any loss beyond the funds lent to the company. Only the proper responsible partners can take part in the conduct of the business. 3d, Anonymous partnership (*société anonyme*) is that which has no social firm, but is merely distinguished by the nature of the enterprise; it can only be established by the authority of Government; the management is conducted by the agents of the company; the shares are transferable, and the holders' liability for loss is limited to the amount of their capital in the concern. Besides these three kinds of partnership, the French law recognises joint adventures between two or more

[1] D. 17. 2. 20.　　　[2] D. 17. 2. 67.　　　[3] I. 3. 25. 4-8.

persons for participating in profit and loss in particular enterprises or transactions, which are regulated by agreement.[1]*

III.—ENGLISH AND SCOTTISH LAW.

In England company not a separate person.

By the law of England, a private partnership of two or more persons is not recognised separately from the partners of which it is composed. In an action at common law, by or against a private partnership, all the partners must concur individually, either as plaintiffs or defendants. But joint-stock companies are usually empowered to sue and be sued by their public officer, who may be appointed to represent the company as distinct from the individuals composing it.[2] In equity, if the partners be numerous, a few may, in certain cases, be permitted to sue and be sued on behalf of the general body, or on behalf of themselves and other partners having a common interest with them ; but all partners having conflicting interests must be represented.[3]

In Scotland rule different.

In Scotland, a private partnership is deemed a separate person in law, capable of entering into contracts, of holding personal property, and carrying on legal proceedings by its distinctive name or firm. When the company firm includes the name of one or more partners, as John Bruce & Co., the partnership may sue or be sued by that appellation. But if

[1] Code de Commerce, art. 18-50.

* Besides the partnerships stated in the text, another kind was authorised by a law of 23d May 1863, promulgated on the 29th, called *Société à Responsabilité Limitée*. This partnership may be formed without the authority of Government. The liability of the partners is limited to their capital in the concern, and they cannot be less than seven in number. The capital cannot exceed 20,000,000 francs. The managers must be proprietors equally of a twentieth part of the capital, and that capital forms a guarantee fund for the right administration of the managers. So long as they are managers their shares are inalienable, and the share certificates are stamped with a declaration that the shares are inalienable, and are deposited in the safe of the company. Within a fortnight after the company is constituted the managers must deposit in the Record Office of the Tribunal of Commerce a copy of the deed of constitution, and a list of the partners, and other details, which may be examined by the public.

[2] Lindley's Law of Partnership, p. 720.

[3] Lindley's Law of Partnership, p. 776.

 ·m be descriptive merely, as the Shotts Iron Company, it is necessary that three at least of the partners, described as suing or being sued on behalf of themselves and all the other partners, should be joined along with the descriptive firm. To these opposite principles in the laws of the two countries many important practical differences may be traced.

When a partnership becomes bankrupt in England, the joint property of the partnership, as well as the separate pro- _{Bank-ruptcy.} perty of each partner, vests in the assignees; but the separate creditors of each partner must be first paid in full before his separate property can be applied to the debts of the partnership. "For the rule as to the application of joint and separate property to the payment of creditors, is, that the joint estate should be applied to the joint debts; the separate to the separate debts; and the surplus of each reciprocally to the creditors remaining on the other."[1]

In Scotland, the partnership estate may be sequestrated and applied in payment of the creditors of the company; and they have a right to be ranked as creditors for the balance unpaid on the private estates of the partners.[2]

As to joint-stock companies with transferable shares, and limited liability companies, they are now chiefly regulated _{Joint-stock companies.} by Acts of Parliament, and particularly by the 25 & 26 Vict. c. 89,* which applies both to England and Scotland. Under that statute, which takes effect from 2d November 1862, any seven or more persons associated for any lawful purpose may, by subscribing their names to a memorandum of association, and otherwise complying with the requisitions of the Act, form an incorporated company, with or without limited liability.[3] The liability of the members of a company formed under the Act may be unlimited, or may, according to the memorandum of association, be limited either to the amount, if any, unpaid on the shares respectively held by them, or to such amount as the members may respectively undertake by the memorandum of association to contribute to the

---

[1] Smith's Mer. Law, 6th ed., 644.   * Amended by 30 & 31 Vict. c. 131.
[2] Bell's Com., 660.   [3] 25 & 26 Vict. c. 89, s. 6.

assets of the company in the event of its being wound up.[1]

There are also numerous railway companies, and other public enterprises, which are governed by special statutes, and certain general acts incorporated therewith.

Sect. 4.—Mandate.

Nature of mandate.

Mandate is a contract by which one person confides the management of some business to another, who undertakes to perform it without pay or reward. He who gives the commission is called the mandant, and he who undertakes it is called the mandatary. It is essential to this contract that it should be gratuitous, because, if any remuneration is given to the agent for his services, the contract is not mandate, but *locatio operarum*.[2]

Under the emperors, when honoraries to advocates were authorised, they could not pursue for payment by the *actio mandati;* the magistrate awarded their fees *extra ordinem*.[3] Brokers, who intervened in the purchase and sale of goods and similar operations (called by the Romans *proxenetæ*) were allowed a premium for their trouble.[4]

How constituted.

A mandate may be constituted verbally, or by letter, and it may even arise *rebus ipsis et factis*, where one permits another to transact his business for him. The mandatary is not bound to undertake the business; but when he does so, he must perform it in terms of the orders given, otherwise he will be liable for the consequences of his neglect. He is answerable, not only for fraud and gross negligence, but also for slight faults.

Powers of mandatary.

A mandate may be general or special. When a mandatary is intrusted with general powers, he must exercise a sound discretion within the scope of his employment. If his orders are special and limited, he must strictly follow them.

The agent who is employed to buy an estate may better the condition of the person who employs him, but cannot

---

[1] 25 & 26 Vict. c 89, s. 7-10. [3] D. 50. 13. 1. 10.
[2] I. 3. 27. D. 17. 1. C. 4. 35. [4] D. 50. 14. 3. Maynz, § 211.

make it worse. Thus he may buy for a lower price than what he was empowered to give; but if he buy at a dearer rate, he cannot recover the excess from his principal.[1]

While the mandatary must act strictly according to the orders given to him, the mandant, on the other hand, is bound to ratify what was done by the agent within the scope of his instructions, and to reimburse the agent for all advances and expenses properly incurred in executing the commission. The rights and obligations arising out of the contract were enforced by the *actio mandati directa*, when the mandatary was called upon to account, and by the *actio contraria*, when indemnity was claimed from the mandant.

Every mandate is revocable at pleasure; it may be renounced by the mandatary while things are entire; and it is put an end to by the death of either party; but if the mandatary, while ignorant of the death of his principal, does any act *in bona fide* within his authority, the representatives of the principal are bound by what is so done. *How mandate terminated.*

In modern times, the law of principal and agent is of constant application in the commercial world, and the rights and duties which belong to that relation are very important. But in mercantile transactions agents are generally remunerated for their services. For this reason their responsibility for diligence in the execution of the business intrusted to them, is more rigorously enforced than in the case of a gratuitous mandate.[2] Still the law of England distinctly recognises the principle that an unremunerated agent, standing in the same position as a mandatary in the Roman law, is liable for ordinary diligence adequate to the performance of the duty he has undertaken, as exemplified in the well-known case of Coggs *v.* Bernard.[3] There the mandatary undertook, without pay, to carry brandy from one place to another, and managed the carriage so negligently that one of the pipes was staved. He pleaded that he had not undertaken to carry it safely; but he was held responsible, on the ground that this was implied, so far as regards ordinary care.[4] *Modern law.*

[1] I. 3. 27. 8.
[2] Code Civil, art. 1992.
[3] 2 Lord Raymond, 909.
[4] Jones on Bailments, p. 58.

CHAPTER V.

I.—ROMAN LAW.

AMONG the *pacta legitima* or special conventions which might be enforced by action by the new Roman law, donation was included. Originally it was subjected to many restrictions which afterwards disappeared.[1]

Nature of donation.

Donation consists in one person giving something from generosity alone, and without any antecedent obligation, to another who accepts it. The subject of the gift may be movable or immovable property, or anything having a pecuniary value, such as the release of a debt. To constitute donation there must be an *animus donandi* on the part of the donor, and acceptance or willingness to accept on the part of the donee. But in pure and simple donations, which confer a benefit without imposing any burden on the donee, acceptance may generally be presumed without any formal act.

By the ancient Roman law a *pactum donationis* gave no right to the donee to sue for performance or delivery of the subject. If the convention was clothed with the form of stipulation it might be enforced; but if not, the donee acquired no right to the thing till the property was transferred to him by actual delivery.

After the time of Antoninus Pius this rigour was relaxed when the donation was between ascendants and descendants, for then any clear declaration on the part of the donor was sufficient to give effect to the gift. Justinian went much farther; he allowed the donee to bring an action for delivery when the donor declared his intention to give a thing, either orally or in writing, even though the form of stipulation had not been observed. The donor, however, continued proprietor till delivery.

Cincian law.

The Cincian law *de donis*, passed in the year of Rome 550, prohibited all donations beyond a certain maximum, the amount of which is unknown. It also prescribed the form

[1] I. 2. 7. D. 39. 5 and 6. C. 7. 54. N. 162.

in which donations were to be made by mancipation and tradition. But certain persons nearly connected by the ties of blood were exempted from these restrictions. One of the provisions of the same law prohibited advocates from accepting presents for pleading causes; and this is frequently referred to by Roman writers. In later times the limitations imposed by the Cincian law entirely disappeared.[1]

Towards the close of the republic, governors of provinces were not allowed to receive presents from persons under their jurisdiction. One prohibitory law on this subject contains an exception of eatables and drinkables for a few days' consumption.[2]

Following a principle which had been adopted in some imperial constitutions from the time of Constantine, Justinian ordained that when the gift exceeded the value of 500 solidi, a formal act stating the particulars of the donation should be drawn up and inscribed in a public register. To this rule there were some exceptions, such as gifts to the emperor, the distribution of prize-money by the military tribunes, sums given for the ransom of captives, and donations *mortis causa*. Donations not recorded in terms of this law were not wholly null, but only in so far as they exceeded the prescribed sum.[3] *Registered donations.*

By the Roman law donations, though perfected by delivery, were revocable by the donor for ingratitude in the donee, as for instance by his threatening the life or offering some violence to the person of the donor.[4] When the donor is not the true owner of the subject, it may be evicted from the donee; but in that case no recourse lies against the donor, who is only liable to warrant the gift against his own future deeds. *Revocable for ingratitude.*

As to donations between husband and wife, we refer to what we have already said in treating of the law of marriage.

Besides donations *inter vivos*, which are intended to take effect during the life of the donor, there is another kind of donation called *donatio mortis causa*, which under Justinian's law partakes almost wholly of the character of a legacy.[5] Such a gift, being made in contemplation of death, is not *Donatio mortis causa.*

---

[1] Fragmenta Vaticana, De donationibus ad legem Cinciam, § 266-316. Huschke, Jurisprudentiæ Antejustinianæ quæ supersunt, p. 674 *et seq.* Ortolan, Institutes, vol. ii. p. 387.

[2] D. I. 18. 18. Modestinus.
[3] Ortolan, Institutes, vol. ii. p. 390.
[4] C. 7. 56. 10.
[5] I. 2. 7. 1.

perfected till death ; it falls by the predecease of the donee,
and it is revocable by the donor at any time during his life,
whether delivery has taken place or not. By a constitution
of Justinian a donation *mortis causa*, whether declared orally
or in writing, required to be made in presence of five witnesses ; and, as already explained, inscription in a public
register was not necessary.[1]

II.—FRENCH LAW.

French
rules as to
donations.

Some peculiarities of the French law regarding donations
are sufficiently interesting to deserve notice here. 1. Every
gift *inter vivos* must be in the form of a contract executed
before notaries, so as to preserve evidence of the transaction.[2]
2. A person who has no descendants or ascendants among his
relations may dispose of his whole estate by gifts *inter vivos*
or by testamentary bequests ; but if he has descendants or
ascendants, he can only so dispose of a certain portion of his
property fixed by law, and varying, according to the state of
his family, from three-fourths to one-fourth of his fortune.[3]
3. Doctors of medicine, surgeons, and apothecaries who attend
a person during the malady of which he dies, though entitled
to proper remuneration for their services, can take no benefit
from any gifts or bequests made by the patient in their
favour during the course of that illness.[4] *

[1] C. 8. 57. 4.
[2] Code Civil, art. 931.
[3] Ibid. art. 913 *et seq.*
[4] Ibid. art. 909.

* This salutary and wholesome rule
is not law either in England or Scotland. Every case in these countries
is determined upon its own special
circumstances, generally giving rise
to long trials as to whether there
was *undue influence* in fact. The
French courts have rigidly enforced
the rule. A legacy to the doctor who
attended the testator during his last
illness has been declared invalid
even though the doctor were a rela-
tive. The nullity of the legacy will
be declared, though the effect would
be to benefit a universal legatee, and
not the relations of the testator.
The presumption of captation is so
absolute and inflexible, that no proof
will be allowed to show that the testator had such superiority of mind
that he would not be the victim of
it. In like manner it is irrelevant
to plead that the legacy was given
not on account of services rendered
or cares bestowed, but by reason of
friendship and relationship. Even
legacies to conjunct persons, such as
the colleague of the minister of religion, or the partner of the doctor of
the testator, are void.—*Les Codes
Annotées de Sirey*, art. 909.

CHAPTER VI.

OF OBLIGATIONS ARISING FROM QUASI CONTRACTS.

CERTAIN engagements are formed by implication from circumstances without express agreement, either on the part of the person obliged or of the person to whom he becomes bound.

Quasi contracts are constituted, without convention, by one of the parties doing something that by its nature either binds him to the other party or the other party to him.

Under quasi contracts we shall take as examples *Negotiorum gestio, Indebiti solutio,* and *Jactus mercium navis levandæ causa,* though this enumeration cannot be considered as complete.

Sect. 1.—*Negotiorum Gestio.*

When a person spontaneously assumed the management of the affairs of another in his absence and without any mandate, this was called *negotiorum gestio.* In such a case the reciprocal obligations of the parties are very similar to those which arise under the contract of mandate. Negotiorum gestio defined.

The *negotiorum gestor* is bound to perform any act which he has begun, as if he held a proper mandate, unless the principal shall relieve him. Though his responsibility may vary according to circumstances, yet, as his interference is spontaneous, he is generally obliged to use exact diligence ; nor, according to Justinian, will it suffice to show that he has bestowed the same care which he usually does in his own affairs, if another more diligent person could have transacted Obligations of the agent.

the business more profitably for the principal.[1] The agent must strictly account for his management.

Obligations of the principal. On the other hand, the principal is bound to indemnify the *negotiorum gestor* for all advances and expenses properly incurred on his account, and to relieve the agent from engagements entered into by him in the course of his administration.

Sect. 2.—*Indebiti Solutio.*

Indebiti solutio defined. Where one, through error, makes payment of what is not due, he may in certain circumstances recover it back by an action, which in the Roman law was called *condictio indebiti.* Thus, if a legacy is paid under a testament supposed to be genuine, but which afterwards turns out to be forged, the person who has received the money may be compelled to restore it.

Conditions required for restitution. As the obligation to restore is founded solely on equity, this action does not lie, if the sum paid was due in equity or by a natural obligation; because in such a case there is nothing against good conscience in retaining the money. Neither can restitution be claimed, if he who made the payment knew at the time that no debt was due, it being presumed when this happens that donation was intended.[2] Some writers mention as another exception to the rule, the case where money is paid in consequence of a transaction or compromise. But when a sum is so paid, "the transaction itself creates a debt, though no prior debt had existed."[3]

Effect of error in law. Whether money paid under an error in law can be recovered back by a *condictio indebiti* is a question which has given rise to much controversy. A constitution in the Code seems to deny restitution where the money has been paid under an error in law,—"Quum quis jus ignorans indebitam pecuniam solverit, cessat repetitio. Per ignorantiam enim facti tantum repetitionem indebiti soluti competere tibi notum est."[4]

Controversy among civilians. Founding on this constitution and other texts, many eminent jurists, such as Cujas, Donellus, and Voet, maintain that no

---

[1] I. 3. 28. 1.   [3] Ersk. Pr. 3. 3. 17.
[2] D. 50. 17. 53.   [4] C. 1. 18. 10.

action lies to recover money paid by mistake in point of law.[1]
Other authors, among whom we find Vinnius, Ulric Huber,
D'Aguesseau, and Mühlenbruch, are of opinion that restitution may be obtained in all cases of error, whether it be an
error of fact or an error of law. They contend that as *condictio indebiti* is founded on equity, it can only be excluded
by an equitable plea; that in the whole title of the Digest
which treats of *condictio indebiti*,[2] though very long, restitution is never confined solely to an error in fact, or denied to
an error in law, but is constantly ascribed to error simply,
whether the payment was made on account of what was
never due, or of some claim which could not be enforced by
reason of a perpetual exception; and that some passages in
the Code in which restitution appears to be denied to an
error in law, occur in rescripts which could only be intended
to apply to cases where a natural obligation existed, so as to
afford a good ground of retention in equity.[3]

In a learned essay, which forms an appendix to the third
volume of his 'System,' Savigny has expressed a decided
opinion that money which has been paid by mistake in matter
of law, cannot be recovered by the *condictio indebiti*, unless
it can be proved that such ignorance is excusable, and not
the result of gross negligence.[4] A minor was entitled to
restitution against the consequences of an error in law, if he
sought relief within the *quadriennium utile*, but not afterwards.[5] In some exceptional cases restitution could be
claimed of what was not due, even when payment was made
with full knowledge—as, for instance, in gambling debts and
donations between husband and wife.[6]

Of this famous controversy among the civilians as to the
effect of an error in law, the framers of the French Code were
well aware; and they sanctioned by their authority the doc-

Modern
French law.

---

[1] Voet ad Pand. lib. 12, t. 6, § 7.
Pothier, Traité de Condict. Indeb.
part 3, sect. 2, art. 3.

[2] D. 12. 6.

[3] Vinnius, Com., lib. 3, t. 28. Quest.
Sel., lib. 1, c. 47. Ulric Huber, Inst.,
lib. 3, t. 28. Among other texts

Mühlenbruch founds on D. 50. 17.
206, and D. 36. 4. 1. See also D. 22.
6. 8.

[4] Savigny, System, vol. iii. app. 8,
s. 35.

[5] C. 2. 33. 2.

[6] Maynz, § 359.

trine of Vinnius and his followers by adopting this general rule :—" When a person who, by error, believed himself to be the debtor, has discharged a debt, he has a right of repetition against the creditor. This right, however, ceases, if the creditor, in consequence of the payment, has destroyed his voucher of debt, recourse in that case being saved to the person who has paid against the true debtor."[1] Under this rule of the French Code restitution may be demanded without distinction, whether the payment was made under an error in fact or an error in law.[2] The Austrian Code adopts the same doctrine.[3] The Prussian Code, on the other hand, allows restitution for an error in fact, but not for an error in law.[4]

English and Scottish law.

In England the law appears to be settled upon the same footing, as explained by Lord Chancellor Brougham in the case of Wilson v. Sinclair. " When a person pays money under mistake, he has no right to recover that money, unless where it was a mistake in point of fact. If he pays by mistake in point of law, there was at one time a little doubt in Westminster Hall; but it is now settled that he has no right to recover it back again."

In Scotland an opinion prevailed, and seems to have received effect in several instances, that restitution could be demanded, even where the payment was made under an error in law. But this doctrine has been discredited, if not overturned, by the opinions delivered in the House of Lords in some recent cases.[5]*

Sect. 3.—Lex Rhodia de Jactu.

Rules of contribution for loss.

To those who suffer by loss of goods voluntarily thrown overboard at sea for the common benefit, recompense is due

[1] Code Civil, art. 1377.
[2] Pailliet, Manuel de Droit Français, 8th ed., p. 358.
[3] Savigny, vol. iii. app. p. 444.
[4] Ibid.
[5] Wilson v. Sinclair, 7th December 1830, 4 Wilson & Shaw's App. Cases, 398. Dixon v. Monkland Canal Co., 17th September 1831, 5

Wil. & Sh. App. Cases, 445.
* In the case of Dickson v. Halbert, 17th Feb. 1854 (16 Dunlop, 586), three judges of the First Division of the Court of Session held that those opinions delivered in the House of Lords did not exclude restitution on the ground of error in law in some cases.

quasi ex contractu. By the *lex Rhodia de jactu,* which was
adopted by the Romans and other commercial nations, the
owners of the ship and goods saved are obliged to contribute
for the relief of those whose property has been sacrificed, so
that all concerned may bear their just shares of the loss.[1] To
found this claim for contribution it is essential—1st, That
some part of the cargo or of the ship, such as the masts or
rigging, should have been voluntarily sacrificed for the common safety; and, 2d, that the sacrifice so made shall have
been effectual in preserving the property of those concerned.
If, therefore, notwithstanding the jettison, the ship perish in
the storm, no contribution will be due. Among the parties
bound to contribute to repair the loss, each is only liable
rateably for his own share, and not for what is due by the
rest.[2]

[1] D. 14. 2.　　　　　　　　[2] D. 14. 2. 2. 6.

Q

CHAPTER VII

OF OBLIGATIONS EX DELICTO AND QUASI EX DELICTO.

OBLIGATIONS arising in consequence of an unlawful act are divided into obligations *ex delicto* and *quasi ex delicto*. Delicts are offences wilfully committed in violation of law. A quasi delict arises in certain cases when the law holds a man personally responsible for injurious acts committed without negligence or intention on his part.[1]

It is a general rule of law, that every wrongful act which causes damage to another, obliges the wrongdoer to make reparation. This responsibility extends to damage arising not only from positive acts, but also from negligence or imprudence. Persons having authority, by permitting or giving orders for an unlawful act, are bound to give satisfaction for the injury thereby occasioned. So also, the owners are responsible for damage done, through their fault, by animals belonging to them. In criminal law, every offender must bear his own punishment; but, as regards civil reparation, when several persons have committed an offence, they are liable, *singuli in solidum*, for the whole damage, without the benefit of division.[2]

Rights from delicts.

The rights arising from private delicts are treated in Justinian's Institutes under four heads: *Furtum, Rapina, Damnum, et Injuria.*

Theft and robbery.

Furtum, or theft, is the felonious taking and carrying away of the property of another for the sake of gain. To constitute theft, the taking must appear to be with intent to steal. By the civil law, a man might steal what was his own,

---

[1] Austin's Jurisprudence, vol. iii. p. 134.   [2] D. 4. 2. 14. 15.   C. 4. 8. 1.

by taking it from the lawful possession of another, as in the case of a pledge in the hands of a creditor.

Theft is divided into manifest and not manifest. When the thief has been taken in the·act, or near the spot, with the stolen property in his possession, this is *furtum manifestum*; and in such a case he is liable to restore fourfold the value of the article stolen to the owner. When the thief was not so taken, the act is called *nec manifestum*, and the penalty is limited to double the value. All the ancient distinctions of theft, as *conceptum, oblatum, prohibitum*, and *non exhibitum*, were abrogated by the law as it stood in the · time of Justinian.

Rapina or robbery is theft of movables, committed with violence against the person. The penalty is fourfold restitution, which includes the thing itself, if the action is brought within the year; but after the lapse of a year, simple restitution or indemnity could alone be claimed.

Damnum injuria datum is the damage sustained from the wrongful destruction of, or injury to, property. It has reference to patrimonial loss, for which redress was given by the Aquilian law. This law consists of three chapters, the first of which provided that if any person wrongfully killed the slave or cattle of another, the offender should be bound to pay the highest price for which the slave or animal could have been sold during the previous year. The second chapter of this law was in disuse in Justinian's time, but an explanation of it will be found in the Institutes of Gaius.[1] The third chapter comprehended all damage done to every kind of property, animate or inanimate, except the killing of slaves and cattle. *Damnum et injuria.*

Under the Aquilian law, every man was responsible for damage done by his fault or negligence, as well as for damage done by fraud or design. But if the damage arose in the exercise of a right, as killing a slave in self-defence, or from some inevitable accident, without blame, no claim for reparation could be maintained.

If any one exercised a profession or trade without being properly qualified to do so, he was liable for all damage his

[1] Gai. 3. 215.

want of skill or knowledge might occasion. Thus a medical man was held answerable, under the Aquilian law, if he occasioned the death of a slave by an unskilful incision, or an improper administration of medicine.

Finally, among delicts was reckoned what the Romans called *injuria*. Generally this means *omne quod non jure fit;* but when used in a specific sense, it had reference to an injury done to the *person*, or *reputation*, as in the case of assault or slander.

Injuries were divided into real and verbal. The Prætorian law softened the rigour of the Twelve Tables, and allowed the injured person to recover such pecuniary compensation as the nature of the case required. In an action for libel or slander, the truth of the allegation might be pleaded in justification, at least in those cases where the public was interested in the exposure.[1] It was optional for the injured person to proceed against the offender either civilly or criminally. Not only the perpetrator of the injury, but he who counselled it, might be prosecuted. In all cases it was necessary to show that the act had been done maliciously; and if it was accompanied by any peculiar circumstances of aggravation, the damages awarded were proportionally increased.[2]

A quasi delict has been defined, "An incident by which damage is done to the obligee (though without the negligence or intention of the obliger), and for which damage the obliger is bound to make satisfaction."[3]

Quasi delicto. If anything was thrown from the windows of a house near a public thoroughfare, so as to injure any one by its fall, the inhabitant or occupier was, by the Roman law, bound to repair the damage, though it might be done without his knowledge by his family or servants, or even by a stranger.[4] This affords an illustration of liability arising *quasi ex delicto*.

Damage done by slaves and animals. In like manner, when damage was done to any person by a slave or an animal, the owner might in certain circumstances be liable for the loss, though the mischief was done without his knowledge and against his will; but in such a

[1] D. 47. 10. 18. pr. C. 9. 35. 5.   p. 134. See Cleghorn, 27th Feb.
[2] I. 4. 4. 9.   1856, 18 D. 664.
[3] Austin's Jurisprudence, vol. iii.   [4] I. 4. 5. 1.

case, if no fault was directly imputable to the owner, he was entitled to free himself from all responsibility by abandoning the offending slave or animal to the person injured, which was called *noxæ dare*.[1] Though these noxal actions are not classed by Justinian under the title of obligations *quasi ex delicto*, yet, in principle, they evidently fall within that category.[2]

All animals *feræ naturæ*, such as lions, tigers, bears, and the like, must be kept in a secure place to prevent them from doing mischief, but the same vigilance is not required in the case of animals *mansuetæ naturæ*, the presumption being, that no harm will arise in leaving them at large, unless they are known to be vicious or dangerous. So where a foxhound destroyed eighteen sheep, belonging to a farmer, it was decided by the House of Lords in an appeal from Scotland, that the owner of the dog was not liable for the loss, there being no evidence necessarily showing either knowledge of the vicious propensities of the dog or want of due care in keeping him; and it was observed that, both according to the English and the Scotch law, " the *culpa* or negligence of the owner is the foundation on which the right of action against him rests."[3] This decision, however, was modified by the Act 26 & 27 Vict. c. 100, applicable to Scotland, which declares that " in any action brought against the owner of a dog for damages in consequence of injury done by such dog to any sheep or cattle, it shall not be necessary for the pursuer to prove a previous propensity in such dog to injure sheep or cattle." " The occupier of any house or place or premises in which any dog which has injured any sheep or cattle has been usually kept or permitted to live or remain at the time of such injury, shall be liable as the owner of such dog, unless the said occupier can prove that he was not the owner of such dog at the time the injury complained of was committed, and that such dog was kept or permitted to live or remain in the said house or place or premises without his sanction or knowledge."

[1] I. 4. t. 8 and 9.
[2] Marezoll, § 150.
[3] Fleeming *v.* Orr, 1855, 2 Macq., pp. 14 and 23. See also May *v.* Burdett, June 1846, 2 B. 101.

CHAPTER VIII.

ON THE TRANSFER OF OBLIGATIONS.

BY the Roman law the right, as well as the engagement resulting from an obligation, passed to the heirs of the creditor and debtor respectively, on the principle of representation; but, by a subtlety of the law, the right of the creditor was considered to be inherent in his person, so that it could not be directly transferred by him to a third person without the debtor's consent. Thus, the creditor who wished to make over the profit of an obligation to another, could only do so by giving him a mandate to raise an action for the claim, and retain what was recovered for his own benefit. This was called *mandare* or *cedere actionem.* The mandatory, after having obtained execution on the judgment, applied the amount for his own benefit, and was therefore called *procurator in rem suam.* In this way claims arising under obligations might be transferred to a third person in virtue of sale, exchange, donation, or any other title. He who made over the obligation to another was called *cedens;* and he who received it was called *cessionarius* or *procurator in rem suam.*

Form of transfer.

The effects of the transfer are such as naturally arise from the transaction :—

Effects of transfer.

1. The claim of the cedent is transferred to the assignee with all accessory rights and privileges thereto belonging.

2. The assignee is liable to all exceptions which would have been competent to the debtor against the cedent, and also to all exceptions personal to the assignee himself, because he is *procurator in rem suam.*

3. The cedent generally guarantees the existence of the debt assigned, but not the solvency of the debtor.

To prevent speculators from purchasing debts at low Anastasian prices, and exposing debtors to vexatious prosecutions, the law. Emperor Anastasius ordained that the assignee should not be entitled to exact from the debtor more than he himself had paid to acquire the debt, with interest.[1] This rule was adopted and confirmed by a constitution of Justinian.[2] The Anastasian law applied only to assignments that were onerous, not gratuitous ; but if an attempt was made to disguise a transaction which was onerous in whole or in part, by representing it as gratuitous, the debtor was entitled to plead the benefit of the law. It was limited to obligations for payment of money or delivery of fungibles—that is, articles which consist in quantity, and are regulated by number, weight, or measure, as corn, money, wine. Where the subject of the obligation is a thing of a given class, the thing is said to be fungible—that is, the delivery of any object which answers to the generic description will satisfy the obligation, —*in genere suo functionem recipiunt.* A thing to be delivered *in specie* is not a fungible. A thing merely determined by the class to which it belongs is styled a *genus*, as a bushel of corn, a pound of gold, and so on.[3]

---

[1] C. 4. 35. 22.   Anastasius.

[2] C. 4. 35. 23.   Justinian.

[3] Mackeldey, § 369-374.   Maynz, § 272-4.   In the Roman law fungible was taken to mean *res quæ pondere, numero et mensura constant;* and, though the term is said to be unknown in England, it is adopted in the same sense by French and Scottish lawyers. 2 Denizart, 449. 1 Bell's Com., note 255.

CHAPTER IX.

OBLIGATIONS are extinguished by actual fulfilment of the engagement, as by payment or performance; by virtual fulfilment, as by compensation, novation, confusion; by acceptilation or discharge; and by prescription arising from the lapse of time, which is considered under a separate head.

Sect. 1.—Payment or Prestation.

This is the most ordinary mode of extinguishing an obligation. The term *solutio* imports every satisfaction of an engagement, whatever its nature may be.[1] The creditor is not bound to accept of payment by instalments, or of anything short of proper payment at the time and place agreed upon.

Payment
made by
any one. It is not material by whom the payment is made, whether by the debtor himself or by another for him; for a debtor becomes free from his debt when another has paid it, either with or without his knowledge, or even against his will.[2] But this doctrine does not apply so absolutely to obligations *ad factum præstandum*. In some cases of that description where skill and ability are relied on, the creditor has an interest to insist that the contract shall be performed by the person specified, and may therefore object to accept performance from any other.[3] In order to be effectual, the payment

[1] D. 50. 16. 176.
[2] I. 3. 30. pr.
[3] D. 46. 3. 31. Code Civil, 1237.

must be made to the true creditor, or to some one duly authorised by him to receive it.

Where several debts are due, the debtor in making the Indefinite
payment may appropriate it to any one he pleases. If no payments.
appropriation was made by the debtor, the creditor, by the
Roman law, was bound to apply it as the debtor himself
would have done, and, consequently, to that debt which bore
hardest upon him.[1] A different rule is followed both in
England and Scotland, the creditor being generally entitled
to apply such indefinite payment in the manner most favourable to himself—as, for instance, to the debt least secured—
unless there be some other debt, which, if left unsatisfied,
would expose the debtor to a rigorous forfeiture.[2] If principal and interest be due, the payment should be imputed first
to the interest, and the surplus, if any, is applied to principal.[3]

When performance has become impossible without any Perform-
fault of the debtor—as, for instance, where the engagement ance impossible.
relates to a specific subject which has perished by unavoidable accident—the obligation is extinguished. But if the
impossibility to fulfil the engagement has been caused by
the fault of the debtor, he will be liable in damages to the
creditor.

When the debtor failed to pay, the creditors, after obtaining judgment, were entitled to proceed with execution both
against his person and his property in the manner afterwards
explained.

Sect. 2.—Compensation.

Compensation is the reciprocal extinction of debts between Nature of
two persons, each of whom is indebted to the other,—Com- compensation.
pensatio est debiti et crediti inter se contributio.[4] If the debts
to be compensated are unequal, the lesser obligation is extinguished and the greater is diminished so far as the concourse goes.

The general requisites of compensation are these :—1st,

---

[1] D. 46. 3. 1.
[2] Roscoe's Digest of the Law of
Evidence, p. 470. Ersk. 3. 4. 2.

[3] C. 8. 43. 1. Code Civil, art.
1253-6.
[4] D. 16. 2. 1. Modestinus.

General requisites.

The two debts, whatever their nature may be, must be exigible, so that compensation cannot be pleaded on a claim which is prescribed.[1] By the Roman law, however, a natural debt might be pleaded as a set-off against a civil debt.[2] 2d, The debts must be of the same nature; so an obligation to deliver grain or goods cannot be set off against a pecuniary obligation. 3d, Both debts must be due and payable, so that compensation is not allowed between a debt presently exigible and one that is future or contingent. 4th, Compensation is not admitted unless the debt founded on be liquid; and a debt is liquid when it is clearly ascertained to be due. So a contested debt is not liquid; but if it can be summarily established without much discussion, it may found compensation, according to the rule, *Quod statim liquidari potest pro jam liquido habetur.*[3]

The rule that one can plead compensation only upon a debt due to himself, is subject to limitations. Thus an heir may found on a debt due to his ancestor as his own. In like manner a surety may set off against the demand of the creditor a debt due by the latter to the principal debtor; but the principal debtor cannot set off a debt due by the creditor to the surety.[4]

When excluded.

There are certain debts against which compensation cannot be pleaded. Thus it is never admitted against a demand for restitution of a thing of which the owner has been unjustly despoiled, according to the well-known rule, *Spoliatus ante omnia restituendus.* In like manner a depositary cannot plead compensation upon any extrinsic debt against a claim for restitution of the deposit.[?]

In order to receive effect, compensation must be pleaded by the debtor against the plaintiff's demand. But when the plea is sustained it operates retrospectively, and stops the currency of interest on both sides from the period when the two debts co-existed.[5]

---

[1] D. 16. 2. 14. "Quæcumque per exceptionem perimi possunt, in compensationem non veniunt."

[2] D. 16. 2. 6. "Etiam quod natura debetur venit in compensationem."

[3] Maynz, § 372. Pothier, Traité des Obligations, part 3, c. 4.

[4] D. 16. 2. 5.

[5] Maynz, § 373.

Sect. 3.—Novation.

Novation operates in two ways : 1st, When the debtor Nature of
novation. grants a new obligation to the creditor in lieu of an old one which is extinguished ; and, 2d, When a new debtor is substituted for an old one who is discharged by the creditor. This last method of extinction is called delegation, and the new debtor thus substituted was in the Roman law styled *expromissor*.[1]

Novation is not to be presumed, and the new obligation is Not pre-
sumed. construed to be merely corroborative of the former one, unless the intention of the parties to the contrary clearly appear.[2] If a new obligation be granted to the same creditor by the same debtor, without the intervention of any other person, there is no novation, unless the new obligation be in some respects different from the former one.   When the principal obligation is extinguished by novation, the sureties are free. In delegation no liability attaches to the old debtor on the supervening insolvency of the substituted debtor, unless his credit be specially guaranteed by the old debtor.[3]

Sect. 4.—Confusion.

Obligations are extinguished by confusion when the same Confusion
defined. person becomes both creditor and debtor, either by succession or singular title—as, for instance, when the debtor succeeds to the creditor, or the creditor to the debtor, or a stranger to both ; for no one can be debtor to himself.

When confusion takes effect in the person of the principal debtor, it liberates the surety.   But when the claim comes into the person of the surety, this obviously does not draw after it the extinction of the principal obligation.[4]

---

[1] I. 3. 30. 3.   [3] D. 46. 2.   C. 8. 42.
[2] Ibid.   [4] D. 46. 3.

Sect. 5.—Acceptilation and Discharge.

Nature of acceptila-tion. When an obligation was discharged by the creditor without payment or performance by the debtor, it was called in the Roman law acceptilation :—*Est autem acceptilatio imaginaria solutio.*

Acceptilatio was a solemn declaration made by the creditor in the form of stipulation in answer to a question put to him by the debtor, that he held the obligation to be satisfied. This form of discharge was strictly applicable only to those obligations which were constituted by stipulation. But an ingenious device was resorted to, called the *Aquiliana stipulatio*, whereby any obligation otherwise contracted could easily be converted by novation into one *ex stipulatione*, so as to admit of its extinction by acceptilation.[1]

Pactum de non peten-do. The *pactum de non petendo* was more extensive in its effects than acceptilation, as it applied to all sorts of obligation, however constituted. Yet this mode of extinction did not operate *ipso jure* but only *ope exceptionis*—the declaration of the creditor being, not that he held the debt paid, but that he would not exact payment.[2] In modern practice the Roman form of acceptilation is no longer in use. But all debts and obligations, however contracted, may be cancelled or discharged by a simple convention between the creditor and debtor.

Discharges. As certain contracts are formed by consent alone, so they may be extinguished by the contrary consent of the contracting parties without any performance on either side. *Obligationes quæ consensu contrahuntur contraria voluntate dissolvuntur.*[3] But in the ordinary transactions of life, discharges are most frequently granted as the consequence and acknowledgment of payment or performance by the debtor. In some cases the mere lapse of time is held to extinguish the obligation, and in others to bar action upon it, as we have already taken occasion to show in the chapter on Prescription.

[1] I. 3. 30. 1 and 2.　　　　[2] D. 2 14.　　　　[3] I. 3. 30. 4.

PART IV.

OF THE LAWS OF SUCCESSION.

CHAPTER I.

OF SUCCESSION IN GENERAL.

THERE are two kinds of succession recognised in the Roman law—testamentary and legal. When a person by testament appoints heirs to succeed to his estate after his death, they are preferred in respect of the special destination of the proprietor; and this is called testamentary succession. If the deceased has left no will, his estate is devolved upon his relations, in a certain order prescribed by law, from a presumption that they would have been called by the deceased had he made a destination; and this is termed legal succession, or succession *ab intestato*. ^{Succession, testamentary and legal.}

When a Roman died, the heir or heirs succeeded to all his property as a universal succession; and this was called *hereditas*.[1] The institution of an heir in a testament was a formality which could not be dispensed with. ^{Hereditas denotes whole succession.}

The testator might appoint any number of heirs, and divide his estate into as many parts as he pleased. The whole inheritance was called *as*, and this was commonly divided into twelve parts called *unciæ*. Hence the *heres ex asse* is heir to one's whole fortune, *heres ex semisse* to the half, and so on.

[1] D. 50. 16. 24.

Bonorum possessio. By the prætorian law, various persons who did not possess the character of heirs according to the strict system of the ancient civil law, were admitted to the succession under the form called *bonorum possessio*. Though not properly heir, the bonorum possessor was regarded and treated as such, in so far as the law accorded to him the rights, and imposed upon him the duties, of heir.[1]

When the prætors by their edicts called to the succession persons who were excluded by the civil law, these magistrates virtually exercised legislative power. The *bonorum possessio* was given *contra tabulas, secundum tabulas*, and, in a great many cases, under particular edicts for the distribution of inheritances. Even the legal heir sometimes found it beneficial to take up the succession as bonorum possessor, though he had the option to do so in the character of heir.

Classes of heirs. There were three classes of heirs—1st, Necessary; 2d, Proper and necessary; and, 3d, Strangers.[2]

When a slave was instituted by his master as his heir, he became free at the testator's death, and was compelled to take up the inheritance, so that he was called a necessary heir. Here it may be explained that when the property of an insolvent person was sold by his creditors after his death for payment of their debts, his memory was covered with infamy. To avoid this disgrace it was common for one who suspected his solvency to institute his slave as heir, so that if he did not leave enough to pay his debts, the goods were sold and divided among his creditors as being the property of his heir.[3]

Proper and necessary heirs are the sons and daughters or other descendants in the direct line who are under the paternal power of the deceased at the time of his death. But grandchildren are not proper heirs, unless they succeed in room of their father by his death or emancipation in the lifetime of the grandfather. By the ancient civil law these heirs were compelled to undertake the representation with all its burdens as well as benefits, whatever might be the amount of the debts and engagements of the ancestor; but, as this was frequently attended with hardship, the prætor permitted

[1] I. 3. 10. pr. D. 37. 1.   [2] I. 2. 19. pr.   [3] I. 2. 19. 1.

children and grandchildren to reject the inheritance, so as to relieve themselves from loss when the debts exceeded the value of the estate. This right was confirmed by the perpetual edict.[1]

Strangers—that is, persons who were not under the testator's power at the time of his death—were at liberty either to accept or reject the inheritance ; but if they once accepted they could not afterwards renounce.[2]

Any one entitled to the succession either under a testament or by law was accountable as heir, as soon as he declared his acceptance, or dealt with the property as heir. By the prætorian law the heir was allowed a certain time to deliberate whether he would undertake the representation of the deceased, and this was fixed by Justinian not to exceed nine months if granted by the magistrates, and a year if granted by the emperor. A still more important privilege was conferred upon heirs by Justinian, when he introduced the principle of limited representation by the benefit of inventory. An heir who accepted with benefit of inventory, protected himself from all liability for the debts of the ancestor beyond the value of the inheritance.[3]

Time for deliberation.

Benefit of inventory.

[1] I. 2. 19. 2.　　　　[2] I. 2. 19. 3.　　　　[3] I. 2. 19. 5.

CHAPTER II.

I.—ROMAN LAW.

TESTAMENTS are of high antiquity, and are mentioned in Roman history before the legislation of the decemvirs. The Twelve Tables recognise the power of disposing of property by will in these terms: " Uti legassit super pecunia tutelave suæ rei, ita jus esto." [1]

Testament defined.

A testament is a declaration of the testator's last will, made according to the formalities prescribed by law, and containing the appointment of a testamentary heir or executor. According to Modestinus: "Testamentum est voluntatis nostræ justa sententia, de eo, quod quis post mortem suam fieri velit." [2]

In the Roman law, the essence of a testament, and that which distinguished it from a codicil, was the institution of an heir. [3] The inheritance could not be disposed of by codicil. Originally, though *fidei-commissa*, or bequests in trust, might be left by codicil, legacies could not, unless it was confirmed by a testament. But, under the law as modified by Justinian, a testator might leave legacies or *fidei-commissa* by codicil (which was attested by five witnesses), whether he made a will or not. It was not uncommon to add to a testament what was called a codicillary clause, declaring that, if from any cause the will should not be valid as such, it should

[1] Ulp. 11. 14.
[2] D. 28. 1. 1. pr.
[3] D. 28. 5. 1. 3. " Quinque verbis *esto.*'"

potest (quis) facere testamentum, ut dicat, ' *Lucius Titius mihi heres esto.*' "

nevertheless be effectual as a codicil, which required fewer
legal solemnities.

Among the Romans the power of making a testament only Persons
belonged to citizens above puberty who were *sui juris*—a making a
rule which excluded a great number of persons. Children will.
under the paternal power generally could not make a will,
having no property of their own; but if the son was a soldier
or public functionary, he might dispose of his *peculium* by
will. Males above fourteen and females above twelve, when
not under power or otherwise specially disqualified, could
make a will without the authority of their guardians. Pupils,
lunatics, prisoners of war during their captivity, criminals
condemned to death or other punishments inferring confiscation of property, as well as various other persons, were
incapable of making a testament. Among the Romans a
married woman was as capable of making a will as one who
was single. But in England a married woman cannot devise
lands; and, as a general rule, she is incapable of making a
testament of *chattels* without the licence of her husband.[1]

Sect. 1.—*Forms of Roman Wills.*

Anciently three modes of making wills were in use among Ancient
the Romans. forms.

1st, In the earliest times wills were made before the
general assembly of the people, called *Comitia Calata,*
which were held twice a-year for the purpose.

2d, When the army was about to set forth to meet the
enemy, soldiers might make their wills in presence of their
companions in arms. This was called a testament *in pro-
cinctu.*

3d, The testament *per æs et libram,* consisted of an imaginary sale of the inheritance by the testator to the intended
successor, in presence of the balance-holder and five witnesses.[2] This ancient mode of testamentary transfer is described by Gaius, 2. 104.

In process of time these forms were superseded by the

---

[1] Williams's Exec., p. 47.   2 Black. Com., 497.   [2] I. 2. 10. 1.

R

Wills in writing. introduction of written wills properly attested, which, after being recognised by the edicts of the prætors, were regulated by the constitutions of the emperors. These wills required to be signed by the testator, or some person for him, in the presence of seven witnesses called for the purpose, who attested the same under their hands and seals. If the will was entirely written by the testator, his signature at the end of it was unnecessary. Justinian required that the name of the heir should be written by the testator or one of the witnesses; but he afterwards dispensed with that formality.[1]

It was necessary that witnesses to wills should be Roman citizens and males above fourteen. Women, persons under the power of the testator, the heir and his family, were all disabled from being witnesses; but this objection did not apply to legatees.[2]

A will might be written on a tablet of wax or any substance capable of receiving legible characters.[3]

Nuncupative wills. Nuncupative wills might be made without writing, by mere verbal declaration in presence of seven witnesses. Wills of this nature are certainly the most ancient; and the liberty which the Romans enjoyed of making testaments without writing, serves to account for the burdensome formalities enjoined by the civil law regarding the number and condition of the witnesses.[4] Two witnesses are sufficient to attest a written will in this country. In England a verbal will or legacy is ineffectual, unless the testator be a soldier in actual military service, or a mariner at sea.—1 Vict. c. 26, s. 11. In Scotland, writing is essential to the nomination of an executor; but a verbal legacy, if proved by parole, will be sustained to the amount of £8, 6s. 8d.—Ersk. 3. 9. 7.

Privileged wills. Among the Romans wills could be made without the usual formalities in certain privileged cases.

1st, When military persons were engaged in actual service against an enemy, they might make their wills without any of the ordinary formalities: all that was required was suf-

---

[1] I. 2. 10. 3 and 4.   C. 6. 23. 29.   [3] I. 2. 10. 12.
N. 119, ch. 9.   [4] I. 2. 10. 14.
[2] I. 2. 10. 6-11.

ficient evidence of their intention regarding the disposal of
their property after death. This privilege was enjoyed by
soldiers only during the time of actual service in the field,
and testaments so made without the usual solemnities continued valid only for one year after their discharge from the
army.[1]

2d, During the prevalence of a pestilence or contagious
disease, the presence of all the seven witnesses at one time
and place was dispensed with; it was sufficient if each in
succession attached his signature and seal to the will.[2]

3d, In rural districts, when seven qualified witnesses could
not be found, the number might be reduced to five, and one
witness might sign for those who could not write.[3]

4th, If a will was made by a parent for distributing his
property solely among his children or other descendants, no
witnesses were required, provided the testator wrote the will
himself, or filled up in his own handwriting the date of its
execution, with the names and portions of the children.[4] But
a legacy left to a stranger in such a will was ineffectual.

Among the Romans the testament was opened in presence
of the witnesses, or the major number of them, who had
signed it; and after they had acknowledged their seals, it
was read, and a copy made; after which the original was deposited in the public archives, from which a fresh copy might
be afterwards obtained if required.

Sect. 2.—Contents of Roman Wills.

By the ancient law, if the father of a family wished to de- Law as to
prive his children of the succession, he was obliged to declare ^{disherison.}
his intention by formally disinheriting them in his will. At
first, sons under the father's power were disinherited by
name, so as to prevent any risk of error; but daughters and
grandchildren might be disinherited in general terms. These
distinctions were abolished by a constitution of Justinian,
which declared that all children, whether emancipated or

---

[1] I. 2. 11. pr. and 3.   [3] C. 6. 23. 31.
[2] C. 6. 23. 8.   [4] N. 107, ch. 1.

not, and all other descendants in the male line, entitled by
law to be called to the immediate succession of the testator,
should either be instituted heirs or disinherited by name.
As regards children adopted by an ascendant, they passed
into his family, so that he was bound either to institute or
disinherit them; but children adopted by a stranger retained
all their legal rights against their natural parent, and had
only a right to the succession of the stranger who adopted
them if he died intestate.

If a person *sui juris* died without descendants, he was
bound in his will to institute or disinherit his ascendants,
without distinguishing between the paternal line and the
maternal line.

The necessity of disinheriting was at first nothing but a
simple form to protect children against the forgetfulness of
their ascendants in the paternal line; and the head of the
family could, from pure caprice, and without any sufficient
reason, entirely exclude his descendants from the succession.
But before the age of Cicero the law only allowed disherison
for grave reasons, without which the testament might be
annulled by an action called *querela inofficiosi testamenti*.
For a long time it was left to the judge to decide what should
be held sufficient reasons for excluding the lawful heirs. But,
to remove all uncertainty, Justinian fixed the only grounds
of exclusion which could be admitted—such as attempting
the life of the deceased, grievously injuring him in his person,
character, or feelings, and other immoral or disgraceful acts
—and required that one or more of these reasons should be
indicated in the testament.[1] If the truth of the charge
against the person disinherited was disputed, the burden of
proving it was laid upon the heir named in the will.

Institution of heirs. According to the strict rule of the Roman law, no will was
effectual unless one or more persons were appointed heirs to
represent the deceased.

The testator might appoint one heir, or any number of
heirs. No one, except a soldier, could die partly testate,
partly intestate; and if a testator appointed an heir for any

[1] N. 115, ch. 3 and 4.

portion of his property without naming heirs for the remainder, such heir became entitled to the whole inheritance. When several heirs are instituted, the property may be divided among them in such proportions as the testator may appoint; and if there be no distribution, all will participate equally in the inheritance. If the shares of some of the heirs are expressed in the testament, and nothing is said as to the shares of the other heirs, they will be entitled to the remainder of the property undisposed of by the testator.

Among co-heirs in testamentary succession there is a right of accretion, so that if one of them cannot, or will not, take his portion, it falls to the other heirs according to their shares in the inheritance, to the exclusion of the heirs-at-law, who are not called by the testament. Thus, where two testamentary heirs are appointed, who are not heirs of blood, and one of them declines to take his portion, or becomes incapable of doing so by his predeceasing the testator, or other supervening incapacity, then the other heir, who was instituted only for a part, becomes heir to the whole estate. *Accretion among co-heirs.*

The heir may be appointed simply or under a condition. Various obligations may be imposed on him, such as to pay legacies, to enfranchise slaves, to erect a monument or public edifice, and the like. All conditions which are impossible, or contrary to law or good morals, are rejected as if they had never been written, without affecting the validity of the testament in other respects.

Three kinds of substitution are mentioned by Justinian in the Institutes—Vulgar, Pupilary, and Quasi-pupilary. A testator might appoint one person as heir, and, if he should die or refuse to accept, then another, by way of substitution, and that for any portion of the inheritance. This was called the common or vulgar substitution of heirs; it was truly a subordinate conditional institution, which was only to come into operation if the first institution failed to take effect. *Roman substitutions.*

Modestinus gives this example of it:—"*Lucius Titius heres esto; si mihi Lucius Titius heres non erit, tunc Seius heres mihi esto.*"[1]

[1] D. 28. 6. 1. 1.   I. 2. 15.

When a person had a child under his power in pupilarity, he might not only appoint such child to be his heir, and substitute another to him in the manner above described, but also declare that, in case such child should become heir and die before puberty, then that another person should be heir, so as virtually to make a testament for the pupil. But this pupilary substitution for children was only effectual when the father made a valid testament of his own. If the pupil succeeded as heir, and afterwards reached puberty, the pupilary substitution became extinct.[1]

By a law of Justinian, a man who had children, or other descendants, who were insane, might make a substitution to them in the manner of a pupilary substitution, even although they had arrived at the age of puberty. But this species of substitution became ineffectual, if the heirs first called were restored to a sound mind, so as to be able to make a will for themselves.[2]

II.—FRENCH LAW.

Forms of wills in France.

By the law of France, a testament is effectual if it is holograph—that is, entirely written, dated, and signed by the testator—without any other forms. It may also be executed *par acte public*, with the aid of two notaries, in presence of two witnesses, or one notary and four witnesses; and it must be signed by the testator, if he can write—and if he cannot, a declaration to that effect must be inserted. A third form is used called *mystique*, or secret. The will is made and signed by the testator, whether written by him or by another. It is then sealed up and presented to a notary and six witnesses, the testator declaring that the sealed packet contains his will, whereupon a note to that effect is made on the envelope, and signed by the testator, the notary, and the witnesses.[3]

A Frenchman in a foreign country may make a testament either by a holograph writing, as prescribed by article 970 of the Civil Code, or by a writing authenticated according to the

---

[1] I. 2. 16. 8.   [2] I. 2. 16. 1.   [3] Code Civil, art. 970 *et seq.*

forms in use in the place where it is executed.[1] An Englishman resident in France is allowed to make his will according
to the French law, if he has obtained the authority of the
Crown to establish his domicile there, under the 13th article
of the Civil Code.

III.—ENGLISH AND SCOTTISH LAW.

Sect. 1. — *English Statute of Wills.*

In England, the statute 1 Vict. c. 26, which came into
operation on January 1, 1838, contains important regulations
regarding wills, some of which may be here noticed :—

1. Every person may, by will executed as required by the
Act, devise, bequeath, or dispose of all real estate, and all
personal estate which he shall be entitled to at the time of
his death. *English will carries real and personal estates.*

2. No will shall be valid unless it be in writing, and
signed at the foot or end thereof by the testator, or by some
other person in his presence, and by his direction : and such
signature shall be made or acknowledged by the testator in
the presence of two or more witnesses, present at the same
time ; and such witnesses shall attest and shall subscribe the
will in the presence of the testator, but no form of attestation
shall be necessary. *Form of execution.*

Thus the English law requires every will to be executed in
the presence of two witnesses, with certain formalities ; and
holograph wills unattested are not valid.   But any soldier in
actual military service, or any mariner being at sea, may dispose of his personal estate by an oral will, as he might have
done before the passing of the Act.

3. Every will shall be construed, with reference to the real
estate and personal estate comprised in it, to speak and take
effect as if it had been executed immediately before the death
of the testator, unless a contrary intention shall appear by
the will.

[1] Code Civil, art. 909.

No will by
minor.

4. No will made by any person under the age of twenty-one years shall be valid.

Revoked by
marriage.

5. As a general rule, every will made by a man or woman shall be revoked by his or her marriage.

6. All gifts or legacies by will to an attesting witness, or the husband or wife of such witness, or any person claiming under them, shall be void; but such witness shall be admissible to prove the execution of the will.

Sect. 2.—*How Testamentary Writings executed in Scotland.*

A Scottish
will carries
only per-
sonal estate.

By the law of Scotland, the expression will or testament is understood to apply only to personal property. But a testament is usually combined with a *mortis causa* disposition, expressed in the technical terms essential for the conveyance of lands or other real estate.* Testamentary writings which are holograph—that is, written and subscribed by the testator—are valid without witnesses. But when they are written by another person, they must be signed by the testator, if he can write, and attested by two subscribing witnesses, and must contain at the close an attestation-clause, in the Scotch form, specifying the names and designations of the writer and the attesting witnesses. A will of personal property by one who cannot write, may be signed by a notary authorised by him and two witnesses; and the parish clergyman may act as notary; but two notaries and four witnesses are required in deeds importing heritable title and "other obligations of great importance."[1]

By the law of Scotland, a minor, male or female, and a married woman having separate personal property, may make a will.

Sect. 3.—*Recent Acts as to Wills by British Subjects.*

Act as to
wills by
British
subjects.

In consequence of some decisions of the Privy Council which were considered of questionable authority, the Act 24 & 25 Vict. c. 114, was passed "to amend the law with respect

---

* The necessity of using technical terms in bequeathing real estate in Scotland is now removed; 31 & 32 Vict. c. 101, sect. 20.
[1] Ersk. 3. 2. 23. 1579, c. 80.

to wills of personal estate, made by British subjects."[1] By this statute, which extends only to wills and other testamentary instruments made by persons who die after it is passed, it is enacted :—

1. Every will and testamentary instrument made out of the United Kingdom by a British subject (whatever may be his domicile), shall, as regards personal estate, be held to be well executed, if the same be made according to the forms required either by the law of the place where the same was made, or by the law of the place where such person was domiciled when the same was made, or by the laws then in force in that part of the British dominions where he had his domicile of origin.[2] *Effect of wills made abroad.*

2. Every will and other testamentary instrument made within the United Kingdom by any British subject (whatever may be his domicile), shall, as regards personal estate, be held to be well executed, if the same be executed according to the forms required by the laws for the time being in force in that part of the United Kingdom where the same is made.[3] *Wills made in this country.*

3. No will or other testamentary instrument shall be held to be revoked, or to have become invalid, nor shall the construction thereof be altered, by reason of any subsequent change of domicile of the person making the same. But nothing in the Act shall invalidate any will or other testamentary instrument, as regards personal estate, which would have been valid if the Act had not been passed, except as such will or other testamentary instrument may be revoked or altered by any subsequent will or testamentary instrument made valid by the Act.[4] *Will not affected by change of domicile.*

---

[1] Miss Calcraft, an English subject resident in Paris, made her will conformably to the English law, which the Privy Council held to be invalid, upon the ground that she was domiciled in France, although she had not obtained any authority under article 13 of the Civil Code. Bremer *v.* Freeman, 1857 (10 Moo. P. C. 361). This decision proceeded on an erroneous view of the French law. According to the French jurists, Miss Calcraft's English will was perfectly valid.—Lord St Leonards's Practical Treatise, 1862, p. 404.

[2] Sect. 1.

[3] Sect. 2.

[4] Sect. 3 and 4.

Prospective Act to regulate domicile.

This statute was accompanied by the 24 & 25 Vict. c. 121, entitled, " An Act to amend the law in relation to the wills and domicile of British subjects dying whilst resident abroad, and of foreign subjects dying whilst resident in her Majesty's dominions" (6th August 1861). But this Act, which extends to intestacy as well as to testacy, only becomes operative after a convention shall have been entered into with any foreign state, and an Order in Council shall have been published in the 'London Gazette.'

British subjects dying abroad.

After the publication of such order, no British subject resident at his or her death in the foreign country named in such order, shall be deemed, under any circumstances, to have acquired a domicile in such country, unless such British subject shall have been resident there for one year immediately preceding his or her decease, and shall also have made and deposited in a public office of such foreign country, a declaration in writing of his or her intention to become domiciled there ; and every British subject dying resident in such foreign country, but without having so resided and made such declaration aforesaid, shall be deemed, for all purposes of testate or intestate succession as to movables, to retain the domicile he or she possessed at the time of his or her going to reside in such foreign country.[1]

Foreigners dying in this country.

In like manner, after the publication of such order in the 'London Gazette,' no subject of any such foreign country, who, at the time of his or her death, shall be resident in any part of Great Britain or Ireland, shall be deemed, under any circumstances, to have acquired a domicile therein, unless such foreign subject shall have been resident within Great Britain or Ireland for one year immediately preceding his or her decease, and shall also have signed and deposited with the Home Secretary a declaration in writing of his or her desire to become and be domiciled in England, Scotland, or Ireland, and that the law of the place of such domicile shall regulate his or her movable succession. But the Act is not to apply to any foreigners who may have obtained letters of naturalisation in any part of her Majesty's dominions.[2]

[1] Sect. 1. [2] Sect. 2 and 3.

CHAPTER III.

I.—ROMAN LAW.

ACCORDING to the law of the Twelve Tables, the powers of a *By Twelve* testator in disposing of his property were unlimited; for the *Tables powers un-* testament of the father of a family had the force of law,—*jus* *limited.* *esto.*

In progress of time various laws were enacted to restrain *Falcidian* immoderate bequests, which, after the general introduction of *portion.* wills, were found to prejudice the heir. Of these the most important was the Falcidian law, in the reign of Augustus and year of Rome 714, whereby it was enacted that no one should leave in legacies more than three fourth parts of his estate, so as to secure to the heir at least one-fourth of the succession. This fourth is called the Falcidian portion· Though this right was given originally to the testamentary heirs, yet as legacies might be left by codicil, so as to be payable by the heir-at-law *ab intestato,* he was equally entitled to the Falcidian portion. The fourth part was estimated according to the value of the estate at the testator's death, after deducting debts and the necessary expenses of the succession. If the legacies exceeded three-fourths of the estate, they suffered a proportional abatement in favour of the heir.

Another limitation of the powers of a testator arose from *Legitim.* the law which enjoined parents to leave a certain portion of their estate to their children, and children to leave a certain portion of their estate to their parents. This was called the

[1] I. 2. 22.

Legitim portion, and was originally a fourth of the succession, so that it was an extension of the principle of the Falcidian law.[1]

There are two orders of persons to whom legitim is due,—1st, The descendants of the deceased, who would have been called to the succession had he died intestate; 2d, Failing descendants, the ascendants of the testator, provided they would have inherited *ab intestato.* Brothers and sisters have no right to claim legitim, except when the testator has appointed an infamous person to be heir.

If in the same succession there are both children and parents of the deceased, legitim is only due to the children; for they exclude parents from the succession.

All the children, without distinction as to sex, have a right to legitim. When there are only children of the first degree, the legitim is divided among them in equal shares. But if there be at the same time children of the first degree alive, and grandchildren descended from others deceased, the legitim is divided according to the number of the children of the first degree who are still alive, and of those who, being dead, have left issue to represent them, and these grandchildren have only among them the legal portion which the person whom they represent would have had if he had survived the testator.

The second order of persons to whom legitim is due, failing descendants, are the nearest ascendants. If there are paternal and maternal ascendants in the nearest degree, the legitim is divided into two parts, one for the ascendants on the father's side, and the other for the ascendants on the mother's side.

At first the legitim, after the analogy of the Falcidian portion, was, in all cases, a fourth of the estate which would have fallen to the heirs-at-law *ab intestato,* whatever might be

Legitim increased by Justinian. their number. But Justinian raised the amount of the legitim for descendants at least to one-third of the succession, if there were four or a less number, and to one-half when there were more than four.[2] Most writers think this regulation

---

[1] I. 2. 18. 6.   D. 5. 2. 8. 6.   [2] N. 18, ch. 1.

applied also to ascendants, to the extent of entitling them to one-third of the succession; but Mackeldey is of a different opinion, holding that their legitim never exceeded a fourth part.[1]

Legitim is only due after the death of the testator, and those who claim it must bring into account whatever they have received under the testament, whether in the character of heirs, or by legacy, or donation *mortis causa*. Generally donations *inter vivos* are not reckoned, unless they are given expressly under that condition. Justinian ordained that the legitim should be left to children in the character of heirs and not as legatees or donees, according to the former practice; but if any part of the inheritance, however small, was left to them, they were only entitled to recover by action what was necessary to make up the legitim.[2]

Querela Inofficiosi Testamenti.—When children or parents are unjustly disinherited or passed over in a testament, it may be challenged as undutiful by the *querela inofficiosi testamenti*. Challenge of undutiful testament.

When this complaint was successful, it had not the effect of entirely annulling the testament under the new law of Justinian; the institution of the heir was rescinded, but the legacies and other provisions of the will remained in force.[3] When the appointment of the heir was wholly set aside, the succession was taken up *ab intestato*, under the burden of the legacies so far as these did not exceed the legitim. If one of the children was found to be justly disinherited, while the others were successful in their challenge, the institution of the heir in the testament could only be partially rescinded, and the result was to make the testator die partly testate and partly intestate, which was contrary to the general rule of law.

If the complaint against a testament as undutiful was rejected, the plaintiff by way of penalty forfeited whatever had been left to him in the will. The action was excluded:

---

[1] See on this subject Domat, part ii. b. 3, t. 3, s. 2; Ortolan, Institutes, § 802; Mackeldey, § 680.

[2] N. 115, ch. 3. I. 2. 18. 3.

[3] N. 115, ch. 3, § 14; ch. 4, § 8.

When excluded. 1st, When those who were entitled to raise it approved directly or indirectly of the testament; 2d, By the heirs of blood surviving the testator, and thereafter dying without instituting a challenge; and, 3d, By prescription, which was at first fixed at two years, and afterwards at five.[1]

II.—FRENCH LAW.

Limits of testamentary power. In modern times the limits of testamentary power vary in different countries. In France, if any one die without issue or ascendants, he may leave his whole property to strangers; but if a man at his death has one lawful child, he can only so dispose of the half of his estate; if he leave two children, the third; and if he leave three or more children, the fourth. If the deceased has no issue, but is survived by ascendants in each of the paternal and maternal lines, he can only dispose of the half of his property; and three-fourths if he leave ascendants only in one line.[2]

III.—ENGLISH AND SCOTTISH LAW.

In England testamentary power unlimited. By the modern law of England, whatever limitations may have formerly existed, the testamentary power is wholly unfettered. For, apart from special contract, any man can by will bequeath his whole real and personal estate to strangers, even though he should leave a wife and children.[3]

In Scotland same, if no wife or issue. In Scotland the law stands upon a different footing. If a man die without either wife or issue, his whole property is at his own disposal; if he leave a wife and issue, his goods or personal property are divided into three equal parts, one of which goes to his wife as *jus relictæ*, another to his children as legitim, and the third is at his own disposal; if he leave no wife, he may then dispose of one-half, and the other half goes to the children; and so, *e converso*, if he leave no children

Jus relictæ and legitim.

[1] I. 2. 18.   D. 5. 2.   C. 3. 28.   [3] Williams's Exec., p. 3-5. Paterson's Compendium, p. 223.
[2] Code Civil, art. 913-916.

the wife is entitled to one-half, and he may bequeath the
other. The legitim can only be claimed by the father's existing children, and not by the issue of a deceased child. The
eldest son has a share of the legitim along with the rest,
but is excluded from it if there be a heritable estate falling
to him as heir-at-law, which he refuses to share with the other
children.[1] The wife's *jus relictæ* may be expressly excluded
in an antenuptial contract, and also the children's right to
legitim, at least when reasonable provisions are made for
them on the dissolution of the marriage.

[1] Bell's Pr. § 1583.

CHAPTER IV.

OF FIDEI-COMMISSA OR BEQUESTS IN TRUST.

HITHERTO we have treated of testamentary writings, the object of which was to transfer the succession directly to the heir. We now come to the subject of trusts. This form of disposition was introduced in order to evade the strict rules of the civil law, by transmitting property to foreigners, exiles, and other persons who were legally incapacitated from taking anything directly under the will of a Roman citizen. Originally all trusts were precarious, and depended entirely on the honour of the trustee, till Augustus authorised them to be enforced by law; and having afterwards become extremely common and highly favoured, they were placed under the permanent jurisdiction of a special prætor.[1]

Trusts at first precarious.

A *fidei-commissum* in the Roman law is a *mortis causa* disposition, by which the testator leaves something to another under an obligation to transfer it to a third person. If the object of the trust was the whole succession or a part of it, this was called *fidei-commissaria hereditas*, or *fidei-commissum universale;* if it was a single thing or definite sum of money, it was called *fidei-commissum singulæ rei*, or *fidei-commissum speciale.* In the first case, the obligation could only be imposed on the heir; in the second, it might be laid on a legatee, or any one who received something under the will.

Fidei-commissum defined.

A universal trust, by which the heir is requested to make over the inheritance or a part of it to another, may be regarded as a species of substitution; for the beneficiary takes

[1] I. 2. 23. 1.

in whole or in part the place of the first heir; but it differs from a vulgar substitution in this respect, that the beneficiary can only take as a substitute after the first heir has entered upon the inheritance.

The person charged with the trust was bound to restore the subject at the time appointed by the testator, and, if no time was mentioned, immediately after accepting the succession. The testator might appoint the subject to be restored by the first heir to the second, by the second to the third, and so forth. When a universal trust was constituted with substitutions in favour of the family of the founder, it was called *fidei-commissum familiæ.*[1]

The heir charged with the trust became proprietor in a certain sense when he entered upon the inheritance; but, without the permission of the testator or the express consent of all parties interested, he could not alienate the estate, except for payment of debts affecting the succession, or preventing the beneficiary from suffering damage. But, if the heir was required to restore what remained of the succession at the period of his own death—(*fidei-commissum ejus quod superfuturum est*), he could under the new law dispose of three-fourths of the estate, and was only bound to account to the beneficiary for the remaining fourth, for which he might be required to find security.[2]

As the direct heir was free to accept or refuse the succession, there were reasons to apprehend that he would always repudiate it when he was required to restore the whole estate without deriving any benefit from it. To obviate this difficulty, the person charged with the trust was allowed by law to retain a fourth part of the inheritance if he was universal heir, or a fourth part of his hereditary portion if he was only heir for a part; but, on the other hand, he was bound to accept the succession in order to discharge the trust. All the debts affecting the succession were divided between the

Obligations of the trustee.

Pegasian portion.

---

[1] N. 159. See Domat, part ii. b. 5, t. 3; Mackeldey, § 748.   [2] N. 108, ch. 1 and 2. Mackeldey, § 756.

S

trustee who retained the Pegasian portion, and the beneficiary, according to their respective interests.[1]

A trust of a particular thing. Particular things may also be the object of a special trust, as a field, a silver cup, or a sum of money; and the person charged with the trust may be the heir or a legatee. But no man can be requested to give more than he has received by means of the testament. A legacy was left in imperative terms, a *fidei-commissum* in words of entreaty; but, notwithstanding the difference in the form of expression, both were binding in law. Justinian assimilated legacies and special gifts in trust by abolishing all ancient distinctions and extending the same rules of law to both, so far as this might be necessary to make them effectual.[2]

[1] The Commentators often call this portion the *Trebellian fourth;* but it originated not under the Trebellian, but under the Pegasian senatus-consultum. Ortolan, Institutes, § 962.

[2] I. 2. 20. 3. C. 6. 43.

CHAPTER V.

HOW TESTAMENTS ARE REVOKED OR ANNULLED.

I.—ROMAN LAW.

A TESTAMENT is null *ab initio*, if it be defective in any of the formalities required by law. _(margin)

A TESTAMENT is null *ab initio*, if it be defective in any of the formalities required by law. *Will null ab initio.*

In all cases a will is revocable during the life of the testator, but, when legally made, it remains valid till it is revoked or rendered ineffectual. By the Roman law a testament was revoked by making a new one, even though it made no express mention of the first. For, as every will implied the disposal of the whole estate, two testaments could not subsist together, so that the second annulled the first; but, in order to have this effect, the second testament required to be complete. Without making a new will, the testator might revoke a testament by cancelling or destroying it with that intention. *Will revocable by testator.*

A will might be annulled in whole or in part in various other ways. *How annulled.*

1. By the subsequent birth, or adoption, of a child who was passed over, the testament was rendered ineffectual, so far as regards the institution of the heir.

2. By the testator changing his status—as, for instance, by losing his liberty or his rights as a Roman citizen—his will became invalid. But if he recovered his status before his death the prætor might sustain the testament, by giving to the instituted heirs possession of the goods *secundum tabulas.*

3. When the heir instituted could not or would not accept, the testament was ineffectual as such; but under the law of

Justinian legacies and fiduciary trusts could not be defeated by the non-acceptance or renunciation of the heir.

4. The testament might be rescinded and declared null by judicial sentence for non-compliance with the rules indispensable to its validity.[1]

In cases where a testament was null from the beginning, or subsequently became invalid, the succession was generally taken up *ab intestato*, unless the prætor gave the possession of goods *secundum tabulas*. But, as already explained, when a testament was challenged as undutiful and only partially rescinded, the succession might be partly testamentary and partly *ab intestato*.

II.—FRENCH LAW.

How will revoked in France.

By the French Civil Code a testament cannot be revoked in whole or in part except by a posterior one, or by an instrument before notaries, declaring a change of will. A posterior testament which does not expressly revoke a former one does not annul it, except in so far as its provisions may be found to be incompatible with, or contrary to, those in the second will.[2]

III.—ENGLISH AND SCOTTISH LAW.

How revoked in this country.

In England we have seen that, as a general rule, every will is revoked by a subsequent marriage; but, with that exception, a will can only be revoked by another will, or codicil, or some writing declaring an intention to revoke, and executed like a will, or by the testator, or some person in his presence and by his direction, destroying the will, with the intention of revoking it.[3]

By the law of Scotland a testament may be revoked by the testator executing any probative writing declaring such to be his intention, or by his making a new testament inconsistent with the former one, or by deliberately cancelling or destroying the will with the intention of revoking it.

---

[1] I. 2. 17. D. 28. 3.
[2] Code Civil, art. 1035-6.
[3] 1 Vict. c. 26, s. 20.

CHAPTER VI.

OF LEGACIES.

I.—ROMAN LAW.

A LEGACY is a donation of a sum or subject which the testa- ^{Nature of legacy.} tor directs to be delivered after his death to the legatee.[1]

Anciently there were four kinds of legacies in use among ^{Ancient forms.} the Romans—*per vindicationem, damnationem, præceptionem, sinendi modo.* To each of these was assigned a certain form of words; but these distinctions were all abolished by the imperial constitutions, and Justinian ultimately reduced all legacies to one kind, which might be left either in a testament or codicil.[2]

All persons capable of making a will may leave legacies. ^{What may be bequeathed.} Not only sums of money, rights, and debts, but lands and all other things subject to commerce, whether corporeal or incorporeal, may be bequeathed. One may leave as a legacy what is the property of another, and, if this was known to the testator, the heir was bound either to purchase the thing for the legatee or to pay its value to him. But, if the testator made a bequest of a thing belonging to another under the erroneous belief that it was his own (which was to be inferred unless the contrary was proved by the legatee), neither the thing nor its value could be claimed from the heir, it being presumed that he would not have bequeathed the thing had he known that it belonged to another.[3] These rules have

---

[1] "Legatum est donatio quædam a defuncto, ab herede præstanda."— I. 2. 20. 1.

[2] I. 2. 20. 2 and 3. Ulp. 24. 1-6.
[3] I. 2. 20. 4.

been adopted in Scotland. In France a bequest of what belongs to another is invariably null, whether the testator believed the thing to be his own or not.[1]

Bequest of debt by creditor.

A creditor may bequeath a debt due to him by a stranger; but the legacy is only effectual if any sum can be recovered from the alleged debtor. When the discharge of a debt was bequeathed to the debtor, which was called *legatum liberationis*, it was effectual, so that no suit could be brought by the testator's heir for the debt either against the debtor or his representatives.[2]

General bequest.

If any one made a bequest generally of his jewels, pictures, statues, or the like, the legacy might be augmented by the testator adding to the things bequeathed after the testament, or diminished by his selling or otherwise disposing of a part of them; but in either case the bequest subsisted for what remained. In like manner, the legacy of a herd of cattle or flock of sheep might be increased or lessened by supervening changes after the testament; and it passed to the legatee such as it was when the bequest fell due, although all the animals composing the original flock might be different from what they were at first. If the flock received an increase after the date of the testament, the legatee got the benefit of it; and, on the other hand, if the flock was reduced to a single sheep, he was entitled to claim it.[3] But if from any cause the thing bequeathed was so entirely changed in its nature or condition as no longer to fall under the original description of it given by the testator, the bequest became ineffectual. Thus, if one left a legacy of a flock of sheep, and none of the animals remained alive at his death, the legatee had no right to claim the hides or the wool. Again, if the testator bequeathed a ship, which was broken up and taken to pieces before his death, the legatee could not claim the materials.

Specific legacy.

In some of its legal consequences the distinction between a specific and a general legacy is important. A specific legacy is one where the object is so particularised as to be distinguished from all others. A general legacy is one where

---

[1] Code Civil, art. 1021.   [2] I. 2. 20. 31.   [3] I. 2. 20. 18.

the object is indeterminate and is not distinguished from other things of the same kind belonging to the deceased. If one bequeath a landscape by Claude, and he has only one picture by that artist, there can be no doubt what is meant; the legacy is specific. But if a testator bequeath simply a horse, to be taken from several in his stable, or a landscape, to be taken from several in his gallery, how is the selection to be made? This may vary according to circumstances. If the right of selection be given to the legatee, he may choose the horse or picture which he considers most valuable; if the choice be left to the heir, he may exercise his discretion with a due regard to the will; and, if no choice be given to either, the heir cannot be compelled to give the best thing, nor the legatee to accept the worst—a rule which has been followed in the modern French Code.[1]

If the same thing was bequeathed to two or more persons, *Accretion among legatees.* either jointly (*conjunctim*) or separately (*disjunctim*), each took an equal share; and if any one of them predeceased the testator, or failed to take his portion, it fell by accretion to the rest.[2] But this right does not take effect when the testator forbids it expressly; and if one of the co-legatees only fails after he has acquired right to the legacy, it transmits to his heirs.[3]

Accretion has no place among the *conjuncti verbis tantum*, being those to whom the thing has been bequeathed, with a severance or division into parts between them—for instance: " I leave to Titius and Seius a particular estate or subject, in equal portions, or one half to each of them," or in any other proportion,—*quoniam semper partes habent legatarii.*[4]

In Scotland it has been repeatedly decided, that where a legacy has been left to two persons, to be divided equally between them, the *jus accrescendi* does not take place in favour of the survivor.[5] But accretion has been found to take place where, in the clause of institution, the legatees

[1] I. 2. 20. 22 and 23. Warn. Inst. § 689. Code Civil, art. 1022.

[2] I. 2. 22. 8.

[3] Mackeldey, § 740.

[4] D. 32. 3. 89. Ortolan, vol. ii.

p. 578, § 870.

[5] Stair, 3. 8. 27. Bankton, 3. 8. 52. Paterson, M. 8070; Rove, M. 8101. Torrie, 31st May 1832, 10 Sh. 597.

were conjunct both as to the matter and the words, according to the rule of the civil law, by which, in such conjunct rights, the survivor takes the whole.[1]

Errors in name or description.
A legacy may be effectually bequeathed in any words which express the desire of the testator that it should be paid. An error in the name of the legatee will not vitiate the legacy, if his description is otherwise sufficient to fix his identity. So also a mistake in the description of the thing bequeathed, or a false inductive clause added to a legacy, will not make it void.[2] But if any one bequeath a specific thing, describing it as "my diamond ring," or "my set of Sevres china," and nothing answering the description can be found among the effects of the deceased, the legacy is null.

Legacy falls by predecease of legatee.
The general rule of law is that a legacy implies *dilectus personœ*, and so is personal to the legatee. From the nature of a *mortis causa* bequest it only becomes effectual at the testator's death, and must necessarily fall by the predecease of the legatee. As a consequence of this rule, it is, in the ordinary case, indispensable to mention other persons intended to be favoured failing the legatee, when it is meant that the legacy shall not lapse by his predecease ; and this is usually done by a clause of conditional institution or substitution.

Legacies pure and conditional.
Whether a legacy has vested in a legatee so as to be disposable as his property, depends upon the particular terms of the bequest, which may or may not contain conditions qualifying the nature of the right and affecting the term of payment. Whatever may be the nature of the legacy, no right to it can belong to the legatee or be transmitted from him to his representatives, if he die before the testator. If the legacy be pure and simple, so as not to depend on any condition for its validity, the right to it vests in the legatee, and will transmit to his representatives by his surviving the testator, even though it should not be payable till a future period and the legatee should die before the term. When the legacy is conditional, so that its efficacy depends upon an event or contingency, and the legatee, though he should survive

---

[1] See Barbour, 6th Feb. 1835, 13   D. 94.
Sh. 422; Tulloch, 23d Nov. 1838, 1   [2] l. 2. 20. § 29, 30, 31.

the testator, dies before the condition is fulfilled, he acquires
no right to the legacy. It is a condition rendering a legacy
contingent if it is made payable on a future event which may
never happen. All legacies for payment of which no term is
prescribed, and which are not conditional, ought to be paid
immediately after the succession is accepted by the heir. In
the Roman law the phrase *dies cedit*, when applied to a
legacy, means that the period of vesting has arrived; and
dies venit means that the time has come when the legacy
may be demanded.[1]

The estate of the testator is primarily liable for his debts,
and if he die insolvent the legacies are not due :—*Bona in-
telliguntur cujusque, quæ deducto ære alieno supersunt.*[2]

Legacies may be revoked by the testator either expressly Revocation
in a will or codicil, or tacitly by disposing otherwise of the of legacies.
thing bequeathed. A bequest to a debtor of a debt due by
him is revoked, if the debtor is afterwards compelled to pay
it in the testator's lifetime. So if the testator, after bequeathing a thing, should sell it or make a gift of it to another person, this would annul the legacy. A legacy is also annulled
when it is transferred to a second legatee in room of the first,
and this holds good even though the second legatee should die
before the testator. If the thing bequeathed should perish in
the lifetime of the testator, or even after his death and before
delivery, without the fault of the heir, the legacy would be
ineffectual; but if the loss was occasioned by the fault of the
heir, he could be compelled to make it good.[3]

II.—ENGLISH LAW.

By the English Statute of Wills, 1 Vict. c. 26, s. 33, " where Direction in
any person, being a child or other issue of the testator to whom Statute of
any real or personal estate shall be devised or bequeathed, for Wills.
any estate or interest not determinable at or before the death
of such person, shall die in the lifetime of the testator leaving

---

[1] " *Cedere* diem significat, incipere   peti possit."—D. 50. 16. 213.
deberi pecuniam. *Venire* diem signi-   [2] D. 50. 16. 39.
ficat, eum diem venisse, quo pecunia   [3] I. 2. 20. 16.

issue, and any such issue of such person shall be living at the time of the death of the testator, such devise or bequest shall not lapse, but shall take effect as if the death of such person had happened immediately after the death of the testator, unless a contrary intention shall appear by the will." Under this enactment the issue do not take directly in their own right under an implied substitution, but the legacy is given to the deceased legatee absolutely, as though he had survived the testator; "and it is therefore disposable by the will of the legatee." [1]

This is an exception to the general rule.

Apart from this special regulation, it is a general rule of the law of England that unless the legatee survive the testator the legacy lapses, and this holds even where the legacy is given to the legatee "and his executors, administrators, and assigns." But it appears to be established that where the bequest is "to A *or* his heirs," or "to A or his personal representatives," the word "or," generally speaking, implies a substitution, so as to prevent the bequest from lapsing.[2]

III.—SCOTTISH LAW.

Rules of Scottish law as to vesting and lapsing of legacies.

In Scotland it has been repeatedly decided that wherever a legacy is given, not merely to an individual, but also "to his heirs and executors," it will not lapse by the legatee named predeceasing the testator, but will belong to his heirs or next of kin in their own right as conditional institutes.[3] It may also be observed that the Scottish law, while it adopts the general rule that a legacy to which heirs are not substituted lapses by the legatee dying before the testator, recognises an implied substitution of grandchildren or direct issue, founded on the principle of *paterna pietas*, in legacies or provisions by a father to a child, either singly or as one of a class, whether there be or be not an express substitution of another, failing the child, to the effect of passing the right to the issue of the child on his predeceasing the testator.[4]

[1] Williams on Exec., p. 1098.
[2] Williams on Exec., p. 1085 and 1088.
[3] More's Stair, vol. ii. p. 344, notes.
[4] Dixon, 10th June 1836, 14 D. 938.

CHAPTER VII.

OF ROMAN INTESTATE SUCCESSION.

An intestate is one who dies without a will, or who leaves a Intestacy defined. will which is not valid. The law appoints the person or persons who are to succeed to his property, according to certain rules, which mainly depend upon their proximity in blood to the deceased.

Relationship between two persons arises either from the Relationship. one being descended from the other, which makes the connection between ascendants and descendants, or from their being both descended from the same common ancestor, which makes the connection between collaterals. All blood relations are either descendants or ascendants or collaterals. Consanguinity is distinguished by two lines, the direct and the collateral. The degrees of direct consanguinity are reckoned by counting the number of descents between the ancestor and the descendant. Thus father and son are related in the first degree, grandfather and grandson in the second degree.

The degrees of collateral consanguinity are differently reckoned in the civil and in the canon law. The civil law reckons the number of descents between the persons on both sides from the common ancestor. By this rule brothers are in the second degree and cousins-german in the fourth. But the canon law counts the number of descents between the common ancestor and the two persons on one side only, and, if they are not equally near, on the side of the one who is most distant from the common ancestor. Thus by the canon law brothers stand related to each other in the first degree, and an uncle and nephew in the second degree.

Full blood and half blood. Among collateral kindred it is necessary to distinguish between the whole blood and the half blood. Persons are connected by full blood who are descended of the same father and mother. The nearest are brothers and sisters german. The half blood may be either consanguinean or uterine; the first are persons descended of the same father but not of the same mother, and the second are persons descended of the same mother but not of the same father.

In regulating succession, the Roman law takes no account of the nature or origin of the property left by the deceased, and in particular it makes no distinction between real and personal estates, which by the modern law of succession in this country are governed by totally different rules.

Intestate succession before Justinian. Under the decemviral law, succession *ab intestato* was based on the *patria potestas*, or the ancient constitution of the Roman family. Hence there were three classes called to succeed.

Rules by Twelve Tables. In the first order were the *sui heredes*, that is, children or grandchildren under the power of the father whose succession had opened. Daughters under power succeeded like males, and took an equal part. Adopted children were under power, and the wife if *in manu*. The *sui heredes* were so called because they belonged to the defunct by the paternal power.

Failing *sui heredes*, the succession belonged to the nearest agnates, who excluded the more remote. Agnates are relations by males; they are those who would have been all subjected to the same power if the common head were still alive. The sister is agnate of her brother when both are born of the same father. Beyond this the right of succession was stopped for women under the decemviral law.

In the third place, failing agnates the succession devolved on the *gentiles*, who inherited together.

Gentiles. According to Cicero, the *gentiles* must bear the same name, such as Scipio, Brutus, and the like. They must be descended from free persons, not from slaves. They must not pass by adoption into another family. If they do so, they take the name of the *gens* to which they have emigrated, and remain

no longer in their original *gens.* Thus community of name
and pure extraction, without any taint of servile blood, are
the essential characteristics of Roman gentility.[1] In the re-
volutions that affected public institutions, the *gentiles* ceased
to be called to the succession, and persons connected by the
tie of blood were preferred.

Gaius has pointed out the harshness of the rules of intes- Harshness
tate succession in the Twelve Tables. A son not under power rules.
from having been emancipated, or from any other cause, could
not succeed, because he was not in the family and no longer
among the *sui heredes.* So agnates who underwent a change
of state lost agnation, and along with it the right of succession. Female agnates, other than sisters, could not succeed.
Finally, cognates or relations by women were wholly excluded, so that even the mother, who was not *in manu mariti,*
did not succeed to her son and daughter, and her son and
daughter did not succeed to her.[2]

The second period of intestate succession before Justinian Prætorian
comprises the innovations introduced by the prætors, who law.
relaxed the severity of the decemviral law. They called to
the succession, by the indirect plan of the possession of goods,
all the children without distinction, whether emancipated or
not, by the edict *unde liberi ;* the wife not *in manu* and the
husband by the edict *unde vir et uxor ;* the more remote
agnates, though emancipated, by the edict *unde legitimi ;* the
cognates by the edict *unde cognati ;* and so forth.

When the prætor called emancipated children to the pos- Collatio
session of goods by the edict *unde liberi* or *contra tabulas,* he bonorum.
obliged them to throw into the succession all the separate
property which, if they had remained under power, would
have belonged to the head of the family, so as to place them
on an equal footing with their brothers who had not been
emancipated. This was called *collatio bonorum.*

The same principle was afterwards extended to a daughter
even though not emancipated, who was bound to bring into
account the marriage portion she received from the head of

---

[1] Cicero, Topic, c. 6. Giraud, Dis-   [2] Gai. 3. 18-24.
sertation sur la Gentilité Romaine.

the family in any accounting with the other children. The Emperor Leo extended this obligation to the *donatio propter' nuptias.*[1]

Finally, Justinian ordained that all the children, without distinction, succeeding *ab intestato* to the property of ascendants, should be obliged to collate all those things which were imputable to legitim in a complaint of a testament as undutiful.[2]

Intestate succession under Justinian.   Notwithstanding all the improvements introduced by the prætorian edicts, Justinian found it necessary, at the close of his reign, to remodel and simplify the rules of intestate succession, and establish a new system by the 118th Novel, which was published A.D. 543. To this an important addition was made by the 127th Novel.

In the Roman law of succession not only is no distinction made between real and personal estates, but primogeniture is disregarded ; and there is no preference of males over females.

Consanguinity being the basis of Justinian's law, blood relations succeed *ab intestato.* Except in the instance of the surviving spouse of the intestate, affinity or relationship by marriage gives no right of succession.[3] There is no difference between agnates and cognates ; the nearer in degree in either excluding the more remote in either. Certain persons, however, unconnected with the deceased by blood, have the right of succession on special grounds.

The following is the order in which relations succeed *ab intestato* under the law of the Novels :—

General rules.   First, the succession is devolved on the descendants of the deceased.

Secondly, failing descendants, the nearest ascendants are called ; but if there be brothers and sisters, and the children of deceased brothers and sisters, they are entitled to succeed together along with ascendants in the same class.

Thirdly, half brothers and sisters consanguinean and uterine, and the sons and daughters of such half brothers

---

[1] De Fresquet, vol. ii. p. 18.   [2] Ortolan, Institutes, § 1127-1130.
Marezoll, § 218.   [3] C. 6. 59. 7.

and sisters as had predeceased the intestate, are called in the third class.

Finally, in the fourth class are comprehended all other collateral relations, without distinguishing whether they are connected with the defunct on both sides or on one side only, but always according to the proximity in degree.[1]

I.—DESCENDANTS.

If a person dies intestate leaving lawful children, they all First class. succeed to him by equal portions without distinction of sex, and if there is only one child, he takes the whole estate. A descendant of either sex, or any degree, is preferred to all ascendants and collaterals.

In the direct descending line the right of representation Representa-takes place *in infinitum.* The effect of this is, that the de-[tion.] scendants of a son or daughter who has predeceased, take the same place and share of the succession that their parent would have done had he been alive. This right is admitted when the children of the intestate in the first degree coexist with the descendants of a son and daughter in whatever degree they may happen to be. Thus the children of the intestate succeed to equal shares *per capita*, while the grandchildren by a son deceased succeed only *per stirpes* to the share which their parent would have had if he had been alive.

Even when grandchildren by different sons or daughters When stand alone, though they are all equally near in degree to the grandchildren take intestate, they take by representation, so that if they happen alone. to be unequal in their numbers as derived from different stocks, the succession is divided among them, not by the head in equal portions, but *per stirpes*, the descendants of each son or daughter having no more among them all than the portion which their father or mother would have taken if alive.[2] In England a different and more equitable rule is

---

[1] Marezoll, § 206. Mackeldey,   art. 3.   Dr Harris, Justinian's Inst.
649-653.   3. 1. 6, p. 186, note.
[2] Domat, part 2, b. 2, tit. 1, § 2,

followed. For if all the children are dead and only grand-children exist, they all take, not by families, but *per capita*, that is, equal shares in their own right as next of kin.[1]

II.—ASCENDANTS WITH OR WITHOUT COLLATERALS.

Second class.

If there are no descendants, the father and mother and other ascendants exclude all collaterals from the succession, except brothers and sisters of the whole blood and the children of deceased brothers and sisters, who may succeed concurrently with ascendants in the manner to be imme-diately explained.[2]

Three cases may possibly occur affecting succession in the ascending line:—First, the succession of ascendants alone, where there are no collaterals falling within the favoured category; secondly, the concurrence of ascendants with brothers and sisters of the whole blood; and, thirdly, the concurrence of ascendants with brothers and sisters of the whole blood and also with the children of deceased brothers and sisters.

Ascendants alone.

1. When ascendants stand   one, the father and mother succeed in equal portions, and if only one of them survives, he or she succeeds to the whole estate.   There is no repre-sentation among ascendants, and the nearest in degree ex-cludes the more remote, so that the father alone, or the mother alone, will exclude grandparents.

When several ascendants concur in the same degree, some on the father's side and some on the mother's side, the suc-cession is divided into two equal parts, one of which is given to the paternal ascendants and the other to the maternal ascendants *per lineas*, though the number of individuals should be less on one side than on the other.

Ascendants along with brothers and sisters.

2. If there be brothers and sisters of the whole blood, they are called to the succession along with the father and mother or other ascendants, and the estate is divided among them *in capita*, that is, according to the number of persons.   So where

---

[1] Williams's Exec., p. 1348, 1349.   [2] N. 118, ch. 2.   N. 127, ch. 1.

the deceased leaves a father and mother, and a brother and sister, each is entitled to a fourth of the succession.

Voet was of opinion that under the 118th Novel, ch. 2, only the father and mother could succeed along with the brother of the intestate, and consequently that the brother excluded the grandfather.[1] This principle was recognised in the law of England in the case of Evelyn, decided by Lord Chancellor Hardwick in 1754;[2] but Domat and other eminent civilians have rejected the opinion of Voet. They say he has given an erroneous version of a passage in the Greek Novel 118, ch. 2, by the words "si aut pater aut mater fuerint," while the clause should be translated, as it is by Warnkoenig, "*etsi* pater aut mater sint," the true meaning of the law being that brothers and sisters are called to the succession along with ascendants, even although these ascendants should be a father and mother.[3]

3. By the 118th Novel the children of a deceased brother or sister german were not admitted to the succession along with ascendants or surviving brothers and sisters; on the contrary, they were excluded by ascendants. This was corrected by the 127th Novel, ch. 1, which allowed those children to succeed along with ascendants and surviving brothers or sisters, so as to take by representation the share which would have fallen to their parent had he or she been alive. *And also with children of deceased brother or sister.*

Whether these nephews are entitled to succeed along with ascendants alone, when there are no surviving brothers of the deceased, is a doubtful question, which has led to much controversy. By the 118th Novel these nephews are excluded by ascendants: and by the 127th Novel they are only expressly called when brothers succeed along with ascendants, from which it is inferred that they are not admitted with ascendants alone. This is the conclusion to which Cujas has

---

[1] Voet, Com. ad Pand., tom. ii. p. 588.

[2] Evelyn *v.* Evelyn, 3 Atkyns, 762.

[3] See Domat, part 2, b. 2, t. 2. s.

1. Muhlenbruch, Doctrina Pandectarum, vol. iii. p. 227. Warn. Inst. § 510. Dr Irving, Introduction to Civil Law, p. 99.

T

arrived, and Pothier says he thinks it is most in accordance with the true meaning of the Novel.[1]

III.—COLLATERALS.

Succession of collaterals.

As a general rule, collaterals who are nearest in the degree of kindred to the deceased are called together to his succession, and exclude those who are in a degree more remote. This rule suffers limitations in the Roman law by the preference given to the full blood over the half blood, and by the right of representation, which in collateral succession is given to the children of brothers and sisters, but extends no further.

Brothers and sisters german.

If a person dies leaving neither descendants nor ascendants, his brothers and sisters of the full blood succeed to his estate in equal shares.[2] But if the intestate leaves brothers or sisters, and also nephews or nieces by a deceased brother or sister, these last will succeed, along with their uncles and aunts, to the share which their parent would have taken if alive. Among collaterals, however, as already explained, this privilege of representation does not extend beyond the sons and daughters of brothers and sisters.

Nephews.

If the intestate's brothers and sisters are dead, and nephews alone succeed, it has been made a question how the estate is to be divided. Azo contends that it must be divided *in capita*, and Accursius *in stirpes*. Vinnius holds that when there are only nephews there is no representation, and consequently that each of them takes an equal share in his own right; and this is the rule of distribution adopted in England.[3]

Half brothers and sisters.

On the failure of brothers and sisters by the whole blood, and their children, the brothers and sisters by the half blood

---

[1] Pothier, Traité des Successions chap. 2, s. 2. Warn. Inst. 2. p. 150 note.

[2] N. 118, ch. 3.

[3] Vinn. Com. lib. 3, title 5, p. 539. Dr Harris, Justinian's Institutes, 3. 2. 4, p. 197, note.

succeed, whether they are by the same father only or by the same mother. And if any of these brothers or sisters by the half blood have died leaving children, the right of representation is extended to them so as to enable them to succeed to the share which would have fallen to their parent if alive, just as in the case of children of brothers-german.[1]

All the other relations of the deceased are called to the succession according to their proximity in degree, the nearer being always preferred to the more remote ; and if many are found in the same degree, whether on the father's side or on the mother's, the estate must be divided among them in equal shares, according to the number of persons.[2] *Other relations nearest in degree.*

For particular reasons the Roman law gives a right of succession to other persons besides relations. *Special cases of succession.*

When one of two married persons dies without leaving any relations, the survivor, whether husband or wife, is called to the succession under the edict of the prætor *unde vir et uxor,* which was confirmed by imperial constitutions.[3] *Husband and wife.*

A widow who was poor and unprovided for had a right to share in the succession of her deceased husband. When he left more than three descendants the widow was entitled to participate with them *per capita;* and if there were only three or fewer descendants, or if other relations of the husband were called, her portion was fixed at a fourth of the estate. If she had children by the deceased, she had only the usufruct of her portion during her life, and was bound to preserve it for these children ; but in all other cases she acquired her share in full property, and could dispose of it at her pleasure.[4]

If a man had no lawful descendants or ascendants, he might by will give his whole inheritance to his natural children—that is, those born of a concubine—or to their mother : but if he had lawful children, he could only leave one-twelfth to the natural children and their mother. If the father died intestate, without leaving a lawful wife or lawful issue, his *Natural children.*

---

[1] N. 118, ch. 3.
[2] Ibid.
[3] I. 3. 9. 6.   D. 38. 11.   C. 6. 18.
[4] N. 117, ch. 5.

natural children and their mother were entitled to receive two unciæ, or one-sixth of the succession, and the remainder fell to the lawful heirs.[1]

Treasury ultimus heres.
On the failure of all heirs and successors, testamentary and legal, the succession devolved on the Treasury, under the burden of paying the debts of the deceased to the extent of the value of the estate.

[1] N. 89, ch. 12, § 2 and 3, and ch. 15.   De Fresquet, vol. ii. p. 41.

CHAPTER VIII.

OF INTESTATE SUCCESSION IN FRANCE, ENGLAND, AND SCOTLAND.

I.—FRENCH LAW.

IN the modern law of France no distinction is made between real and personal estates in the matter of succession; there is no privilege of primogeniture, and no preference of males over females; and many of the rules are similar to those in the Roman law. No distinction between real and personal estates.

Children and other descendants, of whatever degree, male or female, exclude all other relations, whether ascendants or collaterals. Rules of intestacy by Civil Code.

If the intestate die without issue, survived by his father and mother, and brothers or sisters, or their descendants, one half of the succession goes to the parents equally between them, and the other half belongs to the brothers and sisters, and their descendants. If only one of the parents survive, his or her share is limited to a fourth, and the other persons mentioned succeed to three-fourths. If neither parent survive, the brothers and sisters, and their descendants, take the whole estate, to the exclusion of ascendants and other collaterals.

When the intestate leaves no issue, and no brothers or sisters, or their descendants, the succession is divided into two equal portions between the ascendants of the paternal line and the ascendants of the maternal line.

For further information on the rules of intestate succession in France, reference may be made to the Civil Code, articles 745-755.

II.—ENGLISH LAW.

Descent to lands. By the law of England, as well as of Scotland, the rules of succession to lands are quite different from those which relate to personal property. In England, descent signifies the title by which a man acquires an estate in lands as the heir-at-law of a person deceased, and the estate itself is called the inheritance.

Inheritance Act. By the Inheritance Act, 3 & 4 William IV. c. 106, which applies to deaths occurring after 1st January 1834, the heir must trace his descent, not from the person last seised, but from the purchaser—that is to say, from the person who last acquired the land otherwise than by descent, or by any escheat, partition, or enclosure, making the land descendible as if acquired by descent.[1]

It often happens, however, that it is uncertain by whom an estate was originally purchased; and to obviate this difficulty the Act declares that the person last entitled to the land shall be considered to have been the purchaser, unless it be proved that he inherited it; and the same rule is applied at every step upward of the pedigree.[2] Where there is a total failure of heirs of the purchaser, or of an ancestor held as such, the descent is traced from the person last entitled to the land, as if he had been the purchaser.[3] Actual seisin is unnecessary in the purchaser, or the person to be deemed such.[4]

Descent traced from purchaser. The rule, that in every case descent must be traced from the purchaser, though newly introduced by the Inheritance Act, is founded on a maxim peculiar to the English law, that none can claim as heir who is not of the blood of the purchaser. Respect is had to the origin of landed property, and the ancestor who acquired it by purchase, so that land which came by the father shall descend to the heirs on the part of the father, and land which came by the mother shall descend to the heirs on the part of the mother—*paterna paternis et*

---

[1] Sect. 1.
[2] Sect. 2.
[3] 22 & 23 Vict. c. 35, sect. 19.

[4] Lord St Leonards's Practical Treatise on New Statutes relating to Property, 2d ed., p. 257.

materna maternis. No such rule obtains in Scotland, where
the law looks no farther back than to the last owner of the
estate, and assigns him an heir without considering from
what ancestor the estate was derived.[1]

To illustrate the English rule, suppose that John dies
owner of an estate which he inherited from his father George,
who purchased it, the claimant must prove that he is heir by
the right of blood to George the father, instead of John the
last owner. The consequence of this is, that no relation of
John on the mother's side can as such succeed to the estate ;
but, if the estate descended to John from his mother, who is
known to have been the purchaser, the descent in that case
must be traced from her, and John's relations on the father's
side are excluded on the same principle.[2]

According to the law of England, inheritances lineally Canons of
descend to the issue of the person last entitled *in infini-* descent.
tum ; the male issue is admitted before the female ; where
there are two or more males in equal degree, the eldest only
inherits ; but females, where there are several, take together.

The lineal descendants of any person deceased represent
their ancestor; that is, stand in the same place as the person
himself would have done had he been living. So, by right
of representation, the child or grandchild, whether male or
female, of an eldest son, succeeds before the younger son.

On failure of lineal descendants or issue of the person last
entitled, the inheritance ascends and descends to the lineal
ancestors and to the collateral relations of the purchaser.
Thus, next after descendants, the father, as the nearest lineal
ancestor, succeeds in preference to a brother under the sixth
section of the Inheritance Act. On the failure of the father,
the brothers and sisters and their descendants take in their
order in preference to the grandfather, and the estate does
not pass to any remoter lineal ancestor till the issue of the
father are exhausted.

The nearest lineal ancestor is the heir of the purchaser in
preference to any of the descendants of such lineal ancestor,

---

[1] Stephen's Com. on the Laws   Ersk. 3. 8. 10.
of England, 4th ed., vol. i. p. 388.   [2] Stephen's Com. vol. i. p. 389, 390.

and to more remote lineal ancestors and their descendants
(other than himself), and the descendants of such lineal
ancestors succeed next after, or in default of him.[1] Farther,
the paternal ancestors of the person from whom the descent
is to be traced and their descendants, are always preferred to
his maternal ancestors and their descendants.[2]

Between collaterals of a purchaser, a relation of the half
blood succeeds next after any relation in the same degree of
the whole blood and his issue, where the common ancestor
is a male; and next after the common ancestor where such
common ancestor is a female. So the brother of the half
blood on the part of the father inherits next after the sisters
of the whole blood on the part of the father and their issue;
and the brother of the half blood on the part of the mother
inherits next after the mother.[3] Before the Inheritance Act
kinsmen of the half blood were wholly excluded. The collaterals of the half blood of a person last entitled, who was
not a purchaser, will take in a course of descent from the
purchaser of whose whole blood they are, by force of the
direction, that in every case the descent shall be traced from
the purchaser.

Lastly, in lineal ascending and in collateral inheritances
the male stocks are preferred to the female—that is, the
male ancestors and kindred derived from their blood, however remote, are admitted before female ancestors and kindred derived from their blood, however near—unless where
the lands have in fact descended from a female.

These canons of descent have been transcribed almost in
the words of Lord St Leonards from his 'Practical Treatise
on the New Statutes relating to Property,' which contains a
comparative view of the 'Canons according to Blackstone,'
and the 'Canons according to the New Law grafted upon
the Old;' and to this work our readers are referred as the
best exposition of this difficult subject.[4]

There are two anomalous modes of descent (gavelkind
and borough English) which prevail in some parts of

[1] Sect. 6.   [3] Sect. 9.
[2] Sect. 7.   [4] Practical Treatise, 2d ed., p. 264.

England; but the nature of these customs has already been explained.[1]

In the distribution of the personal estate of an intestate, the law of England gives the same preference as the civil law to the children and lineal descendants of the deceased, only taking in the widow, if there is one surviving. After the expiry of a year from the death of the intestate, his personal property is distributed in the following manner :—One-third goes to the widow of the intestate, and the residue in equal portions to his children, or if dead to their representatives, that is, their lineal descendants; if there are no children or descendants of children, then a moiety goes to the widow, and a moiety to the next of kin in equal degree, and their representatives ; if no widow, the whole goes to the children ; if neither widow nor children, the whole is distributed among the next of kin in equal degree and their representatives. Among descendants children represent their parents *ad infinitum ;* but no representatives are admitted among collaterals farther than the children of the intestate's brothers and sisters.[2] In determining the next of kin under the English Statute of Distributions, the degrees of propinquity are reckoned according to the computation of the civil law ; and the relations on the mother's side share equally with the relations on the father's side in the same degree. *(margin: Distribution of personal estate. Descendants and widow. Relations on father's and mother's side share equally.)*

The heir-at-law, if one of the next of kin, has an equal part in the distribution of the personal property with the rest of the children, without taking into account the value of the land which he has received by descent or otherwise from the intestate; but if the heir-at-law has had any advancement from his father out of his personal estate, this is counted as part of his share. If any of the younger children, not being the heir-at-law, has received an advancement either from the real or personal estate of the intestate in his lifetime, this must be reckoned as a part of the distributive share of such child.[3] *(margin: Heir may share in personal property.)*

Where a wife dies intestate the husband is entitled to be

[1] See supra, p. 143.
[2] 22 & 23 Car. II. c. 10.
[3] 22 & 23 Car. II. c. 10, s. 5. Williams's Exec., p. 1352.

Husband's rights to wife's effects.

her administrator, and to recover and enjoy her personal property whether she leave children or not ; but if the husband be judicially separated from his wife, her personality will go to her next of kin, as if she had been a single woman.[1] On the other hand, if personal property is settled on a wife for her separate use, and after her decease on her next of kin, expressly excluding the husband's right, as if she had died unmarried, the wife's next of kin will succeed, to the exclusion of the husband.

Rights of widow.

The widow's right to a share of the effects of her husband who dies intestate has already been explained. At common law the wife has no absolute right to any part of the husband's personal property, and we have shown he can by will bequeath the whole to a stranger; but if he die intestate, she becomes entitled to her share under the Statute of Distributions, unless her claim be expressly barred by antenuptial contract.[2]

Rights of father.

When the intestate dies without leaving wife or child, his father, as the next of kin in the first degree, is entitled to the whole personal estate. If there be no child, but a widow and father survive, the personal estate is divided equally between them.[3]

Rights of mother.

Before the statute of 1 James II. c. 17, if a person died intestate without a wife, child, or father alive, his mother, as his next of kin in the first degree, was entitled to his whole personal estate; but it was declared by that Act, sect. 7, " that if, after the death of a father, any of his children shall die intestate without wife or children in the lifetime of the mother, every brother and sister, and the representatives of them, shall have an equal share with her." The reason assigned for this enactment is that, under the former state of the law, the mother might marry and transfer all the property to a second husband.[4]

If the intestate die without wife, child, or father, and without leaving brother or sister, nephew or niece, the whole

---

[1] Williams's Exec., p. 1340. 20 & 21 Vict. c. 85, s. 25.
[2] Ibid. p. 1342.
[3] Williams's Exec., p. 1357.
[4] Ibid. p. 1357.

personal property devolves, as before the statute, on the mother.[1]

Brothers and sisters of the intestate are preferred to the grandfather or grandmother, though they are all in the second degree of kindred.[2] Grandfathers and grandmothers, being nearer in degree, exclude uncles and aunts. Uncles and nephews, aunts and nieces, are entitled to equal portions, being all in the third degree. If the intestate leave one brother and several children by a deceased brother, these children will only take one-half of the personal estate, and their uncle the other; but if the brothers and sisters of the intestate are all dead, having left children, these nephews and nieces all take in their own right *per capita.*[3]

Brothers preferred to grandfather.

Brothers and sisters of the half blood are entitled to an equal share of the intestate's estate with brothers and sisters of the whole blood.[4] In this respect the English law differs from the civil law and the law of Scotland.

Half brothers and sisters share equally with full blood.

Except in the instance of the wife of the intestate, affinity or relationship by marriage gives no title to a share of his property under the statute.[5]

The Statute of Distributions provides that it shall not prejudice the customs of the city of London, or the province of York or other places, but that these customs shall be observed as formerly. But, though the customs remain in force in the case of intestacy, any one may now by will bequeath his whole goods and chattels, all restraints on testamentary power having been removed by subsequent statutes.[6]

III.—SCOTTISH LAW.

In the succession to lands in Scotland *ab intestato*, the heir must trace his descent, not from the last purchaser as in England, but from the person last seised. Descendants are preferred to all other relations, males being always preferred

Succession to lands.

Heirs of line.

[1] Williams's Exec., p. 1359.
[2] Ibid. p. 1360.
[3] Ibid. p. 1363.
[4] Williams's Exec., p. 1362.
[5] Ibid. p. 1362.
[6] Ibid. p. 1374.

before females, and the eldest male before the younger, while females in the same degree succeed equally, and are called

**Descend-
ants.** heirs-portioners. The estate goes first to the eldest son and his issue male or female ; next to the second son and his issue male or female ; and so on through all the sons with their issue in the order of seniority. On the failure of sons and their issue the daughters succeed equally as heirs-portioners, and the issue of each daughter who has predeceased the defunct takes the mother's place. On the failure of immediate descendants grandchildren are called, and after them great-grandchildren, and so forth *in infinitum*, males always succeeding before females, and the eldest male before the younger.[1]

**Brothers
and sisters
and their
descend-
ants.** When there are no descendants collaterals succeed, among whom brothers-german take the first place. If the deceased was the eldest brother the estate goes to the immediate younger brother ; but where the deceased leaves brothers both older and younger than himself, the estate, if it be heritage, goes to the next younger brother and not to the eldest, according to the maxim that *heritage* descends; and if the deceased happens to be the youngest, the succession goes to the immediate elder brother, as being the least deviation from this rule. If there are no brothers-german, the sisters-german succeed equally ; then brothers consanguinean one after another in the same order as brothers-german, and failing them sisters consanguinean equally. Brothers and sisters uterine—that is, by the mother only—are entirely excluded from the succession to land.[2]

**Father's
rights.** Next in order after brothers and sisters and their descendants, the father succeeds to lands as the nearest relation in the ascending line, and after him his brothers and sisters in their order; then the paternal grandfather, and failing him his brothers and sisters, and so upwards as far as propinquity can **Mother and** be traced. By the law of Scotland, an estate in land never **relations
through her** ascends to the mother or her relations, though her children **excluded.** succeed to her. Even the mother's own estate, after vesting in her son or daughter, never ascends to relations claiming

[1] Ersk. 3. 8. 5 and 6.   [2] Ersk. 3. 8. 8.

through the mother. On the failure of heirs in the three lines of succession, the Crown succeeds as *ultimus heres.*[1]

In the succession to lands there is a right of representation, whereby, if any one has died, who, if alive, would have succeeded as heir, his place is supplied by his lineal descendants in their order. Thus, if an eldest son should die before the succession opens, a grandchild, male or female, by him, will exclude a younger son.[2] Right of representation.

A distinction is made between an estate to which the deceased has succeeded as heir to his father or other relation, and which is strictly termed *heritage,* and an estate which the deceased has acquired by *conquest*—that is, not by succession, but by purchase, donation, or other singular title. This holds where the deceased has died without issue, leaving brothers both older and younger than himself, or the issue of such brothers, or two or more uncles, older and younger than the father of the deceased, or the descendants of such uncles. In such cases, *heritage* descends to the immediate younger brother of the deceased, or to the next younger brother of his father; but *conquest* ascends to the immediate elder brother or uncle. Where the deceased is the youngest brother, and leaves two elder, the younger of the two surviving brothers is heir both of line and of conquest.[3] Heirs of conquest.

There is no room for this distinction in female succession, which the law divides equally among the co-heiresses, or heirs-portioners as they are called in Scotland. If the proprietor be a woman, her brother-german excludes sisters-german, and the immediate elder brother succeeds in conquest, and the immediate younger brother in heritage. Conquest can ascend but once; for, when one succeeds as heir of conquest, the estate becomes heritage in his person, and as such descends in the usual way at his death.[4]

Lord Stair thus explains the state of the law of Scotland as to intestate movable succession before the changes introduced by the 18 Vict. c. 23 (25th May 1855):—"The succession in movables from the intestate belongeth to the nearest Distribution of personal estate.

[1] Ersk. 3. 8. 9.   Stair, 3. 4. 33.   [3] Ersk. 3. 8. 14.
[2] Ersk. 3. 8. 11.   [4] Stair, 3. 4. 33.   Ersk. 3. 8. 15.

of kin, who are the defunct's whole agnates, male or female, being the kinsmen of the defunct's father's side of the nearest degree, without primogeniture or right of representation; wherein those joined to the defunct by both bloods do exclude the agnates by one blood."[1]

Exclusion of cognates. Here it will be observed (and this is the most remarkable feature of the Scottish system, as distinguished from the Roman law and the law of England), that intestate movable succession was confined to the agnates, male or female, being the kinsmen on the father's side, excluding altogether the cognates or relations on the mother's side. Strange as it may appear, the mother was not allowed to succeed to her own children, and all relations claiming through her were equally excluded. Under the statute of 1855, representation in movables was admitted, the position of the father was materially improved, and the mother, in certain circumstances, was admitted to a share of the personal estate of her children. But, with the exception of a provision to brothers and sisters uterine and their issue, to be afterwards noticed, all the relations claiming through the mother of the intestate, whether ascendants or collaterals, are still excluded from the succession, and the nearest of kin must be sought for among the agnates, male or female, being the kinsmen of the deceased on the father's side.

The rules of intestate succession in movables, as the law now stands, may be shortly explained :—

Descendants. *First,* The nearest descendants, male and female, in the same degree, succeed equally, with representation. Formerly there was no representation in movable succession; but it is now provided that the issue of a predeceasing next of kin shall come in the place of their parent in the succession to an intestate, with this restriction, that "no representation shall be admitted among collaterals after brothers and sisters descendants."[2]

Rights of father and mother. Failing descendants, the brothers and sisters german, and their issue, and the brothers and sisters by the father's side, and their issue, were formerly called to succeed before the

[1] Stair, 3. 8. 31.   [2] 18 Vict. c. 23, s. 1.

father; but this has now been modified by the following provisions in favour of the father and mother of the intestate :
" Where any person dying intestate shall predecease his father,
without leaving issue, his father shall have right to one-half
of his movable estate in preference to any brothers or sisters,
or their descendants, who may have survived such intestate." [1]

Again, " Where an intestate, dying without leaving issue,
whose father has predeceased him, shall be survived by his
mother, she shall have right to one-third of his movables, in
preference to his brothers and sisters, or their descendants, or
other next of kin of such intestate." [2]

Where the intestate dies without leaving issue, and his
father and mother have both predeceased him, his brothers
and sisters german, and their descendants, succeed to the
whole personal estate ; and failing these parties, his brothers
and sisters, on the father's side, and their descendants, are
called ; for the full blood still takes precedence of the half
blood in Scotland, though, as we have already shown, a
different rule prevails in England.

As regards brothers and sisters uterine, who, along with all
maternal relations of the deceased, were formerly entirely
excluded from succession in movables, as well as in heritage,
the following rule is now established : " Where an intestate,
dying without leaving issue, whose father and mother have
both predeceased him, shall not leave any brother or sister
german, or consanguinean, nor any descendant of a brother or
sister german, or consanguinean, but shall leave brothers and
sisters uterine, or a brother or sister uterine, or any descendant
of a brother or sister uterine, such brothers and sisters uterine,
and such descendants in place of their predeceasing parent,
shall have right to one-half of his movable estate." [3]   As
already explained, all the relations claiming through the
mother of the intestate, with this exception, are still excluded
from the succession. [4]

Brothers and sisters.

Full blood excludes half.

Rights of brothers and sisters uterine.

[1] 18 Vict. c. 23, s. 3.
[2] Ibid. s. 4.
[3] Ibid. s. 5.
[4] It was a saying of Lord Keeper

Williams, that "old imperfections
are safer than new experiments."
But this doctrine may be carried too
far; and it is not easy to explain

Father may acquire whole personal estate.   When the intestate died without leaving issue, or brothers and sisters, or their descendants, the father, before the statute 18 Vict. c. 23, was entitled to the whole personal estate, as the nearest ascendant; and this right remains entire, and cannot be affected by the provision of the statute, which, on the failure of issue, gives him a right to one-half of the movable estate of the deceased, in preference to the brothers and sisters, or their descendants.

Collation by heir-at-law.   Where the intestate leaves only one child, he is both heir and executor without collation.[1] But every heir who is one of the next of kin, whether he be in the line of descendants or collaterals, is bound to collate the heritable estate before he can claim any share of the movables; and, when he does so, the whole property is thrown into one mass, and divided equally among all the next of kin. This rule was introduced in order that the heir might in no case fare worse than the other next of kin.[2] Where any person who, had he survived the intestate, would have been his heir and one of his next of kin, shall have predeceased him, the child of the predeceaser, being the heir of the intestate, shall be entitled to collate the heritage, to the effect of claiming for himself and the other issue, if any, the share of the movable estate of the intestate, which might have been claimed by the predeceaser, upon collation, had he survived the intestate.[3]

Though the husband is the absolute administrator of the goods in communion consequent on marriage, during his life, yet, upon his death, a certain share of these goods belongs to his widow, *jure relictæ*, and a certain share to the children, called the legitim; and, though these rights may be renounced or discharged, they cannot be defeated by the will of the husband. If the husband leave a widow, but no child, one half of the personal estate goes to the widow; the other

---

how the unjust exclusion of the relations on the mother's side should have remained so long a *blot* on the Scottish system of intestate succession. The distinction between agnates and cognates should be abolished, so as to assimilate the law of Scotland to that of England.

[1] Ersk. 3. 9. 3.

[2] Ibid.

[3] 18 Vict. c. 23, s. 2.

half is the dead's part, which he may dispose of by testament, and which falls to his next of kin if he die intestate. When the husband leaves children, one or more, but no widow, they get one-half as their legitim; the other half is the dead's part, which also goes to the children, if the father has not disposed of it otherwise by his will. If he leaves both widow and children, the widow takes one-third, *jure relictæ*; another falls as legitim to the children, equally among them; the remaining third is the dead's part.[1]

If a wife die intestate, in Scotland, leaving separate personal property, not falling under the communion of goods, and excluded from the *jus mariti*, the succession does not devolve on the surviving husband, but falls to her children, or other next of kin, whoever they may be.

[1] Ersk. 3. 9. 19.

PART V.

OF ACTIONS AND PROCEDURE.

CHAPTER I.

OF MAGISTRATES AND JUDGES IN CIVIL SUITS.

Jurisdiction.

JURISDICTION is a power conferred by the State on a magistrate or judge to take cognisance of and determine questions according to law, and to carry his sentences into execution. Among the Romans jurisdiction was divided into voluntary and contentious. The first was exercised in matters that admitted of no opposition; the second related to disputed questions, which required judicial discussion.

By civil jurisdiction, questions of private right are decided; by criminal, crimes are tried and punished. That jurisdiction is supreme from which there lies no appeal to a higher court.

Jurisdiction is either proper or delegated. Proper jurisdiction is that which belongs to a magistrate himself in virtue of his office; delegated, is that which is communicated by the magistrate to another who acts under his authority. By special commission persons are sometimes delegated to judge in a particular cause, after the decision of which their power ceases.

When jurisdiction was conferred on a Roman magistrate, he acquired all the powers that were necessary to enable him to exercise it. In criminal law the *imperium merum*

was the power to inflict punishment upon offenders ; and the
imperium mixtum was the power to carry civil sentences or
decrees into execution.[1]

From jurisdiction in general must be distinguished the
competency of a tribunal.   By that phrase is meant the right
which a tribunal has to exercise in a particular case the jurisdiction which belongs to it.   From the earliest period it was
an established rule that the plaintiff should raise his action
before the court of the defendant's domicile—*Actor sequitur
forum rei*.   At first, this principle was acted upon whether
the action was real or personal.[2]   It was afterwards declared
by an imperial constitution that a *real action* might be
directed against the possessor in the territory where the subject in dispute was situated, *ratione rei sitæ*.[3]   Under Justinian this rule was followed in actions for vindicating
property ; but a *petitio hereditatis* was brought before the
court of the defendant's domicile, because this related rather
to the abstract right than to the objects of the succession.
By a constitution of the same emperor the authors of a delict
might be pursued wherever the unlawful act was committed,
and all debtors in consequence of a contract, in the place
where the contract was entered into.[4]

*Compe-
tency.*

Sect. 1.—*Judicial System during the Republic.*

Among the Romans the power of determining civil causes
belonged at first to the kings, and after their expulsion to the
consuls.   It then devolved on the prætor; and, in certain
cases, on the curule and plebeian ediles, who were charged
with the internal police of the city.[5]

Judges in
civil causes.

The prætor, a magistrate next in dignity to the consuls,
was elected annually by the Comitia Centuriata.   His chief
duty was to act as supreme judge in the civil court at Rome,
and he was assisted by a council of jurisconsults in determining questions of law.   At first there was only one prætor, A.R. 387.

Jurisdic-
tion of the
prætor.

---

[1] D. 2. 1. 2 and 3.
[2] De Fresquet, vol. ii. p. 401.
[3] C. 3. 19. 3.

[4] N. 69, ch. 1.   De Fresquet, vol.
ii. p. 519.
[5] Ortolan, Institutes, § 1849.

but he was afterwards joined, in the year 508 of Rome, by a colleague, who was invested with power to decide all disputes in which foreigners were concerned.[1]

After the conquest of Sicily, Sardinia, and the two Spains, new prætors were chosen to administer justice in these provinces. Permanent courts, which were usually presided over by a prætor, were established for the trial of certain crimes.[2] It became the practice for these magistrates to remain at Rome during their year of office, after which they proceeded to the provinces, where they dispensed justice as proprætors, the different departments assigned to each being determined by lot. The first among them was always the *prætor urbanus*. He performed the duties of the consuls in their absence, and his functions were considered so important that he was not permitted to leave Rome for more than ten days.

The prætor held his court in the Comitium, wore a robe bordered with purple, sat in a curule chair, and was attended by lictors. Ulpian informs us that his assessors at Rome were ten in number—five senators and five equestrians.[3] These assessors are often called judges, but they did not pronounce the sentence, which was drawn up in the prætor's name by their advice. Beaufort is of opinion that they were the same as the *decemviri litibus judicandis*, so often mentioned by ancient authors.[4]

Proceedings in jure.

According to the judicial system long established at Rome, it was the duty of the prætor, or other magistrate exercising civil jurisdiction, to inquire into matters of law; and whatever business was transacted before him was said to be done *in jure*. When the magistrate took cognisance both of the law and the fact, and decided the whole cause himself, the judgment was called extraordinary. But in the great majority of cases, and particularly where the parties were at issue upon the facts, it was customary for the magistrate merely to fix the question of law upon which the action turned, and then to remit it to a delegate with power to hear

Delegated judges.

[1] D. 1. 2. 3. 27.
[2] Ibid. § 32.
[3] Ulp. 1. 13.

[4] Beaufort, Rep. Rom., vol. ii. p. 35.

the cause, inquire into the facts, and pronounce sentence according to the result of the investigation.

There were three kinds of delegated judges, called respectively Judex, Arbiter, and Recuperatores.

The judex was not a magistrate holding jurisdiction; he was a private citizen invested by the magistrate with a judicial commission in each cause, and for that cause only.[1] Originally he was chosen from the senators, and afterwards from the official list of the judices selecti, which was made up of persons whose qualification varied at different times. In the reign of Augustus, the number of judices was about 4000, and from that period at least the Album Judicum contained all the persons who were qualified to act as judices, both in civil suits and in criminal trials.

When the lawsuit was not one of those which fell to be determined by the centumvirs, or by the prætor himself, that magistrate referred the parties to a judex chosen by themselves from the official list; if they could not agree the prætor proposed a judex, or allowed one to be drawn by lot. Both parties had a right to object to the judex nominated by the magistrate; but we do not know precisely in what form and within what limits that right was exercised.[2]

As the function of the judex was a public one, he could not decline to act without a lawful excuse. After being sworn to do his duty he received from the prætor a formula containing a summary of all the points under litigation, from which he was not allowed to depart; he admitted the demand, or rejected it, purely and simply, and without having power to modify it. To suppose that the office of judex was limited to simple questions of fact would be a mistake. He required not only to investigate facts but to give sentence, and in doing so law was more or less mixed up with the case according to the extent of the powers committed to him. For this reason he was allowed to consult one or more jurisconsults to guide him in cases of difficulty; and, if the question appeared to him so obscure that he could not decide it, he

Powers of the judex.

---

[1] Ortolan, Institutes, vol. i. p. 147.
[2] Ibid. vol. iii. p. 478. De Fresquet, vol. ii. p. 398.

might decline to give judgment, by declaring on oath *sibi non liquere.*[1]

Powers of the arbiter. There were two sorts of arbiters,—those who were named by the parties extrajudicially in a reference or submission, and those who were assigned to them by the prætor in a lawsuit. Here it is only of the last that we are to speak.

The arbiter, like the judex, could hear and determine all ordinary lawsuits, and received a formula from the prætor which enabled him to pronounce a sentence *ex æquo et bono*. Some discussion has arisen as to the difference between the duties of an arbiter and those of a judex; but these difficulties seem to be resolved by the definition of Festus :—*Arbiter est qui totius rei arbitrium habet et potestatem.*[2] All the difference between them seems to have consisted in the formula and its consequences, so that the arbiter in substance was a judex with more extensive powers; and, like the judex, he could call in the aid of legal assessors.

Recuperatores. Besides the judex and the arbiter there were officers called *recuperatores*, to whom the prætor was in use to remit a certain class of cases to be heard and determined. This institution is involved in some obscurity. Beaufort is of opinion that when the prætor appointed one person to hear and decide a case he was called judex, but when three or more persons were named for the same suit they were called recuperatores.[3] Zimmern has adopted this opinion, and he adds that the recuperatores might be chosen from the whole body of the citizens, and did not require to be taken from the list of judices selecti; and farther, that they were only called upon to serve in summary affairs requiring extraordinary despatch. The number of recuperatores appointed for each case was usually three or five, and in the event of difference of opinion a majority had power to decide.[4]

Centumviral court. The centumvirs constituted a permanent tribunal, composed of members elected annually, in equal number, from each tribe, and to this court the decemvirs were attached.

---

[1] De Fresquet, vol. ii. p. 476.
[2] Festus, v. *Arbiter.*
[3] Beaufort, Rep. Rom., liv. v. c. 2.
[4] Zimmern, Traité des Actions, tra-duit de l'Allemand, par M. Etienne, 1843, part ii. ch. 1, § 37. De Fresquet, vol. ii. p. 399.

In the year of Rome 512, when there were thirty-five tribes, and each furnished three members to the centumviral court, the whole number was 105; at a later period, in the time of Pliny the Younger, the number appears to have been 180.

This tribunal was presided over by the prætor. It was divided into four chambers, which, during the republic, were placed under the ancient questors, and after Augustus under the *decemviri litibus judicandis*. These sections gave judgment separately; but they were sometimes united, so as to form one tribunal in affairs of great importance. A spear, the symbol of Quiritarian ownership, was fixed in front of the audience-hall of the centumvirs.

This court had not what the Romans call jurisdiction. All the proceedings *in jure* took place, in the first instance, before the prætor, or other magistrate, who remitted the case to be heard and determined by the centumvirs, if it was one falling within their cognisance.[1] From a passage in Cicero we learn that the centumvirs were competent to decide questions of status, Roman property and succession, embracing a wide range of subjects, which gave great importance to this court.[2]

The date of the institution of the centumvirs is uncertain. Among other celebrated lawyers, Pliny the Younger, as we learn from his letters, was accustomed to plead before this tribunal. It is supposed to have subsisted till near the close of the Western empire; but it had entirely disappeared before the time of Justinian.[3]

From this rapid sketch of the judicial system at Rome during the republic, it will be seen that it laboured under considerable defects. The superior magistrates were changed annually, and their political duties were mixed up with their judicial functions. They were not necessarily lawyers by profession; and the same objection applied to the subordinate officers, who, as judices or centumvirs, were intrusted with the power of hearing and deciding civil causes. There was at that period no class of men among the Romans like the judges in this country, who are appointed by the Crown, hold their offices *ad vitam aut culpam*, and are trained to be

Peculiarities of judicial system.

---

[1] De Fresquet, vol. ii. p. 393-5.   [3] Maynz, § 36.

[2] Cicero, De Orator., i. 38.

interpreters of the law, by making it the business of their lives. One thing, however, greatly contributed to the success of the Roman system—the institution of legal assessors, selected from the most skilful jurisconsults. At first the magistrate had the choice of his assessors; under the empire they became public salaried officers. At all periods the assessors had only a consulting voice in judicial business: the magistrate was not bound to follow their advice; but it cannot be doubted that their opinions exercised the greatest influence upon his decisions.[1]

Italy and provinces.

After Italy was subjected to the Roman supremacy, the jurisdiction of each city and its territory was in the hands of the municipal magistrates. Justice was administered as it was at Rome. In the provinces the governors performed the functions of the prætor, holding circuit courts at stated periods at certain places within their territory, when they decided suits, either directly, or by remitting them to a judex, or to recuperatores. The circuit court was called *conventus*. The governors were accompanied by assessors, and they were assisted by *legati* chosen by themselves, or named by the senate.

Sect. 2.—*Judicial System under the Empire.*

New judicial institutions.

Under the empire the consuls preserved some judicial power till the fourth century. The jurisdiction of the prætors endured still longer. Prætors were appointed to decide questions relating to trusts and guardianship, and exchequer cases; and the number of these magistrates varied considerably at different times. Augustus fixed their number at twelve; Tiberius raised them to sixteen; and Pomponius tells us that, in his time, the magistrates who dispensed justice at Rome were eighteen prætors, besides two consuls, six ediles, and ten tribunes of the people.[2]

The accession of Augustus led to some important changes in the judicial institutions of Rome, and new jurisdictions sprang up under the imperial government.

---

[1] On the Office of Assessors, see D. 1. 22.   [2] D. 1. 2. 34.

Among the magistrates the emperor himself became su- preme judge, and gave decisions in lawsuits by his decrees, sometimes directly, and sometimes by appeal. When the emperor dispensed justice, he was assisted by a council, which, under Augustus, was composed of the two consuls, a magistrate of each grade, and fifteen senators.

Next in dignity to the emperor were the prætorian pre- fects. At first their duties were purely military, but they afterwards discharged the most important judicial functions. Their jurisdiction was established in the reign of Alexander Severus. For a time their judgments might be reviewed by appeal to the emperor, but they afterwards became final, subject only to the condition that they might be made the object of a supplication addressed to the prince. The prætorian prefects were chosen at first from the equestrian order, and afterwards from the senators.

The jurisdiction of the emperor and the prætorian prefects extended over the whole empire. Under Augustus the prefect of the city became a permanent judicial officer, whose jurisdiction was gradually extended till it embraced appeals from decisions of the prætors. There had been eighteen prætors in the time of Alexander Severus; there were only three in the reign of Valentinian. Finally, all the important judicial functions of these ancient republican magistrates were withdrawn from them by little and little, and transferred to the prefect of the city and the prætorian prefect, till the prætors, who had formerly stood nearly on a level with the consuls, were reduced to little more than the insignificant duties of directing the public games.[1]

Beyond Rome, in Italy and the provinces, jurisdiction con- tinued under the empire to be divided between the municipal magistrates and the governors. But the competency of the municipal magistrates, which was formerly unlimited, was restricted to suits not exceeding the value of fifteen thousand sesterces, equal to about £125, and their criminal jurisdiction was in a great measure absorbed by that of the governors.

[1] Maynz, § 50-53.

The *judices pedanei* were appointed by the governor of a province to decide upon affairs of small importance. Cases within their competency were brought directly before them as permanent judges ; but an appeal lay from their decisions to the governor. It has been conjectured that the title *pedaneus* was given to those judges, *qui negotia humiliora disceptant*, because they were placed at the foot of the judicial ladder.[1]

To diminish the influence of the prætorian prefects, whose powers sometimes held in check that of the emperor, Constantine deprived them of their military prerogatives, and limited them to duties purely civil and political ; and, while their number was increased to four, care was taken never to leave them in office for a longer period than a year. The empire was divided into four prefectures—the East ; Illyria ; Italy, which included Sicily, Sardinia, and Africa ; and the Gauls, which comprehended Spain and England. Each of these four departments was administered by a prætorian prefect, who acted as supreme judge, almost always, of the last resort, in lawsuits raised within his prefecture.

Under the prefect, *vicarii*, invested with judicial powers, were placed at the head of each diocese, which comprehended many provinces, each of the latter having a capital or metropolis.

Finally, in the provinces which composed the diocese, the governor, called præses or rector, was judge-ordinary, acting sometimes in the first degree, and sometimes deciding appeals from the municipal magistrates and other inferior judges, such as the *judices pedanei* and the *defensores civitatum*.[2]

Originally the *defensores civitatum* had civil jurisdiction in suits not exceeding 50 solidi, but augmented by Justinian to 300 solidi ; and they also had power to try for petty delinquencies.[3]

---

[1] C. 3. 3. 5. Julian's Constitution. De Fresquet, vol. ii. p. 423.

[2] Beaufort, Rep. Rom., vol. i. p. 418-419. Maynz, vol. i. p. 148.

[3] De Fresquet, vol. ii. p. 517. Dr Colquhoun states that Constantine reduced the weight of the *aureus*, and called it *solidus*. The value of the *solidus* or *aureus* of Justinian's age is said to have been about 11s. 6d. Summary of Roman Civil Law, vol. iii. p. 154-5.

CHAPTER II.

AMONG the Romans the history of civil procedure is divided Civil pro-
into three periods, to which successively belong—1st, The cedure.
actions of the law; 2d, The formulary system; 3d, The system of extraordinary procedure—judicia extraordinaria.

ACTIONS OF THE LAW—LEGIS ACTIONES.

Anciently, a process could only be introduced by means of Actions of
certain sacramental forms called actions of the law, probably the law.
because they were strictly adapted to the laws themselves,
and could not be varied or departed from in any particular
under the penalty of nullity. According to Gaius these
legal actions were five in number:—1. Actio sacramenti;
2. Judicis postulatio; 3. Condictio; 4. Manus injectio;
5. Pignoris capio.[1] Strictly speaking, only the first three
were proper actions, the last two being modes of execution.

The *actio sacramenti* derived its name from a deposit
made by each of the parties of a certain sum of money under
the penal condition that he who lost the cause should forfeit
his part of the stakes for the benefit of public worship—*ad
sacra publica*. This action was both real and personal, and
very general in its application, as it extended to all matters
for which no other form was prescribed by law. By the loss
of a leaf of the manuscript of Verona, we have been deprived

[1] Gai. 4. 11, 12.

of the commentary of Gaius on the action *per postulationem;* and little is known as to the procedure under the *condictio,* being the third action under this system.[1]

Every judgment might be carried into effect by the *manus injectio,* or personal apprehension of the debtor, after the lapse of thirty days, allowed by the law of the Twelve Tables. If the debtor could not find a surety, he was imprisoned in the house of the creditor; and if the debt was not paid after the lapse of sixty days, he might be sold as a slave beyond the Tiber.

The *pignoris capio* was a mode of execution against property, by constituting a sort of pledge. This, however, did not apply to ordinary private debts, but only to a few exceptional claims relating to the public treasury, military service, and sacrifices.[2]

The place where justice was administered at Rome was the Comitium or Forum. There the superior magistrates held their tribunal, seated on curule chairs. The inferior magistrates and the judices occupied the subsellia.

Summons before the judge.

In the earliest times the action was commenced by the plaintiff summoning the defendant to appear before the prætor or other magistrate, which was called *in jus vocatio.* According to the law of the Twelve Tables, if the defendant refused to go quietly, the plaintiff, after calling witnesses, could drag him into court by force, unless he furnished a solvent representative—*vindex.*

Procedure in court.

Before the magistrate the parties went through the ancient forms required by the particular action resorted to. If the affair was such that it could be decided by the magistrate, the suit was terminated before him. But if the litigation was not of that nature, the magistrate had power to remit the case to a judex, to arbiters, or to the court of the centumvirs. Before the judex, or other delegated tribunal, parties were heard, evidence was adduced, and, after pleadings in detail, sentence was pronounced.

---

[1] Gai. 4. 13, 14.

[2] For a more particular account of the *legis actiones* the reader is referred to Gaius, 4. 12, and the Institutes of Ortolan, vol. iii. p. 480 *et seq.*

The system of the actions of the law endured from the earliest times to the period of Cicero. They were abolished in consequence of the excessive nicety required in the pleadings, and the risks of failure arising from the slightest departure from the prescribed forms. A remarkable illustration of this is given by Gaius. A person who complained of his vines having been cut down lost his cause for using the term "vines" in place of "trees," because the law of the Twelve Tables, under which he claimed damages, mentions only trees in general terms.[1]

FORMULARY SYSTEM.

This system was a modification of the preceding one, freed from its mysterious and sacramental forms. The essential feature of the new system consisted in a formula, which the prætor prepared after hearing the parties, and which was remitted to the judex to regulate his decision ; for in this period, as well as in the preceding one, the process was generally divided into two parts, one of which took place before the prætor (*in jure*), and the other before the judex (*in judicio*). All the formulæ generally in use were to be found in the Album Prætoris, and they were multiplied from time to time to suit the exigencies of particular cases. *Formulary system.*

The formula usually consisted of three distinct parts, called *demonstratio, intentio,* and *condemnatio.* *Parts of formula.*

The *demonstratio* stated shortly what had given rise to the litigation,—*res de qua agitur.*

The *intentio* set forth the plaintiff's claim, and the question which the judex was called upon to decide.

The *condemnatio* gave the judge power to condemn or acquit the defendant, according to the result of his examination of the affair. When a process was raised to divide a subject held in common between two parties, the term *adjudicatio* was used in place of *condemnatio.*[2]

In certain cases the matter of the exception pleaded by the defendant required to be inserted in the formula. Sometimes

[1] Gai. 4. 11. Maynz, § 130. [2] Gai. 4. 39-44.

the formula was preceded by claims or reservations favourable to one or other of the parties; these were called *præscriptiones,* because they were written at the head of the formula.[1]

It must also be remarked, that under the formulary system the *condemnatio* was always given for a determinate sum of money, even when the object of the action was to obtain restitution of a particular thing.

To render these explanations more clear, we shall here transcribe the text of a formula given by Gaius, in a case where Aulus Agerius prosecuted Numerius Negidius to restore a silver table deposited with the latter, and failing restitution, to pay damages :—

" (Octavius) Judex esto ;

" Quod Aulus Agerius apud Numerium Negidium mensam argenteam deposuit ; qua de re agitur ;

" Quidquid ob eam rem N. Negidium A. Agerio dare facere oportet, ex fide bona ejus ;

" Id judex N. Negidium A. Agerio condemnato, nisi restituat ; si non paret, absolvito."[2]

According to the principle already explained, the condemnatory sentence was given for a certain sum of money, *nisi restituat.* The sum might be fixed by the prætor in the formula, or left to be fixed by the judex. If the amount decerned for in the judgment was sufficiently high, the defendant generally found it to be for his interest to restore the thing rather than pay the damages, so that indirectly the plaintiff attained his object without infringing the general rule.

Summons and procedure.

Under the formulary system, which marked the finest period of Roman jurisprudence, the summons to appear in court was given at first verbally, and afterwards in writing (*litis denunciatio*). The defendant who refused to follow the

---

[1] Gai. 4. 1. 30, 131.

[2] Gai. 4. 47.   The names Aulus Agerius, and Numerius Negidius, are frequently used in Roman forms to denote any plaintiff or defendant. Maynz, § 132.

plaintiff or to give security to appear on the day specified, was subjected to a fine ; and if he made no appearance the magistrate could put the plaintiff in possession of the defaulter's goods.

When both parties were before the magistrate, the plaintiff pointed out the action he wished to use, and his adversary explained the grounds of his defence, and the exception which he desired to be inserted in the formula. If the prætor considered the claim and exception relevant, he prepared the formula, and appointed the judex for the trial of the cause.

After the delivery of the formula the parties appeared, on a day fixed for the purpose, before the judex ; the cause was pleaded, witnesses were examined, the advocates on both sides were heard, and sentence was pronounced, sustaining or rejecting the claim.   When sentence was given by the judex, his office came to an end, and his power ceased.   For the purposes of execution it was necessary to resort to the magistrate.[1]

Such was the ordinary course of procedure during the formulary system.   But there were cases in which judgment was given by the prætor or other magistrate himself, without any remit to a judex, and these were called *judicia extraordinaria*.

· The formulary system remained in force from near the close of the republic till the reign of Diocletian, A.D. 294.[2]

EXTRAORDINARY PROCEDURE AFTER DIOCLETIAN.

The system of extraordinary procedure was the last and the only one which existed under Justinian.

The distinguishing feature of the *judicia ordinaria* was the separation of the functions of the magistrate from those of the judex.   Even in the time of the republic we have seen that the magistrate sometimes found it useful or necessary in certain cases to unite these functions.   It was then said

[1] Ortolan, Institutes, vol. iii. p. 590. [2] Ibid. vol. i. p. 499. Maynz, § 131-4.

that he acted *extra ordinem*, and all suits so dealt with were called *judicia extraordinaria*. This mode of procedure was invariably followed by the emperors, not only when they judged in appeals, but in all suits brought before them in the first instance. In the time of the classical jurists the new procedure was adopted in numerous cases.

Finally, what had formerly been regarded as the exception was established as the general rule. In the decay of Roman manners private persons were disinclined to undertake the irksome office of judices in civil suits ; and it became every day more and more difficult to find men sufficiently instructed and sufficiently honest to be intrusted with that duty. This difficulty was chiefly experienced in the provinces. By a constitution of Diocletian, A.D. 294,[1] the provincial governors were directed to decide all cases brought before them without remitting them to a judex, unless the pressure of business rendered this absolutely necessary. This was followed by other ordinances which established the new system throughout the empire.

The formulæ were no longer required, and after they had remained for some time in use by the mere force of habit, they were expressly abolished by Constantine, A.D. 342.

Summons and procedure. In Justinian's time the defendant was summoned to appear in court by a writing called *libellus conventionis*, which was served upon him by an officer of the law. There was no longer any distinction between proceedings *in jure* and proceedings *in judicio*. All questions of law and fact were discussed before the same magistrate or judge, and the sentence, if given against the defendant, might either condemn him to pay a sum of money or to restore the subject in dispute.[2]

---

[1] C. 3. 3. 2.   [2] Maynz, § 135. De Fresquet, vol. ii. p. 521.

CHAPTER III.

ACCORDING to Justinian, an action is the right of prosecuting *Action* judicially for what is due to us.[1] But the word action is *defined.* frequently applied to the actual exercise of the right, and in that sense has been defined, a demand made judicially for attaining or recovering a right. He who makes the claim is called the plaintiff, *actor;* and he who is subject to it, is called the defendant, *reus.*

Among the Romans the principal division of actions is into *Actions* real and personal. A real action is that which arises from a *real and personal.* right in the thing itself, *jus in re,* either as proprietor or as holding an inferior real right, such as servitude, pledge, hypothec, or the like. A personal action is founded on an obligation undertaken by another, and is directed against the person bound, or against his heirs or universal successors. What are called *mixed actions,* are those which in one aspect are real and in another personal.

Under real actions the Romans comprehended not only all questions regarding property and other real rights, but all disputes regarding the *status* of persons, sometimes called prejudicial actions.[2] When the object of the action was to recover the property of a corporeal thing, it generally bore the special name of *rei vindicatio.*

There is an infinite variety of personal actions, according to the different character of the obligations intended to be

---

[1] I. 4. 6. pr.   "Actio nihil aliud   quod sibi debetur."
est, quam jus persequendi in judicio,   [2] I. 4. 6. 13.

X

enforced. These actions are founded on contracts or quasi contracts, on delicts or quasi delicts, and sometimes on engagements arising from the law itself or from natural equity. The word *condictio* is frequently used in the Roman law as synonymous with personal action; but before the abolition of the *legis actiones* that term had a more special and technical signification.

Civil and prætorian. Another well-known division of actions among the Romans was into civil and prætorian. A civil action was founded on a law, decree of the senate, or imperial ordinance. A prætorian action was one introduced by edict of the prætor. By the strict rule of the civil law, no one was bound by the contracts or deeds of another. But this rigour was softened by the prætor in many cases where equity or public utility required it. Thus, for instance, the *actio institoria* was allowed against the principal upon the contracts of those whom he employed as managers or superintendents of a farm or any other particular branch of business; and under the *actio exercitoria* a similar remedy was given against the owners of a ship, upon contracts for necessary repairs or provisions entered into by the shipmaster.

Penal actions. A distinction was taken in the Roman law between actions *rei persecutoriæ* and those which were penal. By the first the plaintiff simply asks to recover what is his own, including any loss or damage he may have sustained. In penal actions, which always arise *ex delicto*, something more is demanded by way of penalty.[1]

Bonæ fidei et stricti juris. During the prevalence of the formulary system great importance was attached to the distinction between actions *stricti juris* and those *bonæ fidei*. Under the first, the powers of the judge were limited to the strict letter of the law; under the second, which embraced actions arising from sale, hiring, partnership, mandate, and other mutual contracts, more latitude was allowed, full effect being given to considerations of equity. Mention is also made of the actions *arbitrariæ*, in which large discretionary powers were conferred, more analogous to those of an arbiter than a judge.

[1] I. 4. 6. 17 and 18.

The limitation of actions varied according to circumstances. Limitation of actions. Some penal actions allowed by the prætor required to be brought within the year.[1] Generally speaking, according to the ordinances of the lower empire, every action, whether real or personal, was extinguished if not brought within thirty years; the longest term was for forty years in a small number of exceptional cases. Thus, under Justinian, there was no longer such a thing as a perpetual action, though the term was sometimes applied to the actions of thirty years (formerly perpetual) in opposition to those limited to a lesser period.

[1] I. 4. 12. pr.

CHAPTER IV

OF INTERDICTS.

Nature of interdict.

AN interdict is an order issuing from the prætor or other judge, commanding some person to do or not to do certain acts. It is granted in cases requiring the summary interposition of a judge to preserve property or rights in danger of immediate invasion.

Effect of possession.

Possession of personal property is *prima facie* evidence of ownership, and whenever a right has been *de facto* exercised for a long time, a court of law will always, if possible, refer it to a lawful origin. Where the property of a subject is contested, the lawful possessor is entitled to continue his possession till the point of right be determined; and if he has lost possession by violence or stealth, the judge will summarily restore it to him. A person in possession has a right so to continue against every one who cannot show that he has a better right to possess; and, consequently, *in pari casu melior est conditio possidentis.*[1]

Different kinds of interdicts.

By the Roman law interdicts were: 1. Prohibitory, which prohibited something from being done; 2. Restoratory, which commanded something to be restored; 3. Exhibitory, which commanded some thing or person to be exhibited.[2]

Under exhibitory interdicts we find one, *de libero homine exhibendo*—the guarantee of individual liberty, which had for its object to prevent any free man from being detained by any one whatever. This interdict might be applied for by

---

[1] "Beati in jure censentur possidentes."—Hein. Inst., l. iv. tit. 15. [2] I. 4. 15. 1.

any person; for no one was prohibited from favouring liberty; and it bore some resemblance to the English writ of *habeas corpus*.[1]

Interdicts were granted in order that possession might be acquired, retained, or recovered.[2]   Among interdicts for the purpose of gaining possession were: 1st, *Quorum bonorum,* whereby goods belonging to an inheritance were acquired by the person entitled under the edicts of the prætor to be bonorum possessor; 2d, *Salvianum,* whereby goods belonging to the tenant of a rural subject were secured under the landlord's hypothec for payment of rent.

Among interdicts for the purpose of retaining possession were *Uti possidetis,* which was granted in favour of one who was in possession of lands or other immovable property; and *Utrubi,* which was granted in favour of one who was in possession of movables.   But, in order to entitle any person to this protection, his possession at the date of the litigation must have been lawful, and not obtained from his adversary, *vi, clam, aut precario*—that is, by violence, clandestinely, or upon a precarious concession dependent on the pleasure of his opponent.[3]

An interdict called *unde vi,* was granted to recover possession in the case of one who was ejected by violence from lands or buildings.   This remedy applied only to immovable property.   As regards movables seized by violence, the possessor could obtain redress, either by the interdict *utrubi* or in the form of action *vi bonorum raptorum,* or *vi furti,* or *ad exhibendum.*[4]   Thus, the violent seizure either of movables or immovables was always sternly repressed by the Roman law.   According to Ulpian, if an aggression was made with arms, it might be repelled by arms, not only for defending the possession, but for instantly regaining it when lost; provided this was done during the continuance of one general struggle, and without any interval.[5]   But when such

(margin notes: Uti possidetis et utrubi. Unde vi.)

---

[1] Ortolan, Institutes, vol. i. p. 498.
[2] I. 4. 15. 2.
[3] " Precarium est, quod precibus petenti utendum conceditur quamdiu   is, qui concessit, patitur."—D. 43. 26. 1. pr. Ulpian.
[4] I. 4. 15. 4.
[5] D. 43. 16. 3. 9, Ulpian.

an aggression was successful at the time, the proper remedy of the person ejected was to recover possession by interdict.

After the formulary system was suppressed, interdicts were replaced by actions, which served the same purpose.

English and Scottish law.   In England, injunctions (which are the same as interdicts) are issued from the Court of Chancery, and may now, by recent statutes, be granted by the superior courts of Common Law.[1] In Scotland, interdicts are granted on summary applications, not only by the Court of Session, but by the sheriffs of counties and other local judges in matters falling within their jurisdiction.[2]

---

[1] 15 & 16 Vict. c. 83, s. 42. Common Law Procedure Act, 1854, s. 79.

[2] Bell's Pr. § 2239.

CHAPTER V.

DEFENCES are the pleas offered by the defendant against *Defences.* whom an action is brought, in order to exclude it; and this general term comprehends both objections to the libel and exceptions.

When the action is brought into court, the defendant may admit the facts on which it is founded without offering further opposition, in which case judgment passes against him. If denied, the plaintiff must prove the allegations of fact necessary to support his demand: " Ei incumbit probatio, qui dicit; non qui negat." [1]

Again, the defendant may oppose the demand, not by a simple denial or by objecting to it as incompetent or irrelevant, but by alleging some new matter sufficient to exclude the action in whole or in part; and that defence is an exception. Thus, in personal actions, when the defendant pleads payment, or performance, or set-off, or discharge, he admits the demand to be good but for the new facts alleged by him. If the exception turn on disputed facts, the burden of proving them lies on the defendant, on the principle of Ulpian: " Reus in exceptione actor est." [2]

Exceptions are dilatory and peremptory. Dilatory excep- *Exceptions dilatory and* tions are those whereby an action is opposed which is legally *peremptory.* competent but brought at an improper time or in an improper manner, as, for instance, before a court having no jurisdiction. These dilatory exceptions require to be pleaded *in*

_____
[1] D. 22. 3. 2.   [2] D. 44. 1. 50.

initio litis, otherwise they are held to be waived. Peremptory exceptions enter into the merits of the cause, and are said *perimere causam*, because they not only free the defendant from the depending suit, but totally destroy the plaintiff's right of action upon the claim.

Various examples of exceptions are given in the Institutes of Justinian;[1] such as *res judicata*, when the question between the parties has already been decided by a competent court—prescription, when the action is excluded by the lapse of time—and the common cases of contracts being annulled by fraud, violence, forgery, or essential error.

In actions of strict law, during the prevalence of the formulary system, the judex could not take any cognisance of exceptions competent to the defendant, unless they were inserted in the formula remitted to him by the prætor. But in the class of actions called *bonæ fidei*, which were of common occurrence, this rule was not enforced, it being competent for the judge to entertain all exceptions founded on any violation of good faith, such as fraud, violence, or error, even though no mention was made of them in the formula. When the prætor admitted exceptions, most writers are of opinion that they were inserted immediately after the *intentio*. The term exception is supposed to have been derived from the practice of inserting it as a condition in the formula, the plaintiff's claim being rejected if the condition was proved.

Replication and duplication.
A replication is the plaintiff's answer to an exception. Thus, if the defendant plead compensation as an exception to the demand, the plaintiff may meet this by pleading, in replication, recompensation upon a separate debt not included in the libel. A duplication is the answer to a replication ; a triplication to a duplication, and so forth. In these pleadings the defendant was always entitled to the last word.

Litis-contestation.
In the Roman law litis-contestation was originally, and properly, the termination of the proceedings *in jure*, when the matter in dispute was prepared for the investigation of the judex. At a later period, under the system of Justinian, when all legal disputes were conducted before the magistrate,

[1] I. 4. 13.

litis-contestation took place when the cause was ready for hearing, that is, after the plaintiff had stated his claims and the defendant his answers or defences.   After litis-contestation the subject in dispute became litigious, and both parties were bound under a quasi-judicial contract to submit to the decision of the judge.[1]

All questions of law may be decided by the judge on his own knowledge ; but as regards questions of fact he cannot proceed on his own private knowledge, but must decide according to the evidence adduced,—*secundum allegata et probata.*

[1] De Fresquet, vol. ii. p. 472-3, 520.   Maynz, § 141.

CHAPTER VI.

OF EVIDENCE.

Three modes of proof. ALL disputed averments made by parties to a suit require to be supported by proper evidence. There are three ordinary ways of proving points in issue ; by writings, witnesses, and oath of party.[1]

Onus probandi. The burden of proof lies on the party asserting an affirmative fact if unsupported by any presumption. But if the legal presumption be in favour of one party, the burden of proof is thrown on his adversary.

Proof by writing. Proof by writing is generally considered the most certain, and great importance was attached to documents of a public character, such as those prepared by the officers called *tabelliones*. As parole is inferior in degree to written evidence, the Romans were jealous of admitting it to vary or contradict an instrument in writing. This appears from the text, " Contra scriptum testimonium, non scriptum testimonium non fertur ;"[2] and the principle laid down by Paulus, "Testes cum de fide tabularum nihil dicitur, adversus scripturam interrogari non possunt."[3] In some instances, however, parole evidence was admitted to contradict a written instrument. Witnesses might also be adduced to prove forgery, and probably also to prove that the deed was obtained by fraud or wrong.

Proof by witnesses. Generally speaking, parole evidence was admitted by the Roman law. Every person might be a witness who was not by law expressly disqualified.

---

[1] On the general subject of proof, see D. 22. 3 ; C. 4. 9.

[2] C. 4. 20. 1.

[3] Paul. 5. 15. 4.

Among persons who were declared inadmissible as witnesses were : 1. Pupils. 2. Lunatics. 3. Infamous persons. 4. The parties in the cause, and all persons having a direct interest in it as sureties or otherwise. 5. Near relations of the parties; so a father could not be a witness for his son, nor the son or any one under power for the father. 6. Slaves were not competent witnesses for their masters or against them, except in certain offences, such as treason, fraud against the Treasury, and adultery. Finally, no one who had a strong enmity to one of the parties could be examined against him. *Witnesses disqualified.*

After the time of Constantine witnesses in civil suits were required to give their testimony on oath. In general, two witnesses were sufficient to prove a fact; but, in some exceptional cases, a larger number was required. When the witnesses for the parties gave conflicting testimony on any point, it was the duty of the judge not to count the number on each side, but to consider which of them were entitled to the greatest credit, according to the well-known rule, " Testimonia ponderanda sunt, non numeranda." It rarely happens that the evidence is so nicely balanced as not to preponderate on one side or the other. But questions of fact may be supported and opposed by every degree of evidence, and sometimes by that degree of evidence of which the proper effect is to leave the mind in a state of doubt, or in an equipoise between two conclusions. Where such a case occurred, the Roman law provided that the benefit of the doubt should be given to the defendant rather than to the plaintiff.[1]

A great revolution has taken place in the law regarding the admission of witnesses, both in England and Scotland. Formerly we adopted the rules of the Roman law in rejecting as witnesses the parties to the suit, and all persons who had a direct interest in the litigation, as well as those who were considered infamous from being convicted of certain crimes. These and other disqualifications have been removed by recent statutes.[2] Great apprehensions were entertained *Recent changes in British law.*

---

[1] D. 50. 17. 125. Hein. Pand., lib. 22, tit. 5, §.144.   [2] For England, 6 & 7 Vict. c. 85 ; 14 & 15 Vict. c. 99; 16 & 17 Vict.

that these changes might open the door to perjury; but experience has demonstrated that the latitude allowed under the new system, all objections to credit being duly weighed, is, on the whole, highly beneficial, by enabling courts of law to reach the truth in a multitude of cases where the ends of justice were formerly defeated by excluding the testimony of the parties best acquainted with the facts in dispute.

Generally speaking, the judicial admission by a party of a fact alleged by his adversary is conclusive proof. The value of such an admission arises from its being supposed to be made by the litigant against his own interest. But in actions where collusion ought to be jealously guarded against, such as consistorial causes involving questions of status, independent evidence should be adduced in addition to the admissions on record.

Reference to oath.

On the failure of regular proof, the Roman law, as a last resource, allowed a party to refer the facts in a civil action to the oath of his adversary. The characteristic feature of this proceeding was, that it was considered a species of transaction, whereby the party referring staked the issue on his opponent's oath, which was received as the only evidence on the point referred, and was conclusive, without regard to any offer to prove its falsehood. This appeal to the conscience of the litigant could only be made on matters of fact falling within his knowledge. If the person to whose oath reference was made was not in a position to speak distinctly upon the facts, it was competent for him to defer to the oath of his adversary; and then the judge, in his discretion, ordered that party to depone who was supposed to have had the best opportunities of knowing the facts.

Adopted in France and Scotland.

The oath on reference borrowed from the Roman law has been adopted in France, where it is called *serment decisoire*.[1] It also retains a prominent place in the Scotch law of evidence, notwithstanding recent changes. In some matters the only admissible proof is the writ or oath of party; in others, parole evidence is competent, and, in general, refer-

c. 83. For Scotland, 3 & 4 Vict. c.   Vict. c. 20.
59; 15 & 16 Vict. c. 27; 16 & 17   [1] Code Civil, art. 1357.

ence to oath is resorted to by a litigant when all other evidence has failed, " ubi non deficit jus, sed probatio." By the 16 & 17 Vict. c. 20, s. 5, it is not competent to any party who has called and examined his adversary as a witness, thereafter to refer the cause to his oath, but " in all other respects the right of reference to oath shall remain as at present established by the law and practice of Scotland."

Another species of proof of a somewhat anomalous character was allowed by the Roman law, called the oath *in litem.* A person whose goods were lost or destroyed by the delict or quasi delict of another, was sometimes permitted by the judge to prove their amount and value by his own oath in a civil action against the wrongdoer. Thus, in cases founded on the edict *nautæ, caupones, stabularii,* under which shipowners, innkeepers, and stablers are responsible, *quasi ex delicto,* for loss or damage to goods or luggage intrusted to their care, the plaintiff's oath was received to prove the number and value of the articles lost or destroyed, where proof from other sources could not be obtained. The oath *in litem,* though a very questionable kind of evidence, has been adopted both in the French law and the law of Scotland.[1]

Before leaving the subject of evidence a few observations may be made on presumptions, which are usually divided into three classes according to the degrees of their probative force. The first class are purely artificial rules of law, which admit of no contradiction by contrary evidence, and are called by the commentators *præsumptiones juris et de jure.* Such, for example, is the rule that a child born more than ten months after the dissolution of the marriage is not the lawful child of the husband.

Another class of presumptions, called *præsumptiones juris,* are inferences drawn in pursuance of the pre-appointment of law, and include those cases in which the law presumes a fact of which no evidence is given, in the absence of contrary proof. Many such presumptions are established in the Roman law. The property of movables is presumed from the

---

[1] Code Civil, art. 1366. Dickson on Evidence, 762.

possession of them ; a document of debt found in the custody of the debtor is presumed to have been paid by him,—*debitor non presumitur donare;* and so forth. All these presumptions may be rebutted by evidence to the contrary ; and, if one presumption of law be opposed by another, the court must then decide which is the stronger. As already explained, where the legal presumption is on one side, the burden of proof is thrown on the other. Thus a bill of exchange is always presumed to have been given for a good consideration ; but evidence is admitted on the part of the defendant to show that such was not the fact.

Another class of presumptions, called *præsumptiones facti seu hominis,* are the natural presumptions of mere fact emerging from the special circumstances of each case, and of which the law has left the probative force to the discretion of the judge. They occur when direct proof of a fact is offered to a judge or jury as probable evidence, from which another fact may be inferred.

CHAPTER VII.

OF JUDGMENTS AND THEIR EXECUTION.

I.—ROMAN LAW.

AN interlocutory judgment is a decision on an incidental point which does not exhaust the merits of the cause. A final judgment is one which terminates the action by determining the whole matters in dispute. It is a sacred rule, that every judgment legally pronounced by a competent court, even though it be erroneous, must be obeyed until it is reversed or set aside by superior authority.

(margin note: Judgments interlocutory or final.)

Under the empire every judgment required to be reduced to writing, and signed by the judge. It was entered in a register, and a copy was delivered to the parties. In the East, after Arcadius, the judgment might be drawn up in Greek, but the use of Latin was retained at Constantinople down to Justinian's time.[1]

After sentence the debtor was allowed thirty days for payment of the debt under the law of the Twelve Tables. At the expiry of that time he was assigned over to the creditor by the prætor, and was kept in chains for sixty days, during which he was publicly exposed for three market-days, and the amount of his debt proclaimed; and then, if no person released the prisoner by paying the debt, the creditor could sell him as a slave to foreigners. When there were several creditors, the letter of the law allowed them to cut the body of the debtor in pieces, and divide it among them in pro-

(margin note: Execution in early times.)

---

[1] C. 7. 45. 12. Lydus de Magis., ii. 12; iii. 11. 20. 42.

portion to their debts; but some writers contend that the words *partes secanto* are to be taken in a figurative sense, as referring to a division of the price when the debtor was sold as a slave. There can be no doubt that the debtor, who was *addictus*, might be sold as a slave; but, according to Aulus Gellius, there was no instance in which he was ever put to death.[1]

Such was the state of the law at the time of the Twelve Tables. The law Pœtelia Papiria, of the year of Rome 428, made an important change in the liabilities of the *nexi*, who came under a voluntary engagement of the person for the loan of money.[2] But the *addictio* of the debtor, whereby he was formally declared the property of the creditor by judicial sentence, still continued in force, though other institutions rendered this usage more and more rare.

The prætor allowed a delay of two months for payment of a judgment debt; and Justinian extended the period to four months, both to the defendant and his sureties, after which the debtor might be imprisoned, not in the house of the creditor, as in early times, but in a public prison.

In progress of time the property of the debtor might be attached and sold for payment of the judgment debt, by means of the *missio in possessionem*, which the creditors obtained from the prætor. At first this was followed, after public advertisements, by a sale in mass of the whole goods of the debtor, in favour of any one who offered, by way of price, to pay the largest dividend to the creditors upon their respective claims. Afterwards the goods of the debtor were sold in detail, either by the creditors, or a *curator bonis* appointed by them. All the creditors who presented them-

---

[1] Aulus Gellius, xx. 1.

[2] Among civilians the precise condition of a *nexus* has been a subject of controversy. A *nexum* was a transfer of a thing in the form of a sale *per æs et libram*. Some think that persons *sui juris* could mancipate themselves by way of pawn for debt. By this alienation the person of the debtor became the property of the creditor. *Nexi datio* expressed the contracting, and *nexi liberatio* the release from the obligation. Savigny and other writers reject the notion that a Roman citizen could sell or pledge himself. Maynz, Droit Romain, vol. ii. p. 499, note.

selves in proper time were entitled to be paid a rateable dividend from the produce of the sale, in virtue of the prætorian pledge which the *missio in possessionem* conferred equally upon them all ; but the preferences of hypothecary creditors, under rights acquired before the period of concourse or bankruptcy fixed by the prætor's decree, were reserved entire.

In the time of the classical jurists, a judgment creditor Execution could adopt three modes of execution against his debtor: 1st, law. by imprisoning his person ; 2d, by attaching and selling his movable goods ; and, 3d, by attaching and selling his immovable property. All these modes of execution were concurrent. After the abolition of the formulary system, when any one obtained a judgment ordaining the restitution of a particular thing, he could, if required, be put in possession of the thing *manu militari*.[1]

II.—FRENCH, ENGLISH, AND SCOTTISH LAW.

In France, imprisonment for debt at the end of a suit is French law. forbidden by the Civil Code, subject to a few exceptions ;[2] but it is allowed by the Commercial Code when the debt is commercial, and amounts to not less than 200 francs, or £8. By adopting certain formalities the debt becomes commercial and the law is evaded. Persons above seventy cannot be imprisoned even for commercial debts. The duration of the imprisonment varies from one year to five years, according to the amount of the debts.[*]

In England, no debtor, generally speaking, can be im- English prisoned for a debt under £20; neither can the judgment law. creditor execute all the writs of execution at the same time. " The general rule is, that imprisonment is a satisfaction for the debt, unless the debtor die in prison, or escape, or be

---

[1] I. 4. 17. 2. D. 6. 1. 68. Maynz, § 155.

[2] Code Civil, art. 2059 *et seq.*

[*] By article 2062 of the Code Civil, imprisonment for non-payment of rent could not be enforced unless it was so stipulated for in the lease. But by art. 2 of the law of 13th Dec. 1848, it was enacted that, in future, imprisonment could not be stipulated for in a lease for non-payment of rent of agricultural subjects.

rescued; and hence, after that kind of execution, the creditor cannot seize his goods and lands also: Again, where a writ of execution against the real estate has been executed, the debtor's person, or personal estate, cannot be taken. But after taking the personal estate, either the person or the real estate may be taken." [1]

In the English county courts, a debtor who has no goods, and does not pay at the time ordered, may be committed to prison for not more than forty days, if it be proved that the debt was contracted fraudulently, or without any reasonable prospect of his having the means of payment. This imprisonment, however, is no satisfaction of the debt.[2]

Scottish law.

In Scotland, imprisonment is not permitted for an ordinary debt under £8, 6s. 8d.; [3] but all modes of execution are concurrent, so that the judgment creditor can imprison the debtor, attach his debts and goods, and adjudge his real estate at the same time for the same debt.

[1] Paterson's Compendium, p. 399. [3] 5 & 6 Will. IV. c. 70.
[2] Ibid. p. 417.

CHAPTER VIII.

OF APPEALS.

AN appeal is an application to a superior judge to review the decision of an inferior one, on the ground that it is informal or erroneous. The effect of an appeal is usually to suspend the execution of the judgment till it is confirmed by the superior court. The first title of the 49th book of the Digest treats of appeals.[1]

During the republic there was no appeal in civil suits for the purpose of reversing or altering a decision, for each judge had power to decide finally within the limits of his jurisdiction; and even the sentence of the judex, as a general rule, was not subject to review by the magistrate who appointed him. In such cases the only mode in which a person could obtain relief was by the intercession of certain magistrates of high rank. Cases occur in which one of the prætors interposed to stop the proceedings of his colleague. The tribunes could also use their authority to prevent execution of a judicial sentence. Thus, when the prætor condemned L. Scipio for peculation, the tribune allowed execution to pass against his property, but interfered to prevent Scipio being sent to prison.

During republic no appeals in civil suits.

From the time of Augustus a regular system of appeals was established. At Rome there was an appeal from all the magistrates to the prefect of the city, and then from the prefect of the city to the prætorian prefect or the emperor. M. Aurelius, by a rescript, allowed an appeal from the judgment

Appeals competent under empire.

[1] See also C. 7. 62. N. 23, ch. 1.

of a judex to the magistrate who appointed him.[1] By a constitution of Hadrian there was no appeal from the senate to the emperor, and from the emperor himself there was of course no appeal.

In Italy and the provinces there was an appeal from the municipal magistrates in the first instance to the governors, and from them to the prætorian prefect or to the emperor.

Constantine prohibited appeals before final judgment, except where a question of competency was raised. From his time no appeal was allowed from the decisions of the prætorian prefect; but redress might still be sought against his judgments in the form of supplication addressed to the emperor.

Under Justinian all appeals were appointed to be entered within ten days from the date of the judgment.[2] The same emperor directed that the imperial court (*auditorium principis*) should not entertain any appeal under the value of twenty pounds of gold, and all cases below that standard were remitted to one or more judges, whose decision was declared to be final.[3]

[1] D. 49. 1. 1 and 21.

[2] N. 23, ch. 1.

[3] Walter, Procedure Civile, tra- duite par Laboulaye, Paris, 1841; ch. ix. p. 96.

CHAPTER IX.

OF INSOLVENCY AND CESSIO BONORUM.

BY the Lex Julia, passed either in the time of Julius Cæsar *Cessio*
or Augustus, and subsequently extended to the provinces, *bonorum.*
insolvent debtors were allowed the benefit of *cessio bonorum,*
whereby they were freed from imprisonment on making a
voluntary surrender of all their property to their creditors.[1]

This surrender was made by a solemn declaration, either *Not a re-*
judicial or extrajudicial. The property thus given up was *lease of debts.*
sold, and the price was distributed among the creditors. The
debtor was not released from his debts unless the creditors
were fully paid, but he was protected from imprisonment at
their instance. If the debtor subsequently acquired property, *Future*
his creditors were entitled to attach it, except in so far as it *property attachable.*
was necessary for his own subsistence.[2]

The *cessio bonorum* has been adopted in France [3] as well *Cessio in*
as in Scotland. By the ancient law of France, every debtor *France and Scotland.*
who sought the benefit of *cessio* was obliged by the sentence
to wear in public a green bonnet (*bonnet vert*) furnished by
his creditors, under the penalty of being imprisoned if he
was found without it. According to Pothier, this was intended as a warning to all citizens to conduct their affairs
with prudence, so as to avoid the risk of exposing themselves
to such ignominy; but he explains that in his time, though
the condition was inserted in the sentence, it was seldom

---

[1] D. 42. 3. C. 7. 71.

[2] I. 4. 6. 40. D. 42. 3. 4.

[3] See Code de Proc. Civ., art. 898-906.

acted on in practice, except at Bordeaux, where it is said to have been rigidly enforced.[1]

Formerly, a custom somewhat similar prevailed in Scotland. Every debtor who obtained the benefit of *cessio* was appointed to wear "the dyvours habit," which was a coat or upper garment, half yellow and half brown, with a cap of the same colours. In modern times this usage was discontinued. "According to the state of public feeling, it would be held a disgrace to the administration of justice. It would shock the innocent; it would render the guilty miserably profligate."[2] For a considerable time it had become the practice in the judgment to dispense with the dyvours habit, and by the statute of Will. IV. it is utterly abolished.[3]

[1] Pothier, Traité de la Procedure Civile, part v. ch. iii. § 5.

[2] Per Lord Meadowbank in Smith, 6th Feb. 1813. F. C.

[3] 6 & 7 Will. IV. c. 56. 2 Bell's Com., 6th ed., 1102.

Since the discovery of the Institutes of Gaius at Verona, a considerable number of works have appeared on civil procedure among the Romans. Among the most useful to consult we may mention—Histoire de la Procedure Civile chez les Romains, par Walter, traduite de l'Allemand par M. Laboulaye, 1841; Traité des Actions, ou Théorie de la Procedure Civile Privée chez les Romains, par Zimmern, traduite de l'Allemand par M. Etienne, 1843; Traité des Actions, ou Exposition Historique de l'Organisation Judiciaire et de la Procedure Civile chez les Romains, par M. Bonjean, 3d edit., 1846.

PART VI.

OF CRIMINAL LAW AND PROCEDURE.

CHAPTER I.

OF CRIMINAL COURTS.

THE Institutes of Gaius contain nothing on the criminal law of the Romans, and very little information can be gleaned from the title in Justinian's Institutes, *de publicis judiciis*.[1] Our limits will not permit us to enter into the subject at much length; but a short account of the administration of criminal justice at Rome may not be without its use.

Sect. 1.—Criminal Jurisdiction of the Kings and Consuls.

Though our sources of information as to the regal period are obscure, we have reason to believe that the kings were the supreme judges in criminal trials, and that they were assisted by a council. Kings and consuls.

Tullus Hostilius delegated his authority to two commissioners to try Horatius for killing his sister, and allowed an appeal from their sentence to the Comitia Curiata.[2] Tarquin the Proud dispensed with the aid of a council in criminal trials; but this was considered irregular, and was made matter of complaint against him.

[1] I. 4. 18.   [2] Livy, i. 26.

After the expulsion of the kings, the consuls succeeded to
their judicial authority as regards the trial and punishment
of capital crimes, and they exercised the power of life and
death, as shown in the proceedings against the sons of Brutus.
But this power was of short duration. By the Valerian law,
passed in the year of Rome 245, every Roman citizen had a
right to appeal to the people against any criminal sentence
pronounced by a magistrate; and the direct jurisdiction of
the Comitia was afterwards recognised for the trial and punishment of all the more serious crimes. Further, by an express law of the Twelve Tables, no citizen was to be tried
for any offence involving his life or his rights as a citizen,
except before the Comitia of the Centuries.

By laws of this kind, which, though sometimes attempted
to be evaded, were frequently renewed and confirmed, the
criminal jurisdiction of the consuls and other magistrates was
reduced within narrow limits. In times of civil commotion,
however, when the liberties of the people were endangered,
the senate, by a decree, invested a dictator or the consuls with
extraordinary powers, in virtue of which they might put any
dangerous citizen to death, and execute summary justice upon
all offenders, without regard to the ordinary forms of law.

Sect. 2.—*Criminal Jurisdiction of the Senate.*

Senate as a
criminal
court.

During the republic, the senate possessed no regular jurisdiction in criminal causes in so far as Roman citizens were
concerned. If this body sometimes ordered criminal prosecutions, they did so, after a preliminary investigation, by the
intervention of the magistrates, who prosecuted before the
people according to established forms; and the trial took
place before the ordinary courts, or a special tribunal created
for the purpose.

When the senate was appointed to decide criminal causes,
either by itself or by commissioners taken from its body, this
power was derived from the express or tacit delegation of the
people. On some extraordinary emergencies of extreme peril,
the senate, along with the consuls, assumed the responsibility

of inflicting summary punishment on state criminals. Of this
we have a memorable example in the proceedings against the
conspirators associated with Catiline, some of whom were
strangled in prison without any regular trial, under the consulship of Cicero. This measure, however, was viewed with
great jealousy as a dangerous and unconstitutional stretch of
power; and although it was generally acknowledged that
Rome had been preserved from great peril by the vigorous
conduct of Cicero, he was afterwards driven into exile, under
the law of Clodius, for having put Roman citizens to death
without a trial.

Though the senate, during the republic, had no proper crim- Offences in
inal jurisdiction over the city of Rome, they took cognisance provinces.
of all serious crimes committed in Italy and the provinces.

Under the empire, the senate was invested by the prince, State
exercising the powers of dictator, with criminal jurisdiction, offences.
particularly in all offences against the state and the person of
the emperor, as well as in crimes of extortion by provincial
magistrates, and capital charges against senators. Frequently
the emperor in person attended the deliberations of the senate; the senators held their office during his pleasure; and he
had no difficulty in obtaining any condemnation which he
desired, when his object was to crush men of influence who
had incurred his displeasure. Thus the senate soon became
a mere instrument in the hands of the prince, who absorbed
all its authority.[1]

Sect. 3.—Criminal Jurisdiction of the Comitia.

There were three sorts of popular assemblies at Rome—the Assemblies
Comitia Curiata, the Comitia Centuriata, and the Comitia people.
Tributa.

Of these the Comitia Curiata, the earliest in date, was an Comitia
assembly of the thirty curiæ, composed entirely of patricians. Curiata.
The trial of Horatius, being the first we meet with in Roman
history, took place before this tribunal.

The Comitia of the Centuries, instituted by Servius Tullius,

[1] Maynz, § 51.

Comitia
Centuriata.

comprehended all the citizens, divided into a certain number of classes, according to fortune, age, and rank. In this assembly the great preponderance was given to riches, all the power having been concentrated in the superior classes, without appearing to exclude any one from the right of suffrage. The sentiments of each century were governed by the majority of its members, but in the assembly each century counted only for one vote.

Comitia
Tributa.

The Comitia Tributa was an assembly of the people according to their tribes, and originally consisted only of plebeians. Here the democratic element prevailed. All citizens were afterwards admitted into this assembly; and, at a period not clearly ascertained, the system was modified by the introduction into the tribes of a classification analogous to that of the centuries, so that the votes were no longer given by the head, but by classes in each tribe.

Assembly of
centuries
the chief
criminal
court.

At the commencement of the republic, the assemblies of the people appear to have acted as a court of review in those criminal cases only where an appeal was made from the sentence of a magistrate. But after the power of the magistrates as criminal judges had been restricted by successive laws, the Comitia Centuriata came to be recognised as the regular court for the trial of all the more serious crimes committed by Roman citizens. What chiefly led to this result was the well-known law of the Twelve Tables, that no Roman citizen could be tried for any offence involving his life or privileges, except by the *Comitiatus Maximus*—that is, as we are told by Cicero, the Comitia Centuriata. The judicial power so conferred on the popular assembly was regarded as a fundamental part of the Roman constitution, and the surest safeguard against injustice and oppression down to the close of the republic.

The Comitia Tributa likewise acted as a supreme court of criminal judicature, but the limits of its jurisdiction are not very clearly defined. Originally, it claimed the right of giving judgment on those offences which were regarded as infringements of the privileges of the plebeians; but, as the power of the tribunes increased, they grew bold and unscrupulous, and occasionally brought before the Comitia Tributa capital offences which did not fall under their cognisance. Thus Coriolanus was condemned by the assembly of the tribes; but this was considered a flagrant violation of the constitution. Cicero was convicted and driven into exile by the same tribunal; but he complained that it had no power to try him on the charge of *perduellio*, brought against him by Clodius, which could only be legally tried before the assembly of the centuries. Many writers are of opinion that although the Comitia Tributa sometimes exceeded their powers, they were prohibited by law and established usage from inflicting any punishment more severe than the imposition of a fine.[1]

In criminal trials before the comitia, no one could act as an accuser except a magistrate.

As a general rule, no person could be brought to trial while holding any of the higher offices of state, though this was sometimes departed from; but all magistrates might be called to account for malversation after their year of office had expired. When threatened with a criminal prosecution by Milo, Clodius contrived to stave it off by getting himself elected edile.

In a trial before the comitia, the people gave their votes in the same manner as in passing a law.

Sect. 4.—*Criminal Jurisdiction of Commissioners—Quæstiones Perpetuæ.*

To convene the citizens in the comitia for the trial of offenders, after the population of Rome had increased, was found to be inconvenient, and the expedient was adopted of delegating the jurisdiction of the people to one or more persons, invested with temporary authority, to try particular crimes. These judges were called *quæsitores* or *quæstores*—the trial being termed *quæstio*—and their authority ceased when the trial was over. The ordinary magistrates were most

Standing criminal commissions.

---

[1] See Laboulaye, Essai sur les Lois Criminelles des Romains (Paris, 1845), p. 96.

frequently appointed commissioners, and sometimes private persons. In matters falling under their jurisdiction, the senate usually appointed *quæstores* from their own body.

In the early ages of the republic, it was customary to issue a special commission to try each cause ; but in the beginning of the seventh century, when offences of every description had become numerous, an important change was introduced into criminal procedure by establishing permanent courts for trying crimes of the most frequent occurrence, and these courts were called *quæstiones perpetuæ.* Calpurnius Piso, a tribune of the people in 604, introduced a law *de pecuniis repetundis,* whereby a permanent commission was established for the trial of extortion by provincial governors. This court was composed of a prætor, who acted as presiding judge, without a deliberative voice, and a certain number of judices, resembling in many respects a modern jury, chosen from the senators.

So successful was this new experiment that it was soon extended to other crimes, such as treason, peculation, and bribery. When the criminal code was remodelled by Sylla, new courts of a similar description were instituted for a great variety of offences, till at length the system was brought into general operation, and the whole ordinary criminal business, with few exceptions, was conducted by the *quæstiones perpetuæ* down to the establishment of the imperial government.

Presiding judge at trial. — After the institution of the *quæstiones perpetuæ* in the seventh century, the presiding judge was either one of the prætors, or an officer called *judex quæstionis.* Each court took cognisance of one class of offences only; and the multiplicity of these tribunals rendered it necessary to increase the number of prætors, though these magistrates were authorised to delegate their functions of president to the *judex quæstionis.*

Any citizen might prosecute. — As the *quæstiones perpetuæ* were established under different laws, the forms of procedure were not always the same ; but some general principles were applied in all of them. It was no longer necessary, as it was before the comitia, that a magistrate should act as accuser ; any citizen might now

come forward and prefer a charge before the prætor. Every
case submitted to these courts was tried by a judge and a
jury. It was the duty of the judge to preside and regulate
the proceedings according to law. It was the duty of the
jury, after hearing the pleadings and the evidence, to decide
upon the guilt or innocence of the accused. The number Jury varied in number.
of the jury varied according to the provisions of the law
under which the trial took place, but was always considerable; and we find examples of thirty-two, fifty, seventy,
seventy-five, and other numbers. The presiding judge drew
out the names of the jurors from the urn: each party had
a right to challenge a certain number; and the verdict was
returned by a majority of votes.[1]

During the last century of the republic, the power possessed by those who acted as judices was very great, and was
often abused for party purposes, so that the most serious internal dissensions arose from contests between different orders
of the state for the privilege of acting in that capacity. At How juror chosen.
first the judices were chosen only from the senators, and so
matters stood at the passing of the lex Calpurnia, in 604;
then, by the Sempronian law of C. Gracchus in 630, only
from the equestrians; afterwards, by the Servilian law in
647, from both orders. Sylla, in 671, restored the privilege
to the senators alone. By the Aurelian law, Cotta, in 683,
divided it among the senators, equestrians, and tribunes of
the treasury. Augustus increased the number of the judices,
and extended the qualification to the humbler classes of the
community; but the political importance of the office under
the empire soon passed away.

Sect. 5.—*Criminal Jurisdiction of the Emperor and other Magistrates.*

Under the imperial government, the prince exercised Imperial magistrates.
criminal jurisdiction in concurrence with the senate. We
find frequent examples of the emperor presiding personally
in criminal trials without consulting the senate. When

[1] Maynz, § 35.

Cæsar, the dictator, constituted himself sole judge of Ligarius, it may be said that the old Roman constitution was overthrown.

By the side of the republican courts, Augustus established the jurisdiction of the senate for a large class of crimes, such as treason, and offences committed by magistrates and public functionaries. During the first century of the empire, we find examples of some crimes tried by the *quæstiones perpetuæ;* but these became more and more rare, and criminal jurisdiction was gradually diverted to imperial magistrates.

Prefect of the city.
The prefect of the city usurped many of the duties which had formerly belonged to the prætor and ediles. He punished all ordinary crimes committed in the city of Rome, and within a circuit of a hundred miles around it, having power to banish persons from Italy, and transport them to an island named by the emperor.

Prefect of police.
The *præfectus vigilum,* who commanded the soldiers appointed to watch the city, took cognisance of incendiaries, thieves, vagrants, and the like; but he could only inflict light punishments.[1]

---

[1] Maynz, § 53.

CHAPTER II.

PROCEDURE IN CRIMINAL TRIALS.

ANY Roman citizen might accuse another before the prætor, Authority to prosecute —postulatio. on being authorised to do so by that magistrate. The demand for such authority was called *postulatio*, and was published in the forum, to allow all concerned an opportunity of objecting. At the same time the accuser gave his oath of calumny that his proceedings were adopted in good faith, and with a view to the public interest.

After a reasonable delay, if the title of the accuser was Accusation --inscriptio. sustained, he made a formal declaration of the name of the person impeached, and the crime laid to his charge. A document was then drawn up, called *inscriptio*, stating the name of the accused and the precise nature of the charge: and this was signed by the accuser and those who intended to support him in conducting the prosecution.

The accused was summoned to appear before the prætor and hear the charge preferred against him. If he appeared and denied his guilt, as usually happened, the prætor appointed a day for proceeding with the trial, which was generally fixed after the lapse of ten days.

On the day appointed the parties appeared; and the prætor, Trial. or in his absence the presiding judge, called *judex quæstionis*, drew out of the urn the proper number of names to constitute the jury. A certain number of the jury might be challenged, both by the accuser and the accused. The jury having been sworn, the prosecutor, or his counsel, opened the case; the accused defended himself in person or by his counsel; and then the evidence was taken.

Verdict and
judgment.

When the proof and pleadings were concluded, the jury were called upon by the judge to give their verdict, which was done at first openly, and afterwards by ballot. The judge distributed among the jury small tablets, upon which they wrote secretly either an A. (*absolvo*), or a C. (*condemno*), or N. L. (*non liquet*). After examining these tablets, the judge pronounced sentence, according to the opinion of the majority, in a certain form. If the verdict was guilty, the prætor said, *videtur fecisse;* if it was not guilty, *non videtur fecisse;* and if a majority were unable to decide, he said *amplius*, and the cause was deferred for a new hearing on a future day. When the criminal was condemned, he was punished by law according to the nature of his offence.

Such were the forms of procedure followed in trials before the *quæstiones perpetuæ.* The forms observed before the comitia were very nearly the same, excepting the differences arising from the nature of the tribunal and the mode of giving the vote.[1]

---

[1] Much of our knowledge of criminal procedure among the Romans is derived from Sigonius, a learned writer of the sixteenth century. To this modern discoveries have added very little; but the subject is discussed with great clearness in the 'Republique Romaine' of Beaufort, and more recently by M. Laboulaye in his ' Essai sur les Lois Criminelles des Romains,' Paris, 1845.

CHAPTER III.

IN a general sense, crimes are such transgressions of law as *Nature of crime.* are punishable by courts of justice. The perpetrator of a crime is liable to punishment on grounds of public policy, besides being bound to repair, where that is possible, the injury sustained by the individual. For minor offences the term delict is sometimes used.

By the Roman law, crimes were divided into private and *Crimes private and public.* public. Private crimes could be prosecuted only by the party injured, and were generally punished by pecuniary fines applied to his use. Some offences which we are accustomed to regard as public crimes, such as theft and robbery, were treated as civil wrongs in the same manner as trespass, slander, and various other injuries which have already been noticed under the head of actions arising from wrongs. All these were usually requited by payments in money; and the same peculiarity is observable in the early laws of the Germans.

Ordinary public crimes were those expressly declared to *Ordinary and extraordinary.* be such by some law or ordinance, and which, on account of their atrocious or hurtful character, might be prosecuted by any member of the community. Some public crimes were called extraordinary, when the nature of the punishment was not defined by any specific law, but was left to the discretion of the judge. Of this description were violating a tomb, removing landmarks, forcing prisons, sheltering and abetting thieves, stellionate, and a great variety of innominate offences.[1]

[1] D. 47. t. 11-21.

z

Character of
criminal
system.
The criminal system of the Romans never attained the same degree of maturity and perfection as their law of civil rights. Their law respecting crimes was framed with special reference to their national institutions, their religion, the functions of their magistrates, and the manners and habits of the people, so that many regulations which were natural and convenient in their situation are wholly unsuitable to modern states. Besides, under the empire, the violence, and jealousy of every bad prince, and the short-sighted policy of every weak one, led to numerous inconsistent ordinances often dictated by mere caprice, which threw this branch of Roman jurisprudence into great confusion.

In classifying crimes, a distinction has generally been drawn between offences against the sovereign and the state, and offences against individuals.

I.—OFFENCES AGAINST THE STATE.

Treason—Crimen læsæ majestatis.

Treason.
In the early times of the republic, every act which was injurious to the safety of the state was called *perduellio*, and was punished by death. Numerous offences against the state were comprehended under that term, such as conspiracy against the government, aiming at kingly power, assisting the enemies of Rome, misconduct in the command of the armies. Marcus Manlius, who saved his country during the invasion of the Gauls, was convicted of an intention to seize upon the government, and being condemned, was, as Varro relates, hurled from the Tarpeian Rock, or, as Cornelius Nepos affirms, scourged to death ; his property was also confiscated, and his house razed to the ground.[1] Cn. Fulvius was accused of losing a Roman army ; but he anticipated his condemnation by voluntary exile. Coriolanus was charged with aspiring at tyranny, because he declared in the senate that the office of tribune of the people should be abolished.

[1] Aulus Gellius, lib. xvii. c. 21.

Of all the crimes falling under the description of capital, treason was visited with the greatest severity. The term *perduellio* fell into disuse, and the offences corresponding to treason in English law were comprehended under the *crimen læsæ majestatis*, the penalty of which was death with confiscation of goods, while the memory of the offender was declared infamous.[1] Under the empire, the law was extended not only to all attempts on the life of the reigning prince, but to all acts and words which might appear to be disrespectful to him, so that any indignity offered to a statue of the emperor could be punished as severely as an offence against his person. Every reader of Roman history knows how fearfully this engine of oppression was worked by Tiberius and some of his successors.

One striking peculiarity of the Roman law of treason was that the criminal might be tried even after his death, in order that his memory might be declared infamous and his property confiscated to the state.[2] This barbarous practice, so contrary to the rules of law and the dictates of humanity, was introduced during the despotism of imperial Rome ; and, strange to say, was adopted both in France and Scotland at a period so recent as the beginning of the seventeenth century.

Trials for treason after death.

Nicolas l'Hôte, a clerk of the Secretary of State, having betrayed Henry IV. of France by giving information to the King of Spain of all the deliberations of the French Council, was warned that his crime had been discovered, and in attempting to escape from his pursuers was drowned in the Marne. His dead body was taken to Paris, where he was convicted of high treason on 15th May 1604, and sentenced to have his body drawn on a hurdle, and dismembered by four horses, and the quarters exposed on the four principal avenues of the city. Dismemberment by four horses was then the ordinary punishment for treason in France, but it was sometimes aggravated by the most cruel torments, as shown by the sentences against the regicides Ravaillac and Damiens ; and it is remarkable that in both of these cases

[1] I. 4. 18. 3.   D. 48. 4.   C. 9. 8.   [2] C. 9. 8. 6.

me.

the houses in which the criminals were born were ordered to be razed to the ground according to the Roman custom, the proprietor being indemnified for the loss.[1]

Several trials for treason after the death of the criminals took place in Scotland during the reign of James VI., who piqued himself on a strict adherence to the classical standards of antiquity, though he frequently selected the worst models for imitation. In January 1603, Francis Mowbray, who was accused of "most high, horrible, and detestable points of treason," was killed in his attempt to escape from Edinburgh Castle. By a royal warrant his dead body was brought to the bar of the Court of Justiciary, which, without any evidence, and without the verdict of a jury, sentenced him "to be dismembered as a traitor, his body to be hanged on a gibbet, and afterwards quartered; his head and limbs stuck up on conspicuous places in the city of Edinburgh, and his whole estate to be forfeited."[2] In Robert Lesly's case, and in that of Logan of Restalrig, the bones of the deceased were raised from the grave and presented at the bar, as if to mock the very forms of justice.[3]

During the same reign, Archibald Cornwall, town-officer in Edinburgh, was convicted of treason for the foolish jest of attempting to hang up the king's picture on the gallows. The prisoner was charged with "the ignominiously dishonouring and defaming of his majesty, in taking of his portrait, and laying of the same and setting thereof to the stoops and upbearers of the gibbet." For this offence Cornwall was condemned to be hanged on the same gibbet till he was dead, and to remain on the gibbet "by the space of twenty-four hours, with a paper on his forehead containing that vile crime committed by him, which was pronounced for doom."[4]

Blackstone mentions two instances in the reign of Edward IV. of England, of persons executed for treasonable words,— the one a citizen of London, who said he would make his son heir of the *crown*, being the sign of the tavern in which

[1] Encyclopédie de Jurisprudence, voce *Lèse-Majesté*, Paris, 1785, vol. v. p. 440-1.
[2] Arnot's Criminal Trials, p. 65.
[3] 1 Hume's Criminal Law, p. 540.
[4] Arnot's Criminal Trials, p. 63.

he lived; the other, a gentleman whose favourite buck the king killed in hunting, whereupon he wished it, horns and all, in the king's belly. In the last case, we are told, Chief-Justice Markham rather chose to leave his place than assent to the judgment.[1] It has now, however, been long settled, that words spoken are not treasonable, though they may amount to a high misdemeanour.

Vis Publica et Privata.

Public force was a breach of the peace committed by bodies Public and private force. of men in arms organised for purposes of sedition, or obstructing the constituted authorities in the performance of their duty. In the last century of the Roman republic, violent riots by hired mobs became frequent, and persons convicted of this offence were banished. Private force was an illegal act of violence perpetrated on private account without arms; and this was punished by confiscation of one-third of the offender's estate.[2]

Milo accused Clodius of having opposed by an armed force the decree by which Cicero was recalled from exile; but Clodius escaped from this prosecution by getting himself appointed to the office of edile. He then brought a similar accusation against Milo for having employed force in dispersing Clodius and his satellites when the law for Cicero's recall was passed.

Crimen Repetundarum.

These expressions were used to denote a charge against Extortion. governors, magistrates, or other public functionaries, of extortion or other corrupt practices, such as accepting bribes to pervert the course of justice.[3] In the early ages of Rome there are few traces of this offence; but after the corruption of manners it became extremely common, especially in the provinces. If Cicero's orations can be relied on, they present

[1] Black. Com., book 4, ch. 6.   7. C. 9. 12.
[2] Lex Julia de Vi, D. 48. t. 6 and   [3] D. 48. 11. C. 9. 27.

a vivid picture of the extortions of Verres during his three
years' rule as proprætor in Sicily.   No class of the inhabitants was exempted from his avarice and cruelty.   Both the
producers and farmers of the revenue were laid under contribution; the industrious classes were made to pay heavy im-
posts; and the wealthy were forced to yield up their money
and their works of art, among which were the beautiful
statues and Corinthian vases, the possession of which by
Verres, after his return from exile, is supposed to have led
Mark Antony during the second triumvirate to place his
name on the list of the proscribed.[1]

The *crimen repetundarum* (*pecuniarum*) was punished by
restitution of what was wrongfully taken, and pecuniary
penalties to the extent of double and sometimes quadruple
the value.   Under the empire, the offender generally suffered
degradation, by loss of rank or office; and he was sometimes
condemned to exile.

Peculatus.

**Embezzle-
ment of
public pro-
perty.**   By this is meant the theft or embezzlement of property
belonging to the state.   In early times it was punished by
the interdiction of fire and water; afterwards, when the
offence was committed by public officers during their administration, the punishment was death; and private persons
suffered deportation.   Of the same nature was the *Lex de
Residuis*, which applied to those who had received public
money for public purposes and retained it.   They were compelled to restore what they had appropriated, and to pay
one-third more by way of penalty.

Sacrilege.   Sacrilege is the stealing of sacred or religious things consecrated to the service of God.   It was comprised in the Lex
Julia *de Peculatu*.[2]   The punishment was death, but sometimes a lighter penalty was inflicted.   It was not unusual for
private persons to deposit their money in temples for security;
but the stealing of such money appears to have been regarded
as theft, not sacrilege.

[1] Plin. Hist. Nat., xxxiv. 3.   [2] D. 48. 13.   C. 9. 28. 29.

Ambitus.

During the republic, severe laws were passed to repress Bribery. bribery by candidates in their canvass for election to public offices, not only while the voting was open, but also after the ballot was introduced by the Gabinian law (B.C. 139). Only the briber and his agents appear to have been punished, not the persons bribed. The penalty was sometimes exile, and sometimes a pecuniary fine, exclusion from the senate, and incapacity to hold office.

By the Lex Tullia, passed in the consulship of Cicero (B.C. 63), the punishment of bribery was ten years' exile. This law forbade any person to exhibit public shows for two years before he was a candidate; and prohibited the practice of hiring gladiators and armed men to attend the competitors at the popular elections. Notwithstanding the severity of these enactments, the temptation to purchase the suffrages of the people was too strong to be resisted, and bribery, reduced to a regular system, went on increasing till the close of the republic. Marius, Sylla, Pompey, Julius Cæsar, all lavished money among the venal citizens to procure dignities for themselves and their friends or adherents.

The trials for bribery were numerous in the republican period. When Emilius Scaurus was elected consul, he was accused of bribery by Rutilius, who had been his competitor for that office. Scaurus was acquitted, and immediately afterwards he impeached Rutilius for the same offence, and obtained a conviction. Cicero defended Murena and Plancius when accused of bribery, and his orations have come down to us.

The popular forms of election ceased under Tiberius. The choice of magistrates was then transferred to the senate; but the emperors abolished by degrees the vestiges of republican government, and appointed the magistrates themselves, so that the laws against bribery, as Modestinus observes, became obsolete at Rome. They subsisted only in municipal towns and colonies, where the people continued to enjoy the freedom of elections; and, by a decree of the senate, persons convicted of bribery were subjected to a fine of one hundred *aurei*, with infamy.[1]

II.—OFFENCES AGAINST INDIVIDUALS.

Homicide.

Homicide is the act by which the life of a human being is taken away. There are two degrees of criminal homicide, *murder* and *manslaughter;* and two degrees of homicide which do not expose to punishment, *excusable* and *justifiable.*

Murder.

Murder is the killing of any person wilfully without a necessary cause. By the laws of the Twelve Tables, this crime was punished by death. In the early ages, trials for murder took place before the people in the Comitia Centuriata, or by commissioners appointed by them; and this practice was continued till about the last half-century of the republic, when Sylla established a permanent court (*quæstio perpctua*) to take cognisance of all offences falling under the Lex Cornelia *de Sicariis et Veneficiis.*[2]

At different periods of Roman history, poisoning prevailed to an alarming extent. Livy informs us that two patrician matrons were accused of preparing poisonous drugs, which were found in their possession. They asserted that the drugs were wholesome; and, in order to test their sincerity, they were brought into the forum, and made to drink off the preparation, when they both perished. Their attendants being instantly seized, gave information against a great number of matrons, of whom no less than 170 were condemned. This affair created a great sensation, and, according to the historian, " seemed more the result of madness than of vicious depravity." [3]

Parricide.

Parricide is the murder of parents—a crime against which Solon refused to make any law, lest he should by forbidding it teach the people it was possible. By the Roman law the murderers of a parent or grandparent were scourged till they bled, sewed up in a leather sack with a dog, cock, viper, and

<hr/>

[1] D. 48. 14. C. 9. 26.   [2] D. 48. 8.   [3] Livy, viii. 18.

ape, and thrown into the sea or a river. This extraordinary punishment was originally introduced by the Twelve Tables; it was renewed by the laws of Sylla and Pompey; and it is mentioned in the Institutes as subsisting in the time of Justinian.[1] Under the empire, it was not uncommon to condemn parricides to be burned alive, or to be devoured by wild beasts in the amphitheatre.[2]

By the laws of Sylla and Pompey, parricide was extended to the killing of ascendants and descendants in any degree, of collaterals to the fourth degree, and of the wife, husband, and patron; but the punishment of the sack appears to have been retained only for those who had murdered a father, mother, grandfather, or grandmother, among ascendants, or children among descendants.[3] Publicus Malleolus, who killed his mother, is said to have been the first who suffered this punishment, in the year of Rome 652.[4] Sextus Roscius, of Ameria, was tried for the murder of his father under the Cornelian law (B.C. 80); but he was ably defended by Cicero, and acquitted.

Among civilised nations murder has been generally punished capitally. But it is a remarkable fact, that in almost every barbarous state this atrocious crime might be atoned for by paying a fine to the nearest kinsmen. This custom prevailed among the ancient Germans,[5] and was incorporated as law in the provisions of the barbarian codes.

Plagium.

This offence was the abduction or stealing of a free person, or a slave belonging to another. By the Lex Fabia the Kidnapping.

---

[1] I. 4. 18. 6.
[2] D. 48. 9. 9. 1. "Hodie tamen vivi exuruntur vel ad bestias dantur." Paul, 5. 24. 1, p. 439, ed. Huschke.
[3] C. 9. 17. 1.
Something resembling the ancient form of execution took place at Jaen, in Spain, on 1st March 1832. A man who had murdered his daughter-in-law, was hanged in the usual manner; his right hand was then cut off, and his body "*encubado*," that is, placed in a barrel, with a cock, a snake, a monkey, and a toad, and thrown into the river.—See Quart. Rev., vol. lxi. p. 390.
[4] Beaufort, Rep. Rom., vol. ii. p. 87.
[5] Tac. Ger., c. 12.

penalty was pecuniary; but after kidnapping became common, the punishment was increased to banishment, and in some cases was capital.[1]

Adultery.

Adultery. By the law of most Christian countries, adultery is the violation of conjugal fidelity by either of the spouses, so that the incontinency of the wife and husband stand upon the same foundation. The Romans adopted a different rule; for adultery was defined by them to be sexual intercourse with another man's wife.[2] It was adultery whether the male was married or not; but the sexual connection of a married man with a woman who was not married was not adultery. By the Julian law, passed in the time of Augustus, persons convicted of adultery were banished, besides forfeiting a considerable part of their property.[3] A constitution of Constantine, inserted in the Code, made adultery a capital offence, but it seems to apply only to males; and, at a subsequent period, Justinian ordered the erring wife to be confined in a convent, after being whipped.[4]

In England, during the Commonwealth, adultery in either sex was made a capital offence; but this law was discontinued at the Restoration. A similar law for notorious adultery existed in Scotland under the Act 1563, c. 74; but this statute has expired by long desuetude. In France, a married woman and her paramour, convicted of adultery, are liable to be punished by imprisonment, besides a pecuniary fine in the case of the man.[5]

Raptus Mulierum.

Rape. By the Roman law, rape was punished with death and confiscation of goods.[6] It is the general opinion of civilians

[1] I. 4. 18. 10. D. 48. 15. C. 9. 20.

[2] "Adulterium est alieni thori violatio, sive coitus cum aliena uxore factus. Nam adulterium jure civili cum nupta tantum committitur."—

Vinnius, Com. 4. 18. 4.

[3] D. 48. 5.

[4] C. 9. 9. 30. N. 134, ch. 10.

[5] Code Penal, art. 336, 337, 338.

[6] C. 9. 13.

that this offence might be committed, not only by forcible connection with a woman against her will, but by carrying off her person from her friends with a view to debauch her, even though there should be no actual violation. But in this country it is essential to this crime that the act of connection should be fully consummated.*

Formerly the punishment of rape was capital with us; but by the 4 and 5 Vict. c. 56, it is provided that every person convicted of this crime shall be liable to be transported for life. In France the punishment varies, according to circumstances, from imprisonment to forced labour for life.[1]

Crimen Falsi.

Falsehood has been defined the fraudulent imitation or suppression of truth to the damage of another. The Lex Cornelia *de Falsis*, passed in the time of Sylla, treated chiefly of three offences: 1. Forgery of testamentary writings; 2. Coining base money; 3. Perjury and corrupting witnesses. The penalty attached to this law was the interdiction of fire and water. *(margin: Forgery and falsehood.)*

There were other legislative provisions regarding these offences, whereby the penalties of forgery were extended to the fabrication of all written instruments, as well as wills. Laws were also passed against the use of false weights and measures, and other frauds. The punishments inflicted were arbitrary, and a distinction was sometimes made according to the rank of the offender; for, while persons of condition, called "honestiores," were banished, we find men of low degree, the "humiliores," sentenced to be buried in the mines or executed.[2]

Besides robbery, theft, patrimonial damage, and injury to the person or reputation, which have already been considered as private trespasses, though in modern systems the first two *(margin: Extraordinary crimes.)*

---

* Proof of penetration is now sufficient in England; 24 & 25 Vict. c. 100, § 63: also in Scotland, case of Robertson, 12th March 1836.

[1] Code Penal, art. 331, 332, 333.
[2] I. 4. 18. 7. D. 48. 10. C. 9. 22. 23.

are usually classed under criminal prosecutions, the Digest
treats of a variety of offences called extraordinary crimes, to
which no certain punishment is annexed.[1]

The Cornelian, Pompeian, and Julian laws formed the
foundation of criminal jurisprudence at Rome; but the later
emperors greatly aggravated the severity of punishments, and
Justinian has disguised their rigour by using the names of the
original lawgivers, from a natural desire to conceal from the
people the progress of despotism.

Extinction of Crimes.

How crimes extinguished. By the Roman law, crimes were extinguished—1st, By the
death of the criminal, though in some exceptional cases
during the empire trials of deceased persons were allowed, in
order to confiscate their property; 2d, By remission from the
sovereign, which freed the delinquent from punishment, but
did not cut off the party injured from his claim of damages;
3d, By prescription after the lapse of twenty years without
accusation, and in particular crimes after a much shorter
period fixed by law.

In England it is understood there is no limitation of time
applicable to the prosecution of crimes, except in some special
cases fixed by statute, as treason, smuggling, and the like.[2]
By 7 William III. c. 3, it is declared that no person shall be
prosecuted for treason after three years from the commission
of the offence, except in the case of a designed assassination of
the sovereign. According to the custom of Scotland, crimes
prescribe in twenty years, following the rule of the Roman
law; but in particular crimes the prescription is limited by
statute to a shorter period.[3] Prescription applicable to crimes
is admitted in the French law, according to certain rules laid
down in the Code.[4]

[1] D. 47. t. 11-21.
[2] Paterson's Compendium, p. 322.
[3] 2 Hume's Criminal Law, 136.
[4] Code d'Instruction Criminelle, art. 635-643.

CHAPTER IV.

PUNISHMENTS IN THE ROMAN LAW.

WHEN the penal laws of the decemvirs, which were remarkable for their extraordinary severity, fell into disuse, the Romans, by a very natural transition, passed from the extreme of rigour to the opposite extreme of lenity. For a time the right to sentence any one to die belonged to the general assembly of the people; and the person of a Roman citizen was deemed so sacred that capital punishments became of rare occurrence. A Roman accused of any capital crime might prevent the sentence of the law by voluntary exile; and this indulgence was carried so far, that till the votes of the last century had been declared, he was allowed to withdraw in the open view of all, and retire in safety to Rhodes or Athens, or any other of the confederate cities.[1] It is to this period that Livy alludes when he says, that no people were fonder of moderation in punishments than the Romans. Sylla, the dictator, when invested with absolute power, put thousands of citizens to death by proscription without any form of trial; but in the Cornelian criminal code the usual punishment fixed by him for heinous crimes was *aquæ et ignis interdictio.* Under the empire public executions became frequent, and new and cruel punishments were introduced.[2]

Some of the principal punishments in use among the Romans may here be shortly noticed.

Fine.—The infliction of a fine for certain offences was common from the earliest times. At first, such was the scarcity

---

[1] Polybius, vi. c. 2.   [2] D. 48. 19. De Pœnis. C. 9. 47.

of money that fines consisted of cattle; and, according to some authors, the highest under the Aternian law, B.C. 455, never exceeded two sheep and thirty oxen.[1] But much larger fines, paid in money, were afterwards exacted at different periods of the republic, proportioned to the wealth of the delinquent and the nature of the offence.

Imprisonment.—A person accused of any crime might be detained in prison till he could be brought to trial. If he denied his guilt he might be required to give sureties for his appearance, so as to avoid being detained in custody; and, except in extreme cases, even when ordinary bail was refused, the accused, instead of being thrown into the public jail, was placed *in libera custodia,*—that is, intrusted to the charge of one of the higher magistrates, or of a private person of distinction, who became responsible for his safe keeping. The prison was chiefly used as a place of confinement before trial, and also as a place of execution. Imprisonment appears to have been seldom used among the Romans as a legal punishment for offences.

A prison was first built at Rome by Ancus Martius, near the Forum. Another was subsequently erected by Appius Claudius, the decemvir, in which he was himself put to death. The prison was under the charge of a jailer, who kept an exact roll of the prisoners, which was reported every month to the *triumviri capitales.*

Corporal Chastisement.—Scourging, or flogging, was applied in various ways. The rod was used in the punishment of Roman citizens till it was abolished by the Porcian law. Soldiers guilty of desertion and other offences against military discipline, were liable to the punishment called *fustuarium,* which was analogous to running the gauntlet. Upon a given signal, all the soldiers of the legion fell upon the delinquent with sticks and stones, and generally killed him on the spot;

(margin: Imprisonment.)

(margin: Scourging.)

---

[1] According to Aulus Gellius, there were great numbers of horned cattle in Italy, but sheep were scarce; and he gives that as the reason why the fine was levied in the proportion here stated.—Aul. Gell., lib. xi. c. 1. In his 'Roman Antiquities,' Dr Adam has stated the maximum fine at *two* oxen and *thirty* sheep.—7th ed., p. 260. See Dr Colquhoun's Summary of the Roman Civil Law, vol. iii. p. 682.

but if he made his escape he could not return to his native country. Slaves were punished by the lash. Under the emperors corporal punishment by beating or flogging was frequently inflicted on freemen of the lower orders.

Retaliation.—By the Twelve Tables the punishment of Retaliation. retaliation was authorised for bodily injuries—an eye for an eye, a limb for a limb; but this severe penalty was seldom exacted, because the law allowed pecuniary compensation to be taken in lieu of it.[1]

Ignominy.—This was inflicted in two ways, either by the Infamy. censors or by judicial sentence. The *nota censoria* operated as a stain on the reputation without affecting civil rights; but those made infamous by a judicial sentence were excluded from public offices and dignities, and deprived of various privileges belonging to other citizens.

Penal Servitude.—A Roman citizen might be sold into Penal slavery for various offences chiefly connected with military servitude. discipline; for neglecting to give an exact account of his property to the censors; for refusing to serve in the army when the consul held a levy; and for deserting to the enemy in time of war. Persons guilty of these offences were supposed to have voluntarily renounced the rights of citizens.

During the empire criminals were often condemned to labour in the mines or on public works.

Banishment.—*Aquæ et ignis interdictio* (forbidding the Banish- use of fire and water) was equivalent to the deprivation of the ment. chief necessaries of life, and its effect was to incapacitate a person from residing or exercising the rights of a citizen within the limits embraced by the sentence. He did not cease, however, to be a Roman citizen, unless he procured admission into another state; and, if the interdiction was legally removed, he might return and resume his former position at Rome. Thus Cicero, who had been interdicted

---

[1] I. 4. 4. 7. Among the Athenians, Solon decided that whoever puts out the only eye of a one-eyed person shall, for so doing, lose both his own. But the case has been put, what shall be done where a man having but one eye happens to thrust out one of his neighbour's? Shall he lose his only eye by way of retaliation? If so, he would then be quite blind, and suffer a greater injury than he had caused.

from fire and water within four hundred miles of Rome, was
restored by a *lex centuriata.*

Under the emperors two forms of banishment, in the
ordinary sense of the term, were introduced, *deportatio* and
relegatio. *Deportatio* consisted of confinement in some place
more or less distant, generally in one of the small rocky
islands off the coast of Italy, or in the Ægean, which were
used as state-prisons ; and, although the criminal was not reduced to the condition of a slave, he lost his property and all
his rights as a Roman citizen. Relegation was compulsory
residence in a particular place assigned in the sentence, without being deprived of personal freedom or the rights of a
citizen, and this might be either for an indefinite or a definite
time. Sometimes a person was forbidden to live in Rome, or
in a particular province, leaving him to choose his residence
elsewhere ; and sometimes an island or a particular city was
assigned for his residence. Ovid, who was banished to Tomi,
a town on the Euxine, praises, perhaps without much sincerity, the clemency of the emperor for the mildness of his
sentence.

Capital
punish-
ments.   *Death.*—In early times the punishment of death appears
to have been inflicted by hanging, scourging, and beheading,
and by hurling from the Tarpeian Rock. The ancient usage
of scourging, *more majorum,* is described by Suetonius. "The
custom," he says, "was to strip the criminal stark naked, and
lash him to death, with his head fastened within a forked
stake."[1] This execution generally took place in a field out-
side the Esquiline Gate, at the sound of a trumpet.

Many criminals were also executed in prison, either by
strangling them or precipitating them from a high place
called *Robur.*

Slaves after being scourged were crucified, usually bearing
on their breast a label or inscription intimating the crime for
which they suffered. They were compelled to carry the cross
to the place of execution. No death could be more lingering
and horrible when the suspended culprit was left to perish by
slow degrees without any one to put an end to his torments.

---

[1] Sueton. in Ner., c. 49.

Sometimes he was stifled by the smoke of a fire, lighted expressly for the purpose, at the foot of the cross ; and at other times a merciful bystander plunged a spear into the victim's body to terminate his sufferings. This barbarous punishment, which is said by Cicero to have been invented by Tarquin the Proud, continued in force until Constantine, from reverence to the sacred symbol, abolished it throughout the Roman empire.

During the republic, capital punishments appear to have been inflicted on Roman citizens by the lictors. But there was a public executioner (*carnifex*), one of the most odious of all the officers of justice, who was not permitted to live within the city. It was his duty to execute slaves and persons of vile condition condemned to infamous punishments, such as the cross, or strangling in prison.[1]

Some new and cruel capital punishments were introduced under the emperors, such as burning alive, exposing to wild beasts, and similar tortures. The inhuman practice of exposing criminals to the fury of wild animals, which was in use among the Carthaginians, was adopted at Rome from the time of Tiberius : sometimes the culprit was condemned to engage in mortal strife with a lion for the amusement of the populace ; at other times he was deprived of the chance of life, being tied to a stake that he might be unresistingly devoured by his ferocious assailants. That the early Christians were not unfrequently subjected to this cruel fate, may be inferred from a well-known passage in Tertullian :—" If the Tiber overflow its banks ; if there be a famine or plague ; if there be a cold, a dry, or a scorching season ; if any public calamity overtake us ; the universal cry of the populace is,— To the lion with the Christians—*Christiani ad leonem !* "[2]

Under the empire persons of condition were generally treated with more favour in the matter of punishment than those of lower degree. Beheading and deportation were reserved for the former : while meaner criminals were subjected to the most cruel and degrading punishments. In some

---

[1] Beaufort, Rep. Rom., vol. i. p. 425.

[2] On Roman Punishments, see Beaufort, vol. ii. p. 115-118.

instances criminals. of distinction, convicted of offences
against the state, were permitted to choose whatever form of
death appeared to them least painful, as happened in the
case of Seneca, who was condemned for having been privy to
a conspiracy against the Emperor Nero, and chose to expire
in a warm bath after having his veins opened.[1]

[1] According to popular tradition, when the Duke of Clarence, brother of Edward IV., was condemned to death, he very whimsically chose to be drowned in a butt of Malmsey.—Hume's Hist., vol. iii. p. 363.

CHAPTER V.

I.—FRENCH LAW.

BEFORE the Revolution of 1789 the criminal laws of France Criminal were arbitrary and confused, and stained by the most wanton system. cruelty. The first National Assembly in 1791 improved the penal system, remodelled the criminal courts, and introduced publicity and trial by jury. Since then the body of penal law has been entirely recast, and now consists of the Code d'Instruction Criminelle of 1808, and of the Code Penal of 1810, both of which were revised in 1832, besides numerous laws concerning special matters, forming a collection much more considerable than that of the codes.

According to the French penal system offences are treated under three heads. 1. *Crimes,* which are tried before a jury and punished by severe or infamous punishments. 2. *Delicts,* which are tried by the correctional tribunals without a jury, and are punished by imprisonment for a time in a house of correction, temporary privation of certain civil rights, or a fine. 3. *Contraventions,* which are petty offences tried by the simple police, and punished by imprisonment not exceeding five days, and fines not exceeding fifteen francs.*

---

* There have been additions made to the French Criminal Code since 1832, particularly in 1858 and 1863. One of these we transcribe, as repressing a practice which in England and Scotland has given rise to inconvenience. " Any one who shall publicly wear a costume, a uni- form, or a decoration to which he is not entitled, will be punished by imprisonment for six months. Any one who, without right, and with the view of attributing to himself an honorary distinction, shall have publicly taken "a title, changed, altered, or modified the name which

Trial by jury.

All criminal prosecutions in France are conducted by a public prosecutor appointed by Government. The jury consists of twelve persons. Originally the verdict could be returned by a simple majority; but under the law of 28th April 1832 no decision can be given against the accused except by a majority of more than seven votes. A similar majority of more than seven votes may find the existence of extenuating circumstances so as to reduce the punishment.

Principal punishments.

By the Penal Code all crimes are defined and all punishments are fixed, but with a maximum and a minimum as regards certain punishments. The principal punishments now in force in France are death, forced labour for life or for a limited time, deportation for life to some place beyond the continental territory of France, banishment from the empire for a fixed period, detention in a fortress, imprisonment in a house of correction, privation of civil rights, and pecuniary fine.

Ancient system.

Formerly there were five modes of inflicting capital punishment in France : — Burning alive, breaking on the wheel, hanging, beheading, and quartering. To these were sometimes added extraordinary tortures, such as tearing off the flesh from the living body with red-hot pincers, pouring molten lead and brimstone into the raw wounds, cutting out the tongue, and similar atrocities, which, though carefully recorded in judicial sentences, almost stagger belief.[1] * Un-

is assigned to him in the public registers, will be subject to a fine of from 500 to 1000 francs." The offender must also pay the costs ; and the judgment is to be advertised in the newspapers. — *Loi*, 28th May 1858.

[1] When General Kleber was assassinated by a fanatic in Egypt in June 1800, the murderer was put to death by impalement, which is said to be the punishment of assassins by the law of Turkey.

* The sentence passed in 1610 on Ravaillac, the assassin of Henry IV., was that, after publicly confessing his guilt, "he shall be carried to the Grève, and, on a scaffold to be there erected, the flesh shall be torn to pieces with red-hot pincers from his breasts, his arms, and thighs, and the calves of his legs ; his right hand, holding the knife wherewith he committed the aforesaid parricide, shall be scorched and burned with flaming brimstone ; and on the places where the flesh has been torn with pincers, melted lead, boiling oil, scalding pitch, with wax and brimstone melted together, shall be poured ; after this he shall be torn in pieces by four horses, his limbs and body burnt to ashes and dispersed in the air." His goods and

der the ancient regime nobles were beheaded, while meaner criminals were hanged; but now all are reduced to the same level, as every one condemned to death is beheaded by the guillotine.   This machine, though surrounded by painful Guillotine. associations from the great number of its victims during the Reign of Terror, was introduced and is retained from motives of humanity, because it inflicts less pain than decapitation by the axe or the sword as practised in other countries.

The proposal to abolish the punishment of death, supported by Robespierre, was rejected by the National Assembly. The question as to the mode of execution was a question of equality.   After the Revolution of 1848 the punishment of death was abolished for all political crimes; but it was re-established in 1853 for all criminal attempts against the head of the state.[1]

By the law of 28th April 1832 the Penal Code was greatly Recent im-improved by a general reduction in the scale of punishments; provements. many crimes formerly capital were declared to be so no longer, and the barbarous penalties of mutilation, branding, and the iron collar, were entirely abolished.   The penalty of confiscation of goods was abrogated after the Restoration by a law of Louis XVIII.   Criminals sentenced to death, to forced labour for life, or to deportation, were formerly subjected to what was called *civil death*, involving the loss of property and all civil rights; but that penalty, after being long condemned as inexpedient, was finally abolished by the law of 31st May 1854.[2]

II.—BRITISH CRIMINAL LAW.

By the law of England crimes are classed under the heads Classifica-of felony and misdemeanour.   Treason is a higher kind of tion of crimes.

chattels were declared to be confiscated; the house in which he was born was to be pulled down (the owner being indemnified), and no other ever to be erected there; his father and mother to be banished; his other relatives commanded to change the name of Ravaillac for some other; and before the execution of the sentence, Ravaillac again to undergo the torture for discovery of his accomplices. — Sully's Memoirs, vol. v. p. 234; English translation, 1812.

[1] Ortolan, Eléments du Droit Penal, Paris, 1855, p. 69.

[2] Ibid., p. 715.

felony, and a misdemeanour is an offence lower in the scale
of crime than felony, but separated from it by an arbitrary
line. " The chief practical difference consists in the legal
incidents attaching to conviction of these crimes. In capital
felonies the prisoner forfeits both his real and personal estate.
In felonies not capital he forfeits only his personal estate.
In misdemeanours the prisoner forfeits nothing." [1]

Besides these classes of indictable crimes there are many
statutory offences subject to the summary jurisdiction of
Justices of the Peace. The distinction between felony and
misdemeanour is unknown in the law of Scotland. Sentence
of death by that law involves only a forfeiture of movables.
In all other cases not capital, even the movables are not
forfeited, except in a few crimes where this is made part of
the punishment, and in outlawry. [2]

How pro-
secuted.

One of the great defects in the English system of criminal
procedure, is the want of a public prosecutor, such as exists
in France and Scotland. Any member of the community,
generally speaking, may prosecute for all offences in the
name of the sovereign, but the task is usually devolved on
the person injured by the crime, though, in some cases, the
prosecution is conducted by the Crown. " To leave each
individual in the community," says Lord Brougham, " the
power of prosecuting for all offences in the name of the
sovereign, but at his discretion, subject to the power of stay-
ing his proceedings, vested in the sovereign, and at his own
cost, subject to the court which tries the case allowing his
reimbursement; to burden the injured party with the expense
and trouble of bringing to justice him by whom he has been
injured; to let wealthy offenders buy off their prosecutor, while
poor men must stand their trial; to divide the responsibility of
a culprit's escape, who ought to be convicted, and of an innocent man's vexation and trial, who ought never to have been
tried, among three-and-twenty country gentlemen or trades-
men in towns, while no professional man is answerable at all
either for the omission or the oppression; this is the English

---

[1] Paterson's Compendium, p. 342.   [2] 2 Hume's Criminal Law, p. 483-
Broom's Com., p. 891.   492.

system of prosecution, and anything so bad, we may safely affirm, exists in no other country under the sun." [1]

In Scotland, the Lord Advocate and his deputies, who are barristers, are charged with the duty of prosecuting all crimes, acting with the assistance of procurators-fiscal, who take the initiative, and collect the evidence in all criminal proceedings. Before inferior courts the procurator-fiscal, who is a solicitor, not a barrister, acts as prosecutor. The person injured, or his kinsmen, but not strangers, may also prosecute in certain cases; but they can only do so with the concurrence of the public prosecutor.

The jury which tries the prisoner in England consists of twelve men, and their verdict must be unanimous. In Scotland, the jury in criminal trials consists of fifteen, and the verdict may be returned by a majority. There seems no good reason why the number of the jurymen should not be reduced to twelve; but in no case should a bare majority be allowed to return a verdict against the accused, as involving too great a risk of error: and it might be advisable to adopt the rule followed in France, by requiring, in a jury of twelve, a majority of more than seven votes, which would secure the concurrence at least of two-thirds of the whole jury.[2] *Verdict of jury.*

Since the union of the two kingdoms in 1707, the laws of treason in England and Scotland have been assimilated. The trial proceeds according to the English forms. A bill is found by a grand jury, and the petty jury consists of twelve *Trials for treason.*

---

[1] Lord Brougham, British Constitution, 1861, p. 329.

[2] In Scotland the jury may decide against the accused by a simple majority of 8 to 7, so that the scale is turned against him by *one* vote. Under the French system, the majority must be at least 8 to 4, being in the proportion of two-thirds to one-third, or just double the number of the minority.

In civil causes in Scotland, the jury consists of twelve men; and unanimity was at one time required. But, by the Act 22 & 23 Vict. c. 7, if *nine* of the jury agree, after *three* hours' deliberation, they may return a verdict; and if *nine* cannot agree after *six* hours' deliberation, the jury may be discharged without a verdict. * Though this change was recommended by English lawyers of the highest eminence, the principle of unanimity is still adhered to in all civil and criminal trials before English courts.

* By the Act 31 & 32 Vict. c. 100, § 48, the jury, after being enclosed for three hours, may return a verdict by a majority,—which cannot be less than 7 to 5.

persons. The punishment of treason, in the case of males, is, that the offender shall be drawn on a hurdle to the place of execution, and be hanged by the neck till dead; that the head shall then be severed from the body, and the body be divided into four quarters—the head and quarters being at the disposal of the Crown; and this is accompanied by forfeiture of honours, and real and personal estates, and corruption of blood. Power is reserved to the sovereign, by royal warrant, to change this sentence to beheading. In the time of Blackstone, the traitor, if a male, was hanged by the neck, and cut down before life was extinct, and his entrails were taken out and burned while he was yet alive; and, if a woman, she was drawn to the place of execution, and there burned alive. But, by Acts passed in the reign of George III., the sentence was altered, in the case of males, by abolishing the savage custom of embowelling; whilst women were appointed to be drawn to the gallows and hanged.

Principal punishments.

In Britain the punishment of offences is in some cases governed by the common law only, but is more frequently defined by statute. The principal punishments now in force are—death; penal servitude, now substituted for transportation beyond seas; imprisonment, with or without hard labour; whipping, in certain cases; and fine.

The ordinary mode of capital punishment which has been in use from the earliest times, is that the offender shall be hanged by the neck till dead, with the addition, in the case of murder, that his body (which formerly was sometimes given to the doctors for dissection) shall be buried within the precincts of the prison in which he shall have been last confined after conviction. Treason, as we have seen, is accompanied with other severities; and beheading is sometimes substituted for hanging, especially in the case of criminals of distinction who have committed offences against the state.

Ancient penal system.

In former times burning alive was the inevitable doom of persons convicted of heresy and witchcraft. Trials for witchcraft were common both in England and Scotland down to the close of the seventeenth century. Sir Matthew

Hale passed sentence of death on two poor women for this offence in 1664. A change soon afterwards took place in the feelings of the English judges; and Chief-Justice Holt, in several trials, charged the jury with such firmness and good sense as to obtain verdicts of acquittal. Yet, after all this, in 1716, Mrs Hicks and her daughter, aged nine, were condemned to death at Huntingdon for selling their souls to the devil. In Scotland, where this delusion had full sway, the last execution for this offence took place at Dornoch in 1722, under a sentence of the Sheriff of Sutherlandshire. The penal statutes against witchcraft were repealed in 1736, and the pretended exercise of such arts was made punishable by imprisonment and the pillory.

Among the laws of William the Conqueror, mutilation figures very prominently as a punishment, with such horrible details as plucking out the eyes, cutting off a hand or a foot, and the like.[1] During the reign of the Tudors, fine and imprisonment were the usual penalties inflicted by the Star Chamber; but the pillory, whipping, branding, and cutting off the ears, grew into use by degrees.[2] These abuses attracted notice at the Revolution, and it was declared by the Bill of Rights (1 Will. sess. 2, c. 2), that no cruel and unusual punishments should be inflicted. Mutilation and branding have been long discontinued; the pillory has been abrogated by statute; and even the stocks have fallen into disuse as unsuited to modern manners.

Formerly the law of England assigned capital punishments to many kinds of offences, but inflicted it only in a few examples of each kind. About the beginning of the present century the sentence of death was not executed on more than a sixth part of the persons on whom it was pronounced, even taking into account crimes the most atrocious and dangerous to society; and, if these be excluded, the proportion which the number executed bore to those condemned, was

Capital sentences not enforced.

---

[1] " Interdicimus ne quis occidatur vel suspendatur pro aliqua culpa; sed eruantur oculi, abscindantur pedes, vel testiculi vel manus."—Leg. Gul. I. cap. 7. Fleta, lib. i. c. 38. Brac. lib. 3, c. 32.

[2] Hallam's Constitutional History of England, vol. i. p. 484-493.

probably not more than one in twenty.[1] To relax the
severity of the statutes, the royal prerogative was constantly
invoked, and every year capital executions became more
rare. At length, by 4 Geo. IV. c. 48, when any person was
convicted of a capital crime, and the judge considered him fit
to be recommended to the royal mercy, the court was authorised to abstain from pronouncing sentence of death, and to
order it to be recorded, which entering on record was to have
the same effect as if the judgment had been pronounced and
the offender reprieved. By this extraordinary expedient,
which transferred a portion of the prerogative of the Crown
to the judges, the legislature practically declared that the
statutes creating capital offences were not meant to be carried
into indiscriminate execution.

One great peculiarity of the Scotch criminal system is that
the Lord Advocate, as the responsible Minister of the Crown
in his character of public prosecutor, may pass from any
charge at pleasure, and restrict the penalty to an arbitrary
punishment short of death before moving for sentence.

A theory at one time prevailed, supported by the authority
of Dr Paley, who was fond of devising apologies for existing
abuses, that it was good policy, in framing penal statutes, to
sweep into the net every crime which could possibly merit the
punishment of death, leaving the Crown to relax the severity
of the law as often as circumstances appeared to palliate the
offence. But many writers have demonstrated the flagrant
injustice and mischievous consequences of this practice.
Commenting on the frequency of capital punishment which
disgraced the English law at the time he wrote, Blackstone
observes:—"It is a melancholy truth that among the variety
of actions which men are daily liable to commit, no less
than 160 have been declared by Act of Parliament to be
felonies without benefit of clergy; or, in other words, to be
worthy of instant death. So dreadful a list, instead of diminishing, increases the number of offenders. The injured,
through compassion, will often forbear to prosecute; juries,
through compassion, will sometimes forget their oaths, and
either acquit the guilty or mitigate the nature of the offence;

[1] May's Constitutional History of England, vol. ii. p. 597.

and judges, through compassion, will respite one-half of the convicts, and recommend them to the royal mercy. Among so many chances of escape, the needy and hardened offender overlooks the multitude that suffer; he boldly engages in some desperate attempt to relieve his wants or supply his vices, and if, unexpectedly, the hand of justice overtake him, he deems himself peculiarly unfortunate in falling at last a sacrifice to those laws which long impunity has taught him to contemn." [1]

Notwithstanding this forcible appeal to justice and humanity, capital offences, in place of being diminished, were greatly increased after Blackstone's time. So reckless was the sacrifice of human life, that from the Reformation to the death of George III.—a period of 160 years—no less than 187 capital offences, wholly different in character and degree, were added to the criminal code.[2] At length the opinion advocated by Beccaria, Montesquieu, and Bentham, gained ground, though slowly, that "crimes are more effectually prevented by the *certainty* than the *severity* of punishment." To the exertions of Sir Samuel Romilly we are mainly indebted for having laid the foundation of that reform of our penal jurisprudence which was afterwards commenced by Sir Robert Peel, and carried out so successfully in the reign of her present Majesty. By the acts 7 Will. IV. and 1 Vict. c. 84 to 89 and 91, brought in by Lord John Russell, and passed on 17th July 1837, the punishment of death was removed *Capital* from about 200 offences, leaving it applicable to high treason, *offences greatly* murder, and attempts at murder, rape, arson with danger to *reduced.* life, and to piracies, burglaries, and robberies, when aggravated by cruelty and violence. Rape was taken out of the list of capital offences by a subsequent statute.

As great difficulties were experienced in finding colonies *Penal* willing to receive transported convicts, penal servitude was *servitude.* substituted for transportation under the Acts 16 & 17 Vict. c. 99, and 20 & 21 Vict. c. 3. By the last of these Acts, no person can be sentenced to transportation after 1st July 1857, and any person who might have been previously sentenced to transportation may be sentenced to be kept in penal ser-

[1] Black. Com., book 4, c. 1.   [2] May's Const. Hist., vol. ii. p. 595.

vitude for a term of the same duration as the term of transportation to which such person would have been liable if these
Acts had not been passed, but the discretion of the court as
to alternative punishments is not affected; and in any case
in which, before the passing of the last Act, sentence of seven
years' transportation might have been passed, the court may
in its discretion pass a sentence of penal servitude of not less
than three years.

Every person sentenced to penal servitude may be confined in any prison or place of confinement in the United
Kingdom, or in any river, port, or harbour of the United
Kingdom in which persons sentenced to transportation might
formerly have been confined; and may be conveyed to any
place or places beyond seas to which persons sentenced to
transportation could formerly be conveyed, or to any place
or places beyond seas which may be hereafter appointed.

Any of the principal Secretaries of State may grant licences
to be at large to convicts under sentence of penal servitude;
but if the licence of any convict be revoked, he may be committed to prison, and compelled to undergo the residue of
his sentence.[1]

In modern Acts, when offences are punished by imprisonment, the duration is usually limited, so as not to exceed
three years, or at the utmost four years, and not unfrequently
the imprisonment is accompanied with hard labour.[*]

The principal part of the English criminal law is contained
in the Criminal Law Consolidation and Amendment Acts of
1861, 24 & 25 Vict. c. 94 to 100.[2] .

[1] These two statutes are now modified by 27 & 28 Vict. c. 47 (25th
July 1864). The minimum period
of penal servitude is fixed at five
years, or, in case of previous conviction, at seven years. The Act also
relates to corporal punishment for
offences committed in prison, and to
licences granted under these penal
servitude Acts.

[*] The Habitual Criminals Act,
1869, contains important provisions
applicable to both England and

Scotland respecting that class of
criminals.

[2] See Treatise on these Acts by
Charles S. Greaves, 2d ed., 8vo,
London, 1862.

The principal Acts are—c. 100,
relating to offences against the person; c. 96, relating to larceny and
other similar offences; c. 97, relating to malicious injuries to property;
c 98, relating to indictable offences
by forgery; c. 99, relating to coin-
age offences (United Kingdom).

CHAPTER VI.

OF THE ROMAN BAR.

IN the earliest times the Romans were more addicted to the profession of arms than to the study of law and eloquence. Every head of a patrician house had a number of dependants, who looked up to him as their protector, and owed him certain obligations in return. This was the relation of patron and client. One of the ordinary duties of the patron was to assist his client in lawsuits, and defend him before the tribunals. *First pleaders were patrons.*

The first pleaders who appeared at the Roman bar were not jurisconsults; but when the science of law became more difficult and complicated, the pleaders began to apply themselves to the study of jurisprudence, and a new class of public men arose, who combined the double character of able speakers and great jurisconsults. During the republic, the bar was held in high estimation, and was the principal field for attaining the honours of the state.

Till the close of the republic, pleaders were generally termed *patroni*. Under the empire they were usually called *advocati*, and sometimes *causidici*. In a short rescript of Valentinian and Valens, declaring it to be incompatible for any one to be judge and advocate in the same suit, the three terms *patronus, advocatus,* and *causidicus*, are all used in the same sense.[1] *Advocates under the empire.*

[1] " Quisquis vult esse causidicus, non idem in eodem negotio sit advocatus et judex : quoniam aliquem inter arbitros et patronos oportet esse delectum."—C. 1. 6. 6.

In private causes it was customary to deliver to the advocate a brief drawn up by a jurisconsult, in which questions of law were fully discussed. Besides, the advocates were frequently assisted at the bar by a lawyer of a second order, who was called *leguleius* or *formularius*, and sometimes *monitor*.

Costume. Among the Romans the costume of the advocates was the white *toga*, which at one period was common to all the citizens. By the lower class this began to be given up about the time of Cato the Censor, and it had almost fallen into disuse at the end of the republic, except among the senators and equestrians. Under Augustus advocates were compelled to assume the ancient costume at the bar. Before long the toga was nowhere to be seen except in courts of justice; and the expression *togati*, which Cicero and Virgil had applied to the whole Roman people, became at last the usual designation of the advocates.

Duration of pleadings. Whether any limitation was imposed on the length of the oral pleadings in early times is uncertain; but in the age of Cicero this seems to have been left to the discretion of the judge, especially in private causes. In criminal trials Pompey made a regulation, that the accuser should not be entitled to speak for more than two hours, nor the accused for more than three hours; but the parties were sometimes allowed to exceed these limits when the nature of the cause appeared to require more time. Not long afterwards the judges were again invested with discretionary power to regulate the period to be occupied by the speeches according to the importance of the affair. In criminal causes the time was usually divided in the proportion fixed by the Pompeian regulation, so that if *six* hours were allowed to the accuser, *nine* hours were allowed to the accused.[1]

A clepsydra was used in the tribunals for measuring time by water, similar in principle to the modern sand-glass. When the judge consented to prolong the period assigned for discussion, he was said to give water—*dare aquam*. "As for myself," says Pliny, "whenever I sit upon the bench

[1] Pliny, Ep. iv. 9.

(which is much oftener than I appear at the bar), I always
give the advocates as much water as they require; for I look
upon it as the height of presumption to pretend to guess before a cause is heard what time it will require, and to set
limits to an affair before one is acquainted with its extent,
especially as the first and most sacred duty of a judge is
patience, which, indeed, is itself a very considerable part of
justice. But the advocate will say many things that are
useless. Granted. Yet is it not better to hear too much
than not to hear enough? Besides, how can you know that
the things are useless till you have heard them?"[1]

Marcus Aurelius, we are told, was in the habit of giving a
large measure of water to the advocates, and even permitting
them to speak as long as they pleased.

By a constitution of Valentinian and Valens, A.D. 368, advocates were authorised to speak as long as they wished, upon
condition that they should not abuse this liberty in order to
swell the amount of their fees.

Sometimes the pleadings were very long: for, if we are to
believe Quintilian, it was a species of glory for an advocate
that he had spoken a whole day for one party. Regulus
fatigued the judges with interminable harangues. In the
trial of Marcus Priscus before the senate, Pliny, who opened
the case, spoke nearly five hours. On another occasion, he
tells us, he spoke for seven hours before the centumvirs and
a crowded audience, with success equal to his great fatigue.[2]

According to ancient custom, one counsel only appears to
have been allowed on each side. Afterwards the number
was increased.

Number of counsel.

Cicero defended Celius with Crassus; Cornelius Balbus
with Pompey and Crassus; P. Sextus with Hortensius and
other members of the bar. Scaurus had six advocates—
Cicero, Hortensius, M. Marcellus, P. Clodius, Calidius, and
Messala Niger. Occasionally the number rose so high as
twelve counsel for one party in the same trial.

Of this practice Cicero disapproved, conceiving it to be
attended with great inconvenience, and contrary to the ancient

----

[1] Pliny, Ep. vi. 2.   [2] Pliny, Ep. ii. 11, and iv. 16.

institutions of the bar.   Under the empire the number of
counsel employed was reduced, and seldom exceeded two or
three on each side.   When the accused had no advocate, it
was customary for the judges to appoint one to act for him.
Hortensius and Cicero, we are told, sometimes defended pick-
pockets ; and Asinius Pollio, the friend of Augustus, pleaded
cases about mean-walls.[1]

Remunera-
tion of
pleaders.

For some centuries after the foundation of Rome, the profession of an advocate did not exist ; because the duty of
patron, which included the defence of clients before the
tribunals, was discharged by the patricians, who formed the
first order among the citizens.   No remuneration was then
given for forensic pleading beyond the usual services which
every client owed to his patron.   After the ancient institutions were modified, and law became a complicated and difficult science, presents of various kinds were given by clients
to those persons who devoted themselves to pleading.   This
practice having been regarded as an abuse, a law was passed
by the Tribune Cincius, B.C. 204, prohibiting any one from
taking money or gifts for pleading causes ; but as this law
imposed no penalty on those who contravened its injunctions,
it was little observed, and the opinion gained ground that
advocates who required to devote their time to the special
studies of their profession were entitled to receive some
recompense for their services.

Before the overthrow of the republic it was quite common
to give large fees to advocates.   M. Licinius Crassus, whose
fortune is said to have exceeded three millions sterling, exacted exorbitant sums from his clients, and the same charge
has been made against P. Clodius and C. Curio.   Cicero
himself, who lost no opportunity of boasting of his respect
for the Cincian law, and who is represented by his enthusi-
astic admirers as a model of disinterestedness, is strongly
suspected of not having always put in practice the principles
which he professed.   There are many reasons for believing
that the sum of a million of sesterces (about £8000), which
he received from Publius Sylla, then under impeachment,

[1] Quint. iv. 1.   Grellet-Dumazeau, Barreau Romain, Paris, 1851, p. 38.

and which was employed by Cicero in the purchase of a house, was neither more nor less than the fee given for his forensic services, though it was disguised, according to a common practice, under the form of a secret loan.[1]

Another mode of rewarding members of the bar was by legacies left to them by clients in their testaments. These bequests were considered honourable when they were not obtained by fraud or undue influence, and Cicero boasted that he had received in this form sums amounting to upwards of twenty millions of sesterces, equal to about £166,666. *Legacies to the bar.*

Augustus endeavoured to restore the ancient discipline by a senatus-consultum, which revived the Cincian law, and declared that advocates convicted of having received remuneration from their clients should be compelled to refund the amount fourfold. This injudicious regulation, from the change of circumstances, could not have been enforced with advantage to those parties whom it was intended to protect. The people had ceased to be the dispensers of political power, and it could not be expected that persons qualified to act as pleaders in courts of justice would devote their time and talents to the service of those from whom they could obtain no return.

All attempts to put down the practice of giving fees to counsel proved unavailing. But, in the time of the Emperor Claudius, a regulation was made that the sum given as a fee should not in any case exceed ten thousand sesterces, which is equivalent to about £80 of our money. Trajan renewed this law, with the addition that no fee should be paid till after judgment was given in the cause. This was intended to put a stop to an evil arising from the fraudulent abandonment of a cause by those who had been paid in advance to conduct it. That restriction, however, was removed by Justinian, who allowed counsel to receive their fees from clients *Honoraries authorised.*

---

[1] In the case of Small *v.* Attwood, a fee of £8000 was given to Sir Thomas Wilde (afterwards Lord Truro), which nearly corresponded with the amount handed to Cicero. It is stated by M. Berryer, that Gerbier, an eminent French advocate of the eighteenth century, received from a French colonial governor a fee of 300,000 francs, or £12,000 sterling.

without waiting till judgment was given; and there is a passage in the Digest which mentions a hundred aurei as the lawful amount of honoraries to be awarded in a cause.[1]

By a law of Constantine, advocates were prohibited, under the penalty of deprivation of office, from making with their clients any bargain for acquiring a portion of what they might gain by the lawsuit, which was called *pactum de quota litis*. In most countries into which the Roman law has been introduced, a similar regulation exists, in order to maintain the honour and integrity of the legal profession.

After pleading at the bar became fully recognised as a profession, the right of advocates to pecuniary remuneration was established. In form, however, the fee was merely an honorary consideration, not paid in name of hire, but as the reward of services which could receive no proper estimation. For this reason advocates were not allowed to prosecute for payment of their honoraries under the *actio locati* or the *actio mandati*, but from the time of the Emperor Alexander Severus they might recover by means of an *extraordinaria cognitio*.[2]

In France, ancient laws and decisions, as well as the opinions of the doctors, allowed an action to advocates to recover their fees; but according to the later jurisprudence of the Parliament of Paris, and the actual discipline of the bar now in force, no advocate was or is permitted to institute such an action. In like manner, barristers in England are held to exercise a profession of an honorary character, "and cannot, therefore, maintain an action for remuneration for what they have done, unless the employer has expressly agreed to pay them."[3] Upon this point the authorities in the law of Scotland are not very precise. Lord Bankton says, "Though action be competent for such gratification, advocates who regard their character abhor such judicial claims, and keep in their mind the notable saying of Ulpian upon the like occasion, *Quædam enim tametsi honeste accipi-*

---

[1] D. 50. 13. 1. 12.   [3] Addison on Contracts, p. 507.
[2] D. 50. 13. 1. 10. Maynz, § 301-303.

antur, inhoneste tamen petuntur."[1] But it is maintained by others, whose opinion is entitled to great weight, that no action lies for such fees—the presumption, in the absence of an express paction, being, that the advocate has "either been satisfied, or agreed to serve *gratis.*"[2]

To entitle any one to be admitted to the Roman bar, the first condition was that he should be of competent age, which was fixed at seventeen years by the edict of the prætor, and this was confirmed by Justinian.[3] *(Age for admission to bar.)*

The entrance to the bar was forbidden to all infamous persons. Women were never prevented from pleading their own causes, but they were prohibited from acting for others. Caia Afrania, a bold, impudent woman, was in the habit of molesting the prætor by her violent speeches, and this led to an edict forbidding all females from pleading for others in courts of justice. This prohibition passed from the edict into the Pandects.[4]

Candidates for the bar studied the law for four years, and after Justinian's new regulations for five years. They also required to pass a public examination previous to admission.[5] *(Course of study.)*

It is probable that the Roman advocates were formed into a corporation, called *ordo* or *collegium*, about the time of Ulpian; and they certainly were so under Theodosius and his successors. The names of the advocates authorised to plead before the courts were inscribed upon a tablet in the order of their admission; they enjoyed special privileges; and for breaches of duty they were liable to be suspended from the exercise of their functions for a term, or even to be entirely deprived of their office. *(Advocates a corporation.)*

From Constantine to Justinian the bar was divided into two classes—the advocates in practice, and the supernumeraries. The number of practising advocates was fixed in each tribunal, and new members were only received from the supernumeraries when vacancies occurred. The court of the prætorian prefect of the East could furnish employment for

[1] Bank. 4. 3. 4.   D. 50. 13. 1. 5.
[2] More's Stair, Notes, p. 126. Shand's Practice, p. 80.
[3] D. 3. 1. 1. 5.
[4] D. 3. 1. 5.   Val. Max. viii. 3. 2.
[5] D. Præf. Prim. Const. 2.

150 advocates ; there were 50 at Alexandria, besides a large number who practised at the provincial bars. But even those whose names were not inscribed in the privileged lists were still members of the order, and were at liberty to practise before some inferior courts.[1]

All the judges were chosen from the profession of the law. The members of the bar were often raised to preside in the tribunals before which they had pleaded. Many of them obtained the government of provinces, and by the aid of merit or favour rose by degrees to the highest dignities of the state.

Style of the Roman bar. From the works of Cicero, the Institutes of Quintilian, and the Epistles of Pliny, we are enabled to form a general idea of the style of eloquence that prevailed at the Roman bar during an uninterrupted period of several centuries.

Orators before Cicero. In giving an account of the orators of Rome, Cicero does not go farther back than about 150 years before his own consulate, naming as the first and most ancient of them M. Cornelius Cethegus. He was a contemporary of the poet Ennius ; and though his manner was simple, he was a most persuasive speaker. Cato the Censor came after him in the order of time. His style was concise, pointed, and forcible. He is said to have been the first at Rome who laid down some rules of eloquence. Quintilian says, " His genius, like his learning, was universal; historian, orator, lawyer, he cultivated the three branches ; and what he undertook he touched with a master hand."

Between the death of Cato and the birth of Cicero about forty years intervened. During that period the eloquence of the bar made rapid progress, chiefly through the influence of the literature and philosophy of Greece, which began to be studied by the better classes, whereby they improved their taste and judgment, and enriched their minds with new stores of knowledge. Of all the advocates who appeared at this **Crassus and Marcus Antonius.** epoch, Lucius Licinius Crassus, and Marcus Antonius, the grandfather of the triumvir, were the most illustrious. According to Cicero, they were the two greatest orators of the

[1] Grellet-Dumazeau, p. 79.

bar, and the first Romans who raised eloquence to the same
level which it had attained in Greece.

As success at the bar was the surest mode to gain popu- Orators of Cicero's age.
larity and distinction, and opened up one of the most direct
avenues to political power, it can excite no surprise that the
art of forensic speaking was more and more cultivated, until
it reached its culminating point in the age of Cicero.   In
the 'Dialogue concerning Oratory,' which has been ascribed
by some to Tacitus, and by others to Quintilian—the scene
being laid in the sixth year of Vespasian, A.D. 75—Messala
thus expresses himself: "Cicero stands at the head of our
Roman orators, while Calvus, Asinius and Cæsar, Cælius and
Brutus, follow him at a distance; all of them superior not
only to every former age, but to the whole race that came
after them.   Nor is it material that they differ in the mode,
since they all agree in the kind.   Calvus is close and ner-
vous; Asinius more open and harmonious; Cæsar is distinguished by the splendour of his diction; Cælius by a caustic
severity; and gravity is the characteristic of Brutus.   Cicero
is more luxuriant in amplification, and he has strength and
vehemence.   They all, however, agree in this—their eloquence is manly, sound, and vigorous.   Examine their works,
and you will see the energy of congenial minds, a family
likeness in their genius, however it may take a distinct
colour from the specific qualities of the men."[1]   This opinion
as to the superiority of Cicero and his contemporaries has
been generally adopted by the best critics.

The great Roman orator improved himself, not only by the Cicero.
most laborious exercises, but by a diligent study of the best
models of Greece.   His own native genius and industry supplied the rest.   Yet Cicero had his detractors, who objected
to him that he was diffuse without vigour, and luxuriant
to a fault, and that he wanted the strength, purity, and
elegance of the Attic school.   While vindicating Cicero
from these criticisms, and placing him in the highest rank
among Roman orators, Quintilian candidly acknowledges
that, although it was hardly possible to have added any-

[1] Dialogue concerning Oratory, c. 25.

thing to his eloquence, something might have been retrenched from it.

All the speeches of Cicero which have reached us, being fifty-nine in number, were carefully revised and corrected by him before they were published. Of the seven orations against Verres, the first two only, called the "Divination" and "the First Action," were spoken in court; the other five were published as they were prepared and intended to be spoken if Verres had not abandoned his defence. Like many of his other speeches, Cicero's defence for Milo was much altered and improved; and when a copy of it was sent to Milo in his place of exile, he is said to have exclaimed, "O Cicero, if you had spoken thus, I never should have eaten such good fish at Marseilles!" [1]

Hortensius.
Among the contemporaries of Cicero, though eight years his senior, was Hortensius, who exercised for a considerable time an undisputed sway in the courts of justice. He was much engaged in defending men of the aristocratical party when accused of malversation and extortion in the provinces, or of bribery and corruption in canvassing for public honours. In his work called 'Brutus,' Cicero gives such a graphic account of Hortensius that we cannot resist quoting it. After describing Cotta's way of speaking as calm and easy, Cicero says: "The language of Hortensius was splendid, warm, and animated, and far more lively and pathetic both in his style and action. He had such an excellent memory, that what he composed in private he was able to repeat without notes in the very same words he made use of at first. He employed this natural advantage with so much readiness, that he not only recalled whatever he had written or premeditated himself, but remembered everything that had been said by his opponents without any notes. He was inflamed with such a passionate fondness for the profession, that I never saw any one who took more pains to improve himself; for he would not suffer a day to elapse without either speaking in the forum or composing something at home, and very often he did both on the same day. He had, besides, a turn of ex-

[1] Dio. Cass. Hist. Rom., xl. 54.

pression which was far from being lax and unelevated, and possessed, too, other accomplishments in which no one could equal him; an uncommon clearness and accuracy in stating the points he was to speak to; and a neat and easy manner of collecting the substance of what had been said by his antagonist and by himself. He had likewise an elegant choice of words, an agreeable flow in his periods, a copious elocution, with a sweet and sonorous voice, which he was partly indebted for to a fine natural capacity, and partly acquired by the most laborious rhetorical exercises. In short, he had a most retentive view of his subject, and always divided and parcelled it out with the greatest exactness; and he very seldom overlooked anything which the case could suggest that was proper either to support his own allegations, or to refute those of his opponents."

Hortensius had no rival in the forum till he encountered Cicero. Having first run through the career of public honours and amassed a large fortune, Hortensius remitted his intense application, and began to enjoy a life of ease and affluence; while Cicero, redoubling his exertions, obtained at last, by general consent, the palm of eloquence. The orations of Hortensius, though published, have not reached us, and some other works written by him have also perished. His eloquence appears to have been of the florid or "Asiatic" style, and was probably fitter for hearing than for reading. With a soft and musical voice, his action was graceful and elaborate. Ancient writers have recorded the pains he bestowed in arranging the folds of his toga; and Roscius, the actor, is said to have followed him into the forum to take a lesson in his own art. Hortensius possessed immense wealth. He had several villas, splendidly furnished, a gallery of valuable paintings, and a large stock of wines; he had also parks with fish-ponds, and all sorts of animals. He was renowned for his sumptuous entertainments, and, it is said, was the first person at Rome who brought peacocks to table. He died at the age of sixty-four, in the year of Rome 703, some months before the passage of the Rubicon.

According to Quintilian, Calvus was preferred by some to

all the orators of his time. His manner was grave and solid;
his style chaste, and often animated. To be thought a man
of Attic eloquence was the height of his ambition. His chief
fault was, that in labouring to refine his language he was too
attentive to little niceties. Had he lived to correct this error,
and to give more scope to his eloquence, he would have
reached the summit of his art ; but he was cut off by a pre-
mature death. Asinius Pollio was an accomplished pleader
in extensive practice. Of all the eminent advocates he was
considered the most happily endowed with the power of speaking on a sudden question with unpremeditated eloquence.
As to Brutus, Quintilian says he was fitter for philosophical
speculations than for the career of eloquence.

At this brilliant period the members of the Roman bar
embraced with ardour all branches of knowledge; their literary
exertions were remarkable ; and many of them left behind
them esteemed works on a great variety of subjects. When
we consider the career of Cicero, who prepared such elaborate
pleadings, and published them with so much care after they
were delivered—who took so large a part in public business
during the most stormy period of the republic—who was successively quæstor, edile, prætor, consul, proconsul, and general
of an army—and reflect on his numerous works in almost
every department of literature and philosophy, we are aston-
ished at his power and versatility, and can hardly conceive
how one man was capable of such vast labours. Varro, who
also belonged to the bar, earned for himself the title of " the
most learned of the Romans ; " and St Augustin declares
that the life of man is hardly sufficient to enable one to read
all he has written. Cato the ancient, Lelius, Crassus, the
Antonies, Curio, Philippus, Hortensius, Catulus, Asinius
Pollio, Messala Corvinus, and most of the celebrated pleaders
of the empire, composed histories or other treatises evincing
literary taste and varied erudition; to say nothing of Quintilian, Tacitus, Suetonius, and Pliny, who were all advocates.[1]

After the age of Cicero, eloquence declined, and a decla-
matory, redundant, and affected style of speaking was intro-

[1] Grellet-Dumazeau, pp. 197, 198.

duced. It had become usual to complete the education of Decline of eloquence after Cicero. young men destined for the bar in some of the towns of Asia, where professors of rhetoric abounded ; there a new kind of speaking was taught, called the Asiatic style. This was a compound of Greek subtlety and Oriental pomp, very seductive in appearance, but founded on false taste ; it was not simple or natural, but diffuse and ostentatious, and affected to dazzle by strokes of wit, far-fetched metaphors, and superfluous ornament. To Hortensius is ascribed the blame of having first introduced this vicious style at the bar. He had many admirers, who, without his oratorical talents, imitated his faults, and the Asiatic school came by degrees into fashion in the courts of justice.

The eloquence of the bar, already much impaired under Augustus, declined still farther under his successors. From Tiberius to Trajan the advocates who appear most prominently on the scene are those who attained a bad eminence by making a traffic of their talents in conducting criminal prosecutions to satisfy the vengeance of some of the worst emperors. But even during that period a few names occur which recall the best days of the old Roman bar.

Domitius Afer, who was born under Augustus, and died at Domitius Afer. an advanced age in the reign of Nero, was the most celebrated advocate of his time. He spoke slowly, and with gravity ; his arrangement was clear and logical ; and his style was concise, earnest, and energetic, with nothing idle or redundant about it; but he could enliven his discourse with touches of irony and humour, and was always heard with pleasure. One day Julius Gallicus was pleading before the Emperor Claudius, who held his court near the banks of the Tiber. The advocate, having irritated the prince, was by his orders thrown into the river. Some days afterwards a client of Gallicus brought his case to Afer, requesting him to plead it before the emperor : "Who told you," said Afer, "that I was a better swimmer than Gallicus ?"[1]

The great blot on the fame of Afer was, that he lent himself to the vengeance of Tiberius. But in those days no

[1] Dio. Cass., lx. p. 790.

man's head was safe on his shoulders, and Domitius may
have acted on compulsion. A declared enemy to all charla-
tans, he encouraged a manly style of eloquence ; and the bar,
raised by his example from a long lethargy, produced some
eminent men, who appeared as his adversaries, or acted along
with him in all causes of importance. Crispus Passienus,
Decimus Lelius, and Julius Africanus, might be seen by his
side, all of them men of mark, and the last almost worthy to
walk as his equal.

Pliny the younger. Pliny the younger was the last of the Roman bar who tried
to restore to it a portion of its ancient glory. He was the
pupil of Quintilian. Not content with the eloquence of his
own times, he aspired to follow the best examples of a
former age. In his nineteenth year he began to speak in the
forum, and he was frequently employed as an advocate before
the court of the Centumvirs, as well as before the Roman
senate. He soon acquired a high position at the bar. His
pleading for Accia Variola, a noble lady disinherited by her
father, was regarded as his masterpiece.[1]

Pliny and Tacitus the historian were most intimate friends.
They were both appointed to conduct the prosecution of
Marcus Priscus, proconsul of Africa, before the senate. The
impeachment was opened by Pliny ; and, after an able defence by Salvius Liberalis, we are told, " Tacitus replied
to him with great eloquence, and a certain dignity which
distinguishes all his speeches." [2] Such was the debasement
of the bar at this period, that Pliny declares he was ashamed
of the corrupt effeminate style that disgraced the court of the
Centumvirs, and he thought of withdrawing from it altogether.[3] Pliny wrote a history of his own times, and numerous pleadings, which have perished ; but his letters, and his
panegyric on the Emperor Trajan, have reached us.

If Pliny under Nerva and Trajan was a model of good
taste, his example was not followed by his brethren of an
inferior order, who are justly reproached for indulging in
foolish quotations and irrelevant digressions. To this habit
Martial alludes in his well-known epigram : " Advocate—

[1] Pliny, Ep. vi. 33.   [2] Ibid. Ep. ii. 11.   [3] Ibid. Ep. ii. 14.

We have nothing to do here with violence, or murder, or poison. I accuse my neighbour of having stolen *three goats*, and the judge wants me to prove this. You, with all the force of your lungs, and striking the bar with your hand, only make a noise about the battle of Cannæ, the war of Mithridates, and the perfidy of the Carthaginians,—about Sylla, Marius, and Mucius. Speak, then, I pray you, of my *three goats*." [1]

Only one pleading of the second century has been pre- Apuleius. served. It is the defence which Apuleius, an advocate of the Roman bar, made at Carthage, before the proconsul Claudius Maximus, upon an accusation brought against him of having had recourse to magic to secure the love of a woman older than himself. In this singular discourse Apuleius, who was born some years after the death of Pliny, professes himself to be a follower of Plato; and, in order to vindicate himself from the charge of magic, he discusses questions of grammar, natural history, and physics; he cites Moses and Zoroaster; and he passes under review all the orators, poets, and philosophers of the world.

To push our inquiries on this subject farther would only lead us into a region of conjecture. Pliny the younger, and Apuleius, are for us the last known representatives of the Roman bar; after them, forensic pleading as an art disappeared before the science of jurisprudence.

Much has been written on the qualifications necessary for Qualifica-
an advocate, on the legal knowledge required in conducting tions re-
causes, on composition, action, and delivery, the style which the bar. quired for
he may adopt with the greatest advantage, the collateral studies to be pursued, and other kindred topics. Cicero has treated this subject with judgment and discrimination. But the great work of Quintilian, written during the reign of Domitian, is the most complete system of rhetoric that the Romans have left to us.

In the 'Dialogue' of M. Loisel, an eminent advocate of the Parliament of Paris in the sixteenth century, we have some striking sketches of the most celebrated men who then

[1] Martial, vi. 19.

practised at the French bar.[1] M. Pasquier, who takes part in the discussion, says: " I do not desire for an advocate all the perfections which Cicero, Quintilian, and others require for their orator; for I do not consider high eloquence to be the principal qualification for an advocate. It is, indeed, one of them, and very useful in great pleadings; but it is not what is most required for the bar. What I desire in my advocate is, that he should learn to conduct well any suit in which he may be engaged ; to prepare the written pleadings in proper form ; and, when he comes to plead, that he should handle judiciously all the circumstances of the cause, seize well the point on which it hinges, and express himself in well - chosen language, plain and sententious rather than redundant and copious, supporting his argument with perti-nent reasons and formal and precise authorities, texts of law, ordinances, customs, and determinations of the jurists, with-out obscuring the subject with superfluous matter, sometimes embellishing it with a touch of sentiment, or a passing illustration from the Greek or Latin, but so significant and to the point that it could not be better expressed in French. . . . . In short, I desire in my advocate the contrary of what Cicero requires in his orator, which is eloquence in the first place, and then some knowledge of law ; for I declare, on the contrary, that an advocate should above all be learned in law and practice, and moderately eloquent—more a dialectician than a rhetorician, and more a man of business and judg-ment than of great or long discourse."

There is much good sense in these reflections ; and, after the lapse of three centuries, they apply with equal force to the business of an advocate in our day, though few of that profession, however high their scholarship, now venture to season their speeches with Greek.[2]

---

[1] ' Pasquier, ou Dialogue des Avo-cats du Parlement de Paris.' This dialogue, which gives an account of the principal advocates from 1524 to 1599, has been reprinted by M. Dupin, in an edition of the 'Lettres sur la Profession d'Avocat,' by Ca-mus. Paris, 1818. 2 vols. 8vo.

[2] For a full account of the Roman bar we refer our readers to an able work from which we have derived much aid—' Le Barreau Romain de-puis son Origine jusqu'à Justinien.' Par Grellet-Dumazeau. Paris, 1851.

INDEX.

THE END.

PRINTED BY WILLIAM BLACKWOOD AND SONS, EDINBURGH.

www.ingramcontent.com/pod-product-compliance
Lightning Source LLC
Chambersburg PA
CBHW032301280326
41932CB00009B/651

* 9 7 8 3 7 4 4 7 7 3 3 0 0 *